Lesson Planner

WORLD**LINK**

Developing
English Fluency

Level 3

Nancy Douglas

James R. Morgan

Australia • Brazil • Mexico • Singapore • United Kingdom • United States

World Link Lesson Planner 3: Developing English Fluency, Third Edition
Nancy Douglas, Author
James R. Morgan, Author
Susan Stempleski, Series Editor

Publisher: Sherrise Roehr

Executive Editor: Sarah Kenney

Senior Development Editor: Brenden Layte

Associate Development Editor: Alison Bruno

Assistant Editor: Patricia Giunta

Media Researcher: Leila Hishmeh

Senior Technology Product Manager:
Lauren Krolick

Director of Global Marketing: Ian Martin

Senior Product Marketing Manager:
Caitlin Thomas

Sr. Director, ELT & World Languages:
Michael Burggren

Production Manager: Daisy Sosa

Content Project Manager: Beth Houston

Senior Print Buyer: Mary Beth Hennebury

Composition: Lumina

Cover/Text Design: Brenda Carmichael

Art Director: Brenda Carmichael

Cover Image: Reed Saxon/Associated Press

Inside Front Cover Image: AFP/Getty Images

Photo Credits are listed on the inside back cover.

> For product information and technology assistance, contact us at
> **Cengage Learning Customer & Sales Support, 1-800-354-9706**
> For permission to use material from this text or product,
> submit all requests online at **www.cengage.com/permissions**
> Further permissions questions can be emailed to
> **permissionrequest@cengage.com**

World Link Level 3 Lesson Planner ISBN: 978-1-305-65129-6

National Geographic Learning
20 Channel Center Street
Boston, MA 02210
USA

Cengage Learning is a leading provider of customized learning solutions with office locations around the globe, including Singapore, the United Kingdom, Australia, Mexico, Brazil, and Japan. Locate your local office at **international.cengage.com/region**

Cengage Learning products are represented in Canada by Nelson Education, Ltd.

Visit National Geographic Learning online at **NGL.cengage.com**
Visit our corporate website at **www.cengage.com**

Printed in China
Print Number: 02   Print Year: 2017

STUDENT BOOK WALK-THROUGH

Each unit now opens with an engaging, real photograph designed to generate interest while introducing the unit topic.

To introduce the unit topic and facilitate meaningful communication, Lesson A now features all-new exercises designed to support the Warm-Up video.

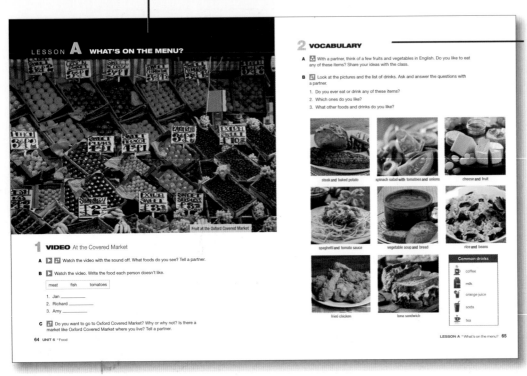

Vocabulary sections dynamically introduce the vocabulary through the use of word families and useful expressions.

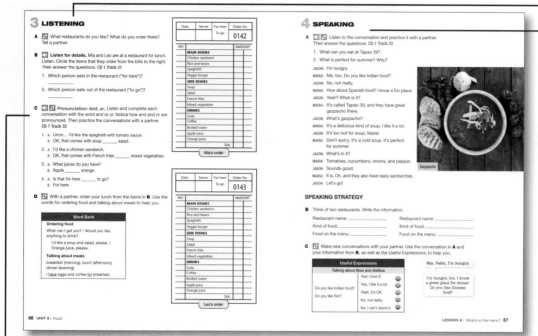

Listening sections use listening tasks to focus students' attention, and are accompanied by open-ended discussion and critical thinking opportunities.

Speaking and **Speaking Strategy** sections give students guided support while leading them to produce the language fluently.

Pronunciation exercises give students item-specific practice with reductions, stress, rhythm, intonation, and troublesome minimal pairs.

An updated **Grammar** presentation increases meaningful classroom communication. Within the unit, learners apply the target grammar in new relevant, communicative exercises and are supported by expanded explanations and traditional practice exercises found in the appendix.

Writing sections reinforce the structures, vocabulary, and expressions taught in the unit.

Communication sections include fun tasks and engaging exercises to provide learners with opportunities for realistic, meaningful communication using target language.

STUDENT BOOK WALK-THROUGH (Continued)

Updated **readings** feature engaging, relevant topics in a highly visual design.

Audio of the readings is now included on the Audio CD!

3 READING

A Find the words in *italics* below in your dictionary. Then answer the questions with a partner.
1. Which *illness*—*cancer* or a *cold*—is very bad?
2. Where is your *stomach*? Where is your *skin*? Point to each one.

B **Scan for information.** Read and answer questions 1–3 about your food only.
Student A: Read about chili peppers.
Student B: Read about licorice.
1. Where does the food come from?
2. How do people use it today?
3. Why is it good for us?

C Ask your partner the questions in **B** about his or her food. What are the answers? Take notes.

D **Read for details.** Are statements 1–9 about chilies (C), licorice (L), or both (B)? Write the correct letter.
_____ 1. is / are high in vitamin C
_____ 2. is / are in cold medicine
_____ 3. give(s) you energy
_____ 4. come(s) from Asia and Europe
_____ 5. can help people with cancer
_____ 6. is / are in sweet foods and drinks
_____ 7. make(s) you less hungry
_____ 8. come(s) from the Americas
_____ 9. can stop stomach and skin problems

E Name another healthy food. Answer the questions in **B** about it. Tell a partner.

72 UNIT 5 ° Food

TWO
POWERFUL
HEALTH
FOODS

Red chili peppers.

Chili peppers are a type of fruit from the Americas. They were first used 6,000 years ago! Today, people all over the world, from Mexico to Thailand, use chilies in their cooking.

Chili peppers taste good, but they're also good for us. They are high in[1] vitamin C. This keeps you healthy. Many chilies are also spicy. This spice gives you energy. It also makes you less hungry, so you eat less. Doctors think chili peppers can stop some kinds of cancer, too.

[1] If something is high in vitamin C, it has a lot of vitamin C.

Licorice, a type of plant, comes from southern Europe and Asia. Today, when people hear the word *licorice*, they think of candy. In fact, licorice is in some sweet foods (like candy) and drinks (like soda), but it is also a very old medicine.[2] Two thousand years ago, people used licorice for colds and other illnesses. Today, it is still in some cold medicines. People also use it for stomach and skin problems. And now doctors think licorice—like chili peppers—can help people with cancer!

[2] *Medicine* is something you drink or eat to stop an illness.

Red licorice candy has no real licorice in it. Black licorice is much healthier!

LESSON B ° Eating right **73**

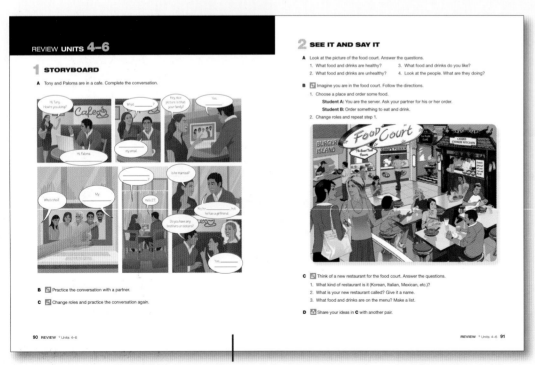

REVIEW UNITS 4–6

1 STORYBOARD

A Tony and Paloma are in a cafe. Complete the conversation.

B Practice the conversation with a partner.
C Change roles and practice the conversation again.

90 REVIEW ° Units 4–6

2 SEE IT AND SAY IT

A Look at the picture of the food court. Answer the questions.
1. What food and drinks are healthy?
2. What food and drinks are unhealthy?
3. What food and drinks do you like?
4. Look at the people. What are they doing?

B Imagine you are in the food court. Follow the directions.
1. Choose a place and order some food.
    Student A: You are the server. Ask your partner for his or her order.
    Student B: Order something to eat and drink.
2. Change roles and repeat step 1.

C Think of a new restaurant for the food court. Answer the questions.
1. What kind of restaurant is it (Korean, Italian, Mexican, etc.)?
2. What is your new restaurant called? Give it a name.
3. What food and drinks are on the menu? Make a list.

D Share your ideas in **C** with another pair.

REVIEW ° Units 4–6 **91**

Review sections appear every three units and actively engage students in utilizing the language learned with the intention of mastering fluency.

LESSON PLANNER FEATURES

The *World Link* Lesson Planner for each level makes preparation simple and effective through updated page-by-page teaching tips, pacing guides, expansion activities, new teaching options, audio and video scripts, and all of the answers for the student book and workbook.

What's new?

- **About the Photo** sections provide background information on the new unit opener photos.

- **Video** sections offer video-viewing support for the new Warm-Up videos.

- WORLDLINK The point-of-use **My World Link Online** symbol reminds instructors where they can integrate additional instruction and practice tied to the student book lessons.

- Updated **Teaching Option** sections target where and how instructors can implement different teaching styles, including the flipped classroom approach, which is designed to increase meaningful communication.

- **Listening and Reading Strategies** support skill-building and offer implementation techniques.

About the Photo sections provide fascinating background information on the photo so instructors can lead dynamic and informed classroom discussions.

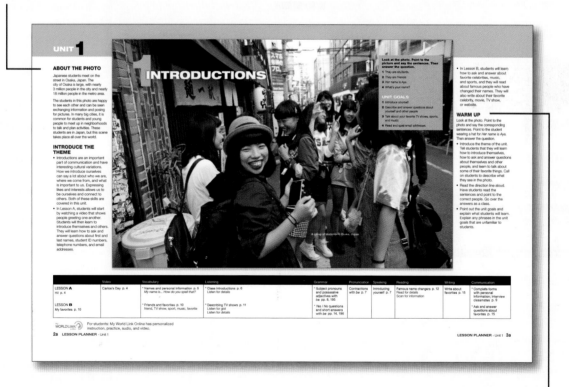

The **Warm-Up** prompts facilitate meaningful conversation about the photograph and the unit topic.

Each unit begins with an all-new page designed to support the **Warm-Up video**.

The new **Warm-Up videos** featuring authentic language are easy to integrate into your instruction with step-by-step video-viewing support! Use the video-viewing techniques, background information, additional vocabulary, and updated pacing guide to reinforce the unit topic and generate meaningful discussion about the unit topic.

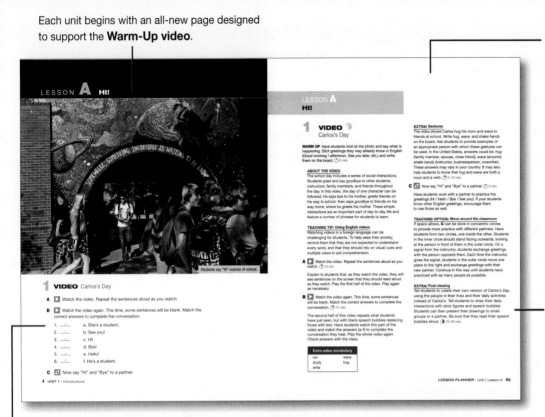

Extra! expansion activities offer additional reading practice and communication activities.

Overlay answers make it easy for instructors to check learners' work.

Interleaved Lesson Planner pages with answers on the student book pages make navigation easy for instructors.

The point-of-use **My World Link Online** symbol reminds instructors where they can integrate additional instruction and practice tied to the student book lessons.

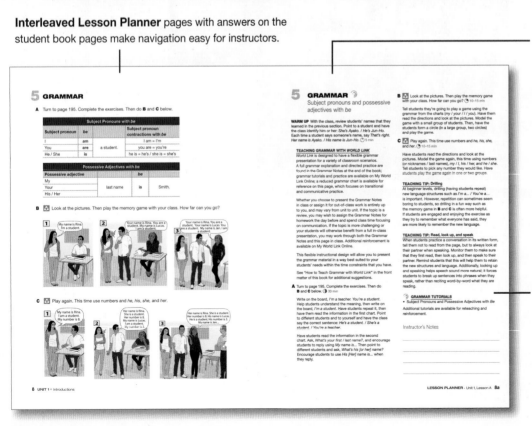

All-new Grammar Tutorials located on My World Link Online and the Classroom Presentation Tool support the updated, communicative grammar presentation.

New **Strategy** sections for all areas of fluency explain each strategy taught in the student book while providing meaningful classroom implementation techniques.

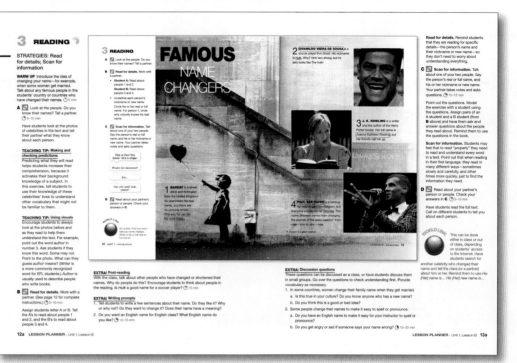

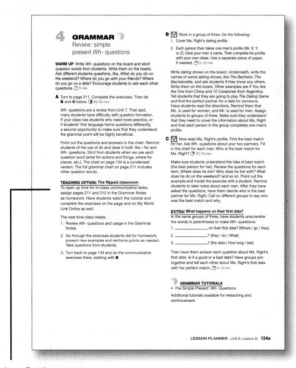

Updated **Teaching Option** sections maximize the enhanced instructional design by helping instructors implement varied teaching approaches, like the flipped classroom model, to increase meaningful in-class communication.

For a more comprehensive approach to integrating writing, the expanded **Process Writing** sections provide instructional support.

INSTRUCTOR RESOURCES

The new **Classroom Presentation Tool** (download instructions in the front of this Lesson Planner) promotes classroom communication through new grammar presentations, engaging games, and interactive student book pages! Instructors also have seamless access to the audio and video from the series.

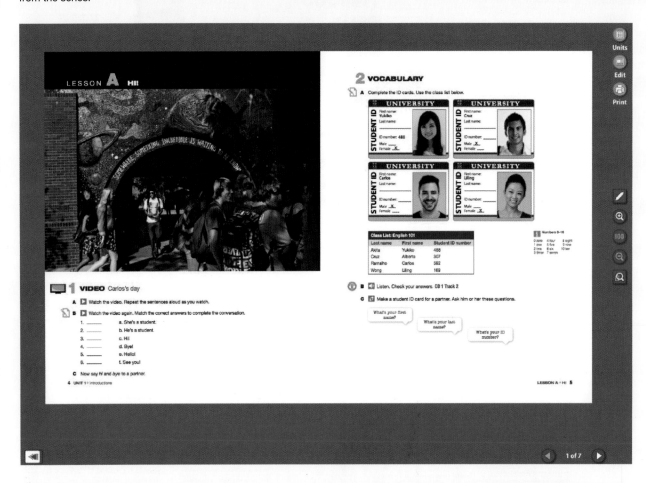

Assessment CD-ROM with Exam*View*®

The Assessment CD-ROM with Exam*View*® is a test-generating software with a data-bank of ready-made questions designed to allow teachers to carry out assessment quickly and conveniently.

Includes Placement Test!

TEACHING GRAMMAR WITH *WORLD LINK*

Maximize classroom time and increase meaningful communication with a new approach to teaching grammar!

The new approach supports the ***flipped classroom*** model, where instruction through video and traditional practice are completed independently, freeing up class time for communicative application of key structures.

Explore how *World Link*, Third Edition provides flexible instructional options:

For the learner:

Learners are directed to the detailed *Grammar Notes* section in the appendix of their books for a comprehensive explanation of and practice with the target grammar. These notes can be used as reference points in class, as a starting point for a more traditional grammar presentation, or as a homework assignment.

Clear, contextualized grammar charts summarize the main points of the grammar structure. Learners use these as models as they complete the communicative activities that follow.

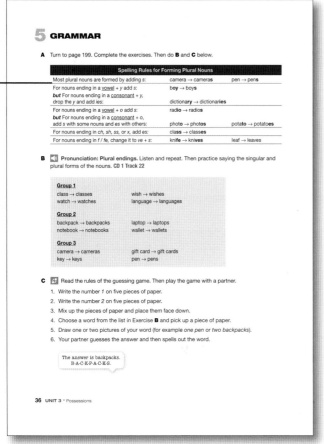

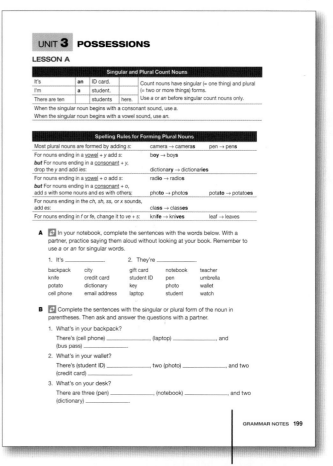

from the related *Grammar Notes* section

Point-of-use **My World Link Online** icons remind instructors when additional instruction and practice is available that support key lessons.

For the instructor:

Updated **Teaching Option** sections provide implementation tips for the flipped classroom model.

New video grammar tutorials on **My World Link Online** support independent learning and practice of key grammar structures.

The new video grammar tutorials are also available on the updated Classroom Presentation Tool for flexible instruction opportunities!

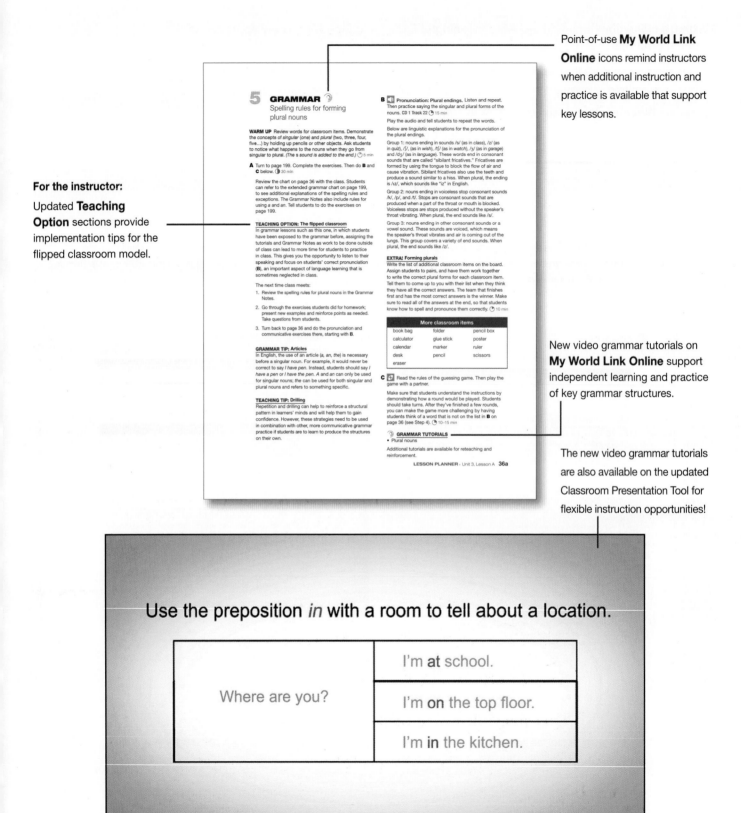

MY WORLD LINK ONLINE

My World Link Online offers **personalized** instruction and practice that **prepares** learners for meaningful classroom communication!

With My World Link Online, learners can access:
- Their personalized learning path
- An interactive eBook
- Grammar tutorials
- Speech recognition technology
- All video and audio resources

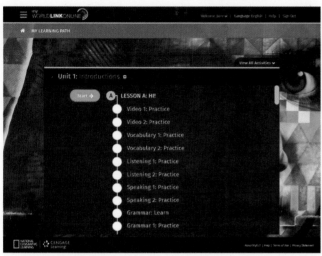

Each learner is given a core set of instruction and practice activities in reading, writing, listening, speaking, grammar, and vocabulary.

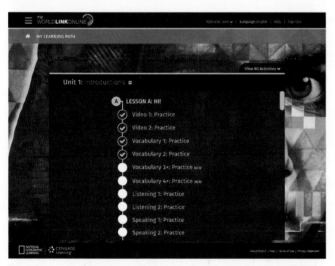

Based on unique learner performance, the personalized learning path adjusts to add the instruction and practice needed for fluency. Learners will receive additional **reteaching** as needed in grammar and vocabulary, and **level-specific practice** in all areas of fluency!

With My World Link Online, instructors can:

- Track individual learner and class progress through the gradebook.
- Create assignments and monitor learner progress.
- Access all of the audio, video, and instructional support materials needed for classroom preparation.

USING THE WARM-UP VIDEOS IN *WORLD LINK*

This edition of *World Link* now features a new Warm-Up video for each unit from authentic sources like National Geographic and YouTube. Each video has been carefully selected to:

- bring the world to the classroom.
- engage learners in the topic of the unit.
- introduce thematically-related, authentic language.
- encourage meaningful discussion.

While the authentic content and language in these new videos may be a challenge for some learners, the use of video engages learners at all proficiency levels. *World Link* offers complete learner and instructor support.

Remember that additional exercises for the new Warm-Up videos are available on My World Link Online and the Classroom Presentation Tool!

The updated lesson planner provides step-by-step video-viewing implementation tips and instructions, making using the video easy for instructors to integrate into their lessons and helpful to learners as they build confidence and oral fluency.

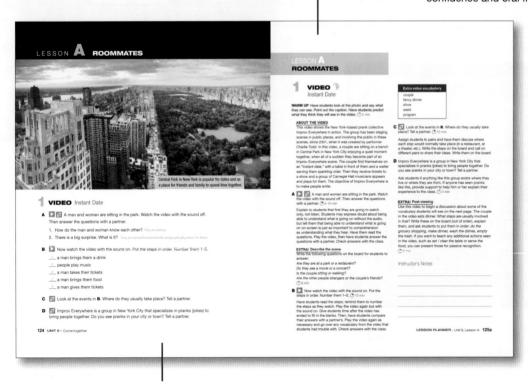

The student book offers related vocabulary, comprehension activities, and discussion questions that support the video.

THE *WORLD LINK* VIDEO PROGRAM

The video clips for each unit are available on the Classroom DVDs and My World Link Online. The Warm-Up videos and grammar tutorials are available on the Classroom Presentation Tool.

The all-new **Warm-Up videos** are supported by new content in the student books and are from authentic sources like National Geographic and YouTube. These videos offer engaging examples of authentic English while providing a springboard for meaningful communication.

Good Morning World features interviews, discussions, and performances in the style of a TV talk show. The hosts, Jay and Kim, welcome guests and discuss topics related to the unit themes and recycle the language learned in *World Link*.

The sitcom style of **City Living** expands on the language practiced in the lesson, providing an opportunity to see it used in natural settings and situations.

Global Viewpoints videos feature interviews with students and professional people from around the world, sharing their opinions on issues related to the topic of each unit.

Emma

Kim

Emma is younger than Kim.   Kim is **young**.

The new grammar tutorials empower students through straightforward instruction.

Websites

Visit NGL.Cengage.com/worldlink for teacher and learner resources.

Visit NGL.Cengage.com/generalenglish for instructional support videos and access to level-specific units and videos.

It is important to stress that "professional development" does not only mean going to conferences, reading books, or writing papers. Although these are very helpful professional development activities, they are just three possible ways from a large number and a wide variety of different ways, which we will learn more about in this section of the book.

Task 8

Check (✓) the professional development activities that you have tried. If you have tried the activity, what did you learn? If you have not tried this activity before, why not?

☐ Keeping a teaching journal/diary

Tried and learned _____

_____

Not tried because _____

☐ Watching yourself teaching on video

Tried and learned _____

_____

Not tried because _____

☐ Watching another teacher teaching

Tried and learned _____

_____

Not tried because _____

☐ Having another teacher watch you teaching

Tried and learned _____

_____

Not tried because _____

☐ Teaching together with another teacher

Tried and learned _____

_____

Not tried because _____

☐ Creating a teaching portfolio

Tried and learned _____

_____

Not tried because _____

☐ Writing a "teaching philosophy" (a statement of your pedagogic beliefs)

Tried and learned _____

_____

Not tried because _____

_____

The first few tasks in this section helped you to think about who you are and what you do. Then we asked you to think about what you understand by the term professional development, what developmental activities you've engaged in, and what you have learned from those activities.

Let's now return to the question we asked at the very beginning: What is professional development?

Professional development is anything you choose to do because you want to be better at what you do. Choice and trust are two essential features of professional development. You can be required to have another teacher in your classroom, observing you. But if you didn't choose to have that person there, and if you don't trust the person, there will be little or no development.

Professional development is also about change. But it's not always about changing what you do. It can be about changing the way you think about what you do. In this section, you have completed various tasks. If you carried out these activities carefully and thoughtfully, then you were engaged in professional development. If you learned anything about your professional self from doing these activities, then you were engaged in professional development.

DRAWING RELATIONSHIPS: BRINGING TOGETHER THE DIFFERENT PARTS OF OUR WORK

As we mentioned earlier, English language teachers (and learners) are often very visual. So, another way of thinking about professional development is to use simple shapes to show complex relationships. Here's an example, based on three key aspects of professional development we've discussed:

```
                    Trust
                     /\
                    /  \
                   /    \
                  / Professional \
                 / Development \
                /_____\
            Choice              Change
```

One interpretation of this diagram might be: Trusting yourself and others, engaging in professional development because you choose to do so, and willingness to change are all necessary for professional development to take place.

Another example:

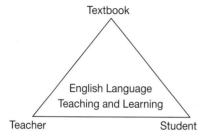

An interpretation of the diagram above might be: English language teachers and students work together, using English language textbooks, to teach and learn the language.

Task 9

Try to put into your own words what this next diagram shows:

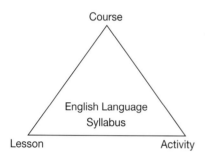

In professional development, teachers often talk about *reflective practice*. This means thinking about what we do so we can understand more, and then make changes so we can do what we do better.

Task 10

Think of three aspects of what you do as an English language teacher, and label the three corners of the triangle below. In the middle of the triangle, write what it is that connects the three corners, then write a brief description of how the three are connected.

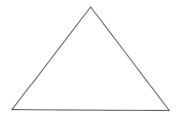

MAKING CONNECTIONS: PICTURING PROFESSIONAL DEVELOPMENT

English language teachers also often make use of analogies in their teaching so that simple language can be used to express complex thoughts.

Analogies are powerful ways of helping us understand what we think and mean and say. For example, we could say, "Being an English language teacher is like being the captain of a ship, because we are all working together on a voyage of discovery."

Task 11

Complete the same sentence, but with your own analogy:

In my teaching and learning context, being an English language teacher is like _____

_____

because _____

_____

An activity like this can be part of your professional development because, even though it seems short and simple, it may require a lot of thought to create a good analogy and then describe it in clear and concise language.

CHANGE AND PROFESSIONAL DEVELOPMENT

As we said earlier, development is all about change—changing what we do, how we do it, and how we think about what we do. Before we can engage in professional development, we should take some time to look at our feelings about change.

Task 12

Circle a number for each statement below to show how you feel about the statement.

> 1 = Strongly Disagree
> 2 = Disagree
> 3 = Agree
> 4 = Strongly Agree

Change is difficult.

1   2   3   4

Change takes a long time.

1   2   3   4

Change takes a lot of energy.

1   2   3   4

Change is complex.

1   2   3   4

Change is painful.

1   2   3   4

Change is usually negative.

1   2   3   4

Once you have read all the statements on page T15 and circled a number for each one, add up your total score. If you have a total score of more than 20, you have probably had a lot of experience of dealing with challenging change. If you have a total of between 12 and 15, the changes you have experienced may have been largely positive, and with a score of 10 or less, you may have experienced relatively little change or few changes, so far.

Most of us tend to naturally resist change, as we are often creatures of habit—we like things to stay the same. But change is one of the only things we can be sure of in modern life. It is sometimes even said that "change is the only constant"!

Task 13

Think of an important change in your life—either personal or professional. Was it difficult and complicated? Did it take a lot of time and energy? Are things better now, because of the change?

Make a few brief notes about this change. How would you describe it to a friend? Once you have made a few notes, use these to describe your change to a friend or colleague, and ask them to do the same with you.

_____

_____

_____

_____

_____

Change may be difficult, and it may even be painful, but the one thing worse than changing is *not* changing. As teachers, we are preparing our students for a constantly changing world. If we are to help them, we must be willing and able to change, grow, and develop. It is even possible that change is at the heart of all teaching and learning.

Here are some ways to make change less difficult:

1. Break it down into small steps.
2. Set yourself realistic, achievable goals at each step.
3. Expect resistance and identify where there will be areas of resistance.
4. Think of ways to overcome this resistance; for example, think of the benefits of the change.
5. Allow enough time for each step to be completed.
6. Reward yourself as you achieve each goal and complete each step.

D The Language of Professional Development

Like all professions, teaching has its own language which teachers can use to talk about teaching. Within this language of the profession there are a number of words and phrases that are commonly used when talking about professional development.

As a language teacher you know that when learning a language, it is not necessary to remember all the meanings of all the words, but it is important to be familiar with them. This task has, then, been created to help you become more familiar with some commonly used terms related to teacher professional development.

As English language teachers, we often ask our students to complete "matching" activities, linking a word with its meaning. So, let's do one of those activities here.

Task 14

Match some simple definitions with some of the words and phrases most commonly used to describe different approaches to professional development for language teachers. (Check your answers on page T22.)

WORD OR PHRASE

1. Case studies

2. Action research

3. Teaching portfolio

4. Mentoring

5. Development

6. Reflective practice

7. Teaching journal

8. Shock language

9. Peer observation

10. Team teaching

11. Training

12. Coaching

13. Awareness

14. Attitude

a. Structured, systematic ways of thinking about what we do and who we are

b. A diary of significant events and moments in our teaching day

c. Short stories based on real teaching and learning events with different endings

d. Sudden and complete immersion in a new and unfamiliar language

e. Being conscious of your psychological state and of your external environment

f. A set of skills acquired for the completion of particular tasks

g. Two (or more) teachers observing each other's teaching and giving feedback

h. A collection of documents and texts that illustrate different aspects of our work

i. Two (or more) teachers planning, preparing, and teaching together

j. A senior teacher helps a junior teacher to develop his or her knowledge and skills

k. A structured, step-by-step investigation of some aspect of our teaching, our students, and so on

l. Two teachers at the same level help each other to develop in a number of different and agreed-upon areas

m. Becoming better at what you do through growth and change

n. Ways of understanding and responding to ourselves, others, and events

E   Painless Professional Development: *Is It Really Possible?*

There are many reasons why many English language teachers do not engage in as much professional development as they might like to do. As we discussed earlier, development requires change, and change can be difficult. Two other common problems are a lack of time and a lack of money. What are some of the obstacles to professional development that you face in your teaching and learning context?

Although there may be challenges to overcome, there are many reasons why we should engage in professional development.

Task 15

Circle a number for each of the statements that follow to show whether each reason for engaging in professional development is important for you or not.

> 1 = Not Important
> 2 = Important
> 3 = Very Important

To keep up to date with new developments in ELT

1   2   3

To maintain an interest in and enthusiasm for teaching

1   2   3

To keep our teaching creative and enjoyable

1   2   3

To meet and exchange ideas with other teachers

1   2   3

To develop new skills needed for new technology

1   2   3

To avoid teacher burnout

1   2   3

To increase and improve job security

1   2   3

To be promoted to a more senior position

1   2   3

To improve salary and status

1   2   3

To learn about new approaches to English language teaching and learning

1   2   3

There are many other reasons for engaging in professional development. Can you identify some of them?

_____

_____

_____

In the same way that change does not have to be painful, professional development does not necessarily need a lot of additional time and money. It is possible to engage in professional development by doing what we are already doing, but doing it with more awareness and more reflection than we usually do.

F Making Your Textbook Part of Your Professional Development

To review some of the main points we have discussed so far:

Professional development is anything you choose to do because you want to be better at what you do.

Professional development does not only mean going to conferences, reading books, or writing papers. There are many different ways to grow professionally.

We also touched upon various types of professional development activities, such as the following:

Teaching journal	Team teaching
Case studies	Mentoring
Action research	Coaching
Teaching portfolio	Peer observation

But one method that few English language teachers think of is using their English language textbook as part of their professional development.

In these pages, you have so far completed 15 different tasks. If you completed each of these tasks carefully and thoughtfully, you were actively engaged in professional development.

But what about the textbook itself? How can an English language textbook be part of an English language teacher's professional development?

Most English language teachers do not think of their textbooks as tools for professional development. Some of the reasons are:

1. Textbooks are used to teach students, so they are not thought of as ways for teachers to learn about teaching.

2. Textbooks are part of our regular, routine, everyday classroom work.

3. Professional development is still often thought of as doing something different, something "extra," or going somewhere else, away from where we are now.

But here are some reasons why you should think of your textbooks as a part of your professional development.

1. Careful and thoughtful use of any kind of teaching material can be part of a teacher's professional development process.

2. Deciding which textbook to use is in itself a professional decision, drawing on your knowledge, skills, and experience.

3. The way in which a textbook is used—which units are used, which are not, what supplementary material you provide, and so forth—also requires a lot of knowledge, skills, and experience.

Part Two: Pursuing Professional Development Using Your Textbook

At the end of Part One, we said:

Careful and thoughtful use of any kind of teaching material can be part of a teacher's professional development process.

Also in Part One, we defined *reflective practice* as a set of structured and systematic ways of thinking about what we do as English language teachers, including the ways in which we use materials.

Reflective practice is an important component of professional development, and can be thought of as a kind of "stepping back." As we do this, we create the necessary distance to see ourselves, and what we do, more clearly.

If you take time to reflect on the ways in which you use your English language textbook, you can make this part of your professional development. Part Two: Pursuing Professional Development Using Your Textbook has been created and designed to help you do this.

At the end of Part One, we also said:

Deciding which textbook to use is in itself a professional decision, drawing on your knowledge, skills, and experience.

It is true that not all English language teachers are allowed to choose the textbooks they believe would work best for them and for their students. Many teachers are simply given books selected by someone else, or textbooks assigned according to standardized, national exams. But even if we do not choose the textbook we work with, there are ways, even in this situation, to create opportunities for professional development. In Part Two, we will explore some of these opportunities.

If you do decide or help to decide which English language textbooks you and your students use, then you are making important decisions because the textbooks we choose and use can directly affect the quality and quantity of English language teaching and learning in our classrooms.

A What Is Teaching?

Task 16

In the space below, write your own personal definition of teaching.

Teaching is...

_____

_____

_____

There are as many different meanings of teaching as there are teachers, because teaching—like learning—is a personal experience. As it is a unique experience, it is never exactly the same for any two teachers or for any two students. Compare your definition with the description below of how teaching and learning happens.

Teaching and learning are the result of a series of choices and decisions, made by the teacher and by the students. Sometimes, the choices and decisions are made together, between students and teachers, and sometimes they are made independently. Teaching—like learning—is about making choices and making decisions.

In a single English language lesson, the teacher—and the students—may make hundreds of moment-to-moment choices and decisions.

B Making Choices and Decisions about Textbooks as Part of Our Professional Development

Although choices and decisions are similar, they are not exactly the same. For example, in an English language class, a teacher may choose between one student and another, both of whom have raised their hands to answer a question. But decisions in classrooms are often a little more complicated, for example, deciding whether or not to continue with a particular activity, as your decision here will affect the timing for the rest of the lesson.

In the English language classroom, there are so many decisions being made that teachers are unaware of many—or even most—of them. But away from the classroom, we can reflect on our decisions so we can understand better why we decided to follow one course of action rather than another.

So, if we think carefully about why we decide to use one textbook over another, we are engaged in a professional development process.

If we think and talk with other teachers about the strengths and weaknesses of one textbook compared to another, we are engaged in professional development.

If we read a short article about how to evaluate textbooks, so that our decisions are informed not only by our knowledge, skills, and experiences, but also by a systematic way of assessing textbooks, then we are also engaged in professional development.

Thinking about the decisions we make when we select an English language textbook can become part of our professional development. But once the decision about which textbook to use has been made, there are many other decisions that need to be made as well.

C Sharing and Charting Your Professional Development

These activities are designed so that they can be carried out by one person, but as teaching and learning are interactive events, you will learn more from these activities if you work on them with another teacher, or with a group of teachers, that you know and trust.

Sharing is an important part of your professional development. Even if you are all using different English language textbooks, you can still learn a lot from each other by exchanging ideas and experiences, as the challenges you face and the decisions you make are often similar.

We have left spaces for you to write your responses to the different tasks and activities in this section for two reasons.

First, your notes will help you share your thoughts with other teachers. But your notes may also form an important part of documenting your professional development, even if you work by yourself.

Development, growth, and change—like teaching and learning—are often invisible, so it is important to keep a record of your development, for yourself and for others.

D Comparing Textbooks

Task 17

If you decided to use this *World Link* textbook, on what did you base that decision?

I decided to use this *World Link* textbook because…

_____

_____

_____

_____

_____

If the decision to use this textbook was made by someone else, talk with them about that decision.

Task 18

Think of some other English language textbooks you have used recently. How is this *World Link* textbook similar to those other textbooks, and in what ways is it different from those textbooks?

Similarities

1. _____

2. _____

3. _____

Differences

1. _____

2. _____

3. _____

A good English language textbook should help the teacher and the students learn more, and learn more effectively and more enjoyably. Your textbook should add to your lesson, not detract from it.

Task 19

How could this *World Link* textbook help develop your English teaching?

_____

_____

_____

_____

E   Getting to Know Your *World Link* Textbook

When we make decisions, we generally base those decisions on our knowledge, skills, and experiences.

If we are to make the most of our textbooks and use them as part of our professional development, we must have a thorough knowledge of the textbook.

How well do you know your *World Link* textbook?

Task 20

Complete this short quiz and see how much you know!

Q1. How many units are there in your *World Link* textbook?

_____

Q2. True or False? The first part of each unit is called Lesson A and is made up of six main parts. _____

Q3. Can you name all the parts of Lesson A in the right order?

1. _____

2. _____

3. _____

4. _____

5. _____

6. _____

Q4. True or False? The second part of each unit is called Lesson B, and is made up of six main parts. _____

Q5. Can you name all the parts of Lesson B in the right order?

1. _____

2. _____

3. _____

4. _____

5. _____

6. _____

Q6. Can you give the unit number and title of two of the units in your *World Link* textbook?

Unit number: _____

Unit title: _____

Unit number: _____

Unit title: _____

Q7a. How many Review Units are there in this textbook?

_____

Q7b. How many units are reviewed in each Review Unit?

_____

Q8. Who are the writers of this textbook?

_____

_____

Q9. Where, when, and by whom was this textbook published?

_____

F Exploring Our Decisions by Asking Questions

The key to making your textbooks part of your professional development is to keep asking questions that explore the decisions you make as you use the textbook.

Before you use a textbook, it is important to consider it in its entirety, then make decisions about individual units, and finally make decisions about the different parts within each unit.

Task 21

Here are some examples of questions you should consider before starting to use your *World Link* textbook.

Q1. Do you plan to use all 12 of the units in the textbook? If so, why? If not, which units will you not use, and why?

_____

_____

Q2. Do you intend to use the units in the order in which they are presented? If yes, why?

_____

_____

_____

Q3. If you plan to change the order of the units and present them in a different sequence, why, and what sequence do you plan to use?

Reason(s) for changing the sequence:

_____

_____

_____

Alternative sequence:

_____

_____

_____

G Adopting and Adapting Your English Language Textbook

The questions in Task 21 are related to adapting your *World Link* textbook to your local teaching and learning context, as every student and every teacher is unique, as we discussed earlier, and every teaching and learning context is unique. Because of this uniqueness, once a textbook has been chosen, or adopted, it may also then need to be "localized," or adapted.

Task 22

What are some aspects of your English language teaching and learning environment that make it different from others?

_____

_____

Task 23

Describe the students with whom you expect you will be using this book.

Q1. First language: _____

Q2. Age range: _____

Q3. Number of years they have studied English:

_____

Q4. English language ability levels:

_____

Q5. Reasons for learning English:

_____

Q6. What makes these students different from other students?

_____

_____

_____

_____

Q7. You are unique, too! What makes you different from other English language teachers you work with?

_____

_____

_____

_____

In Part One, we talked about the importance of change in professional development.

Task 24

Are there any changes you plan to make to your *World Link* textbook to adapt it to your English language teaching and learning environment?

If so, what kinds of changes will you make?

_____

_____

_____

Task 25

Are there any changes you will make to your *World Link* textbook to adapt it to your English language students?

If so, what kinds of changes will you make?

_____

_____

_____

Task 26

Are there any changes you will make to your *World Link* textbook to adapt it to your teaching style(s)?

If so, what kinds of changes will you make?

_____

_____

_____

There are other questions you could ask yourself as well, including: What local objects and artifacts can I—and my students—bring in to supplement and localize the material in the textbook? These "pedagogical artifacts" are sometimes called "realia."

H   Before, During, and After

Another way of using our textbooks as part of your professional development is to make it a focus of your pre-lesson, during-lesson, and post-lesson reflection.

We have already looked at many examples of some of the questions you might ask before and during the lesson, related to your textbook. But there are many questions you should ask afterwards. These include:

- Did that unit or lesson work the way I thought it would? If not, how was it different? It is important to remember here that a lesson may go better than you thought it would, so "different" can be "different but better" as well as "different and worse" than you thought it would be!

- If I had to reteach the same lesson, using the same unit, what would I do the same, what would I do differently, and why?

- Were the materials at the right level for my students? If so, how do I know? If not, what changes can I make so that the material matches the students' levels more closely?

- Did students appear to understand all of the instructions for all of the exercises?

I   Conclusion

We hope we have helped you to start thinking of your *World Link* textbook as part of your professional development. By using your textbook carefully, thoughtfully, and reflectively, your textbook can help you learn as well as help you teach. Good luck! Enjoy!

Dr. Andy Curtis is the 50th President of the TESOL International Association (2015-2016). He is also a professor in the Graduate School of Education at Anaheim University in California.

Answers to Task 14

1. c, 2. k, 3. h, 4. j, 5. m, 6. a, 7. b, 8. d, 9. g, 10. i, 11. f, 12. l, 13. e, 14. n

THIRD EDITION

WORLDLINK

Developing
English Fluency

Level 3

Nancy Douglas

James R. Morgan

NATIONAL
GEOGRAPHIC
LEARNING | CENGAGE
Learning·

Australia • Brazil • Mexico • Singapore • United Kingdom • United States

World Link Level 3: Developing English Fluency, Third Edition

Nancy Douglas, Author

James R. Morgan, Author

Susan Stempleski, Series Editor

Publisher: Sherrise Roehr

Executive Editor: Sarah Kenney

Senior Development Editor: Brenden Layte

Associate Development Editor: Alison Bruno

Assistant Editor: Patricia Giunta

Media Researcher: Leila Hishmeh

Senior Technology Product Manager:
  Lauren Krolick

Director of Global Marketing: Ian Martin

Senior Product Marketing Manager:
  Caitlin Thomas

Sr. Director, ELT & World Languages:
  Michael Burggren

Production Manager: Daisy Sosa

Content Project Manager: Beth Houston

Senior Print Buyer: Mary Beth Hennebury

Composition: Lumina

Cover/Text Design: Brenda Carmichael

Art Director: Brenda Carmichael

Cover Image: Reed Saxon/Associated Press

Inside Front Cover Image: AFP/Getty Images

Photo Credits are listed on the inside
  back cover.

For product information and technology assistance, contact us at
Cengage Learning Customer & Sales Support, 1-800-354-9706
For permission to use material from this text or product,
submit all requests online at **www.cengage.com/permissions**
Further permissions questions can be emailed to
permissionrequest@cengage.com

World Link 3 ISBN: 978-1-305-65120-3

World Link 3 + My World Link Online ISBN: 978-1-305-65121-0

National Geographic Learning
20 Channel Center Street
Boston, MA 02210
USA

Cengage Learning is a leading provider of customized learning solutions with office locations around the globe, including Singapore, the United Kingdom, Australia, Mexico, Brazil, and Japan. Locate your local office at **international.cengage.com/region**

Cengage Learning products are represented in Canada by Nelson Education, Ltd.

Visit National Geographic Learning online at **NGL.cengage.com**
Visit our corporate website at **www.cengage.com**

Printed in China
Print Number: 02   Print Year: 2017

Acknowledgments

We would like to extend a very special thank you to the Instituto Cultural Peruano Norteamericano (ICPNA) academic management staff in the central office, branches and teachers, for the helpful insights and suggestions that contributed toward the development of this series.

We would also like to thank Raúl Billini, Educational Consultant, Santo Domingo, Dominican Republic, for his contributions to this series.

Thank you to the educators who provided invaluable feedback throughout the development of the *World Link* series: Rocio Abarca, Instituto Tecnológico de Costa Rica / FUNDATEC; David Aduviri, CBA (Centro Boliviano Americano) - La Paz; Ramon Aguilar, Universidad Tecnológica de Hermosillo; Miguel Arrazola, CBA (Centro Boliviano Americano) - Santa Cruz; Cecilia Avila, Universidad de Xalapa; Isabel Baracat, CCI (Centro de Comunicação Inglesa); Daniel Sanchez Bedoy, Calfornia Language Center; Andrea Brotto, CEICOM (Centro de Idiomas para Comunidades); George Bozanich, Soongsil University; Emma Campo, Universidad Central; Andrea Carlson, Aichi Prefectural University; Martha Carrasco, Universidad Autonoma de Sinaloa; Herbert Chavel, Korea Advanced Institute of Science and Technology; J. Ventura Chavez, Universidad de Guadalajara CUSUR; Denise de Bartolomeo, AMICANA (Asociación Mendocina de Intercambio Cultural Argentino Norteamericano); Rodrigo de Campos Rezende, SEVEN Idiomas; John Dennis, Hokuriku University; Kirvin Andrew Dyer, Yan Ping High School; Marilena Fernandes, Alumni; Mark Firth, J.F. Oberlin University; Daniela Frillochi, ARICANA (Asociación Rosarina de Intercambio Cultural Argentino Norteamericano); Joseph Gabriella, Toyo University; Marina Gonzalez, Instituto Universitario de Lenguas Modernas; Robert Gordon, Korea Advanced Institute of Science and Technology; Scott Grigas, Youngsan University; Gu Yingruo, Research Institute of Xiangzhou District, ZhuHai; Kyle Hammel, Incheon National University; Mariana Gil Hammer, Instituto Cultural Dominico Americano; Helen Hanae, Toyo University; Xu Heng, Nantong Polytechnic College; Amiris Helena, Centro Cultural Dominico Americano; Rafael Hernandez, Centro Educacional Tlaquepaque; Yo-Tien Ho, Takming University; Marie Igwe, Hanseo University; Roxana Jimenez, Instituto Tecnológico de Costa Rica / FUNDATEC; Liu Jing, Shanghai Foreign Language Education Press; Lâm Nguyễn Huỳnh, Van Lang University; Hui-Chuan Liao, National Kaohsiung University of Applied Sciences; Pan Lang, Nanjing Sport Institute; Sirina Kainongsuang, Perfect Publishing Company Limited; Karen Ko, ChinYi University; Ching-Hua Lin, National Taiwan University of Science and Technology; Simon Liu, ChinYi University; Maria Helena Luna, Tronwell; Ady Marrero, Alianza Cultural Uruguay Estados Unidos; Nancy Mcaleer, ELC Universidad Interamericana de Panama; Michael McCallister, Feng Chia University Language Center; José Antonio Mendes Lopes, ICBEU (Instituto Cultural Brasil Estados Unidos); Tania Molina, Instituto Tecnológico de Costa Rica / FUNDATEC; Iliana Mora, Instituto Tecnológico de Costa Rica / FUNDATEC; Fernando Morales, Universidad Tecnológica de Hermosillo; Vivian Morghen, ICANA (Instituto Cultural Argentino Norteamericano); Aree Na Nan, Chiang Mai University; He Ning, Nanjing Mochou Vocational School; Paul Nugent, Kkottongnae University; Niu Yuchun, New Oriental School Beijing; Elizabeth Ortiz, COPEI (Copol English Institute); Virginia Ortiz, Universidad Autonoma de Tamaulipas; Marshall Presnick, Language Link Vietnam; Justin Prock, Pyeongtaek University; Peter Reilly, Universidad Bonaterra; Ren Huijun, New Oriental School Hangzhou; Andreina Romero, URBE (Universidad Rafael Belloso Chacín); Leon Rose, Jeonju University; Chris Ruddenklau, Kinki University; Adelina Ruiz, Instituto Tecnologico de Estudios Superiores de Occidente; Eleonora Salas, IICANA (Instituto de Intercambio Cultural Argentino Norteamericano); Jose Salas, Universidad Tecnológica del Norte de Guanajuato; Mary Sarawit, Naresuan University International College; Jenay Seymour, Hong-ik University; Huang Shuang, Shanghai International Studies University; Sávio Siqueira, ACBEU (Asociação Cultural Brasil Estados Unidos) / UFBA (Universidade Federal da Bahia); Beatriz Solina, ARICANA (Asociación Rosarina de Intercambio Cultural Argentino Norteamericano); Mari Cruz Suárez, Servicio de Idiomas UAM; Bambang Sujianto, Intensive English Course (IEC); Howard Tarnoff, Health Sciences University of Hokkaido; Emily J. Thomas, Incheon National University; Sandrine Ting, St. John's University; Tran Nguyen Hoai Chi, Vietnam USA Society English Training Service Center; Ruth Tun, Universidad Autonoma de Campeche; Rubén Uceta, Centro Cultural Dominico Americano; Maria Inés Valsecchi, Universidad Nacional de Río Cuarto; Alicia Vazquez, Instituto Internacional; Patricia Veciño, ICANA (Instituto Cultural Argentino Norteamericano); Punchalee Wasanasomsithi, Chulalongkorn University; Tomoe Watanabe, Hiroshima City University; Dhunyawat Treenate, Rajamangala University of Technology Krungthep; Haibo Wei, Nantong Agricultural College; Tomohiro Yanagi, Chubu University; Jia Yuan, Global IELTS School; Selestin Zainuddin, LBPP-LIA.

Grammar	Pronunciation	Speaking	Reading	Writing	Communication
Stative passive voice pp. 8, 193 Giving permission and expressing prohibition pp. 14, 194	Saying a series of items p. 6	Making informal suggestions p. 7	Creating public spaces p. 12 Make and check predictions Scan for information Infer information Read for details	Write about an annoying behavior p. 14	Describing and planning a presentation about how to fix a room p. 9 Talking about annoying behaviors p. 15
Review of future forms pp. 22, 195 Modals of future possibility pp. 28, 196	Content word emphasis p. 20	Talking about plans and needs p. 21	John Francis: The planet walker p. 26 Make predictions Infer meaning Scan for details	Write about your future plans p. 29	Predicting the future p. 23 Talking about future plans p. 29
Participial and prepositional phrases pp. 36, 197 Review of the present perfect pp. 42, 198	Stress: Verb + preposition p. 34	Interrupting someone politely p. 35	Viral news p. 40 Use background knowledge Sequence events Make connections Summarize	Share personal information p. 43	Ranking behaviors p. 37 Catching up at a reunion p. 43
Adverbs used with the present perfect pp. 54, 199 Phrasal verbs pp. 60, 200	Coarticulation p. 60	Disagreeing politely p. 53	Dating around the world p. 58 Use background knowledge Read for details Infer information	Continue a love story p. 60	Discussing social norms over time p. 55 Taking and discussing a dating survey p. 61
It + *be* + adjective + infinitive; Gerund + *be* + adjective pp. 68, 201 Present and future time clauses with *before, after, when, as soon as / once* pp. 74, 202	Linking the same sounds p. 66	Asking about culturally appropriate behavior p. 67	Welcome to Bogotá p. 72 Use background knowledge Understand purpose	Prepare a "how-to" presentation p. 75	Designing a poster to improve public behavior p. 69 Explaining how to do something p. 75
The passive voice: simple present and simple past pp. 82, 203 Connecting ideas with *because, so, although / even though* pp. 88, 204	Stress on nouns and verbs with the same spelling p. 80	Asking about companies / Emphasizing important points p. 81	Life without ads? p. 86 Identify a point of view Draw conclusions Scan for details	Write a product review p. 88	Presenting facts about your city or region p. 83 Creating a commercial p. 89

Grammar	Pronunciation	Speaking	Reading	Writing	Communication
Describing symptoms pp. 100, 206 **Reported speech: commands and requests** pp. 106, 207	The schwa sound p. 100	Giving, accepting, and refusing serious advice p. 99	**Modern health problems** p. 104 Scan for information Make predictions Check predictions Read for details Infer meaning	Write about a healthy change p. 106	Suggesting an alternative treatment p. 101 Giving tips for a healthy life p. 107
The present perfect vs. the present perfect continuous pp. 114, 208 **Review: The simple past vs. the present perfect vs. the present perfect continuous** pp. 120, 209	Stress in compound nouns p. 112	Explaining the set-up and rules of a game p. 113	**A star in the X Games** p. 118 Use background knowledge Scan for information Read for details	Write about a hobby p. 121	Talking about a new skill p. 115 Interviewing classmates about hobbies p. 121
Too and *enough* pp. 128, 210 **Future real conditionals** pp. 134, 211	Using pauses in public speaking p. 127	Language for presentations p. 127	**People of all ages** p. 132 Use background knowledge Make predictions Infer information Infer meaning Read for details Draw conclusions	State your opinion about a future event p. 134	Completing and talking about a lifestyle survey p. 129 Giving a speech about a solution to a problem p. 135
Wish **statements** pp. 146, 212 **Negative modals** pp. 152, 213	Word final /t/ and /d/ p. 152	Apologizing and accepting an apology p. 145	**Money from unusual sources** p. 150 Make predictions Read for details Infer meaning Compare and evaluate	Give an opinion on the best way to donate money p. 153	Renting an apartment p. 147 Persuading someone to donate money p. 153
Present unreal conditionals pp. 160, 214 **Reported statements with** *say* **and** *tell* pp. 166, 215	Repeating with rising intonation to show surprise p. 158	Giving strong advice p. 159	**The kindness of strangers** p. 164 Make connections Make predictions Sequence events Infer meaning	Describe a lie p. 167	Talking about dishonest actions p. 161 Explaining your actions p. 167
Embedded questions pp. 174, 216 **The passive with various tenses** pp. 180, 217	Negative questions to confirm information p. 177	Offering another opinion p. 173	**When the seas rise** p. 178 Use background knowledge Make predictions Take notes on key details Infer meaning Summarize Give opinions	Give an opinion on new construction p. 181	Taking a quiz about the world p. 175 Choosing a civic project p. 181

Language Summaries p. 186   **Grammar Notes p. 193**

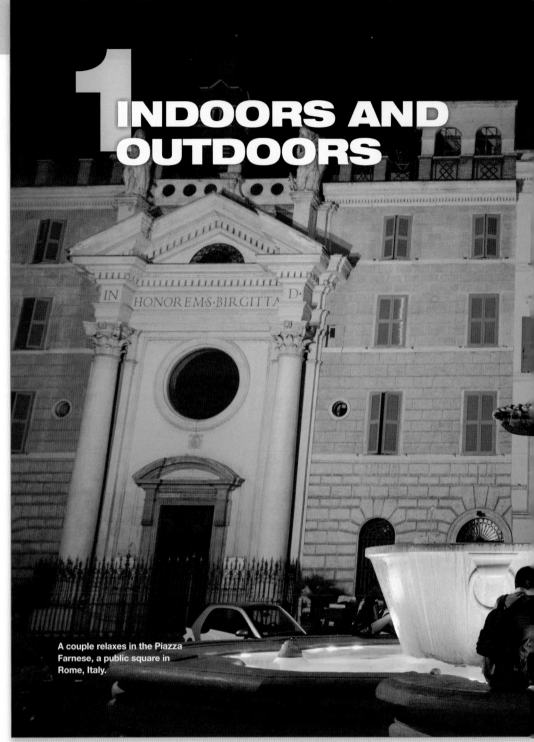

1 INDOORS AND OUTDOORS

A couple relaxes in the Piazza Farnese, a public square in Rome, Italy.

ABOUT THE PHOTO

The city of Rome, Italy, is famous for its fountains. This photo shows one of the two bathtub-shaped fountains in the Piazza Farnese, one of the squares in Rome's historic center. The Piazza Farnese houses the Church of St. Bridget, which can be seen in the background of this photo, and the Renaissance-era Palazzo Farnese. The two granite stone basins were placed in the square in the 16th century. They are believed to have been in the Roman baths of Caracalla before being moved to the piazza. Piazzas, such as the Piazza Farnese, serve as places to meet, to relax and cool off from the summer heat, and to admire the beauty, architecture, and history of the city all year long.

Did you know?
Between monumental fountains, such as the famous Trevi Fountain, decorative fountains, like the Farnese fountain in this photo, wall fountains, and other smaller fountains, Rome has more than 2,000 fountains—the most of any city.

INTRODUCE THE THEME

- In this unit, students will discuss private and public spaces and private versus public lives. The language in the two lessons will help students communicate on these themes, including discussing home improvements, making and responding to suggestions, comparing public and private life, and discussing appropriate and inappropriate behavior in public places.

	Video	Vocabulary	Listening
LESSON A At home p. 4	The Rise of Open Streets p. 4	Home improvements p. 5 *repaint, color, repair*	The color wheel p. 6 Make and check predictions Listen for details
LESSON B Public spaces p. 10		Public and private life p. 10 *general public, privacy, disturb*	Privacy p. 11 Listen for main ideas Infer information

 For students: My World Link Online has personalized instruction, practice, audio, and video.

Look at the photo. Answer the questions.

1 Where are the people in the photo?

2 Is there a public space like this in your city? Why do people gather there?

3 What is something you *shouldn't* do in public?

UNIT GOALS

1 Discuss home improvement ideas

2 Make and respond to informal suggestions

3 Talk about public versus private life

4 Discuss rules and appropriate behavior

- In Lesson A, students will watch a video which talks about open streets in cities around the world. Students will then learn to talk about making home improvements. They will also practice making and checking predictions and listening for details, and they will learn how to suggest solutions to problems. Finally, they will discuss problems and propose solutions.

- In Lesson B, students will learn to talk about public versus private lives. They will read about creating public spaces, practicing making and checking predictions, scanning for information, inferring information, and reading for details. They will also learn how to express permission and prohibition. Finally, they will write and talk about inappropriate behavior in public places.

WARM UP

- Call on students to describe what they see in the photo.

- Have students answer the questions individually or in pairs, then compare answers with the class.

- Point out the unit goals and explain what students will learn. Elicit any key vocabulary students already know (words to describe homes, rooms, and furniture, etc.), and write it on the board. Explain any unfamiliar phrases in the unit goals.

Grammar	Pronunciation	Speaking	Reading	Writing	Communication
Stative passive voice pp. 8, 193	Saying a series of items p. 6	Making informal suggestions p. 7	Creating public spaces p. 12 Make and check predictions Scan for information Infer information Read for details	Write about an annoying behavior p. 14	Describing and planning a presentation about how to fix a room p. 9
Giving permission and expressing prohibition pp. 14, 194					Talking about annoying behaviors p. 15

1 **VIDEO** The Rise of Open Streets

A What do you see in the photo? What do you think the video is going to be about? Tell a partner.

B Watch the beginning of the video. Check (✓) the things that are mentioned.

☐ dancing   ☐ getting a haircut   ☐ driving   ☐ walking

☐ catching the bus   ☐ practicing songs   ☐ yoga   ☐ playing soccer

C Watch the next part of the video and complete the sentences.

Open Streets are when you temporarily _____ a street to people _____ and then _____ it up for people _____, walking, skating, running—pretty much do anything but drive a car.

D Watch the full video and complete the quotes.

1. "You get young and old, _____ and _____, fat and skinny—you get everybody!"
2. "All you need is two _____ and a _____."
3. "Summer Streets celebrates the concept that streets are for _____."
4. "It's showing people that the streets can have different _____ according to the time of the _____, the day of the _____, the week of the _____…"
5. "It's a great way to bring in new folks who are maybe interested in _____ more and _____ more and adding more physical activity to their lifestyle but aren't sure how."

E What do you think of Open Streets and events like it? Where would you create an open street in your city? Discuss with a partner.

1 VIDEO
The Rise of Open Streets

WARM UP Ask students about exercise they do outside, not indoors. Prompt with specific questions as necessary, *Do you have a bike? Do you go jogging? Do you walk? Do you skate?* Once you have a list of activities on the board, ask where they do these activities. Write the places on the board, too. ⏱ 5 min

ABOUT THE VIDEO

From Bogotá to Mexico City to Portland, many cities around the world are organizing open street, or *ciclovia*, days. On these days, main avenues are closed to cars and open to people. They can walk, ride, skate, run, dance, do yoga, and many other activities, as well as socialize with people from all over the city. The concept began in Bogotá in the 1970s and has successfully spread to other countries, with strong *ciclovia* programs in Mexico, the United States, and Canada. Closing the streets to cars gives citizens a chance to take back the streets and see their city, and their fellow citizens, from a different point of view. Furthermore, it promotes physical activity and exercise by allowing people access to more open public space.

A ⮕ What do you see in the photo? What do you think the video is going to be about? Tell a partner. ⏱ 5–10 min

Have students look at the photo and discuss the questions with a partner. Elicit their ideas and write them on the board to help students when they watch.

B ▶ Watch the beginning of the video. Check (✓) the things that are mentioned. ⏱ 10–15 min

Go over the items with the class and explain vocabulary as necessary. Remind students that they don't need to understand everything they hear. Play the beginning of the video ("part one"). Give students time to check the items mentioned, then have them compare their answers with a partner's. Play the video again and check answers with the class.

Extra video vocabulary	
advice on nutrition	run a lemonade stand
civic pride	social integration
folks	temporarily
heartbeat	

C ▶ Watch the next part of the video and complete the sentences. ⏱ 10 min

Go over the sentence parts with the class. Have them think about what kind of word they might need in each blank by looking at what comes before and after the blank. Point out the *you* before *temporarily* and help students see that the blank needs a verb to go with *you*. Play the second part of the video ("part two"), telling students to write as they watch. Remind them that at this stage they shouldn't worry about spelling, they can correct mistakes later. Play the second part again. Have students compare their answers with a partner's, then check answers with the class.

D ▶ Watch the full video and complete the quotes. ⏱ 10 min

Go over the quotes with the class and again, have them work out what kind of word they need for each blank by looking at what comes before and after the blank. For example, in number 1, they can work out that they need adjectives, and possibly opposites. Play the whole video. Tell students to write as they watch. Have students compare their answers with a partner's, then play the video again. Check answers with the class, playing the video again as necessary.

E ⮕ What do you think of Open Streets and events like it? Where would you create an open street in your city? Discuss with a partner. ⏱ 10–15 min

Go over the questions with the class and give students a moment to think about their answers. Encourage them to write a few notes to help them when they are speaking (key words, not complete sentences). Assign students to pairs to discuss the questions. Have pairs share their ideas and lead a class discussion on the topic of open streets.

EXTRA! Post-viewing

1. Have students research on the Internet where the idea for Open Streets came from and how it began in that country.

2. Assign pairs of students to different countries to investigate how *ciclovias*, *vias recreativas*, or open street projects are organized. Possible countries include: Colombia, Mexico, the United States, and Canada. Students can try to find others. ⏱ 10 min

2 VOCABULARY

WARM UP Write *house*, *apartment*, and *dormitory* on the board. If your class is small enough, each student can say his or her name and if they live in a house, apartment, or dormitory. If your class is large, students can interview the other students near them, asking their names and where they live. ⏱ 5 min

A Two people are asking the Home Helper, a **home improvement** expert, for advice. Follow the instructions below. ⏱ 10–15 min

(See Student Book page 5 for complete instructions.)

Have students look at the photo and the caption, then go over the words in the Word Bank. Have students point out the bright and neutral colors in the photo. Point out dark colors in the classroom, and have students say their favorite colors. Go over the instructions. Make sure students understand that the people writing are asking for advice. As possible, elicit example advice columns students are familiar with and have them say what problems people write about in it. These are often found in magazines, newspapers, and websites. A beauty and fashion magazine, for example, might include such a column responding to questions about brands of makeup; a computer magazine or website might respond to questions about technical problems, and so on. Then elicit how to give advice (*You should / could…*, *You ought to…*, etc.). Make sure students understand they don't read the answer to the question, they should give their own answer. Assign students to pairs to ask the questions and give each other advice.

TEACHING TIP: Working with a partner
Exercises that give students the opportunity to practice language with a partner are valuable for building fluency. Working with a partner gives students more opportunities to practice speaking and listening. It also gives students a chance to work with students who have different levels of ability from their own. When pairing students, be sure to give them clear instructions on what they are to do. While students are working, walk around the room, offering help and making sure that they are focused on the task.

ℹ Point out the information about the prefix *re-* (*repair* and *replace* don't fit into the category because although they imply changing something, the *re-* is not prefixing a verb, therefore the meaning is not *to do that action again* as it is in *redo*, *recreate*, etc.). Remind students to try to work out meaning from the context and use their dictionaries.

TEACHING TIP: Using a dictionary
Students can build their vocabulary by using a learner's dictionary. Online or phone-based dictionaries can also be used. Tell your students to look up unfamiliar words and learn the definitions, pronunciation, and usage.

B Now read the responses from the Home Helper. What is the advice? Is it similar to what you said in **A**? Do you agree with it? Tell your partner. ⏱ 10 min

Have students read the advice, paying attention to the words and phrases in blue. Go over the meanings with the class, having students explain as much as possible. Then model the example with a student. Assign students to pairs to discuss the advice. Call on several pairs to share their opinions. Was their advice similar? Do they agree with the Home Helper's advice?

EXTRA! Prefixes
Students can increase their vocabulary by learning to use prefixes. Write this list of examples on the board:

Prefix	Meaning	Example words
un-	not	undecided, unclear, uninteresting
pre-	before	prepare, predict, predetermine
mis-	wrong	misunderstand, misspell, mistake

Ask students to think of other words that begin with these prefixes. ⏱ 10 min

C Discuss the questions with a partner. ⏱ 10–15 min

Go over the questions with the class. Give students time to think about their answers. Encourage them to write a few notes with key words. Model the exercise by asking a student the first two questions, then having the student ask you the questions. Assign students to pairs to ask each other the questions. Monitor and encourage them to ask follow-up questions to find out more about their partner's ideas. Call on different students to share something about their partner's home and home improvement plans with the class.

More home improvement words	
armchair	pattern
couch	rug
cushions, pillows	light
fabric, leather	contrast, complement, accent
home furnishings	attractive

CULTURE TIP: Visiting a home
In the United States, if you visit someone's house, they are likely to take you on a tour of the whole house. In other countries, like Korea, you are usually escorted to a well-decorated room. Food is brought to you, and you will not be shown the rest of the house. In some Arab countries, like Syria, it is considered rude to use the bathroom in a person's home. In many countries around the world, you will be expected to take your shoes off. And in Japan, you will sit on a very clean floor.

2 VOCABULARY

Word Bank
Words to describe a color
bright, dark, favorite, neutral, primary

Bright colors, when combined with neutral colors, create a wonderful look.

A ⟳ Two people are asking the Home Helper, a **home improvement** expert, for advice. Follow the instructions below.

Student A: Ask your partner question ❶.

Student B: Don't read the answer below. Give your own advice. Then switch roles and repeat for question ❷.

❶ *Dear Home Helper, We want to* **repaint** *our bedroom. I want to paint it my* **favorite** **color***: purple. My husband hates the idea. What do you think?*

Answer: **Dark colors** can make a room look smaller. Some colors, like orange and purple, can be **overwhelming** when used alone. **Combine** them with **neutral colors**, like beige and gray, when you **redo** your room.

❷ *Dear Home Helper, My sofa is broken, and the rest of my furniture doesn't* **work well** *in my apartment: it's too large. Should I* **get rid of** *all my furniture and start over?*

Answer: **Repair** your sofa, but you don't have to **replace** everything else. Have you tried **rearranging** your furniture? You may find a new **option** that works better for you and your room.

B ⟳ Now read the responses from the Home Helper. What is the advice? Is it similar to what you said in **A**? Do you agree with it? Tell your partner.

> I agree with her husband. Purple is a terrible choice.

ℹ️ The prefix *re-* can indicate that something is done in a second and, sometimes, different way.

rearrange   recreate   repaint

rebuild   redo   restart

Other words, like *replace* and *repair*, do not fit into this category.

C ⟳ Discuss the questions with a partner.

1. What works well in your bedroom right now? What doesn't?

2. What is one thing you would rearrange in your home?

3. You can repaint your bedroom any color. What color do you choose and why?

4. What colors go well together? What colors should not be combined?

3 LISTENING

A 🔄 Look at the color wheel. Answer the questions with a partner.

1. When do you use a color wheel?

2. Which colors do you think are *warm*? Which ones are *cool*?

B 🔊 **Pronunciation: Saying a series of items.** Read and listen to these sentences. Then listen and repeat. **CD 1 Track 2**

1. The three primary colors on the color wheel are red, yellow, and blue.

2. White, black, and gray are neutral colors.

3. Our living room has a sofa, table, and two chairs.

4. You can enlarge a space by using mirrors, light colors, and small furniture.

C 🔄 Complete the chart below. Read and explain your answers to a partner.

My three favorite colors	
The three hardest subjects in school	
My three favorite singers / actors	

> I really like red, yellow, and orange. They're my favorites because I like bright colors.

D 🔊 **Make and check predictions.** You are going to hear a lecture about the color wheel. Read the chart and predict the answers. Then listen and complete the notes. **CD 1 Track 3**

What the color wheel does	shows us how to (1.) _____ colors in an attractive way
People who use the color wheel	painters, decorators, and (2.) _____ designers
Primary colors Use of these colors	red, (3.) _____, and (4.) _____ can (5.) _____ them together to create (6.) _____
Warm colors Their effect	yellow and (7.) _____ They have a lot of (8.) _____. They come (9.) _____ the viewer.
Cool colors Their effect	blue and (10.) _____ They are quiet and (11.) _____. They move (12.) _____ from the viewer.

E 🔊 **Listen for details.** Listen to the information about combining colors. Which chart illustrates the speaker's point? **CD 1 Track 4**

1

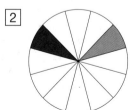

2

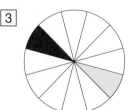

3

F 🔄 Look back at your answers in **D**. Explain the lecture in your own words. What is your favorite color combination? Why? Tell a partner.

3 LISTENING

STRATEGIES: Make and check predictions; Listen for details

WARM UP Ask students to look around the classroom and name all of the colors that they can see. Include students' clothing, images on the wall, the color of the paint in the classroom, etc. Write all of these colors on the board. ⏱ 5 min

A Look at the color wheel. Answer the questions with a partner. ⏱ 5–10 min

Introduce the idea of the color wheel and say that artists and others use it to select colors to work with. Give students a few minutes to look at the color wheel and think about the questions. Then assign students to pairs to discuss the questions. With the class, discuss students' answers but don't provide the correct answers. The students will hear the answers in the listening.

B **Pronunciation: Saying a series of items.** Read and listen to these sentences. Then listen and repeat. **CD 1 Track 2** ⏱ 10 min

Read the sentences, then play the audio. Review intonation. Remind students that *intonation* is the way that our voice goes up or down as we speak. In a normal sentence, we speak at a normal level of pitch, then our voice rises to a high level near the end before falling to a low level at the very end. When we have a series of items, our voice goes up on the first items and then down on the final item. Play the audio again for students to repeat. Practice the sentences several times with the whole class. You can have the class repeat chorally as a whole, in halves, or in rows.

LANGUAGE TIP: Intonation in a series of items
When listing a series of items, the intonation pattern rises on the items at the beginning of the list and falls on the item at the end of the list. If a noun in a list has an adjective in front of it, the pattern changes on the stressed syllable of the noun, not on the adjective.

TEACHING TIP: Intonation patterns
To help students hear intonation patterns in different types of sentences, first write the sentences on the board. Then, draw a line under and over the sentence to show how the intonation pattern rises and falls. Ask students to repeat your pronunciation of the sentences as you trace the line on the board with your hand.

C Complete the chart below. Read and explain your answers to a partner. ⏱ 10 min

Assign pairs to share their answers using the intonation pattern that they practiced in **B**. Monitor and help students with intonation as necessary. Call on different students to tell the class one of their partner's lists.

D **Make and check predictions.** You are going to hear a lecture about the color wheel. Read the chart and predict the answers. Then listen and complete the notes. **CD 1 Track 3** ⏱ 10–15 min

Go through the chart with the class, then have them predict the answers. Compare predictions as a class. Tell the class that they are going to hear a short lecture and that they should listen to confirm their predictions. Play the audio, then check answers with the class.

Make and check predictions. Remind students that predicting content before listening helps them be more prepared for what they are going to hear, as they will have activated prior knowledge of the topic and language related to it. Checking these predictions after they have listened enables them to see how predicting is useful, or if their predictions weren't correct, to analyze why the answers were not what they had predicted.

E **Listen for details.** Listen to the information about combining colors. Which chart illustrates the speaker's point? **CD 1 Track 4** ⏱ 10 min

Ask students, *What color is the opposite of white? Black.* Ask if students think other colors have opposites, like yellow or blue. Take responses from a few students. Then tell students they are going to listen to a short lecture about opposites and color. Tell students to look at the three pie charts. Play the audio twice. Ask the students to explain opposite colors, and how the correct color wheel shows opposites.

Listen for details. Remind students that they do not need to understand every word in order to understand specific details. Encourage them to get into the habit of identifying key words to listen for before they listen.

F Look back at your answers in **D**. Explain the lecture in your own words. What is your favorite color combination? Why? Tell a partner. ⏱ 10–15 min

Go over the directions and the questions with the class. Give students time to think about their answers. Encourage them to write a few notes with key words. Assign students to pairs to talk about the lecture and their favorite color combinations. Monitor and provide help as necessary. Call on different students to tell the class about their partner's favorite color combination and why they like it.

4 SPEAKING

WARM UP Talk with students about giving advice. Ask, *Who do you ask for advice? Who asks you for advice? What do you ask for and give advice about? Do you like giving advice?* ⏱ 5 min

A 🔊 Emilia has just moved into a new apartment. Listen to and read the conversation and answer the questions. **CD 1 Track 5** ⏱ 10 min

Tell students to look at the picture and describe the building. Play the audio. Then ask two students to read the conversation. Review answers to the questions with the whole class. For additional practice, you can read the conversation out loud for the class to repeat.

LANGUAGE TIP: Asking someone to wait

In the conversation, Felipe asks Emilia to *hold on a second* while he gets Sam's telephone number. You can combine any of the words on the left below with the words on the right to give students other examples of how to ask someone to wait. It is common to use the terms *minute* or *second*, even though the wait may be considerably longer! A *moment* is a very short period of time; it does not have a specific measurement.

hold on	*a second*
wait	*a sec*
just	*a moment*
hang on	*a minute*

When using the two-word verbs *hold on* or *hang on*, be sure to put the stress on the word *on*.

B 🔄 Can you think of another way to solve Emilia's problem? What would you do? Tell your partner. ⏱ 5–10 min

Pair students to talk about what they would do. Then call on pairs to share their ideas while you list them on the board. If pairs repeat one another's ideas, write a check mark to represent each additional pair. When all ideas have been listed, point out the most popular suggestions. Ask students to comment on this.

SPEAKING STRATEGY

C 🔄 Read these two situations. Choose one and role-play it with a partner. Then switch roles and role-play the other situation. ⏱ 10–15 min

(See Student Book page 7 for complete instructions.)

Review the Useful Expressions. Point out the use of the base form of the verb with the expressions on the left and the use of verb + *-ing* with the expressions on the right. Call on a few students to respond to the question *Why don't you fix it yourself?* Then assign students to pairs to practice the two problem role plays. Call on one or two pairs to perform their role play for the class.

ℹ️ Point out the different ways to respond. Ask, *What is something that would cause you to respond strongly?*

TEACHING TIP: Using role play effectively

Remind students that in a role play, they are actors taking on the role of another person. Try for more energetic performances by having students stand, rather than sit, while performing. Tell them to speak directly to each other and not to read from their books or papers. You may choose to give students time to prepare their conversations by writing down some ideas. Stronger classes can prepare their role plays without writing. Students should practice their role play one or more times. In smaller classes, all role plays can be presented to the whole class. In larger classes, students can perform their role play for another pair or group. Comment on the successful usage of language and on any problems you observed.

LARGE CLASS OPTION

Before the role play in **C**, brainstorm with students about possible suggestions for what could be done in the case of each problem. Write these suggestions on the board. Be sure that students clearly understand the assignment by modeling the role plays with one or two students at the front of the room. Give students five to ten minutes to prepare and practice their role plays. Then form small groups of two to five pairs. Students should perform the role plays for others in the group.

Instructor's Notes

_____

_____

_____

_____

_____

_____

_____

_____

4 SPEAKING

A 🔊 Emilia has just moved into a new apartment. Listen to and read the conversation and answer the questions. **CD 1 Track 5**

1. How does Emilia like the apartment? What's the problem?
2. How does Felipe make suggestions to solve the problem? Underline the sentences.
3. How does Emilia accept and refuse the advice? Circle the sentences.

EMILIA: Thanks for your help, Felipe.

FELIPE: No problem. How do you like your new apartment?

EMILIA: It's great. I love it. There's just one thing...

FELIPE: Yeah?

EMILIA: I found a small crack in the wall.

FELIPE: The wall is cracked? Really?

EMILIA: Yeah. It's not too big, but it's in the living room, and everyone can see it.

FELIPE: Why don't you fix it yourself?

EMILIA: Um... I don't think so. I'm not good at repairing things.

FELIPE: I know! Try calling my friend, Sam. He can help you. He's a nice guy, and he's very capable.

EMILIA: That sounds like a great idea. Do you have his phone number?

FELIPE: Sure. Hold on a second while I get it...

B 🔁 Can you think of another way to solve Emilia's problem? What would you do? Tell your partner.

SPEAKING STRATEGY

C 🔁 Read the two situations. Choose one and role-play it with a partner. Then switch roles and role-play the other situation.

Student A: Tell your friend about your problem. Practice accepting and refusing suggestions.

Student B: Use the Useful Expressions to help you make suggestions.

Useful Expressions: Making informal suggestions	
With base form	With verb + -ing
Why don't you <u>fix</u> it yourself? I think you should <u>fix</u> it yourself.	Have you thought about <u>fixing</u> it yourself?
I know what you should do. <u>Call</u> my friend.	Try <u>calling</u> my friend.
Speaking tip	
You can respond to an informal suggestion with a strong or weak *yes* or a *no*.	

Problem: It's 2:00 AM. You return home and can't find the key to your house. You're locked out! Your roommate is sleeping and will be angry if you wake him.

Problem: You have just moved into a new apartment. It has very few windows and is dark. You don't have a lot of money to spend on home improvement.

ℹ️ **Responding:**
Strong yes: *Good idea! / That's a great idea. / Sounds good to me.*
Weak yes / maybe: *I guess it's worth a try. / Maybe I'll do that.*
No: *I don't think so. / No, I don't like that idea.*

5 GRAMMAR

A Turn to page 193. Complete the exercises. Then do **B–E** below.

Stative Passive Voice			
Subject	**Verb**	**Object**	
I	broke	the window.	This sentence describes an action.
Subject	***be***	**Past participle**	
The window	is	broken.	This sentence describes a state.

B Complete the chart with the correct forms of the verbs.

Base	Simple past	Past participle		Base	Simple past	Past participle
bend					flooded	
	broke			freeze		
clog				jam		
	cracked				stained	

C Complete the sentences with the correct form of the word in parentheses.

1. This room needs a lot of work. The walls (crack) _____ and the floor (stain) _____.

2. It rained a lot and now the basement (flood) _____.

3. Someone (break) _____ the window last week. I can't believe it _____ still (break) _____.

4. He (throw) _____ something into the sink. Now the drain (clog) _____.

5. This key doesn't work because it (bend) _____.

D Think of something in your home, your classroom, and your school that is broken or not working properly. Write the problems in the chart below.

	Problem	Advice	Advice
Home			
Classroom			
School			

E Tell two of your classmates about your three problems. Ask for their advice and write it in **D**. Which suggestions do you like? Why?

> A light bulb is burned out in our bathroom at home.

> Why don't you buy a new one and replace it?

5 GRAMMAR
Stative passive voice

WARM UP Write the words *regular* and *irregular* on the board. Ask students for examples of past tense verbs that are regular and irregular. Write them on the board. ⏱ 5 min

A Turn to page 193. Complete the exercises. Then do **B–E** below. ⏱ 20–30 min

Go over the examples in the chart. Then have students identify the forms of the verb *break* in the two sentences (past simple and past participle). Refer students back to the verbs listed in the Warm Up as necessary. The grammar chart on page 193 includes active and passive forms, usage explanations, and a list of common verbs in their base, simple past, and past participle forms, expanding on the information in the chart on page 8.

B Complete the chart with the correct forms of the verbs. ⏱ 5–10 min

Students can complete this exercise individually. Refer students to the Grammar Notes on page 193 if needed. To check answers, copy the verb chart on the board with the empty spaces. Ask for volunteers to come to the board to write the correct answers. Then, using choral repetition, the class can repeat each series of verbs after you.

GRAMMAR TIP: Past participles
The past participle is almost always the same as the simple past form of the verb, but some other forms exist, such as *written* or *taken*. The past participle is used for the stative passive voice as seen here. More commonly, the past participle is used with auxiliary verbs in the perfect tenses. Example: *I have broken my leg twice. I had broken my leg, so I couldn't move quickly.*

C Complete the sentences with the correct form of the word in parentheses. ⏱ 10–15 min

Remind students that the base form of the verb they should use will be found in parentheses. Students can complete the sentences individually. If students are struggling with the verb forms, let them know that the answers may be one of the forms in the verb chart in **A**. Check answers with the class.

TEACHING OPTION: Support / challenge
Students complete the answers in **C** individually, then check answers in pairs. One student reads his or her answers out loud while the other student compares them with his or her answers. Students should use this as listening practice. Do not allow students to look at each other's books. They should listen and compare.

D Think of something in your home, your classroom, and your school that is broken or not working properly. Write the problems in the chart below. ⏱ 10–15 min

Go over the directions and the chart with the class. Then give students a minute or two to think about whether there is anything in their home, classroom, or school that is broken or not working properly. They should write their ideas in the chart. Help with vocabulary as necessary. Write new vocabulary on the board to help other students.

E Tell two of your classmates about your three problems. Ask for their advice and write it in **D**. Which suggestions do you like? Why? ⏱ 10–15 min

Go over the directions with the class, then elicit the expressions they saw in Speaking for making and responding to suggestions and write them on the board. Refer students back to the Useful Expressions on page 7 as necessary. Assign students to groups of three or four students to talk about the problems in their charts. Monitor and provide help as necessary. Ask students follow-up questions to encourage them to talk more. Call on different groups to share some of their advice with the class.

GRAMMAR TUTORIALS
• Participles Used as Adjectives

Additional tutorials are available for reteaching and reinforcement.

Instructor's Notes

_____

_____

_____

_____

_____

_____

_____

_____

_____

_____

6 COMMUNICATION

WARM UP Remind students of the color wheel they read about on page 6. Ask students their opinions about the role of color in design. *What colors would make a room feel friendly and warm? How might color be used to improve the room in the photo?* 🕐 5 min

A 🔁 Look at the photo of a room in an old hotel. Answer the questions with a partner. 🕐 10–15 min

Ask students if they have ever been to a hotel. If so, what was it like? Put students in pairs to answer the questions. Provide vocabulary as necessary and write it on the board. Ask some students to share their answers with the whole class.

B Read about a contest. 🕐 5 min

(See Student Book page 9 for complete instructions.)

Give students a few minutes to read about the contest. Answer any questions they have about it.

C 🔁 Work with a partner. On a separate piece of paper, make a chart with two columns: *Ideas to make the room more welcoming* and *Ideas to make the room more comfortable*. Think of ideas for the design contest. Write them in the chart. 🕐 10–15 min

Assign students to pairs. Remind them to brainstorm ideas, and that, when brainstorming, they should avoid criticizing each other's ideas. They should write down as many ideas as possible. Remind students of the words and expressions to describe rooms, both good and bad, on pages 5 and 6. They can use these words and expressions in their brainstorming. Walk around the room and offer help as needed while students are working.

D 🔀 Get together with another pair. Introduce yourselves and present your ideas to them. When you listen, take notes. Then explain what you like most about the other pair's design ideas. 🕐 15–20 min

Go over the examples of language for presentations. Introduce yourself. Then call on a few volunteers to introduce themselves. Tell students they will introduce themselves to the pair they are going to work with and then present their ideas for the hotel. Remind students to speak clearly and make eye contact with the pair they are presenting to. Remind them to try to speak without looking at their notes. As they listen, they need to take notes about the other pair's presentation. After they have presented, have them tell each other what was good about their presentation. Write down any suggestions that you have for students to improve their language in the areas of speaking, pronunciation, grammar, expressions, or presentation skills. Share these observations with students privately after class or as general feedback to the group.

TEACHING TIP: Starting and ending pair, group, and class exercises

To make pair, group, and class exercises go smoothly, it's helpful to use clear signals for beginning and ending the task. Some ideas:

Write starting and ending times on the board. (Group work starts: 10:15. Group work ends: 10:25.)

Tell your students that the exercise ends when you clap your hands three times.

Train your students to understand that when they see you raise your hand, they should also raise their hands and stop talking. The room will fall silent without you interrupting.

LARGE CLASS OPTION

Place students in groups of 6–12 for **D**. If possible, move the desks and chairs in your classroom so that students can sit in a circle and face each other. Appoint one student in each group to decide on the order of the speakers. Appoint another student to be timekeeper with authority to stop speakers who go on for too long. Give each speaker a time limit of 2 or 3 minutes. Then ask students to present their ideas to their groups. Walk around the classroom and listen for errors that are repeated by multiple students. After all of the students have presented, share your observations with the class, and offer suggestions for improvement.

EXTRA! Writing prompt

Assign students to work in groups to prepare a written entry for the design contest described in **B**. Tell them to use pictures and illustrations and to put their ideas in writing. The class can vote on the most creative design proposal. You can award them a small prize, if desired. 🕐 20–30 min

Instructor's Notes

_____

_____

_____

_____

_____

_____

6 COMMUNICATION

A 🔁 Look at the photo of a room in an old hotel. Answer the questions with a partner.

1. Would you like to stay in this hotel? Why or why not?
2. What are some of the problems with this room?

B Read about a contest.

- A local company wants to restore the old hotel. They plan to start with the room in **A**. They are sponsoring a design contest.
- You are going to enter the design contest. Using the photo in **A**, come up with at least five ideas for improving the room.
- Your goals are to make the room more welcoming and comfortable.
- The winning design team will receive $25,000!

C 🔁 Work with a partner. On a separate piece of paper, make a chart with two columns: *Ideas to make the room more welcoming* and *Ideas to make the room more comfortable.* Think of ideas for the design contest. Write them in the chart.

D 👥 Get together with another pair. Introduce yourselves and present your ideas to them. When you listen, take notes. Then explain what you like most about the other pair's design ideas.

Language for Presentations	
Introducing yourself	Stating the purpose
Hello, everyone. I'd like to thank you for coming. My name is... and I'm from (school / company).	Today, we're going to talk to you about...

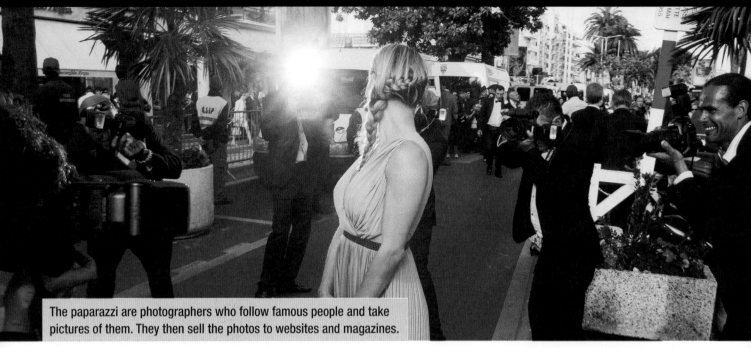

The paparazzi are photographers who follow famous people and take pictures of them. They then sell the photos to websites and magazines.

1 VOCABULARY

A Look at the photo and read the information. Who are the paparazzi and what do they do? Why do they do it? Tell a partner.

B Read the opinions below. Match a person to each statement. Explain your choices to a partner.

> a. My **private life** is my own. What I do in my free time is **no one else's business**.

> c. I like to know any news about famous people right away! But I feel sorry for them. When they go out **in public**, the paparazzi follow them. Celebrities never **have** any **privacy**. That's hard.

> b. Singers and actors are **public figures**. **The general public** is interested in them. It's natural to have paparazzi following them. I work with the paparazzi all the time.

> d. Movie stars, like all people, have certain **rights**. For example, you can't **disturb** (= bother) them in their own homes.

1. Clark, entertainment blogger _____

2. Desiree, lawyer _____

3. Cesar, actor _____

4. Hong-li, student _____

1 VOCABULARY

WARM UP Ask students to name their favorite celebrities. Write the names on the board. Ask students what they know about the private lives of their favorite celebrities. How do they know these things? ⏱ 5–10 min

A 🔁 Look at the photo and read the information. Who are the paparazzi and what do they do? Why do they do it? Tell a partner. ⏱ 5–10 min

Direct the students' attention to the photo and tell them to read the caption. Give the correct pronunciation of the term *paparazzi* (ˌpɑpɑˈrɑttsi) with students repeating after you. Have students discuss the questions with a partner. Call on different pairs to share their answers.

LANGUAGE TIP: Paparazzi
Nowadays, the word *paparazzi* refers to freelance photographers who pursue celebrities in their private lives to get candid photographs of them. Originally, the word comes from Italian, and its etymology is disputed. One claim is that it comes from the famous Italian film *La Dolce Vita* (in English, *The Sweet Life*) by Federico Fellini, where Paparazzo (the singular of *paparazzi*) is the last name of a character who is a photographer.

B 🔁 Read the opinions below. Match a person to each statement. Explain your choices to a partner. ⏱ 15 min

Tell students that they must figure out which statement was made by each person listed below. Make sure they understand what each person does. Tell students to think about these four people in terms of how they might feel about the paparazzi. Pair students to read the speech bubbles and match the opinions to the people. Tell students to try to figure out new vocabulary from the context. Check answers as a class. Ask students how they were able to figure out unfamiliar words. Answer any remaining vocabulary questions.

TEACHING TIP: Assigning partners
It's a good idea to show students very early in the course how you want them to move into pairs and how to change partners. This will save a lot of valuable class time and help make larger classes more manageable. You can ask students to work with a partner on one side, then turn to work with a different partner on the other side. If the class is seated in rows, you can also ask half the students to turn around and work with the student behind them.

TEACHING TIP: Vocabulary notebooks
Recommend that your students keep lists of new words in a special pocket notebook or in a separate vocabulary section of their class notebook. Have them write down new English words from class or outside activities that are interesting or useful for them. Along with the new word, students should write down a definition or translation and a sentence using the word. You may want to give students a minute or two at the end of class to add any new items to their notebooks. Remind them to go back and review the items on each page as it is completed and to review previous pages frequently.

EXTRA! Class contact list
Have each student make a class list in their notebook of each student's name, last name, email address, and telephone number. They should go around the class asking for people's information until they have the complete list. ⏱ 15 min

TEACHING TIP: Social media group
If appropriate, have students exchange contact details and set up a group on the social media site they prefer. Tell them that this can be a way to stay in touch and an opportunity to use English outside of class. If students are happy for you to be part of the group, join too. During the course, encourage students to share useful links in English (sites or apps for practicing English, interesting videos or articles in English, etc.).

Instructor's Notes

_____

_____

_____

_____

_____

_____

_____

1 VOCABULARY (Continued)

C Complete the phrases in the chart with words in **blue** from **B**. Then tell a partner: How are the *public* and *private* phrases different? ⏱ 10 min

Direct students' attention to the speech bubble. This is an example of how they can talk about the ways in which the *public* and *private* phrases are different. As students work in pairs, walk around and listen for clear explanations. Call on different students to share one of their explanations with the class.

D 💬 Which opinion(s) in **B** do you agree with? Why? Tell a partner. ⏱ 10–15 min

Direct students to the opinion statements in **B**. Note that opinion statements a. and d. are in agreement with each other. Be sure to remind students to give reasons for their opinions. Call on several students to share their opinions and lead a class discussion on the topic.

EXTRA! Debate

Tell students they are going to debate the issue of public figures and privacy. Divide the class into an even number of teams of about three students each. Assign the teams numbers 1, 2, 3, 4, etc. Even-numbered teams will argue in favor of the statement below. The odd-numbered teams will argue against the statement. Give the teams about ten minutes to brainstorm a list of reasons to support their opinions. Then match up even- and odd-numbered teams to debate. During the debate, each team member should speak. Here is the debate topic: "Because celebrities are public figures, they should not object to having their pictures taken in public places." ⏱ 30 min

2 LISTENING

STRATEGIES: Listen for main ideas; Infer information

WARM UP Talk with students about privacy in terms of their own lives. Be careful not to make students feel put on the spot about any personal subjects. Form questions so that answers can be more impersonal, such as, *Is it appropriate to ask another student how he or she did on a test? where he or she lives? whether he or she has a boyfriend or girlfriend?* ⏱ 5 min

CULTURE TIP: Taboo topics

Every culture is sensitive to different topics. Americans generally do not openly discuss money, religion, and politics, and they also don't typically ask about a person's age or weight. The former topics may be talked about amongst close friends, but the latter should not be brought up without risking offending the person to whom you are speaking. Ask your class what topics are taboo in their culture. Ask students to share any other taboo subjects they know of from around the world.

A 🔊 **Listen for main ideas.** You are going to listen to three conversations. Which statement (a, b, or c) is true about each conversation? Listen and circle the correct answer. CD 1 Track 6 ⏱ 5–10 min

Play the audio two or more times. The third time, stop after each conversation and give students a minute or two to answer the question. Then discuss the correct answer with the students.

Listen for main ideas. Remind students that listening for main ideas means focusing on the general ideas of what they are listening to, without worrying about details. Understanding main ideas will then help them be able to work out the details more easily, even if they don't recognize all the words used.

B 🔊 **Infer information.** Read the sentences below. Then listen again. What might the person say next? Choose the best ending for each conversation. Two sentences are extra. CD 1 Track 6 ⏱ 5–10 min

Go over the sentences with the class. Remind students that two of the five sentence options are extra. Play the audio. Briefly pause the audio after each conversation to give students time to consider their answers. Have students compare their answers with a partner's. Play the audio again as necessary. When checking the answers, ask students to give reasons for their answer choices.

Infer information. Remind students that *inferring information* means to use the information you have and background knowledge to work out something that isn't stated explicitly. They can guess what someone might say next by inferring how the person feels, or what their opinion is, from what the person has already said.

C 💬 What information do you share with friends and family? with classmates or coworkers? online? Tell a partner. Then say one thing you don't share. ⏱ 10–15 min

Go over the directions and the questions with the class. Give students time to think about their answers. Encourage them to write a few notes with key words. Assign students to pairs to talk about what information they share with whom, and what information they don't share. Monitor and provide help as necessary. Call on different students to share one of their answers with the class. Lead a class discussion on online information sharing and being safe online.

Instructor's Notes

_____

_____

_____

_____

C 🗨 Complete the phrases in the chart with words in **blue** from **B**. Then tell a partner: How are the *public* and *private* phrases different?

Opposites	
Public	**Private / Individual**
1. a public ___figure___	1. a private citizen
2. the _____	2. one person
3. (do something) _____	3. (do something) in private
4. your public life	4. your _____

> A public figure is someone famous, like a movie star. But a private citizen...

D 🗨 Which opinion(s) in **B** do you agree with? Why? Tell a partner.

2 LISTENING

A 🔊 **Listen for main ideas.** You are going to listen to three conversations. Which statement (a, b, or c) is true about each conversation? Listen and circle the correct answer. **CD 1 Track 6**

1. a. The two friends are fighting.
   b. The boy wants to talk to the girl.
   c. The girl is talking to her boyfriend.

2. a. Paula is studying.
   b. Paula has met Carla Smith.
   c. Carla Smith is a public figure.

3. a. The woman is a singer.
   b. They are talking in private.
   c. They are meeting for the first time.

B 🔊 **Infer information.** Read the sentences below. Then listen again. What might the person say next? Choose the best ending for each conversation. Two sentences are extra. **CD 1 Track 6**

Conversation 1 _____
Conversation 2 _____
Conversation 3 _____

a. She doesn't have any privacy. It's terrible!
b. They shouldn't speak to her in private like that. It's rude!
c. Sorry, but I don't talk about my private life on television.
d. Celebrities shouldn't do that in public.
e. Excuse me, but that's none of your business!

C 🗨 What information do you share with friends and family? with classmates or coworkers? online? Tell a partner. Then say one thing you don't share.

> I like to post pictures online, but I never talk about my private life.

STRATEGIES: Make and check predictions; Scan for information; Infer information; Read for details

WARM UP Introduce the idea of changing your name—for example, when you get married. Talk about any famous people in the students' country or countries who have changed their names. ⏱ 5 min

A Make and check predictions. Look at the photo and title. Then choose the best definition to complete the sentence. Read the article to check your answer. ⏱ 5 min

After students have selected their answers, discuss the correct answer with the class. Introduce the words *landscape* and *architect*. Normally an architect is someone who designs buildings. A *landscape architect* changes the natural surroundings to make them more attractive.

Make and check predictions. Remind students that checking predictions after they have read a text enables them to see how predicting is useful, or if their prediction wasn't correct, to analyze why the answer was not what they had predicted.

B 🔄 **Scan for information.** What three public spaces are talked about in the reading? Where are they? What do they have in common? Tell a partner. ⏱ 5–10 min

Go over the questions with the class, then have students read the text quickly to find the specific information they need. Have students compare their answers with a partner's, then check the answers with the class. Ask, *What is a public space? What are some examples in this city or country?*

Scan for information. Remind students that *scanning* means looking over a text quickly in order to find specific information. Scanning is often used on standardized tests that have a time limit.

Central Park, New York City, US

3 READING

A Make and check predictions. Look at the photo and title. Then choose the best definition to complete the sentence. Read the article to check your answer.

A *landscape architect* _____.
a. designs parks and gardens
b. builds schools
c. gives tours

B 🔄 **Scan for information.** What three public spaces are talked about in the reading? Where are they? What do they have in common? Tell a partner.

C Infer information. Read again. Would the people agree or disagree with these statements? Check (✔) your answers. Underline the information that supports your answers.

1. **Jin Hee Park:** I'm always studying. I don't have time to appreciate the campus.
   ☐ agree ✔ disagree

2. **Alejandro Vega:** Central Park is large, but it has a cozy feeling.
   ☐ agree ☐ disagree

3. **Ross Howard:** Niagara Falls is totally open to the public.
   ☐ agree ☐ disagree

4. **Olmsted:** We should keep the natural feeling of these places.
   ☐ agree ☐ disagree

D 🔄 **Read for details; Infer information.** Reread the last paragraph. Discuss the questions with a partner.

1. What place is talked about?
2. What problems is this place having?
3. How would you answer the question at the end?

12 UNIT 1 ● Indoors and outdoors

CREATING PUBLIC SPACES

EXTRA! Discussion questions

1. Why is it important for cities to have beautiful public spaces? How do they benefit the people who live there?

2. Is landscape design a needless luxury? Should cities spend money to make things look beautiful, or should that money be used for more basic services, such as public transportation, schools, or social programs? ⏱ 15–20 min

EXTRA! Post-reading

1. In groups, have students research one of the places mentioned in the article. Have the group prepare and give a short oral presentation to the class.

2. In groups, students can prepare an information guide for tourists to a favorite park or public place in their city. If practical, make copies to distribute to visitors or foreign residents, or post the information guides on the Internet. ⏱ 60 min

Jin Hee Park is a student at Stanford University in California. She studies hard. "Of course, I came here for the academics," she says. "But it doesn't hurt that the campus is so beautiful. I walk around
5 sometimes just to relax."

Alejandro Vega, a banker in New York City, jogs almost every evening after work in Central Park. "I never get bored. The park is so big. It's got gardens, ponds, bike and walking paths,
10 restaurants, and beautiful architecture. And yet, in some places, it can feel completely private."

Niagara Falls was on Ross Howard's list of places to visit in upstate New York. "There are these wonderful footpaths in the park that make the
15 waterfalls so accessible to the general public. You can get really close. The walking paths near the falls are also great for hiking and picnics."

All of these people have one man to thank for these beautiful public spaces: Frederick Law
20 Olmsted. In 1858, a design contest was held for a new park in New York City. Olmsted and his partner, Calvert Vaux, won the contest. Central Park was the finished product—the first landscaped public park in the United States.
25 Today, no trip to New York is complete without a visit to this beautiful park.

Later in his life, Olmsted designed landscapes for college campuses, including Stanford University. He also designed footpaths at Niagara Falls to
30 give visitors better views of the falls. In all his work, Olmsted tried to preserve[1] the natural beauty of an area.

Today there are new pressures on Niagara Falls: some businesses want to develop the area. On
35 Goat Island, an island in Niagara Falls State Park, there are now souvenir shops. There may be signs that say *No Littering*,[2] but there is still a lot of trash on the island. And most of the animals have disappeared. If Olmsted could see these
40 changes, what would he think?

[1] To *preserve* is to save and protect
[2] To *litter* is to throw trash on the ground

LESSON B   Public spaces   **13**

C Infer information. Read again. Would the people agree or disagree with these statements? Check (✓) your answers. Underline the information that supports your answers. 🕐 10–15 min

Go over the statements with the class, then have students read the text again. Remind students to give evidence to support their answers. Tell them to underline the sentence(s) in the reading that support their answers. Check the answers with students by a show of hands to indicate whether they think the person would agree or disagree with the statement. Then have students say how they knew whether each person would agree or disagree.

Infer information. Remind students that *inferring information* means using the information you are given and your background knowledge to work out something that isn't stated explicitly in the text. They can infer someone's opinion about something from other things they say in the text.

D 🔁 Read for details; Infer information. Reread the last paragraph. Discuss the questions with a partner. 🕐 10–15 min

Go over the questions with the class, then have students read the last paragraph again. Assign students to pairs to discuss the questions. Call on different students to answer the questions. Discuss as a class what Olmsted would think and why.

Read for details. Remind students that *reading for details* means reading a text more slowly and in depth.

TEACHING TIP: Supporting answers
Students should always be able to explain why they give the answers they do. Instead of asking students to supply an answer and move on, take the time to ask the student to explain *how* they know that is the correct answer. This is done in **C** on page 12 when students are asked to underline the evidence to support their answers. Extend this to all kinds of questions.

EXTRA! Writing prompts

1. Tell students to write a few sentences agreeing or disagreeing with this statement: "Parks should always preserve natural beauty." Students should plan their argument with supporting reasons. Remind them to be sure to focus on only one point of view.

2. Have students write a description of a park or other public space that they are familiar with. Tell them to use as many descriptive words as they can to help their readers understand the look and feel of the place they are describing.

3. Students can write about how public parks and other public spaces can be preserved. 🕐 15–20 min

4 GRAMMAR

A Turn to page 194. Complete the exercises. Then do **B** and **C** below.

Giving Permission and Expressing Prohibition				
	be	*allowed / permitted / supposed to*	Base form	
You	are(n't)	allowed to / permitted to	park	here.
		supposed to		
	Modal		**Base form**	
You	can('t)		park	here.
No	**Gerund**	*be*	*allowed / permitted*	
	Talking	is(n't)	allowed / permitted	during the test.
No	talking			

B  With a partner, write a rule for each public place using the language in the chart above.

Public transportation (a bus, the subway)

You're supposed to give your seat to an older person.

A swimming pool

A movie theater

Your school or classroom

C Get together with another pair. Take turns telling each other your rules in **B**. Do you always follow these rules? Why or why not?

> Running isn't allowed at a swimming pool.

> I never run at the pool, but some people do.

5 WRITING

A Read the list of items below. Then answer the questions with a partner.

1. Do you ever see people doing these things in public? Discuss.

2. What other annoying things do people do in public? Add two ideas.

Annoying things people do in public

Smoke

Cut the line in a store

Double park on the street

Eat on public transportation

Talk loudly on their phones

Litter

_____

_____

Word Bank
If something is *annoying*, it bothers or disturbs you.

4 GRAMMAR
Giving permission and expressing prohibition

WARM UP Ask students to think about the family rules that they had growing up. What were they not allowed to do as children? What rules did they have to follow? ⏱ 5 min

A Turn to page 194. Complete the exercises. Then do **B** and **C** below. ◑ 20–30 min

Go over the examples in the chart. Elicit more examples from the students of things that they are and aren't allowed to do (prompt with places as necessary, *at home, at school, when driving,* etc.). The grammar chart on page 194 includes additional examples and usage notes, expanding on the information in the chart on page 14.

TEACHING OPTION: The flipped classroom
To open up time for in-class communicative tasks, assign the Grammar Notes on page 194 as homework. Have students complete the exercises on My World Link Online as well.
The next time class meets:
1. Review the expressions for permission and prohibition in the Grammar Notes.
2. Go through the exercises students did for homework; present new examples and reinforce points as needed. Take questions from students. Have students talk about their answers in **C** on page 195 in pairs or small groups.
3. Turn back to page 14 and do the communicative exercises there, starting with **B**.

GRAMMAR TIP: Base form and *–ing* form
Note that to express prohibition, *be allowed to* and *be supposed to* are followed by the base form of the verb. Modal auxiliaries *can't* and *mustn't* (chiefly used in British English) are also followed by the base form of the verb. But we can also use the *–ing* form of the verb: *no smoking; talking is not permitted.* Be sure that students use the correct form of the verbs with the expressions for prohibition.

B With a partner, write a rule for each public place using the language in the chart above. ⏱ 10 min

Tell students to work together to come up with the rules. Remind them to look at the chart above and the one on page 194 to help them. Monitor and help students make corrections as necessary.

C Get together with another pair. Take turns telling each other your rules in **B**. Do you always follow these rules? Why or why not? ⏱ 10 min

Have pairs join to form groups of four to share their rules for each place. Remind them to also discuss for each place whether they always follow these rules or not. Have each group share their rules and write them on the board. Were some of their rules the same? Which ones do they always follow? Which one don't they always follow? Why not?

GRAMMAR TUTORIALS
• Expressing Prohibition

Additional tutorials are available for reteaching and reinforcement.

5 WRITING

WARM UP Review the rules of a public place, such as the school, that students discussed in the last class. What are they permitted to do? What are they not supposed to do? Some ideas to get students started could be cell-phone use, homework policy, number of absences, lateness, etc. Does everyone agree with the list, or are there some disagreements? What happens when someone breaks one of the rules? ⏱ 5 min

A Read the list of items below. Then answer the questions with a partner. ⏱ 10 min

Point out the explanation of *annoying* in the Word Bank and give an example: *People talking at the movie theater is annoying.* Elicit more examples from the students. Go over the list, then assign students to pairs to answer the questions. Monitor and provide vocabulary as necessary. Have different pairs share their answers. Then write a list on the board of other annoying things people do in public.

Instructor's Notes

_____

_____

_____

_____

_____

_____

_____

5 WRITING (Continued)

B 🔁 Read the paragraph. Then answer the questions with a partner. ⏱ 10 min

Remind students to try to guess any new words from the context. After they have read, assign students to pairs to answer the questions. Check answers with the class, having students explain how they found the answers in the text. Point out the use of *for example* in the text if students don't mention it.

C Choose a topic in **A** and answer the questions in **B** about it. Then use your notes and the example to help you write your own paragraph. ⏱ 20–25min

Choose one of the annoying things from **A** and model the exercise by explaining your answers to the questions in **B** to the class and writing them in note form on the board; for example:

1. *smoking in public places, I dislike it*
2. *a student smoking outside the classroom last week*
3. *people should think more about other people, respect the rules*

Then have students help you begin writing a paragraph using the one in **B** as a model:

I hate it when people smoke where they aren't supposed to. When you smoke where there are people who don't smoke, it isn't good for their health. Last week, for example, a student was smoking outside the classroom. Smoking is allowed in special areas on campus; it isn't permitted near the classrooms….

Then have students choose an item from the list in **A** and write notes to answer the questions. Once they have their notes, they should write their paragraph. Monitor and help students with vocabulary and permission and prohibition expressions.

PROCESS WRITING: Planning before writing
An important stage of the writing process is planning. Students will write more effectively if they plan what they are going to say before they begin writing. Modeling the planning stage with students, as in **C** above, will help them get into the habit of doing it themselves.

D 🔁 Exchange papers with a partner. ⏱ 10 min

(See Student Book page 15 for complete instructions.)

Assign students to pairs and have them exchange papers and identify any mistakes in their partner's paragraph. Tell them to focus on the use of permission and prohibition expressions and verb forms. Then have students go back to the questions in **B** and answer them about their partner's paragraph. Encourage students to talk about their paragraphs together, *What was clear? What was confusing? What could be better?* Remind them that the objective is to help each other improve their writing by reviewing each other's work. To complete the writing process, have students write a corrected version of their paragraph. If possible, collect these to give students feedback.

6 COMMUNICATION

WARM UP Write *smoking* on the board and elicit the rules about smoking in the students' country/countries: *Where is it allowed? Where is it prohibited? How old do you have to be to be allowed to buy cigarettes?* Write their answers on the board. Then ask, *Do people follow these rules? Do you agree with these rules? Should there be any other rules about smoking?* ⏱ 5 min

A 🔂 Work in a small group. Answer the questions with your group. ⏱ 15–20 min

Assign students to small groups to discuss the annoying behaviors in Writing **A**. Tell them to go through the list one by one and answer question 1 for each behavior first. Then have them discuss their opinions of the behaviors, whether they do them or not, and how they make people feel. Monitor and provide help as necessary, asking questions to encourage students to talk more. To wrap up, have each group share their answers and have a class discussion on annoying behavior and how we can deal with it.

TEACHING TIP: Encouraging fluency and participation
It is important that all students feel encouraged to speak up during a group exercise. Do not correct students while they are working in groups. Instead, listen and make notes of common errors to discuss as a class. If you notice one student is dominating a group, step in and ask the other students what their opinions are. Tell groups that each student must give his or her opinion and speak for at least one minute. Nominate a timekeeper to time speakers with a phone or watch.

Instructor's Notes

_____

_____

_____

_____

_____

_____

_____

_____

B 🔁 Read the paragraph. Then answer the questions with a partner.

I hate it when people talk loudly on their phones in public. When you talk loudly on the phone, you disturb those around you. Yesterday, for example, I was on the bus, and the man near me was talking to his friend on the phone. I could hear everything, and his call continued for almost 15 minutes. I don't understand this kind of person. It's OK to talk on the phone, but you're supposed to do it quietly. The bus is a public space, and other people don't want to know your business. Some things aren't allowed on the bus, like eating and smoking. Sometimes, I think we should ban talking on the phone, too.

1. Which topic in **A** is the writer talking about? How does he feel about this behavior?

2. What example does he use to illustrate his opinion?

3. What does he think people should do about this problem?

C Choose a topic in **A** and answer the questions in **B** about it. Then use your notes and the example to help you write your own paragraph.

D 🔁 Exchange papers with a partner.

1. Circle any mistakes in your partner's paper. Answer the questions in **B** about your partner's paragraph.

2. Return the paper to your partner. Make corrections to your own paper.

6 COMMUNICATION

A 👥 Work in a small group. Answer the questions with your group.

1. Look again at the list of annoying behaviors in Writing **A**. Are these behaviors allowed or not allowed by law in your country?

2. What do you think of these behaviors? Do you do any of them? How do you think they make people feel?

> You're not allowed to smoke in most indoor places.

> Yeah, but smoking is still permitted in some clubs. I hate it!

> I think people have the right to smoke in some public places.

UNIT 2

ABOUT THE PHOTO

This photo is part of a series taken of a wedding in Cuba. The wedding itself took place at a resort in Varadero, but the day after, the photographer, Dmitri Markine, and the newlyweds went to Havana, the capital, for what wedding photographers call the "trash the dress" session. Here the bride sits on a stone bench with a group of old Havanan women taking a break from their daily business. The contrast of the smooth-skinned young woman in her beautiful bridal gown with the elderly ladies in their everyday pants and sneakers creates an interesting comparison of the different stages in our lives.

INTRODUCE THE THEME

- In this unit, students will explore life's milestones. The language in the two lessons will help students communicate on this theme, including talking about the different stages in life, making predictions about future needs and plans, discussing milestones, and talking about future possibilities.

- In Lesson A, students will watch a video about a retired woman. Students will then learn to describe each stage in life. They will also practice listening for gist and listening for details, and they will learn how to talk about plans and necessities. Finally, they will make predictions about the future.

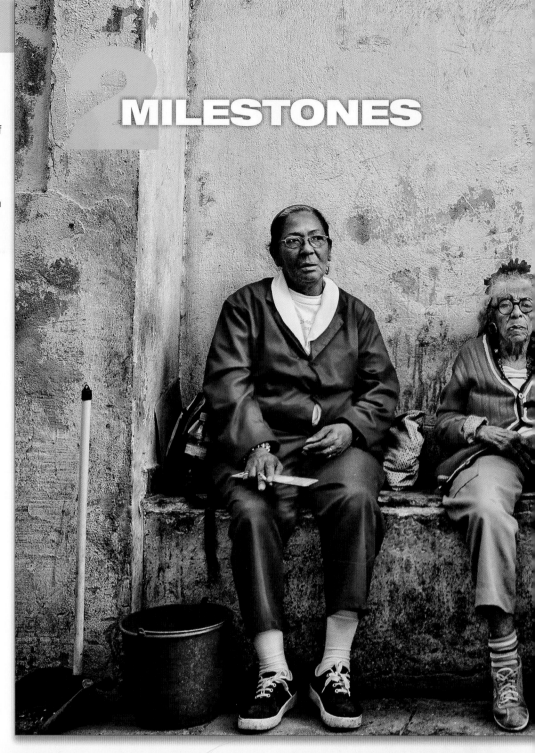

MILESTONES

	Video	Vocabulary	Listening
LESSON A Small steps p. 18	I Like Being 98 p. 18	Life cycle p. 19 *infant, toddler, adult*	A skilled public speaker p. 20 Listen for gist Listen for details
LESSON B Big changes p. 24		Life changes and milestones p. 24 *in love, went to school, left home*	Life events p. 25 Listen for gist Listen for details

For students: My World Link Online has personalized instruction, practice, audio, and video.

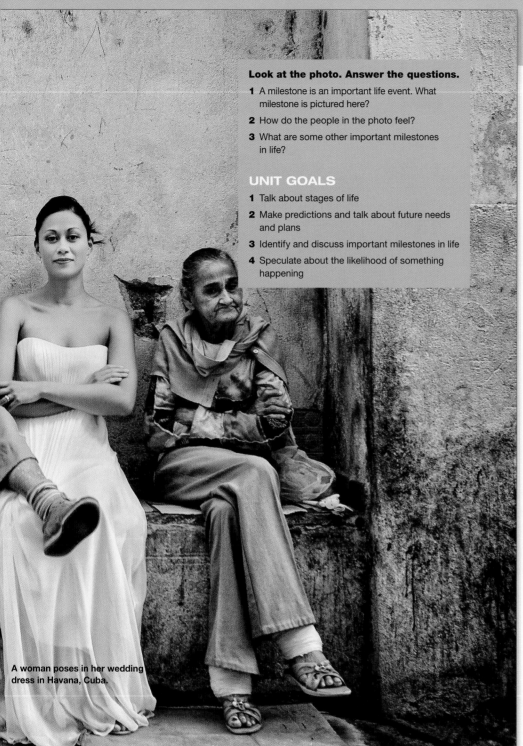

Look at the photo. Answer the questions.

1 A milestone is an important life event. What milestone is pictured here?

2 How do the people in the photo feel?

3 What are some other important milestones in life?

UNIT GOALS

1 Talk about stages of life

2 Make predictions and talk about future needs and plans

3 Identify and discuss important milestones in life

4 Speculate about the likelihood of something happening

A woman poses in her wedding dress in Havana, Cuba.

- In Lesson B, students will learn to talk about changes in life. They will read about John Francis, practicing making predictions, inferring meaning, and scanning for information. They will also learn how to express future possibility. Finally, they will write and talk about their future plans.

WARM UP

- Call on students to describe what they see in the photo.

- Have students answer the questions individually or in pairs, then compare answers with the class.

- Point out the unit goals and explain what students will learn. Elicit any key vocabulary students already know (words to describe life events and plans, for example), and write it on the board. Explain any unfamiliar phrases in the unit goals.

Grammar	Pronunciation	Speaking	Reading	Writing	Communication
Review of future forms pp. 22, 195	Content word emphasis p. 20	Talking about plans and needs p. 21	John Francis: The planet walker p. 26 Make predictions Infer meaning Scan for information	Write about your future plans p. 29	Predicting the future p. 23
Modals of future possibility pp. 28, 196					Talking about future plans p. 29

People in a retirement community

1 **VIDEO** I Like Being 98

> **Word Bank**
>
> *retirement* = when someone gets older and leaves working life
>
> *community* = a group of people living together
>
> *retirement community* = a place where older people live

A Read the information in the Word Bank. Why do you think some people "feel stuck" in retirement communities?

B ▶ Watch the first part of the video. Complete the information about Evelyn. What happened to her? How did she feel?

"I lost my _____ _____ because somebody thought I was too _____. But I didn't have a mark against me at all. I was _____ at that, I really was. It made me feel old. It made me feel _____."

C ▶ Watch the full video. What do the words in *italics* refer to? Match them to the descriptions on the right. You will use one description twice.

1. We used to have a bus *here*. _____
2. They gave *it* up. _____
3. A lot of people were stuck around *here*. _____
4. Joyce didn't want to go *anywhere else*. _____
5. I went to get *it* back. _____
6. I passed *it*. _____
7. *That* will give you joy. _____
8. I don't do *this* so you think I'm great. _____

a. another place to live
b. bus to the supermarket
c. driver's license
d. help Joyce
e. driving test
f. loving your neighbor and being a friend
g. retirement community

D What words describe Evelyn? Do you know anyone like her? Tell a partner.

VIDEO
I Like Being 98

WARM UP Have students look at the photo and describe the scene. Who are the people? What are they doing? Where are they? Write their ideas on the board. ⏱ 5 min

ABOUT THE VIDEO
Evelyn and Joyce, 70, live in the same retirement community. When the bus service which took them once a week to do their grocery shopping is terminated, Joyce feels she will have to move, even though she doesn't want to. Without the bus, she has no way of getting her shopping done. Evelyn believes in helping others, so she decides she will solve her friend's problem and drive her to the supermarket once a week. However, to do this she needs to get her driver's license back—it was taken away from her because she was considered too old to drive. Evelyn passes her driving test again and is able to keep her promise to Joyce. Evelyn's message is simple: give to others however you can; age does not need to be a restriction!

TEACHING TIP: Using English videos
Remind students to look at what is happening around the person who is talking in a video: where the person is, what objects or other people are around, and what the other people are doing. Noticing these aspects will help students understand the context of what they are listening to, and therefore help them understand what is being said. Additionally, it will help them guess the meaning of words they are not familiar with.

A Read the information in the Word Bank. Why do you think some people "feel stuck" in retirement communities? ⏱ 5–10 min

Have students read the definitions in the Word Bank, then call on a student to explain what a retirement community is. Find out if retirement homes and communities are common in the students' country or countries. Have students read the directions and try to explain *feel stuck*; tell them to look up the expression to find more examples and explain why people might feel that way in a retirement community. As a class, discuss the question.

B ▶ Watch the first part of the video. Complete the information about Evelyn. What happened to her? How did she feel? ⏱ 10 min

Go over what Evelyn says with the class and make sure they understand that they need to take notes as they watch to complete it. Play the beginning of the video (up to 1:15) twice. Give students time to complete their notes, then have them compare with a partner's. Play the first part again as necessary and check answers with the class.

C ▶ Watch the full video. What do the words in italics refer to? Match them to the descriptions on the right. You will use one description twice. ⏱ 10–15 min

Go over the sentence with the class and point out the words in italics. Make sure students understand they need to listen and decide what each word in italics refers to. Play the whole video. Have students compare their answers with a partner's, then play the video again. Check answers with the class.

Extra video vocabulary
contribute
heartbroken
make / keep a promise
obey the rules

D 🔄 What words describe Evelyn? Do you know anyone like her? Tell a partner. ⏱ 10 min

Go over the questions with the class and give students a moment to think about their answers. Remind them to write a few notes to help them when they are speaking (key words, not complete sentences). Assign students to pairs to share their answers. Share answers as a class and write a list of words to describe Evelyn on the board. Have students tell the class about anyone they know like Evelyn. Talk about Evelyn's philosophy as a class and ways that students can help other people that don't involve money.

EXTRA! Post-viewing
In small groups, have students think of the advantages and disadvantages of living in a retirement community. Tell each group to write a pros and cons list. Then have them share these lists in groups or with the whole class. ⏱ 10 min

2 VOCABULARY

WARM UP Go over the words for the stages in life with the images and in the Word Bank. Have students repeat the words. Ask, *Which stage is the most difficult?* ◷ 5 min

Draw a Venn diagram (see Teaching Tip below) on the board. Label one circle *parent* and the other *friend*. What words do students think of for each one? Write the words in the appropriate circle. Are there any words they think about with both parents and friends? Write those in the space where the circles overlap. Ask students if they think that their parents want to be their friends.

TEACHING TIP: Venn diagrams
A Venn diagram is a graphic organizer that shows two overlapping circles. It is a simple way to present and understand the similarities and differences in two things. Similarities are in the central section, while differences are on the two sides. There is a Venn diagram in the resources on My World Link Online.

A How would you describe your relationship with your parents? Check (✓) the box. Explain your answer to a partner. ◷ 5–10 min

Help students understand the vocabulary, including *relationship* and *strict*. Then read the sentences with the class, and explain any other vocabulary as needed. Pair students to discuss their answers.

TEACHING TIP: Keeping students on task
When students are assigned to work together with a partner or in a small group, some students may become distracted. Help students stay on task by giving very clear directions about what you want them to do. Then, while they are working, walk around the classroom from group to group. Often, your presence alone is enough to help students get back on task. At other times, you may need to talk to students to make sure they are on task.

B Read the article. What is it about?

Give students five minutes to read the article. Tell students to pay attention to the words in blue and look up new vocabulary words in their dictionaries. Ask some comprehension questions so students can explain the article; for example:
How many people did the survey?
Why does Peggy want to give her son everything?
What does Fred want his children to do?
What is the problem with parents wanting to be their children's best friend?
Did the young adults agree with the parents' opinions?

These questions can be given to students on a worksheet or displayed on the board or screen. Ask students to explain the meanings of the words in blue and any other words they didn't know to the class. Answer any remaining vocabulary questions. ◷ 10–15 min

C Discuss the article in **B** with a partner. Then answer these questions. ◷ 10–15 min

Go over the questions with the class. Give students time to think about their answers. Tell them to write a few notes with key words. Assign students to pairs to talk about the article and discuss the questions. Monitor and remind them to ask follow-up questions to find out more about their partner's opinion. Call on different students to share their answers with the class. As a class, talk about whether parents should be their children's best friends or not.

EXTRA! Dictation
Dictate these sentences to students and tell them to write an age after each one. ◷ 20 min

She's too young to get married. / He's too old to ride a bicycle. / He's too old to change jobs. / He's too young to get married. / He's too old to learn a new language. / She's too young to drive a car. / He's too old to work. / She's too young to travel alone.

Adjectives that describe the quality of an age
babyish, newborn, infantile
boyish, girlish, childish, childlike
young, youthful, juvenile, immature
full-grown, grown
mature
elderly, old, senior

Instructor's Notes

_____

_____

_____

_____

_____

_____

_____

_____

_____

2 VOCABULARY

| infant (baby) | toddler | child (kid) | adolescent (teenager) | adult (grown-up) |
| 0–18 months | 18 months–3 yrs | 3–12 | 13–19 | 20+ |

A How would you describe your relationship with your parents? Check (✓) the box. Explain your answer to a partner.

☐ We're all busy. We don't see each other that much.

☐ I think my parents are too strict. They should relax a little.

☐ We're like best friends. We talk about everything.

☐ other (your idea): _____

> **Word Bank**
>
> **Stages**
> infancy → childhood →
> adolescence → adulthood

B Read the article. What is it about?

- In a survey of 1,000 parents and 500 children, 43 percent of the **grown-ups** said they wanted to be their **children**'s "best friend."

- 40 percent said they wanted to buy their children everything they wanted.

Peggy, a parent with a 15-year-old **teenager**, said, "My **childhood** was difficult. We didn't have any money. I want to give my son everything he asks for."

Fred, a single dad, said, "**Adulthood** is all about responsibility. **Adolescence** is all about having fun. I don't want my children to work too hard."

Dr. Julio Garcia, a childcare specialist, says, "Children need an **adult** to rely on. They need rules—and a best friend isn't going to give you rules."

Interestingly, the **young adults** in the survey didn't share their parents' values.

- When they are ready to **start a family**, only 28 percent of them want to be their children's best friend.

- Only 10 percent want to buy their **kids** everything.

C 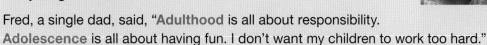 Discuss the article in **B** with a partner. Then answer these questions.

1. Who do you agree with: Peggy, Fred, or Dr. Garcia?

2. When you are ready to start your own family, how will you raise your children?

3 LISTENING

A 🔊 **Pronunciation: Content word emphasis.** Listen to and repeat the following sentences. Notice how the underlined words are stressed. **CD 1 Track 8**

1. My <u>name</u> is <u>Deena Ravitch</u>, and I'm the <u>CEO</u> of <u>Symtax</u> <u>Corporation</u>.

2. I'm <u>happy</u> to be <u>here</u>.

3. <u>Today</u> is also a <u>time</u> to <u>look</u> to the <u>future</u>.

B 🔁 With a partner, take turns reading the sentences in **A**. Be sure to stress the content words.

Many skilled public speakers use inspiring sayings to move their audience.

C Look at the photo and read the caption. Do you know any inspiring sayings?

D 🔊 **Listen for gist.** You are going to hear a speech. Listen and answer the questions below. **CD 1 Track 9**

1. This speech is being given at a(n) _____.

   a. wedding   c. birthday celebration

   b. office party   d. graduation ceremony

2. What information in the speech helped you choose your answer? Write the key words below.

_____

E 🔊 **Listen for details.** Listen again to parts of the speech. What does the speaker mean when she says these things? **CD 1 Track 10**

1. "You are joining the work world with all its responsibilities. In short, you are leaving your comfort zone."

   a. You will face many unfamiliar situations.

   b. Your life will become more comfortable.

   c. It's not so difficult to find a job.

2. "No matter what, though, you were always driven to succeed. And now you are here today. Congratulations."

   a. Your classes were difficult and required a lot of thinking.

   b. You never gave up, and you should feel proud.

   c. You worried about today and not being successful.

3. "Shoot for the moon. Even if you miss it, you will land among the stars."

   a. Make a plan and ask for help.

   b. Travel a lot and experience new things.

   c. Try your hardest at everything you do.

F 🔁 Think about a speech that you heard or gave. Where were you? What was the speech about? Tell a partner.

3 LISTENING

STRATEGIES: Listen for gist; Listen for details

WARM UP Ask the class to think about graduation ceremonies they have attended. What happened? What kind of advice was given to the graduates? 🕐 5 min

A 🔊 **Pronunciation: Content word emphasis.** Listen to and repeat the following sentences. Notice how the underlined words are stressed. **CD 1 Track 8** 🕐 10 min

Review the idea of stressed words. Tell the students that a syllable in a word that is stressed is longer, louder, has a clear vowel sound, and is higher in pitch. An unstressed word or syllable is shorter, spoken at a normal volume, has a reduced or obscured vowel sound, and a normal pitch. The words in the sentences that are not stressed are spoken very quickly.

LANGUAGE TIP: Sentence stress
The stress on a sentence in spoken English falls on the "content words"—nouns, verbs, adjectives, and adverbs. Words that serve a grammatical purpose, rather than carry meaning, are called "function words"—pronouns, prepositions, conjunctions, and auxiliary verbs. Function words are usually not stressed and receive a weak pronunciation, with short vowels reduced to schwa sounds and weak consonants dropped.

B 🔄 With a partner, take turns reading the sentences in **A**. Be sure to stress the content words. 🕐 10 min

With a partner, students should practice speaking the sentences, making sure to stress the content words. Walk around the class, listening for good pronunciation of the stress patterns. If necessary, remind students of the qualities of stressed versus unstressed words.

C Look at the photo and read the caption. Do you know any inspiring sayings? 🕐 10–15 min

Have students look at the photo and caption and explain what the woman is doing. Write an example of an inspirational saying on the board (see the Culture Tip below if necessary). Elicit others from students and talk about what they mean.

CULTURE TIP: Inspirational quotes:

Strive not to be a success, but rather to be of value. –Albert Einstein

I attribute my success to this: I never gave or took any excuse. –Florence Nightingale

If we did all the things we are capable of, we would literally astound ourselves. –Thomas Edison

The mind is everything. What you think you become. –Buddha

The best time to plant a tree was 20 years ago. The second best time is now. –Chinese proverb

Your time is limited, so don't waste it living someone else's life. –Steve Jobs

You can never cross the ocean until you have the courage to lose sight of the shore. –Christopher Columbus

Understand that the right to choose your own path is a sacred privilege. Use it. Dwell in possibility. –Oprah Winfrey

D 🔊 **Listen for gist.** You are going to hear a speech. Listen and answer the questions below. **CD 1 Track 9** 🕐 5 min

Read the questions with the class. Play the audio. Check the answers with the class.

Listen for gist. Remind students that the purpose of listening for gist is to understand the general idea.

E 🔊 **Listen for details.** Listen again to parts of the speech. What does the speaker mean when she says these things? **CD 1 Track 10** 🕐 10 min

The audio has three questions. You may pause after each question and repeat that portion of the audio for your students. Discuss the answers as a class, and explain vocabulary as needed.

Listen for details. Teach students to get into the habit of identifying key words to listen for before they listen.

TEACHING TIP: TOEFL©
Listening items that require students to paraphrase something they've heard are commonly found on standardized tests such as the TOEFL© iBT. When students do exercises without pausing, they get a feel for taking a standardized test. After students have selected their answers, play the audio again, this time allowing more time for pausing.

🔊 **EXTRA!** More listening comprehension

Give students a chance to answer additional comprehension questions about the listening. Write the following questions on the board. Then play the audio again. Tell students to write their answers on a piece of paper. Check the answers as a class. **CD 1 Track 9**

1. Who is the speaker? *(She is the CEO of Symtax Corporation.)*

2. According to the speaker, why are we here today? *(To celebrate the graduates and their accomplishments.)*

3. What are some of the things that the students did in the past? *(Studied hard for exams; spent hours in the library doing research to write essays; spent hours sitting in class learning new ideas; did a lot of work.)* 🕐 10 min

F 🔄 Think about a speech that you heard or gave. Where were you? What was the speech about? Tell a partner. 🕐 5 min

Go over the questions with the class, then give students a moment to think about their answers and write some notes. After they discuss in pairs, call on different students to tell the class about the speech their partner talked about.

5 GRAMMAR

A Turn to page 195. Complete the exercise. Then do **B** and **C** below.

Review of Future Forms	
Make a prediction	She **will go** to a good school. / She**'s going to go** to a good school. She**'s going to have** a baby.
State a future plan	The teenagers **are going to work** part time this summer. The teenagers **are working** part time this summer.
Scheduled events	The kids **are going to go** / **are going** / **go** to summer camp on August 2nd.

> **i** Use *will* for quick decisions / offers: (phone ringing) *I'll get it!*

B Unscramble the questions.

1. you'll / think / a / do / life / you / have / happy

   _____?

2. happen / what / think / going / to / is / do / you / week / next

   _____?

3. how / the / life / in / different / will / future / be

   _____?

4. today / does / time / class / what / end

   _____?

5. doing / you / this / for / vacation / what / year / are

   _____?

6. are / what / this / to / weekend / you / do / going

   _____?

C 🔁 Work with a partner. Take turns asking and answering the questions in **B**.

> What are you doing for vacation this year?

> I'm going to go to Cozumel!

Cozumel, Mexico

1 VOCABULARY

WARM UP Have students look at the photo and describe the scene. Ask, *What is the woman doing? Where is she? Why do you think she went there?* ⏱ 5–10 min

A Match the words in column A with those in B. Then read the story about Fran Turner. Use the expressions to complete the story. (Remember to use the past tense if necessary!) ⏱ 10 min

Students can match the words individually. When they have finished, write the words from column B vertically on the board. Ask students for the answers, and write the correct words from column A directly in front of the words in column B. Read the expressions, with students repeating. Tell students to read the story about Fran Turner and to fill in the blanks. Remind them that the answers require them to use the expressions on the board. Call on students to give the answers, and check the exercise with the whole class.

B Look again at the expressions in **blue** in **A**. When do these events typically happen in one's life: childhood, adolescence, or adulthood? Complete the rest of the box with present tense forms. ⏱ 15 min

Write the following sentence on the board with blank lines: *People usually _____ in _____.* List the three times of life: *childhood, adolescence,* and *adulthood.* Explain to students that these words go in the second blank. With the students, find the blue expressions in the reading, and write them on the board. Explain to students that these go in the first blank. Tell students to write the expressions in the box next to the appropriate time of life. Check the answers as a class.

C 🔁 Don't look at **A**. Use the expressions in **B** to retell Fran's story with a partner. ⏱ 10 min

Keep the information from **B** on the board. In pairs, students should take turns using the expressions on the board to retell Fran's story. Remind students not to look at **A** and to use the past tense.

TEACHING TIP: Speaking exercises
In a speaking exercise such as **C**, be sure that you are asking students to work on their language skills, not testing their memory. Students may have difficulty remembering the story exactly. You can help by jotting an outline on the board. This will help prompt students, and keep them from looking at their books when they are practicing speaking. Remind students to look at each other when they speak, rather than looking at the page.

TEACHING OPTION: Support / challenge
If your students need a review of past tense forms, work together with them to convert the words on the board from **B** into past tense forms. Let students use these expressions to retell the story. If students need additional help, they can refer to the reading in **A** while they retell the story.

Instructor's Notes

_____

_____

_____

_____

_____

_____

_____

_____

_____

_____

_____

2 LISTENING

STRATEGIES: Listen for gist; Listen for details

WARM UP With the class, brainstorm a list of major life events, such as birth, graduation, marriage, trips overseas, children, etc. If students need help, use a famous person as an example, and write a timeline on the board with major events and dates. ⏱ 5 min

A 🔄 Look at the **blue** vocabulary words on page 24. Which of life's events are you looking forward to? Which ones do you want to avoid? Tell a partner. ⏱ 10 min

Have students go back to the vocabulary on page 24 to remind themselves of the various life changes. Then have them discuss their answers to the questions with a partner. Tell them to explain their reasons. Monitor and provide help as necessary. Call on different students to share one of their partner's answers with the class.

B 🔊 **Listen for gist.** Lindsay is reading a magazine quiz. Listen and choose the best title for the quiz. **CD 1 Track 12** ⏱ 5–10 min

Play the audio for the students at least twice. The second time, stop and discuss the correct answer with the students. What helped them decide the answer?

Listen for gist. Remind students that when listening for gist, they don't need to worry about understanding everything they hear. The purpose is to understand the general idea.

C 🔊 **Listen for details.** Listen. Check (✓) the life event each person chooses. Write key words that explain the reasons for the person's answer. **CD 1 Track 13** ⏱ 10 min

Play the audio. Pause the audio after each conversation to give students time to write. Remind students to take notes on the key words that explain the reasons for the person's answer. Have students compare their answers with a partner's, then play the audio again. Check answers with the class and answer vocabulary questions.

Listen for details. Remind students that they do not need to hear and understand everything in order to understand specific details. Encourage them to get into the habit of identifying key words to listen for before they listen.

D 🔄 Who are you most similar to: Mark, Lindsay, or their dad? Tell a partner. ⏱ 10 min

Go over the question with the class. Give students a moment to think about their answer and their reasons, then assign them to pairs to tell their partner. Monitor and provide help as necessary. Call on different students to tell the class who their partner is most similar to and why.

TEACHING TIP: Focus on strategies

It is a good idea to focus students' attention on the strategies they are being asked to use, such as listening for details and listening for gist, and to ask them after the task if using the strategy helped them. This makes students more aware of language-learning strategies and more likely to use them more often.

Instructor's Notes

2 LISTENING

A 🔄 Look at the **blue** vocabulary words on page 24. Which of life's events are you looking forward to? Which ones do you want to avoid? Tell a partner.

B 🔊 **Listen for gist.** Lindsay is reading a magazine quiz. Listen and choose the best title for the quiz. **CD 1 Track 12**

    a. Is Your Life Happy?

    b. How Can You Get the Best Job?

    c. Which Life Event is the Most Exciting?

    d. Are You a Happy Teen?

C 🔊 **Listen for details.** Listen. Check (✓) the life event each person chooses. Write key words that explain the reasons for the person's answer. **CD 1 Track 13**

Person	Event		Reasons
Mark	☐ get a job	☐ leave home	_____
Lindsay	☐ get married	☐ have a big family	_____
Dad	☐ get a promotion	☐ retire	_____

D 🔄 Who are you most similar to: Mark, Lindsay, or their dad? Tell a partner.

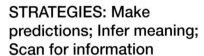
STRATEGIES: Make predictions; Infer meaning; Scan for information

WARM UP Elicit examples of *global problems* from students. Write them on the board (pollution, climate change, poverty, etc.). Then ask students, *What are people doing about these problems? How do people share information about these problems?* ⏱ 5 min

A 🔁 **Make predictions.** Read the title and look at the photo. What do you think this man does? Tell a partner. Then read the article to check your ideas. ⏱ 10 min

Assign students to pairs to make their predictions based on the title and the photo. Have pairs share their predictions and write ideas on the board. Then have students read the article quickly to check their predictions. Point out the footnotes to help them with key words and phrases.

Make predictions. Remind students that predicting before they read helps them to activate prior knowledge of the topic and language related to it.

B **Infer meaning.** Match the words in *italics* in the article with the correct definitions below. ⏱ 10 min

Have students read the definitions then read the article again and work out the meaning of the words in italics. Have students compare their answers with a partner's. Tell them to go back to the article for any they disagree on and try to work out the correct answer together. Check answers with the class.

Infer meaning. Remind students that it is often possible to work out the meaning of a new word from how it is used in the text.

---

3 READING

A 🔁 **Make predictions.** Read the title and look at the photo. What do you think this man does? Tell a partner. Then read the article to check your ideas.

B **Infer meaning.** Match the words in *italics* in the article with the correct definitions below.

1. a talk given to teach people something _____
2. disagreed _____
3. a group of people with a specific purpose _____
4. communicate an idea _____
5. nature _____

C 🔁 **Scan for details.** Find answers to the questions and underline them in the article. Ask and answer the questions with a partner. Answer in your own words.

1. Why did John stop using cars?
2. Why did he stop talking?
3. What did John learn by not talking? What did he teach people?
4. What places did John visit? How did he get to them?
5. Why did John start talking again?
6. What things did he do after he started talking again?

D 🔁 Discuss with a partner.

1. Do you think John's walk has helped the environment?
2. Have you ever experienced a "life-changing event"? What happened? How did the event change your life?

WORLD LINK

Plan a planet walk in your country. Where will you go? What will the message be?

26 UNIT 2 • Milestones

JOHN FRANCIS: THE PLANET WALKER

John Francis was born in 1946, in Philadelphia, in the United States, but in his early twenties, he left home and moved to the San Francisco area. In many ways, John's life in his new city was pretty typical. He got a job and made friends. He planned for his future. But then, two years after he arrived, something happened, and the event changed John's life forever. One day, there was a big oil spill[1] that caused a lot of damage to the local *environment*. The spill killed hundreds of animals and polluted the water in the area terribly. John was so upset by this that he decided to stop using automobiles altogether. Instead, he started walking everywhere.

When John told people he didn't ride in cars, people *argued* with him. John didn't like to fight, so he decided to stop talking for an entire day. One day became two, two days turned into a week, and finally, John decided to stop talking completely. After several weeks, he discovered something: He realized that he didn't always listen to people. By not talking, he started to really hear what others had to say.

John remained silent for 17 years. During this time, he tried to teach others about protecting the environment. He was in the newspaper several times, and he even gave *lectures* at universities. Although he didn't talk, John was still able to *get his message across* to listeners. He explained his ideas through hand motions, paintings, and the music of his banjo.

[1]If there is an *oil spill*, oil comes out of a ship and goes into the water.

TEACHING TIP: Organizing group work

Here are some ways to group students:

- Location: Put students sitting near one another together.
- Random: Count each student off with a group number (1 – 2 – 3 – 4, 1 – 2 – 3 – 4) and then say, *All number 1s sit here. All number 2s sit there.*
- Similar ability: Put stronger students together and weaker students together. The instructor can help those who need it most.
- Mixed ability: Put stronger and weaker students together in the same group. The stronger students can help the weaker students.

John eventually enrolled in college (he walked hundreds of kilometers to get there), and he got a degree in environmental studies. After he graduated, John continued his journey around the United States. He also traveled on foot and by boat to South America, the Caribbean, and other places around the world, trying to educate people about caring for the environment and each other.

John wanted to share his story with more people, so in 1990 he started to talk again. John also started to ride in cars, but his work continued. He helped write environmental laws, worked for the United Nations as a goodwill ambassador, and started Planetwalk, an *organization* that helps raise awareness[2] for environmental and humanitarian[3] issues. He also started working with National Geographic.

Today, John Francis is still trying to make the world a better place. He has written a book to inspire a new generation of planetwalkers. In it, he explains how anyone can make their own walk. He also continues to teach people about the environment. The environment, he says, is not just about animals and plants. It's about how we treat each other. If we're going to make the world a better place, we need to do it for each other, not just ourselves.

[2]To *raise awareness* is to bring attention to something.
[3]*Humanitarian* issues have to do with improving human lives.

LESSON B Big changes **27**

C **Scan for details.** Find answers to the questions and underline them in the article. Ask and answer the questions with a partner. Answer in your own words. 🕐 10–15 min

Have students read the questions and then scan the article to find the answers. Once they have underlined them, they should work with a partner and ask and answer the questions. Remind them that they need to explain the answers in their own words, not repeat what they underlined. If they disagree on any answers, they should go back to the text to confirm the answer. Check answers with the class.

Scan for information. Remind students that they can use key words from the questions (*stop* and *car* in 1) to find the details they need.

D Discuss with a partner. 🕐 10–15 min

Go over the questions with the class, then have students think about their answers and write down some notes. Assign students to pairs to discuss the questions. Monitor and help with vocabulary as necessary. Call on different pairs to share their answers. Finally, discuss life-changing events as a class.

WORLD LINK Plan a planet walk in your country. Where will you go? What will the message be?

Students can do this in pairs or small groups. First, have them decide what their message is. Then, have them think about what would be important places to include on their walk and why. Students should plan the walk and represent it visually to share with their classmates. Remind them that they need to be able to explain the reasons for their message and the places they will visit. Have pairs or groups present their message and route to the class or in groups.

EXTRA! Discussion
In small groups, talk about how effective or not they think actions like John Francis's are. 🕐 15 min

EXTRA! Post-reading
In pairs, have students research a celebrity activist or a UN Goodwill Ambassador online and prepare a short presentation about them to give to the class (in large classes, presentations can be given in small groups). 🕐 30 min

EXTRA! Writing prompt
Have students write about the person they researched. They should include their opinion on public figures doing this kind of work. 🕐 15–20 min

4 GRAMMAR

A Turn to page 196. Complete the exercises. Then do **B** and **C** below.

Modals of Future Possibility			
Subject	**Modal**	**Main verb**	
I / He / They	**may / might / could**	go	to college in the fall.
	may / might not		

Yes / No questions and short answers			
With *be*	Will you <u>be</u> home by midnight?	I **may / might / could be.** I **may / might not be.**	I don't know. I'm not sure.
With other verbs	Are you going to <u>go</u> to college?	I **may / might / could.** I **may / might not.**	It's hard to say right now. We'll see.

Remember: If you are certain about something in the future, answer like this:

Will you be home by midnight?   *Yes, I will.* or *No, I won't.*

Are you going to go to college?   *Yes, I am.* or *No, I'm not.*

B How possible is it that the predictions below will come true in your lifetime? Complete the sentences with *will / won't*, *may / might (not)*, or *could*. Then add two ideas of your own.

1. Scientists _____ solve the global warming problem.

2. World hunger _____ end.

3. We _____ travel to other planets.

4. The world's population _____ decrease (go down).

5. _____.

6. _____.

C  Work in a small group. Take turns asking about the situations in **B**. Each person should explain his or her answers.

> Will scientists solve the global warming problem in our lifetime?

> They probably won't. A lot of people still drive cars and use oil.

> They could. Many countries are working on it. We'll see.

As our planet warms, hurricanes and other storms are becoming stronger in some places.

4 GRAMMAR
Modals of future possibility

WARM UP To get students thinking about possibilities, tell them to list things that will probably happen in the future and things that will probably not happen. Which are possible? Which are probably not possible? Which might happen? Which will probably not happen? ⏱ 5 min

A Turn to page 196. Complete the exercises. Then do **B** and **C** below. ◑ 20–30 min

Go over the examples in the chart, pointing out the modals. Elicit what form of the verb we use after all modals (base verb). Ask students the questions in the chart and have them reply according to whether they are certain or not. Ask other questions related to the students' context; for example, *When are we going to have our next exam? Will you study here next semester?* The grammar chart on page 196 includes additional examples and usage notes, expanding on the information in the chart on page 28.

TEACHING OPTION: The flipped classroom
To open up time for in-class communicative tasks, assign the Grammar Notes on page 196 as homework. Have students complete the exercises on My World Link Online as well.

The next time class meets:
1. Review the modals for future possibility in the Grammar Notes.
2. Go through the exercises students did for homework; present new examples and reinforce points as needed. (You may wish to do **B** on page 28 together as a class.) Take questions from students.
3. Turn back to page 28 and do **C**.

GRAMMAR TIP: The meaning of modals
Note that there is a slight difference of meaning in these modal verbs, although they can be used almost interchangeably. The word *may* suggests a slightly stronger possibility than the word *might*. The word *may* can be used for possibility, but it is also used to ask permission: *May I have the day off tomorrow? Can* and *could* are sometimes used in similar ways.

B How possible is it that the predictions below will come true in your lifetime? Complete the sentences with *will / won't, may / might (not)*, or *could*. Then add two ideas of your own. ⏱ 10 min

Write the words *will / won't, may / may not, might / might not*, and *could* on the board. Be sure that students know the meanings of the terms *global warming, world hunger, planets, population,* and *decrease*. Demonstrate to students how to fill in the blanks. Remind them that they must come up with their own ideas for numbers 5 and 6.

C 👥 Work in a small group. Take turns asking about the situations in **B**. Each person should explain his or her answers. ⏱ 15–20 min

Model the exercise by reading the example with a student. Point out the responses. Walk around the room and offer help as needed. Tell students to comment on or otherwise respond to the suggestion given by their partner. Finish with a class discussion of which problems might be solved or not.

GRAMMAR TUTORIALS
• Modals of Future Possibility

Additional tutorials are available for reteaching and reinforcement.

Instructor's Notes

_____

_____

_____

_____

_____

_____

_____

_____

_____

_____

_____

_____

_____

_____

5 WRITING

WARM UP Write a timeline on the board of your own life. Put in only the years. Ask students to guess what important events happened in your life during the years listed. Write these on the timeline. ⏱ 5 min

A Look at the timeline and read about one person's plans for the future. What things… ⏱ 10 min

(See Student Book page 29 for complete instructions.)

Go over the directions and the questions with the class. Have students look at the timeline. Ask, *When this person is 20, what does he or she want to do? When does he or she want to get married?* Then have students read about the person's plans and answer the questions. Point out the sequencing words in bold and the usage note in the Information Box. Have students compare their answers with a partner's, then check answers with the class.

B Make a future timeline of your own. Put at least five events on it. List things that you know *will* happen and some that *may* happen. Then use your notes and the example to help you write your own paragraph. Use the words from the example to show a sequence. ⏱ 20–25 min

Draw another timeline for yourself on the board, this time about the future. Then have students help you begin writing a paragraph, using the one in **A** as a model: *What will my future be like? It's hard to know for sure, but I do have some plans. This year, for example, I'm going to visit my sister in Canada. I'm really excited because I've never been to Canada. Next year I'm planning to start studying again, so I need to apply to…*

Then have students make their own timeline. Help with ideas and vocabulary as necessary. Once they have their ideas on the timeline, they should write their paragraph. Monitor and help students with vocabulary and modals for future possibility. Remind them to use the sequence words.

C 🔄 Exchange papers with a partner. ⏱ 10 min

(See Student Book page 29 for complete instructions.)

Assign students to pairs and have them exchange papers and identify any mistakes in their partner's paragraph. Tell them to focus on the use of modals for future possibility, future forms, and the sequence words. Then have students go back to the questions in **A** and answer them about their partner's plans. Tell students to talk about their paragraphs together, by having them ask questions, such as *What was clear? What was confusing? What could be better?* Remind them that the objective is to help each other improve their writing by reviewing each other's work. To complete the writing process, have students write a corrected version of their paragraph. If possible, collect these to give students feedback.

PROCESS WRITING: Editing

An important stage of the writing process is *editing*. Students will improve their writing if they get into the habit of editing their work to correct mistakes. Including the editing stage, as in **C** above, will help them get into the habit of doing this whenever they write.

6 COMMUNICATION

WARM UP Ask students if they have ever taken a magazine quiz like the one described in the listening exercise on page 25. Where did they find the quiz? What questions were asked? How did they answer? ⏱ 5 min

A Complete the quiz about your future life. ⏱ 10–15 min

Students should complete the quiz independently by placing a checkmark (✓) in the column that best indicates the probability of each of these events happening in their future.

B 🔄 Interview your partner. Ask and answer questions about events in the chart above. ⏱ 10 min

Model this using the question and answer in the speech bubble. Then write on the board some other possible answers: *I don't know. Maybe. I probably will. I definitely won't. Probably not.* Practice some of these with the students by calling on a few individuals.

LARGE CLASS OPTION

For large classes, students can fill in the quiz individually and then write 12 grammatically accurate, complete sentences about themselves. Students can read their sentences to a partner or hand them in.

EXTRA! Writing prompt

Ask students to write a story about a friend of theirs, either real or invented. In the story, they should describe what happens to the person in the future. If they prefer, they can write more about themselves, using the timeline they made for **B** in the Writing section. ⏱ 15–20 min

C 🔄 Join another pair. Explain how you are similar to or different from each other. ⏱ 10 min

Students should share the results of their quizzes. In what ways are they similar or different? Students may not have time to compare all of their answers. Tell them to focus on just a few of the items.

Instructor's Notes

_____

_____

_____

5 WRITING

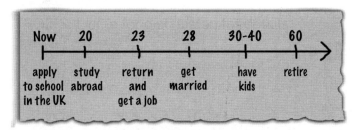

Now   20   23   28   30-40   60

apply to school in the UK   study abroad   return and get a job   get married   have kids   retire

What will my future be like? It's hard to know for sure, but I do have some plans. **This year,** for example, I'm going to apply to the London School of Economics. I want to study there **next year.** I hope I get accepted! If this happens, I want to spend two years in the UK. **Then,** when I'm 23, I may come home and look for a job, or I might stay in the UK. It's hard to know. **Later,** when I'm 28…

i   Notice how the writer uses the words in bold to explain a sequence of events.

A Look at the timeline and read about one person's plans for the future. What things…

1. is the writer definitely going to do?

2. may or may not happen?

B Make a future timeline of your own. Put at least five events on it. List things that you know *will* happen and some that *may* happen. Then use your notes and the example to help you write your own paragraph. Use the words from the example to show a sequence.

C Exchange papers with a partner.

1. Circle mistakes in your partner's paper. Answer the questions in **A** about your partner's plans.

2. Return the paper to your partner. Make corrections to your own paper.

6 COMMUNICATION

A Complete the quiz about your future life.

	I may / might	I will	I won't
1. have at least three children			
2. get married more than once			
3. retire in 30 years			
4. graduate early			
5. get a promotion			
6. live alone			
7. travel somewhere fun or exciting			
8. see or meet a famous person			
9. get a job using English			
10. get a driver's license			
11. leave home before age 20			
12. buy a home			

B Interview your partner. Ask and answer questions about events in the chart above.

> Will you have at least three children?

> I know I won't. It's challenging to raise a large family.

C Join another pair. Explain how you are similar to or different from each other.

3 GETTING INFORMATION

ABOUT THE PHOTO

Coffee shops are a key element in the social fabric of many towns and cities around the world. Menus may vary, but in many cultures, coffee shops and tea houses are part of people's daily routine. Coffee shops can often be the heart of a community, a place for meetings, social gatherings, and neighborly interactions. The coffee shop in this photo is one of Montevideo's most well established. Founded in 1877, it is considered a symbol of the city and its coffee-drinking culture. At the heart of the city in the historic Old Town area, Cafe Brasilero is frequented by both locals and visitors to the city. With its modern and bohemian mix, the Brasilero is a haven for people from all walks of life to enjoy a coffee, and perhaps something to eat, while they soak up the atmosphere.

Did you know?

According to the National Coffee Association's annual survey, Americans consume 400 million cups of coffee per day, which makes the United States the leading consumer of coffee in the world.

INTRODUCE THE THEME

• In this unit, students will talk about getting and sharing information. The language in the two lessons will help students communicate on this theme, including identifying people and places, interrupting politely, talking about how we get news and information, and sharing news about yourself and others.

	Video	Vocabulary	Listening
LESSON A Talk to me p. 32	A Unique US Town p. 32	**Personal communication** p. 33 *argue, chat, discuss*	**A new online service** p. 34 Infer information Listen for details
LESSON B The latest news p. 38		**Types of news** p. 38 *in the news, word of mouth, news sites*	**Popular stories** p. 39 Make predictions Check predictions Listen for details Infer information

 For students: My World Link Online has personalized instruction, practice, audio, and video.

Look at the photo. Answer the questions.

1 Where are these people?

2 What do you think they're talking about?

3 What do you talk about most often with your friends?

UNIT GOALS

1 Identify who someone is and where something is

2 Interrupt someone politely

3 Talk about how you get news and information

4 Share recent news about yourself and others

People talk at a cafe in Montevideo, Uruguay.

- In Lesson A, students will watch a video that shows life in a town without cell phones in the US. Students will then learn to describe ways of talking to people. They will also practice inferring information and listening for details, and they will learn how to interrupt politely. Finally, they will learn how to describe people based on where they are, what they're doing, or what they're wearing, and to describe objects based on where they are.

- In Lesson B, students will learn to talk about news programs and news stories. They will read two unusual news stories, practicing using background knowledge, sequencing events, making connections, and summarizing. They will also write and talk about recent news and events in their lives and in others' lives.

WARM UP

- Call on students to describe what they see in the photo.

- Have students answer the questions individually or in pairs, then compare answers with the class.

- Point out the unit goals and explain what students will learn. Elicit any key vocabulary students already know (words to describe news stories, for example), and write it on the board. Explain any unfamiliar phrases in the unit goals.

Grammar	Pronunciation	Speaking	Reading	Writing	Communication
Participial and prepositional phrases pp. 36, 197 Review of the present perfect pp. 42, 198	Stress: Verb + preposition p. 34	Interrupting someone politely p. 35	Viral news p. 40 Use background knowledge Sequence events Make connections Summarize	Share personal information p. 43	Ranking behaviors p. 37 Catching up at a reunion p. 43

Pocahontas County, West Virginia

1 **VIDEO** A Unique US Town

A The video is about a town in a *quiet zone*. What do you think a quiet zone is?

B ▶ What do people say about life in Green Bank, West Virginia? Watch the video and complete the sentences.

1. "Just listen to _____ all around you."

2. "No one here has a _____."

3. "There's a long list of _____ conveniences that we can't utilize here."

4. "We can't _____ because I don't have service."

5. "I really enjoy it because it's _____, it's peaceful, it's _____."

C 🔁 Would you want to live in a quiet zone? Why or why not? Tell a partner.

1 VIDEO
A Unique US Town

WARM UP Have students look at the photo and describe the scene. What do they see? What adjectives would they use to describe the place? How would they feel if they were there? How far is the nearest town? Write their ideas on the board.
⏱ 5 min

ABOUT THE VIDEO

The small town of Green Bank, West Virginia, in the United States, is home to the Robert C. Byrd Green Bank Telescope, an almost 500-foot (152-meter) high radio telescope with a dish as big as a football field. This sophisticated, high-tech telescope is used by astronomers to detect and study objects in space, so it is therefore extremely sensitive to even very faint radio waves from space. This, however, means that it is also very sensitive to interference from the electronic gadgets that most people nowadays can't imagine living without, such as cell phones, digital cameras, televisions, and Wi-Fi modems. Consequently, people who live in the 13,000-square-mile area of the Green Bank Telescope have to agree, by law, to live without these electronic devices. In this video, some of the residents of Green Bank share their views on life in the quiet zone and the irony of being without technology right next door to some of the world's most sophisticated technology.

TEACHING TIP: Cultural context clues

Videos can also provide an entry point for talking about culture. When you watch something, how do you know which country it is in, or where the people are from? What are the cultural clues? the way people talk? how they are dressed? the buildings and landforms? How do students know that these people / clothes / buildings / landforms are from a certain country or culture?

A The video is about a town in a *quiet zone.* What do you think a quiet zone is? ⏱ 5–10 min

Elicit ideas from students about what a quiet zone could be. Write their ideas on the board.

B ▶ What do people say about life in Green Bank, West Virginia? Watch the video and complete the sentences.
⏱ 10 min

Go over the sentences with the class and make sure students understand that they need to take notes as they watch to complete the sentences. Remind them to try to work out what kind of word they need in each blank and have them explain how they know (a noun after *listen to*, a noun after *a*, etc.). Play the video twice. Give students time to complete the sentences, then have them compare them with a partner's sentences. Play the video again and check answers with the class.

C 🔗 Would you want to live in a quiet zone? Why or why not? Tell a partner. ⏱ 10 min

Go over the questions with the class and give students a moment to think about their answers. Encourage them to write a few notes to help them when they are speaking (key words, not complete sentences). Assign students to pairs to discuss their opinions. Call on different students to share their opinions and discuss the concept of living in a quiet zone as a class. Provide extra video vocabulary as needed.

Extra video vocabulary	
atmosphere	odd
be obliterated	peaceful
maintain	(a) setup
modern conveniences	signal

EXTRA! Post-viewing

Have students find out more about the Green Bank Telescope online and answer these questions:
How many people live in Green Bank?
What do local people call the Green Bank Telescope (GBT)?
What states are part of the National Radio Quiet Zone?
How many telescopes are in the zone?
When did the GBT first start listening to space?
What problem does Green Bank have?
How much money does the GBT observatory bring to the area every year?

For more information, go to: https://science.nrao.edu/facilities/gbt

2 VOCABULARY

WARM UP Ask students to suggest some synonyms for *talk*. Write them on the board. Work down the list of synonyms, asking students to give examples of when or with whom they talk in each way. For example, *chat: I chat with my friends after class; argue: I argue with my sister.* Ask follow-up questions as appropriate. 🕐 5 min ·

A 🔄 Look at the verbs in the Word Bank. All of them are related to talking. Answer the questions with a partner. 🕐 10 min

Have students look at the photos and read the captions. How do the people feel in each photo? Say the verbs in the Word Bank and have students repeat them. Then assign students to pairs to answer the questions. Model the example with a student. Have them talk about what the words mean and look up any they don't know. Remind them to circle the words that can have a negative meaning. (These include *gossip* and *argue*.) Check answers by having students explain what each word means and give examples if they can. Point out the footnotes.

LANGUAGE TIP: Noun endings
Some word endings or suffixes can change a word's part of speech. Common suffixes that change verbs into nouns include: *-ment, -tion, -sion,* and *-ion*.

LANGUAGE TIP: Collocations
Two or more words that are often used together are called a *collocation*. Some examples of *collocations* within the context of communication:

have: *have a conversation, have a chat, have a discussion, have an argument, have a talk*
get into: *get into a conversation, get into a discussion, get into an argument*
carry on: *carry on a conversation, carry on a debate*

Collocations help build students' vocabulary and make their speech and writing sound more fluent.

TEACHING TIP: Dictionary use
At this level, students can make good use of a monolingual intermediate-level dictionary. Teach students how to use the grammatical information and pronunciations included in each entry. Learning to use a dictionary will help your students to become independent learners and explore vocabulary that is relevant to their own interests.

B 🔄 Ask and answer the questions with a partner. 🕐 10–15 min

Pair students to ask and answer these questions. Model the example with a student. Remind them about the vocabulary words found in the sentences. After students have had time to discuss their answers, ask a few students to share their partner's most interesting answers with the class.

EXTRA! Writing prompt
Have students choose one topic from **B** and write a paragraph. 🕐 15 min

Instructor's Notes

_____

_____

_____

_____

_____

_____

_____

_____

_____

_____

_____

_____

_____

_____

_____

_____

2 VOCABULARY

When we were younger, my brother and I **argued** a lot...

... but now we **share** everything. We have great **conversations**.

Word Bank			
Verbs			**Nouns**
argue converse chat gossip talk[1]	<u>with</u> *someone* <u>about</u> *something*	get into an ~ strike up / start a ~, carry on a ~ have[2] a ~, stop by for a ~ a ~ of (the plan) give a ~, listen to a ~	argument conversation chat discussion talk
discuss share	*something* <u>with</u> *someone*	the latest ~, juicy ~, a piece of ~	gossip

[1]You can also *talk <u>to</u> someone.*

[2]*Have* can also be used before *argument*, *conversation*, *discussion*, and *talk*.

A 🔁 Look at the verbs in the Word Bank. All of them are related to talking. Answer the questions with a partner.

> What does "argue" mean?

> It means to fight or disagree with someone when you are talking.

1. How are the verbs similar? How are they different? Ask your partner. Use your dictionary to help you if necessary.

2. Which verbs have a negative meaning? Circle them.

3. Which verbs have an identical noun form? Underline them.

B 🔁 Ask and answer the questions with a partner.

1. When is the last time you **got into an argument** with someone? Who was it with? What was it about?

2. Are you good at **striking up conversations** with people you don't know well? Why or why not?

3. How often do you **chat** with your neighbors?

4. Think of a well-known celebrity. What is **one piece of** juicy **gossip** about him or her?

5. What is one thing you want to **discuss** with your instructor?

6. Who do you **share** your personal thoughts with? Why do you choose that person?

7. Who do you **talk to** on a daily basis? What do you **talk about**?

> I got into an argument with my mom yesterday. She's always telling me to clean my room!

3 LISTENING

A  Look at the names of the websites below with a partner. Add one more. Which one(s) do you know? Which one(s) do you use?

Facebook	Qzone	Twitter
Instagram	LinkedIn	Mixi
Sina Weibo		

our idea: _____

B 🔊 **Infer information.** Read the questions. Then listen to an advertisement for a new online service. Which question might you ask with the service? **CD 1 Track 15**

a. Do you own a phone?

b. Can I borrow your phone?

c.) What's an affordable phone?

d. What's the best thing about phones?

C 🔊 **Listen for details.** Listen again. Complete the summary about InstaHelp and how it works. **CD 1 Track 15**

When you have a question, it's easy to waste time looking for (1.) _____ online.

InstaHelp is an (2.) _____ service. You ask an important (3.) _____ by

(4.) _____ or instant message. InstaHelp (5.) _____ it on to some of your online

(6.) _____ (and their acquaintances, too). You then get live answers back in

(7.) _____ minutes or so.

D  Look back at your answers in **C** and explain to a partner how the InstaHelp service works. Would you use it? Why or why not?

E 🔊 **Pronunciation: Stress: Verb + preposition.** Look at the two underlined words in each question. Which one is stressed? Circle it. Listen and check your answers. **CD 1 Track 16**

1. Who do you <u>talk</u> <u>to</u> when you have a problem?

2. What do you <u>talk</u> <u>about</u> with your friends?

3. What is everyone <u>gossiping</u> <u>about</u> these days?

4. Do you need to <u>discuss</u> anything <u>with</u> your teacher?

5. Who do you <u>chat</u> <u>with</u> the most on the phone?

F  Practice saying the questions in **E**. Ask and answer the questions with a partner.

3 LISTENING

STRATEGIES: Infer information; Listen for details

WARM UP Ask the class what they do when they need to get answers to questions. Make a chart on the board. How many students said they use dictionaries? the Internet? libraries? newspapers or television news? ask someone?
⏱ 5 min

A 🔄 Look at the names of the websites below with a partner. Add one more. Which one(s) do you know? Which one(s) do you use? ⏱ 5 min

Assign students to pairs to talk about the different websites. As a class, discuss which ones they prefer and why.

B 🔊 **Infer information.** Read the questions. Then listen to an advertisement for a new online service. Which question might you ask with the service? **CD 1 Track 15** ⏱ 5–10 min

Read the possible answers (a–d). Tell students that in this exercise they must listen for the answer to one specific question. Play the audio. Students can circle their answer individually. Check the answer with the class. Before explaining any unfamiliar vocabulary, ask if anyone has figured it out from the context. Ask for volunteers to use some of the new words in sentences.

Infer information. In this exercise, students have to understand the purpose of the online service in order to answer the question. The answer is not explicitly given in the audio.

LANGUAGE TIP: The language of advertising
The advertisement for InstaHelp includes expressions often found in advertisements and commercials. The goal of this language is to get you to buy a product. Here are some of the common expressions:

Imagine this...	*What would you do?*
If you're like most people...	*I'm here to tell you...*
It works like this...	*It's that easy!*
with _____'s help, of course.	*Sit back and wait...*

C 🔊 **Listen for details.** Listen again. Complete the summary about InstaHelp and how it works. **CD 1 Track 15** ⏱ 10 min

Play the audio again while students listen only. Then play the audio again, pausing at the end of each sentence for about 30 seconds to give students time to write the answer. Have students compare their answers with a partner's. Check answers as a class.

Listen for details. Students should read the summary with the blanks before they listen. What types of answers do they expect (nouns, verbs, numbers, etc.)? They may even remember some of the information from the previous exercise, and can write it in before they listen, and then check the answers.

🔊 **EXTRA! More listening practice**
Write the following questions on the board. Then play the audio again. Tell students to write their answers on a piece of paper. Check the answers as a class. **CD 1 Track 15**

1. *What is the problem with finding information online? (Sometimes websites don't have the exact information you need. That can be frustrating.)*

2. *How does InstaHelp work? (You send an email or instant message. InstaHelp sends the question to your online friends. One of your friends will know the answer and will tell you.)*

3. *What are some of the things that InstaHelp can help you find? (Directions to a club or a suggestion for a new cell phone.)* ⏱ 10 min

D 🔄 Look back at your answers in **C** and explain to a partner how the InstaHelp service works. Would you use it? Why or why not? ⏱ 10 min

Go over the questions with the class and have students think about their answers. Assign students to pairs and tell them to first explain together how the service works, then discuss whether or not they would use it. Monitor and provide help as necessary. Call on different pairs to tell the class their opinion about InstaHelp. Do most students think it is a useful service or not?

E 🔊 **Pronunciation: Stress: Verb + preposition.** Look at the two underlined words in each question. Which one is stressed? Circle it. Listen and check your answers. **CD 1 Track 16** ⏱ 10 min

Review stressed words. A syllable in a word that is stressed is longer, louder, has a clear vowel sound, and is higher in pitch. An unstressed word or syllable is shorter, spoken at a normal volume, has a reduced or obscured vowel sound, and a normal pitch. The words in the sentences that are not stressed are spoken very quickly.

Answers: In each case, it is the first word that is stressed because it is a content word that carries meaning. The second word is a function word and should not be stressed. Note that the word *gossiping* has three syllables and is stressed on the first syllable. *Discuss* has two syllables and is stressed on the second syllable.

F 🔄 Practice saying the questions in **E**. Ask and answer the questions with a partner. ⏱ 10 min

Say the sentences, or play the audio again, and have students repeat, making sure that they stress the content words. Remind students of the qualities of stressed versus unstressed words, as needed. Have them ask and answer the questions with a partner. Call on different students to share one of their partner's answers with the class.

4 SPEAKING

WARM UP Ask if any students in the class are comfortable striking up a conversation with a stranger in their own language. What are some topics that they use to begin the conversation? ⏱ 5 min

A 🔊 Listen to and read the conversation. Answer the questions. **CD 1 Track 17** ⏱ 10–15 min

Read the questions. Tell students they need to read and listen to the conversation to answer these questions. Play the audio as they read. Discuss the answers as a class. Students may not know that the *VP of Marketing* is the vice president in charge of advertising. Before explaining the meaning, ask if anyone can figure it out from the context.

B 🔁 Practice the conversation with a partner. ⏱ 5–10 min

For additional practice, you can play the audio or read the conversation out loud for the class to repeat for accuracy of pronunciation. Then assign students to work in pairs to practice the conversation, and switch roles to practice it again. Remind students to look at their partner while speaking.

EXTRA! Writing prompt
Direct students to write an email asking for an appointment to meet a potential employer. They should mention their interest in the company and ask if it would be possible to visit the company to learn more about it. ⏱ 10–15 min

SPEAKING STRATEGY

C 🔁 Think of a time you interrupted someone. Who were you talking to? What were you talking about? Tell a partner. ⏱ 5 min

Put students in pairs to explain what the situation was to a partner. Model the example with a student. Remind them to stay focused on the task.

D 👥 Role-play. Work in groups of three. Use the Useful Expressions to help you. ⏱ 15 min

(See Student Book page 35 for complete instructions.)

Direct students' attention to the Useful Expressions. Practice the expressions by reading them aloud with students repeating after you. Point out the difference between introducing yourself to a new person and interrupting someone who you already know. Model the exercise with two students in front of the class. As students do their role plays, be sure that they are using the expressions from the box. Tell students to switch roles so that each student has the chance to be the one who interrupts.

LARGE CLASS OPTION

Tell all of the students to stand up. Direct students to count off with letters: A, B, or C. Tell all of the A and B students to find a partner and begin a conversation. When you clap your hands, student C should try to interrupt A and B. After a few seconds, clap again. Now each C should move on and interrupt a different A and B. After C has had three attempts, tell them to stay with the B member of the A–B pair. Now B and C talk and A is the one to interrupt. Again, give A three chances. Then pair A with one of the Cs and give B three chances to interrupt different pairs.

Instructor's Notes

_____

_____

_____

_____

_____

_____

_____

_____

_____

_____

_____

_____

_____

_____

_____

_____

4 SPEAKING

A 🔊 Listen to and read the conversation. Answer the questions. **CD 1 Track 17**

1. What does Jared need?

2. What is Ana's advice?

3. Does Jared know Ms. Ruiz? How do you know?

ANA: Oh, look... there's Gloria Ruiz. Do you know her?

JARED: No, I don't. Who is she?

ANA: She's the VP of Marketing for Global Industries. She's standing right over there.

JARED: Is she the tall woman in the sweater?

ANA: No, Gloria is the woman with glasses. She's chatting with the man in the suit.

JARED: You know, I *am* looking for a job.

ANA: You should talk to her. Maybe she can help you.

JARED: That's a good idea. Thanks!

....

JARED: Excuse me, Ms. Ruiz? May I interrupt for a moment? My name is Jared Levy....

B 🔁 Practice the conversation with a partner.

SPEAKING STRATEGY

C 🔁 Think of a time you interrupted someone. Who were you talking to? What were you talking about? Tell a partner.

> My friend and I were having a discussion about our homework. I interrupted because my bus was coming!

D 🔵 Role-play. Work in groups of three. Use the Useful Expressions to help you.

Student 1: You are at a party. You need to interrupt two people who are having a conversation. Choose a reason below.

- You think you know Student 2. You want to introduce yourself.

- You need directions from the party to another place.

- Your idea: _____

_____

_____

Useful Expressions: Interrupting someone politely
Introducing yourself
Excuse me. May I interrupt for a moment? My name is...
I'm sorry to interrupt. / I beg your pardon.
I just wanted to introduce myself. My name is...
Interrupting someone you know
Excuse me. Sorry to bother you, (name), but I have a question.
Could I interrupt for a second? I just wanted to say / ask something.

Students 2 and 3: You are chatting. Student 1 will interrupt your conversation. Ask him or her at least two questions.

5 GRAMMAR

A Turn to page 197. Complete the exercises. Then do **B–D** below.

Participial and Prepositional Phrases		
Who is Joe Ortega?	He's the guy	**chatting on the phone.** **on the phone.**
Who is Ms. Anh?	She's the woman	**wearing glasses.** **in front of the class.**
Which books are mine?	They're the ones	**lying on the floor.** **in the drawer.**

Prepositions

against the wall
alongside the house
between the desks
by the road
in the suit
on the table
opposite the door
under(neath) the tree
with the glasses

B Match the questions with their answers. Then use the words in the box to complete the answers with the correct prepositions and verb forms.

argue	between	discuss	hide	~~in~~	in
in	on	~~play~~	with	with	under

1. Who's the leader of the band?
2. Which one is your sister?
3. Which one is my package?
4. Which one is your cat?
5. Who are your friends?
6. Who's Tom?

a. He's the student _____ his grade _____ the instructor.
b. He's the guy __in__ the hat __playing__ the guitar.
c. They're the people _____ the cafe _____ about politics.
d. She's the girl _____ the ponytail _____ the skateboard.
e. It's the one _____ _____ the bed.
f. It's the one _____ the hall _____ the two tables.

C 🔁 Work with a partner. Follow the steps to play a guessing game.

1. Think of an object and a person that you can see in your classroom. Don't tell your partner!

2. Ask *Yes / No* questions to identify your partner's object and person.

> Is it someone wearing glasses?

> Is it something on the wall?

> No, it isn't.

> Um, not exactly. It's against the wall, though.

> Is the person standing near...?

> Is it...?

D 🔁 Switch roles and play the game again.

5 GRAMMAR
Participial and prepositional phrases

WARM UP Use a book, ball, or other object to review prepositional phrases with students: *The book is on the table. The ball is next to the book. The pencil is under the paper.* After working with the whole class, have students practice prepositional phrases with a partner by moving different objects near their seats. ⏱ 5 min

A Turn to page 197. Complete the exercises. Then do **B–D** below. ◐ 20–30 min

Go over the prepositions in the box and clarify the meaning of any words students aren't familiar with by modeling them in the classroom or with pictures. Then go over the examples in the chart. Provide more examples using information about students and objects in the classroom to help them understand how participial and prepositional phrases are used. Elicit further examples from the students as possible. The grammar chart on page 197 includes more examples and rules, expanding on the information in the chart on page 36.

TEACHING OPTION: Foundation building

Many students will find prepositional phrases very difficult because they are used differently in other languages. Knowing what each English preposition means and when it is used takes time. You will want to carefully go over the extended chart, show the Grammar Tutorial in class, and have students complete the exercises in the Grammar Notes. Then, you can move on to the exercises in the Student Book. This extra support will help students feel more comfortable with these new prepositions and their usage.

LANGUAGE TIP: Guys

The word *guy* is very commonly used in informal speech to indicate a male. The female equivalent is *girl*, though this is considered inappropriate for women over 18 and may cause offense. Use *woman* or *lady* for females over 18. Women are sometimes called *guys* when someone is referring to a group of people.

B Match the questions with their answers. Then use the words in the box to complete the answers with the correct prepositions and verb forms. ⏱ 10 min

Go over the example with the class, then have students complete the rest individually. Remind them to put the verb in the correct form. Refer them to the chart on page 197 as necessary. Have them compare their answers with a partner's, then check answers with the class.

C 🔁 Work with a partner. Follow the steps to play a guessing game. ⏱ 10 min

(See Student Book page 36 for complete instructions.)

Go over the directions and the examples with the class, then model the exercise by thinking of an object yourself and having students ask you questions. Write their questions on the board to help other students, correcting them as necessary with help from the class. Have students choose their person and object; help with vocabulary as necessary. Remind them to keep their choices a secret. Then assign students to pairs to play a round of the game. Monitor and help with vocabulary and question forms as necessary.

D 🔁 Switch roles and play the game again. ⏱ 10 min

With the same partner, have students change roles so they both have an opportunity to guess. If time allows, have students switch partners and play the game again. After everyone has guessed correctly, have students share what the easiest and most difficult ones to guess were.

EXTRA! Who's the man in the photo?

Tell students to bring in an image (newspaper or magazine photo, image from the Internet) that includes several people. Match students with a partner who brought in a different picture to take turns asking and talking about the people in the photos. ⏱ 10–15 min

GRAMMAR TUTORIALS
• Participial and Prepositional Phrases

Additional tutorials are available for reteaching and reinforcement.

Instructor's Notes

_____

_____

_____

_____

_____

_____

_____

_____

6 COMMUNICATION

WARM UP Write *communication* in the middle of the board and have students create a mind map with the different verbs related to communication that they have seen in this lesson. Have them do it without looking at their books first, then let them review the lesson to complete their list. ⏱ 5 min

TEACHING TIP: Starting and ending group work

To make group and partner work go smoothly, it's helpful to use clear signals for beginning and ending the task. Some ideas:

- Write starting and ending times on the board: *Group work starts: 10:15. Group work ends: 10:25.*

- Tell your students that group work ends when you clap your hands three times.

- Train your students to respond when you raise your hand, by raising their hands and stopping all conversation. The room will fall silent without you interrupting.

A 👥 What do the quotes mean? Discuss with a small group. Share your ideas with the class. ⏱ 10–15 min

Read through the quotes with the class, explaining the vocabulary as necessary but not the meaning of the quotes. Assign students to groups of three to four and have them discuss what the quotes mean. Monitor and help with other vocabulary they need. Nominate a spokesperson in each group who will report the group's ideas to the class. Have groups share their ideas and explain as necessary.

B 🔄 Think about the ways you communicate. Do you agree with any of these quotes? Explain your opinions to a partner. ⏱ 10 min

Go over the question with the class then assign students to pairs to discuss their opinions. Monitor and help with ideas and vocabulary as necessary. As a class, discuss whether they agree with the quotes or not.

C Read the situations below. Which behaviors bother you the most? Put them in order from 1 (most annoying) to 5 (least annoying). ⏱ 5 min

Elicit ideas for annoying behaviors related to communication and write them on the board. Then have students look at the list in the book and rank them according to most and least annoying.

D 👥 Form a small group. Tell your group members your answers for the most and least annoying behaviors in **C**. Explain your answers. ⏱ 10–15 min

Assign students to new groups of three or four to discuss how they ranked the annoying behaviors. Make sure each person gives their opinion and remind them that they need to give their reasons. Monitor and help as necessary. As a class, try to agree on the ranking for the behavior and write a list on the board. Ask students, *What do you do when you see any of these behaviors? Do you say anything?*

EXTRA! Writing prompt

Students can write a paragraph about one of the annoying behaviors, explaining why it is rude and giving advice on how to avoid doing it, and on what to do if you find yourself in the situation. ⏱ 20 min

Instructor's Notes

_____

_____

_____

_____

_____

_____

_____

_____

_____

_____

_____

_____

_____

_____

_____

_____

_____

_____

6 COMMUNICATION

A What do the quotes mean? Discuss with a small group. Share your ideas with the class.

"Great minds discuss ideas. Average minds discuss events. Small minds discuss people."
—Eleanor Roosevelt

"Never argue with stupid people. They will drag you down to their level and then beat you with experience." —Mark Twain

"Silence is one of the great arts of conversation." —Chinese proverb

B Think about the ways you communicate. Do you agree with any of these quotes? Explain your opinions to a partner.

C Read the situations below. Which behaviors bother you the most? Put them in order from 1 (most annoying) to 5 (least annoying).

A person / People…

_____ talking loudly on the phone on the train.

_____ having an argument in a restaurant.

_____ gossiping loudly about someone else.

_____ chatting during a movie.

_____ discussing sensitive political issues during dinner.

> Which situation is most annoying to you?

> It's definitely when a person talks loudly on the phone on the train. That behavior really bothers me!

D Form a small group. Tell your group members your answers for the most and least annoying behaviors in **C**. Explain your answers.

1 VOCABULARY

A 🔄 Look at the words below in **blue**. Are there any you don't know? Work with a partner to learn their meanings. Then take the quiz on your own.

1. How do you typically **get your news**? ☐ TV ☐ radio ☐ online ☐ other

2. I am most interested in... because _____.
   ☐ **international** (world) **news**   ☐ **local news** (about my town or city)
   ☐ **national news** (about my country)

3. What's one popular **news program** or **news site** in your country? _____
   What kind of news show or site is it?

   entertainment / international / local / national / sports / tabloid news

   Do you ever watch this news program or visit the site? _____

4. When you read an interesting news **story**, do you post it online? _____

5. Think of someone famous who was **in the news** recently. Who was it? _____
   Was the news about this person **bad**, **good**, **great**, **sad**, or **sensational**? _____
   Did the news about the person **spread** from place to place quickly? _____

6. Think again about the **news story** in #5. How did you **hear the news**?
   ☐ on TV   ☐ on the radio   ☐ on social media   ☐ online
   ☐ by **word of mouth** (= someone told me)
   Did you **tell anyone** else **the news**? If so, how many people did you tell? _____

B 🔄 Explain your quiz answers to a partner.

> How do you typically get your news?

> Usually online, I guess. I never watch TV.

1 VOCABULARY

WARM UP Ask students about a recent story in the news. What happened? Who was involved? How did students learn about it? Why was the story newsworthy? ⏱ 5–10 min

A 🔄 Look at the words below in blue. Are there any you don't know? Work with a partner to learn their meanings. Then take the quiz on your own. ⏱ 15 min

Say the words in blue for students to repeat. Then assign students to pairs to go through the words and explain their meaning. They should use a dictionary for words they don't know. Students should then write answers to the quiz individually. Check the vocabulary by having students explain and give examples where possible. Do not correct this quiz or ask students for their answers. Students will share their answers in **B**.

CULTURE TIP: TV news
National evening news programs present important news stories for the country and the world. Some areas also have local news broadcasts. These present some local news stories, weather forecasts, and regional sports stories. Morning news programs are popular in many countries. On these programs, the hosts chat with one another, interview guests, and have demonstrations, such as cooking. There are often brief news segments, but the tone of these shows is not as serious as the evening news programs. On the other end of the spectrum, light-hearted entertainment news programs follow the lives of celebrities and talk about TV shows and movies.

B 🔄 Explain your quiz answers to a partner. ⏱ 10 min

Put students in pairs. Ask one pair to read the speech bubbles as a model. Point out to students that they should explain their answers using *I...* Also point out that their answers to items 1, 2, 3, and 4 should be in the present tense. Their answers to items 5 and 6 should be in the past tense. Take a class survey to find out the most popular answers for each question.

CULTURE TIP: Magazine quizzes
Popular magazines often have just-for-fun, non-scientific quizzes for their readers. These quizzes, often focusing on romance, lifestyles, and personal goals, "measure" the reader's personality, opinions, or relationships with others. Readers answer some brief personal questions and, based on the answers, the magazine tells them something about themselves or about their knowledge of the world.

TEACHING TIP: Learning new words
In **A**, the word *news* is used as a noun (*I am most interested in local news.*) and as an adjective (*Think again about the news story in question number 5.*). Point this out to students and remind them to record and memorize parts of speech and pronunciation along with the definition of new words. Dictionaries include this type of information because it is an important part of learning new words.

Instructor's Notes

_____

_____

_____

_____

_____

_____

_____

_____

_____

_____

_____

_____

2 LISTENING

STRATEGIES: Make predictions; Check predictions; Listen for details; Infer information

WARM UP Write *the news* on the board and draw four columns below it: *local*, *national*, *international*, and *entertainment*. In pairs, have students complete the columns in their notebooks with as many stories as they can think of in two minutes. Then complete the columns on the board as a class. ⏱ 5 min

A 🔄 **Make predictions.** You will hear two reporters talk about three stories that were in the news recently. Which one (a, b, or c) do you think most people wanted to read or hear about? Circle your answer and then tell a partner. ⏱ 5 min

Go over the directions and the options with the class, then have students make their predictions. Have students raise their hands to see which option is the most popular. Call on a few students to explain the reasons for their choice.

Make predictions. Remind students that predicting before they listen helps them be more prepared for what they are going to hear, as they will have activated prior knowledge of the topic and language related to it.

B 🔊 **Check predictions.** Listen and check your answer in **A**. **CD1 Track 18** ⏱ 5 min

Preteach the words *cheating*, *breaking*, and *viral*. Play the audio for students to check their predictions. Confirm the answer with the class. How did they know what the right answer was from what they heard? What confirmed their guess?

Check predictions. It is important to always go back to the predictions students made and help them see what they guessed correctly, and talk about why incorrect guesses were wrong.

C 🔊 **Listen for details; Infer information.** Read the sentences. Then listen to the full conversation and circle *True* or *False*. Correct the false sentences. **CD1 Track 19** ⏱ 10 min

Go over the sentences with the class, clarifying vocabulary as necessary. Play the audio twice, then have students compare their answers with a partner's. Play the audio again as necessary and check answers. Then have students correct the false sentences.

Listen for details. Remind students that they do not need to hear and understand everything in order to understand specific details. Encourage them to get into the habit of identifying key words to listen for before they listen.

Infer information. Usually when a statement says something like "The woman believes," students will need to use the information they have to guess, or infer, what the person's opinion is.

D 🔄 Discuss the questions with a partner. ⏱ 10–15 min

Go over the questions with the class. Give students a moment to think about their answers and their reasons. Encourage them to write notes (for example, key information about the news story) to help them when they are speaking. Then assign them to pairs to discuss the questions with their partner. Monitor and provide help as necessary. Call on different students to tell the class their opinion, and call on others to share their news story and why they thought it was important or not.

Instructor's Notes

_____

_____

_____

_____

_____

_____

_____

_____

_____

_____

_____

_____

_____

_____

_____

_____

_____

_____

_____

_____

2 LISTENING

A 🗣 **Make predictions.** You will hear two reporters talk about three stories that were in the news recently. Which one (a, b, or c) do you think most people wanted to read or hear about? Circle your answer and then tell a partner.

a. news about jobs and the economy

b. the president's meeting in Asia

c. a scandal involving a soccer player

B 🔊 **Check predictions.** Listen and check your answer in **A**. CD 1 Track 18

C 🔊 **Listen for details; Infer information.** Read the sentences. Then listen to the full conversation and circle *True* or *False*. Correct the false sentences. CD 1 Track 19

1. The woman feels that a lot of news today is too sensational.	True	False
2. The man says news today is trying to educate the public.	True	False
3. The man says the least popular news stories are about murder and sports.	True	False
4. The woman believes there should be more news about the economy and the environment.	True	False

D 🗣 Discuss the questions with a partner.

1. Do you agree with the opinions in **C**? Why?

2. Think of a story that was in the news a lot recently. Do you think it was important? Why or why not? How long was it in the news?

3 READING

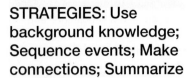

STRATEGIES: Use background knowledge; Sequence events; Make connections; Summarize

WARM UP Ask students to think for a minute about a strange news story they've heard. Ask volunteers to share them with the class, but be prepared to share one or two in case students can't think of any (you can find examples on the Internet).

⏱ 5 min

A ⚡ **Use background knowledge.** Look at the title. What is a viral news story? Can you think of one example? Tell a partner. ⏱ 5–10 min

Have students look at the title and explain what a viral news story is. Then assign them to pairs to share viral stories they have read or heard about. Call on different students to tell the class about the viral news story their partner told them about. Have other students heard the story? Where did they hear about it? Why do stories go viral?

Use background knowledge. Students bring to any text the knowledge they already have about life and the world in general, as well as any knowledge they have about the specific topic of the text. Students need to know that they should draw on this knowledge to help them understand what they are reading. It should come naturally to students, but it's always good to reinforce it as a strategy they can use.

B ⚡ **Sequence events.** Read the first news story. Number the events in the order they happened. Then retell the story to a partner using the appropriate verb forms. ⏱ 10–15 min

First call on students to read the events lettered a–g. After students have finished reading, tell them to check their answers with a partner, then retell the story using the correct verb forms. Walk around the room, verifying that students are using the correct verb forms.

---

3 READING

A ⚡ **Use background knowledge.** Look at the title. What is a viral news story? Can you think of one example? Tell a partner.

B ⚡ **Sequence events.** Read the first news story. Number the events in the order they happened. Then retell the story to a partner using the appropriate verb forms.

a. _____ Lulu barks like a dog.

b. _____ Lulu is adopted.

c. _____ Ken is unconscious.

d. _____ The family finds Ken.

e. _____ Lulu goes everywhere with Ken.

f. _____ Lulu's mother dies.

g. _____ Ken has an accident.

C ⚡ **Make connections.** Read the second news story. What do these pairs of items have in common? Write your answers and then compare them with a partner's.

1. visit waterfalls / go horseback riding
   These are things you can do in Vanuatu.

2. scuba diving / snorkeling _____
   _____

3. three meters below the surface / near Port Vila _____
   _____

4. buy waterproof postcards / receive a special stamp _____
   _____

D ⚡ **Summarize.** Why do you think each news story went viral? Give a reason for each story. Discuss with a partner.

VIRAL NEWS

A viral news story spreads quickly, usually online, and becomes very popular.

40 UNIT 3 ● Getting information

EXTRA! Post-reading

Students can work with a partner to research adventure travel. Across the world, many tourist destinations are taking advantage of people's interests in adventure travel. Instead of going to a new country as tourists and visiting museums and historic sites, adventure travelers want to have a very active vacation. After students have gathered their research, ask them to present their information to the class. Students can prepare posters or other visual aids to help with their presentation. ● 60 min

EXTRA! Writing prompt

1. Write about an interesting animal story you saw or heard about.

2. Ask students to write about an adventure or interesting experience they had on a vacation. ⏱ 15–20 min

Lulu to the Rescue!

Lulu is a kangaroo. For ten years she has lived with the Richards family. Lulu was adopted by the family after they found her next to her dead mother, not far from the Richards family's home in New South Wales, Australia.

Ken Richards is a farmer. He was working on his farm when a heavy tree branch suddenly fell on top of him and he passed out.[1]

Lulu stood next to Mr. Richards's body. She started barking and didn't leave Mr. Richards's side.

"I've never heard Lulu bark like that—she sounded like a dog. She barked and barked, and she didn't stop," said Celeste, Mr. Richards's daughter.

After 15 minutes, the Richards family went to investigate.[2] They found Ken on the ground.

"Lulu is a hero," said Celeste. "She saved my father."

Craig Middleton, a veterinarian, says that Lulu's story is rare. "I have never seen a kangaroo act like that. Maybe Lulu helped Ken Richards because the Richards family is the only family she has ever known."

Lulu is a loyal, friendly, and very intelligent kangaroo. After Ken leaves the hospital, he is planning to go everywhere with Lulu.

This Post Office is All Wet

The Republic of Vanuatu has recently been in the news—but not for the usual reasons.

Approximately 175,000 people live in the Republic of Vanuatu, an island chain east of Australia. It is a popular tourist destination because there's a lot to do there: you can visit waterfalls, go horseback riding, or visit a traditional Ni-Vanuatu village. Vanuatu is most famous for its scuba diving and snorkeling.

In an effort to draw attention to these popular water sports, Vanuatu has created a world's "first": the government has opened an underwater post office. You have to be a trained scuba diver to work there. The office is three meters below the surface in an area outside Port Vila, the capital city.

So far, the post office has hired four workers. They will work in a room surrounded by the beauty of Vanuatu's underwater world. Customers will buy waterproof postcards on land and then dive down to the post office to receive a special waterproof stamp!

[1] If you *pass out*, you fall down and lose consciousness.
[2] If you *investigate* something, you look at it carefully.

EXTRA! Discussion questions

1. What kind of newspapers or online news sites print these types of news stories? Do you like these kinds of stories?

2. What are some unusual behaviors you've heard of in animals? List as many as you can.

3. Do you know of an animal hero story? What is it?

4. Have you ever been scuba diving or snorkeling? What's it like? ⏱ 15 min

Sequence events. Remind students that identifying the sequence of events will help them understand what they are reading. Students need to pay attention to sequencing words, such as *when* and *after*, and time references.

C 🔁 **Make connections.** Read the second news story. What do these pairs of items have in common? Write your answer and then compare them with a partner's. ⏱ 10–15 min

Explain that *to have something in common* means to have the same features or characteristics. Give an example using the students in the class who have something in common. You could choose two students who are the same height or who play on the same sports team. Review the example with the class. Give students five to ten minutes to complete the task, then check the answers.

Make connections. Explain to students that they should always try to think about how different elements in a text are related, as this will help them understand the text more fully.

D 🔁 **Summarize.** Why do you think each news story went viral? Give a reason for each story. Discuss with a partner. ⏱ 10 min

Go over the question with the class, then have students think about their answer and reasons. Assign students to pairs to discuss the questions. Monitor and help with vocabulary as necessary. Call on different pairs to share their opinions. Finally, discuss viral news and the kinds of stories that go viral, and why, with the class.

Summarize. Explain to students that *summarizing* means to explain the main ideas and supporting details of a text in your own words. Doing this pushes students to understand a text at a deeper level because in order to explain it in their own words they have to analyze and synthesize the information they have read. To explain something in your own words demonstrates understanding.

4 GRAMMAR

A Turn to page 198. Complete the exercise. Then do **B–D** below.

Review of the Present Perfect					
Question word	*have / has*	Subject	Past participle		Answers
	Have	you	heard	the news?	Yes, I **have**. I heard it this morning.* No, I **haven't**. What happened?
How long	**have**	you	been	a reporter?	(I**'ve been** a reporter) **for** six months.
	has	she			(She**'s been** a reporter) **since** May.

*When you answer a present perfect question with a specific time expression, use <u>the simple past</u>:
Have you heard the news? Yes, I <u>heard</u> it <u>this morning</u>.

B Unscramble the questions.

1. read / you / any funny / have / recently / news stories

   _____

2. in English / ever / have / you / watched / the news

   _____

3. studied / how long / you / English / have

   _____

4. studied / another / have / language / ever / you

   _____

5. known / your best friend / have / you / how long

   _____

C 🔁 Ask and answer the questions in **B** with a partner. Write your partner's answers below. Then ask a follow-up question.

Example: *Yoshi has known his best friend for ten years. They met in elementary school.*_____

1. _____
2. _____
3. _____
4. _____
5. _____

So you've known your best friend for ten years. Where did you meet?

In elementary school.

D 👥 Tell another pair one thing you learned about your partner.

4 GRAMMAR

Review of the present perfect

WARM UP Write *Have you ever...?* on the board, and have students complete the question. Answer the question they give you about yourself. Quickly review past participle forms. Arrange students in groups of six to eight. Give each group a soft ball or crumpled piece of paper. A student should ask a question using the form: *Have you ever....* The student then tosses the ball to another student in the group. That student answers the question, then poses a new question and tosses the ball to another student. Continue until all students have had a chance to answer and ask a question using the present perfect tense. 🕐 5–10 min

A Turn to page 198. Complete the exercise. Then do **B–D** below. ◗ 20–30 min

Go over the examples in the chart, pointing out *have / has* and the past participles. Point out the note about using the simple past in answers. Ask students questions related to their context; for example, *How long have you been a student here? How long have you lived in this city? Have you had lunch yet?* The grammar chart on page 198 includes additional examples and usage notes, expanding on the information in the chart on page 42.

TEACHING OPTION: The flipped classroom
To open up time for in-class communicative tasks, assign the Grammar Notes on page 198 as homework. Have students complete the exercises on My World Link Online as well.

The next time class meets:
1. Review the present perfect tense in the Grammar Notes.
2. Go through the exercise students did for homework; present new examples and reinforce points as needed. Take questions from students.
3. Turn back to page 42 and do the exercises there, starting with **B**.

GRAMMAR TIP: Present perfect
The present perfect is formed with the verb *have / has* + past participle. It is used when something happened in the past, but when it happened is not stated. Additionally, it is used when the action is ongoing: *She has been a student for a year (and she still is a student today).*

GRAMMAR TIP: Present perfect with *ever*
Students often mistakenly use the term *ever* by putting it in positive statements, such as:

*I have ever been to Spain.

This construction is correct as a question or in the negative:

Have you ever been to Spain?
I have never been to Spain.

It is incorrect, however, when used in a positive statement. *Ever* should be used only for questions. *Never* is used only in negative statements. *Ever* means at any time, even once: *Have you ever been sky diving?* Students sometimes confuse *ever* with *always,* which means all the time. *I have always enjoyed music.* Not: **I have ever enjoyed music.*

B Unscramble the questions. 🕐 10 min

Do the first question together with the class. Have students work individually, and then compare their answers with a partner's. Check the answers with the class. Write the questions on the board to make sure everyone has them correct for **C**.

TEACHING OPTION: Support / challenge
Prepare slips of paper with the words from each question in **B** on them. Put students together in groups of five, and give a slip of paper to each student. Students can then try to construct the questions by talking without looking at each other's pieces of paper. Check the answers as a class. If your students would respond well, make this a competition between groups.

C 🔀 Ask and answer the questions in **B** with a partner. Write your partner's answers below. Then ask a follow-up question. 🕐 10–15 min

Elicit possible follow-up questions for each question in **B**. Then assign students to pairs to ask and answer the questions. Monitor and provide help as necessary. Make sure they are asking follow-up questions, and ask additional follow-up questions yourself.

D 🔳 Tell another pair one thing you learned about your partner. 🕐 10–15 min

Have pairs join to make groups of four and share information. Monitor and provide help as necessary. Call on different students to share something about one of the members of his or her group with the class.

GRAMMAR TUTORIALS
• Review of Present Perfect

Additional tutorials are available for reteaching and reinforcement.

5 WRITING 🎧

WARM UP Write the year ten years from now on the board (for example, *2027*) and ask students what they think they are going to do during the next ten years. Write their ideas on the board (plans might include: *take the TOEFL©, finish college, travel, get a job / change jobs, meet someone special, get married, have children, etc.*). ⏱ 5 min

A Read the message Sofia sent to her college roommate Emma. ⏱ 10 min

Go over the directions and the questions with the class. Then have students read the message and work individually to answer the questions. Point out the information in the Word Bank. Have students compare their answers with a partner's. Check answers with the class.

B Imagine it's ten years in the future and you are doing something interesting in your life. Answer questions 2a–c in **A** about your future life. Use the present perfect tense. Then use your notes and the example to help you write an email to a classmate. ⏱ 20–25 min

Go over the directions with the students. Then model the exercise. Write your answers to questions 2a–c on the board in note form. Remind students that planning this way is helpful to organize your ideas before you begin writing. Then have students help you begin writing an email using the one in **A** as a model:

Hi Lucca,

How are you? I haven't seen you in a long time. What are you doing these days? A lot has changed for me since college. At the moment, I'm living in _____. I've been here for five years and I really like it. I work at _____, I've worked here since last year. In other news,…

Then have students answer the questions in **A** about themselves in note form. Help with ideas and vocabulary as necessary. Once they have their notes, they should write their email. Monitor and help students with vocabulary and the use of the present perfect and the simple past tenses.

PROCESS WRITING: Models
Seeing a model of what they are going to write is very helpful for students. It helps them understand the instructions and what is expected. Following a model also helps students to organize their writing more coherently.

C Exchange papers with a partner. ⏱ 10 min

(See Student Book page 43 for complete instructions.)

Assign students to pairs and have them exchange papers and identify any mistakes in their partner's email. Tell them to focus on the use of the present perfect, simple past, and *for* and *since*. Then have students go back to the questions in **A** and answer them about their partner's future life. Encourage students to talk about their emails together, asking *What was clear? What was confusing? What could be better?* Remind them that the objective is to help each other improve their writing by reviewing each other's work. To complete the writing process, have students write a corrected version of their email. If possible, collect these to give students feedback. If time allows, have students reply to each other's emails.

6 COMMUNICATION

WARM UP Ask students what they do when they are at parties. How do they start talking to people? How do they break the ice if it is someone they don't know or haven't seen for a long time? Ask, *Has anyone been to a class reunion? What was it like?* ⏱ 5 min

A Imagine it's ten years in the future and you are at a class reunion. Talk to six different people and find out what they're doing these days. Use your notes from Writing. ⏱ 15–20 min

Go over the directions with the class and model the example about Sofia with a student. Then have a student ask you the questions to model the exercise again. Encourage students to ask follow-up questions to make the conversations more realistic. If space allows, have students walk around the class and talk to six people. Alternatively, they can talk to the six people nearest to them. Tell students they need to remember what they find out about their classmates. Monitor and provide help as necessary.

B Think about the people at the reunion. Which of your classmates has changed the most? Tell a partner. ⏱ 10 min

Go over the directions with the class, then assign students to pairs to discuss the changes in their classmates' lives. Call on different students to share with the class who they think has changed the most and why.

Instructor's Notes

_____

_____

_____

2 SEE IT AND SAY IT

A 🔀 Look at the picture below. Answer the questions with a partner.

1. Where are the people?

2. What are they doing? Why are they doing it?

B 🔀 With a partner, describe what each person is planning to do in the future. Say as much as you can about each person's plans.

> Daisuke is thinking about buying a houseboat. He wants to live on the water. He's probably going to become an artist.

C 🔀 Tell a new partner about your future plans. Where are you going to live? What kind of work are you going to do?

3 GET AND HAVE

A Follow the steps below.

1. Match the words in A, B, and C to make expressions with *get* and *have*.

2. Write your answers in the chart below.

3. Use the column letters (A, B, and C) in the chart as clues to help you.

A	B	C
get have	a divorced into married your	baby an argument friendly chat happy childhood news

get	**have**
(A + B) _____get divorced_____	(A + B + C) _____
(A + B) _____	(A + B + C) _____
(A + B + C) _____	(A + B + C) _____
(A + B + C) _____	(A + C) _____

B 🔁 Compare your answers with a partner's.

C 🔁 Take turns choosing an expression in **A**. Make a sentence using that expression.

4 LISTENING

A 🔊 Listen as John and Amy talk about the photo. Use the names in the box to label the people.
CD 1 Track 21

a. ~~John~~	d. Joseph
b. Olivia	e. Randy
c. Tina	f. Tom

3 GET AND HAVE

WARM UP Review the use of the words *get* and *have* with the class. Although their meanings are similar, *get* usually has the sense of obtaining something that you don't already possess, while *have* suggests that it is already in your possession. Ask students for example sentences with the two verbs. ⏱ 5 min

A Follow the steps below. ⏱ 5–10 min

(See Student Book page 46 for complete instructions.)

Copy the *A-B-C* chart onto the board. Model this exercise for students by choosing one word from each column. Note that it is sometimes only necessary to use two columns. If students are struggling with this, tell them that if they use the words *divorced* or *married* from column B, they do not need additional words from column C. Practice one or two expressions with a student volunteer. Then direct students to write their answers in the blanks in the second chart. Point out that the column on the left is for expressions beginning with *get* and that the column on the right is for expressions beginning with *have.*

B 🔁 Compare your answers with a partner's. ⏱ 5–10 min

After students have compared their answers with a partner's, work with the whole class to be sure that all of the expressions are correct. You may wish to write the two-column chart with *get* and *have* on the board and complete it with the class.

C 🔁 Take turns choosing an expression in **A**. Make a sentence using that expression. ⏱ 5–10 min

Suggest to students that their responses to **C** might take the form of either a statement or a question. They might ask *Do you plan to have children?* Or they might say *My sister got into an argument last night.* Tell students to be sure that their answers are complete sentences.

EXTRA! Review tic-tac-toe

This is a whole-class review game. Preparation: Choose nine vocabulary- or grammar-related tasks. (Examples: Write three home improvement verbs. Write three sentences expressing permission or prohibition. Write three sentences about plans with *going to*.) On paper, make a tic-tac-toe grid, number the squares, and write one task in each square. Make one copy for each student. To play, divide the class into two teams, X and O. Each team must prepare answers for all the tasks (this can take a half-hour or longer, depending on the tasks). For large classes, have students work in pairs or groups on specified tasks within the teams. When all are ready, draw a big tic-tac-toe grid on the board. In order to put their X or O on a space, the team must correctly complete the task for that space. The first team to get three in a row wins. (Example: The X team chooses square 1, and answers correctly. Mark X in square 1. The O team chooses square 5. Their answer contains two errors. Say, *Two mistakes*, and the turn passes to the X team. The X team can correct those mistakes to claim square 5, or they can try a different square if they choose.) ◗ 30 min

4 LISTENING

WARM UP Ask students to tell you the names of different family members and relatives (*mother, father, brother, sister, son, daughter, uncle, aunt*). Draw a quick sketch on the board of a family as in the photo on page 46—alternatively, draw a family tree. Find out from students who has the most brothers and sisters. Who is the only child in their family? ⏱ 5 min

A 🔊 Listen as John and Amy talk about the photo. Use the names in the box to label the people. **CD 1 Track 21** ⏱ 5 min

Practice the pronunciation of the names in the box. *Joseph, Randy,* and *Tina* are all stressed on the first syllable. *Olivia* is stressed on the second syllable. Also review with students the pronunciation and meaning of the word *mustache*—the hair that grows on a man's upper lip. Play the audio more than once if students need more time to write their answers. You can also pause the audio to give them time to write. If students have difficulty in identifying the two boys, point out that the speaker, John, is the one standing in front of his parents. His brother, Tom, is the boy wearing the tie.

4 LISTENING (Continued)

B 🔊 Listen again. Complete the chart about where the people are now. **CD 1 Track 21** ⏱ 10 min

Play the audio one or two more times to give students time to complete the chart. Have students compare their answers with a partner's. Review the answers by playing the audio a final time.

TEACHING TIP: Listen and repeat
To give students extra practice in listening, speaking, and pronunciation, go back and play the audio one sentence or one phrase at a time. Pause after each sentence or phrase, and ask students to repeat what the speaker just said. As an alternative, you can have some students repeat only half of the dialog. For example, for this track, you can have one group of students repeat only the words that John says, while another group repeats only the words that Amy says.

C 👥 Do you have a photo of family members in your wallet or on your phone? Show your photo to the class and talk about it. ⏱ 10–15 min

This exercise provides students with the opportunity to talk rather freely about their family photos. Don't be too strict about what students can discuss as long as they are speaking about the topic of their families. If you think of it, ask students the day before the lesson to bring in pictures of their families. If students don't have photos of family members, they can describe the people in the illustration on page 46, or from another picture in the book. If students don't want to talk about their own families, they can talk about families they know.

TEACHING TIP: Guest speakers
A frequent student complaint about listening is that though they can understand their instructor easily, they can't understand other English speakers in conversation. One way to deal with this is by occasionally inviting English-speaking "guest speakers" to class for short periods of five to ten minutes. These guest speakers could be colleagues, people from the community, or even students from more advanced classes. Before the guest speaker's appearance, give the class a little information about him or her, and brainstorm a list of interview questions. Assign one student to ask each question. Have the guest speaker make a very short self-introduction, and then have the class interview him or her. Students should take notes on the information they hear. After the guest's departure, have a whole-class discussion of what they heard, or have students write short reports on the guest speaker, individually or with a partner.

5 SWIMMING POOL RULES

WARM UP With the class, talk about rules for behavior in public places. It may be helpful to bring in a photo of a typical *Do not* sign with a red circle with a line, such as *No Smoking* or *No Dogs*. ⏱ 5 min

A 👥 Look at the picture. Take turns saying the rules at the swimming pool. Point to the people breaking the rules. What are they doing? ⏱ 10–15 min

Explain that this picture is similar to the kind found on some international English tests that they might take in the future. Sometimes on these tests, students are required to describe a picture. Model the example, then assign students to pairs to say what the rules are. Check answers with the class, writing the rules on the board. Make corrections as necessary with the class's help.

TEACHING TIP: Pair work
Students working in pairs may sometimes be distracted and talk about subjects other than the ones that they are assigned. You can help students stay on task in the following ways:

- Give clear directions about what students are to do.

- Be sure that the assigned task is challenging enough to be interesting, but not so challenging that they can't do it.

- Don't put two easily distracted students together in the same pair.

- Periodically remind students of the task and ask them to stay focused.

- Circulate around the classroom, offering help to students who need it and encouraging students to complete their work.

- For students who finish early, have an additional task ready to keep them engaged.

B 👥 Make up a list of rules for your classroom, and share them with the class. ⏱ 10–15 min

Have students work together in small groups to write down rules that might be used in the classroom. After each group is finished, have them write their ideas on the board or on a poster (one per group). Discuss the rules with the class, then tell students to vote on the rules that they think should be put into effect. What should happen if the rules are broken?

B 🔊 Listen again. Complete the chart about where the people are now. **CD 1 Track 21**

Joseph and Olivia	They are _____ now. Olivia lives in _____. Joseph is _____ in Florida.
Randy	He just had _____.
Tom	He just _____.
Tina	She's _____ high school.

C 👥 Do you have a photo of family members in your wallet or on your phone? Show your photo to the class and talk about it.

> The person standing in front of me is my sister. Her name is...

5 SWIMMING POOL RULES

A 🔁 Look at the picture. Take turns saying the rules at the swimming pool. Point to the people breaking the rules. What are they doing?

> No dogs are allowed in the pool.

NO YOUNG CHILDREN WITHOUT ADULTS

PLEASE SHOW ID CARD

B 👥 Make up a list of rules for your classroom and share them with the class.

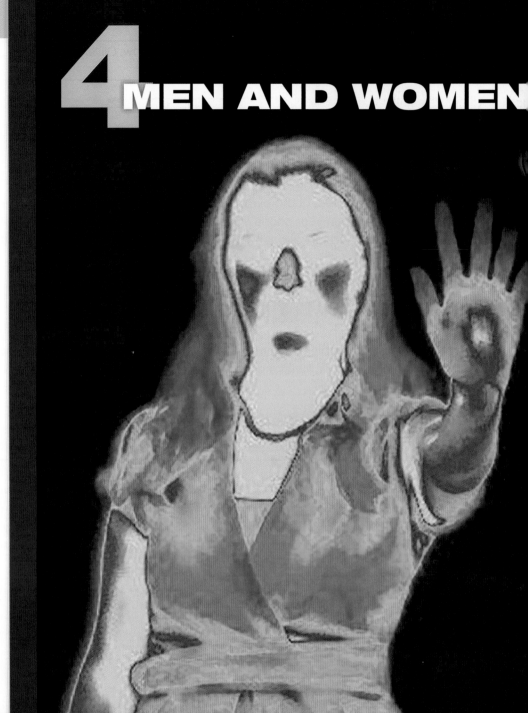

4 MEN AND WOMEN

ABOUT THE PHOTO

Thermal imaging cameras can be used to detect elevated body temperatures and are often used in airports, hospitals, and even in schools, to screen people when there is risk of a virus epidemic. This image shows how body temperatures differ between males and females. Studies have shown that on average, women have a core body temperature that is 0.4 degrees Celsius higher than men's. However, women's extremities, such as hands and feet, are colder than men's. This is because women have less muscle, so they need a more efficient way of protecting their core body temperature. Their bodies do this by restricting the flow of blood to their skin and extremities when they start to feel cold in order to conserve heat.

Did you know?

According to some studies, a woman's core temperature fluctuates from 36.9 degrees to 37.4 degrees Celsius (98.4–99.3 Fahrenheit), while a man's core temperature remains almost constant at about 37 degrees Celsius (98.6 Fahrenheit).

INTRODUCE THE THEME

- In this unit, students explore the concepts of physical appearance and relationships. The language in the two lessons will help students communicate on this theme, including describing changes to appearance, disagreeing with ideas and opinions, and describing relationship and dating events.

	Video	Vocabulary	Listening
LESSON A Appearances p. 50	Battle of the Sexes p. 50	Personal appearance p. 51 *brush your hair, dye your hair, wear makeup*	Taking selfies p. 52 Use background knowledge Listen for specific information Listen for details Take notes
LESSON B Dating p. 56		Dating p. 56 *go out, get along, break up*	A group's relationships p. 57 Understand relationships Complete a chart Listen for details

 For students: My World Link Online has personalized instruction, practice, audio, and video.

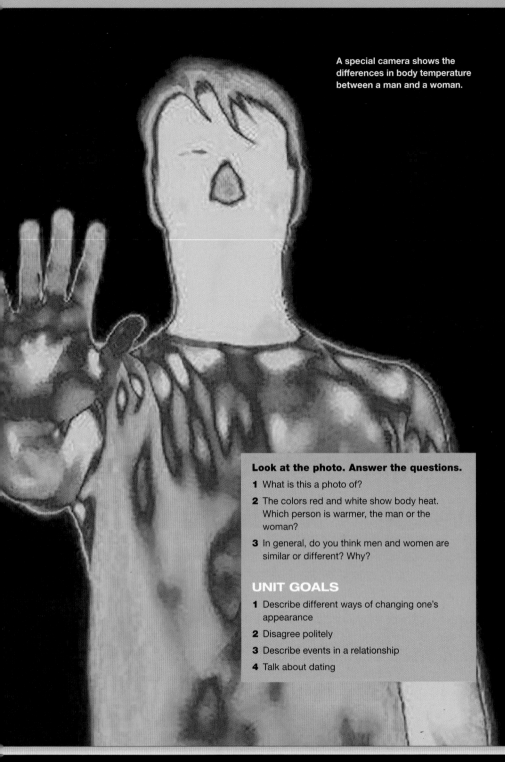

A special camera shows the differences in body temperature between a man and a woman.

Look at the photo. Answer the questions.

1 What is this a photo of?

2 The colors red and white show body heat. Which person is warmer, the man or the woman?

3 In general, do you think men and women are similar or different? Why?

UNIT GOALS

1 Describe different ways of changing one's appearance

2 Disagree politely

3 Describe events in a relationship

4 Talk about dating

- In Lesson A, students watch a video about how men and women listen. Students then learn to describe appearances and talk about changing their appearance. They will also practice the listening strategies of using background knowledge, listening for specific information and for details, and taking notes. They will learn how to disagree politely with someone's idea or opinion. Finally, they will learn how to talk about their planning for an event.

- In Lesson B, students will learn to talk about dating and relationships. They will read about dating habits around the world, practicing the reading strategies of using background knowledge, reading for details, and inferring information. They will also write about an imaginary relationship and how it develops.

WARM UP

Look at the photo. Answer the questions.

- Call on students to describe what they see in the photo.

- Have students answer the questions individually or in pairs, then compare answers with the class.

- Point out the unit goals and explain what students will learn. Elicit any key vocabulary students already know (words to describe appearance, expressions used to disagree, words to describe relationships, etc.), and write it on the board. Explain any unfamiliar phrases in the unit goals.

Grammar	Pronunciation	Speaking	Reading	Writing	Communication
Adverbs used with the present perfect pp. 54, 199	Coarticulation p. 60	Disagreeing politely p. 53	Dating around the world p. 58 Use background knowledge Read for details Infer information	Continue a love story p. 60	Discussing social norms over time p. 55
Phrasal verbs pp. 60, 200					Taking and discussing a dating survey p. 61

1 VIDEO Battle of the Sexes

A 🔁 Do you think you're a good listener? Why or why not? Discuss with a partner.

B ▶ Watch the first part of the video. Don't write anything, just watch.

C Before you watch the full video, try to choose the correct answers.

1. The man's name is _____.   a. Tom   b. Todd   c. Thad
2. The woman's name is _____.   a. Jane   b. Jen   c. Jill
3. What kind of pets do they own?   a. dog   b. bird   c. both
4. What does the wife do for a living?   a. teacher   b. mother   c. both
5. What did the wife say she was better at?   a. playing tennis   b. grilling   c. remembering details
6. What sport do they play?   a. soccer   b. tennis   c. golf

D ▶ 🔁 Watch the full video and check your answers in **C**. What is the conclusion at the end of the video? Circle your answer below. Do you agree or disagree? Tell a partner.

a. Women are better listeners.   b. Men are better listeners.   c. Men and women listen differently.

1 VIDEO
Battle of the Sexes

WARM UP Have students look at the photo and describe the scene. Who do they think the people are? What is their relationship? What are they doing? What adjectives would they use to describe how the man feels and how the woman feels? Write their ideas on the board. ⏲ 5 min

ABOUT THE VIDEO
Women often complain about men not being good listeners. This video shows a husband and wife talking about themselves and their family. The viewer is asked to remember the details in order to then answer some questions. The objective is to show that female viewers are likely to remember more details than men. However, this is not simply because men do not pay attention; rather it is because men and women often listen differently due to how the brain is functioning as they listen. Research has shown that men use only the left side of their brain when they are listening, while women use both the left and right sides of the brain. Consequently women retain more information.

TEACHING TIP: Using English videos
As with reading, students should try to get into the habit of activating background knowledge before they watch a video in order to help them be more prepared for the content and therefore likely to understand more. This activation of background knowledge is done here through the Warm Up and **A**.

A Do you think you're a good listener? Why or why not? Discuss with a partner. ⏲ 5–10 min

Have students read the questions and think about their answers. Then assign them to pairs to discuss their answers. Call on different students to share their partner's opinion with the class. As a class, discuss some characteristics of a good listener.

B Watch the first part of the video. Don't write anything, just watch. ⏲ 5 min

Make sure students understand they don't need to write, just listen. Play the first part of the video.

C Before you watch the full video, try to choose the correct answers. ⏲ 5–10 min

Go over the items with the class and have them choose their answers.

D Watch the full video and check your answers in **C**. What is the conclusion at the end of the video? Circle your answer below. Do you agree or disagree? Tell a partner. ⏲ 10 min

Play the full video and give students time to confirm or correct their answers in **C**. Play the video again, then check answers with the class. Point out the question, *What is the conclusion at the end of the video?* Have students choose their answer. Play the video again as necessary. Assign students to pairs to discuss their opinions. Call on different students to share their opinions and discuss as a class.

EXTRA! Post-viewing
In small groups, have students write a list of tips to be a better listener and present them to the class or to another group, explaining their reasons for each tip. If time and access to technology allow, have students research online to find other tips to add to their lists before they present. ⏲ 10 min

Extra video vocabulary	
accuse	neurons
be better at	parakeet
cliche	primarily
count on	sign language
debatable	stimulated
do for a living	temporal lobe
gender	to back it up

Instructor's Notes

_____

_____

_____

_____

_____

2 VOCABULARY

WARM UP Write the proverb *beauty is only skin deep* on the board, and ask students what it means. The usual interpretation is that physical beauty is only on the outside, but a person's character, on the inside, is more important. Ask students if they agree with the proverb. ⏱ 5 min

A Use the verbs in the box to complete the descriptions. Which description was probably said by a woman? Which was said by a man? Are either of them true for you? ⏱ 10 min

Go over the directions with the class. Tell students they will need to use one of the verbs twice. Have students complete the sentences individually. Encourage them to look up any words they don't know, or can't figure out from context. Then have them compare their answers with a partner's and discuss the questions. Check answers with the class and share opinions about who said each description, a man or a woman.

B Look at the Word Bank on the left. Use your dictionary to look up any unfamiliar words. Then match the verbs on the left with as many nouns as possible on the right. Make a list of the phrases you form on a piece of paper. ⏱ 10–15 min

Go over the words and phrases in the two Word Banks and have students repeat them. Then have them work individually to match the verbs and the nouns. Remind them to look up words as necessary. Have students compare their answers with a partner's, then check with the class, writing the list on the board. Check meanings by having students explain and/or give examples.

TEACHING TIP: Dictionary use
At this level, students can make good use of a monolingual intermediate-level dictionary, along with the bilingual dictionary they probably already own. Point out to students the advantages of a monolingual dictionary, which lets them work entirely in English. Learning to use a dictionary will help your students become independent learners and explore vocabulary that is relevant to their own interests. Students can also access dictionaries online.

TEACHING OPTION: Support / challenge
Students can write a paragraph using the word combinations that they made in **B**. It's easiest if the paragraph is about just one or two people. Tell students to use a variety of sentence structures. Then they should share their paragraphs with a partner.

C 🔁 Discuss the questions with a partner. ⏱ 10–15 min

Go over the questions with the class and model the example with a student. Model again by asking another student a question and then having the student ask you a question. Assign students to pairs to answer the questions. Monitor and provide help as necessary. Call on different students to tell the class one of their partner's answers.

EXTRA! Proverb dictation and discussion
Dictate these proverbs about appearance to students. *Don't judge a book by its cover. Beauty is in the eye of the beholder. Good clothes open all doors. A pretty face costs money. The first appearance deceives many. A pleasing face is no small advantage.* Check the dictation with the class. Then put students in small groups to discuss the proverbs. Which do they think are true? Which do they disagree with? ⏱ 20–30 min

Instructor's Notes

_____

_____

_____

_____

_____

_____

_____

_____

_____

_____

_____

_____

_____

_____

_____

_____

_____

_____

_____

_____

2 VOCABULARY

A Use the verbs in the box to complete the descriptions. Which description was probably said by a woman? Which was said by a man? Are either of them true for you?

get	wash	wear	shave	brush

1. I _____wash_____ my hair every day. Sometimes I _____ makeup, but I don't _____ perfume.

2. I _____ a haircut pretty often, and I _____ every couple of days, but I don't like to _____ my hair. I like it to look a little messy.

B Look at the Word Bank on the left. Use your dictionary to look up any unfamiliar words. Then match the verbs on the left with as many nouns as possible on the right. Make a list of the phrases you form on a piece of paper.

Word Bank			
brush		ears pierced
color / dye		face
get	your	hair
shave		head
straighten		teeth

Word Bank
Other expressions
get a (haircut / manicure / tattoo)
wear (cologne / deodorant / makeup / perfume)

C Discuss the questions with a partner.

1. When do you brush your teeth?

2. Imagine you are going to dye your hair. What color do you choose and why?

3. Where do you get your hair cut? How much does it cost? How often do you get it cut?

4. Have you ever gotten a manicure? Why or why not?

5. Do you like tattoos? Why or why not?

6. Would you ever get your ears pierced? Why or why not?

> So, what color are you going to dye your hair?

> I think I'll go with blue and white, our school colors!

3 LISTENING

A  **Use background knowledge.** Discuss the questions with a partner.

1. Do you think this is an attractive photo?

2. Do you take a lot of selfies? Why or why not?

B 🔊 **Listen for specific information.** You are going to hear an interview and complete an outline. Listen and complete the title for the outline below. **CD 1 Track 22**

Title: _____ to _____ the
_____ Selfie

I. ____Before____ you _____ the photo

   A. _____ different _____ in front of the _____

      1. see which ones look best

   B. neaten up your appearance

      1. _____ your hair

      2. check your _____

      3. wear _____ _____ to stand out

   C. take a selfie to _____ off something _____

      1. just gotten a _____

      2. _____ your _____ done

II. As the _____ is being taken

   A. consider the _____

      1. you want a _____ scene

   B. _____ the camera a bit

   C. watch out for _photobombers_

   D. _____ take a photo alone

      1. it's more fun with _____

Word Bank
neaten up = make neat; clean up
stand out = be noticed
strike a pose = get in position for a photo

C 🔊 **Listen for details; Take notes.** Listen and complete the rest of the outline. **CD 1 Track 23**

D  Strike your typical selfie pose. What face would you make to photobomb someone's picture? Show a partner.

WORLD LINK

Find a selfie online that you like and bring it to class. Who took the picture and where are they? What do you like about it?

3 LISTENING

STRATEGIES: Use background knowledge; Listen for specific information; Listen for details; Take notes

WARM UP Ask the class to think about how they feel when they get their picture taken. Do students feel comfortable? Uncomfortable? What do students do to try to get a good photograph of themselves? ⏱ 5 min

A 🔁 **Use background knowledge.** Discuss the questions with a partner. ⏱ 5–10 min

Go over the questions with the class, then assign students to pairs to discuss them. Compare answers as a class.

Use background knowledge. Students bring to any text the knowledge they already have about life and the world in general, as well as any knowledge they have about the specific topic. Students need to know that they should draw on this knowledge to help them understand what they are going to listen to.

B 🔊 **Listen for specific information.** You are going to hear an interview and complete an outline. Listen and complete the title for the outline below. **CD 1 Track 22** ⏱ 5 min

Have students read the directions, make sure they understand they only need to listen for the title. Play the audio and have students complete the title. Play the audio again, then check the answer with the class.

Listen for specific information. Remind students that listening for specific information means to focus your attention on key words or concepts. Students should identify before they listen what words they should be listening for, in this case *selfie* as part of a title.

C 🔊 **Listen for details; Take notes.** Listen and complete the rest of the outline. **CD 1 Track 23** ⏱ 10–15 min

Go over the outline with the class. Point out the two sections (I and II) and the explanations in the Word Bank. Remind students that they need to take notes as they listen. Play the audio twice, then have students compare their answers with a partner's. Play the audio again, then check answers with the class. Complete the outline on the board.

Listen for details. Remind students that they do not need to hear and understand everything in order to understand specific details. Encourage them to get into the habit of identifying key words to listen for before they listen.

Take notes. Taking notes helps students identify main ideas and be able to clarify what they heard later on. Taking notes as they listen is a skill that can help them in other classes as well as when listening in English.

🔊 **EXTRA! More listening comprehension**
Give students a chance to answer additional comprehension questions about the listening. Write the following questions on the board. Then play the audio again. Tell students to write their answers on a piece of paper. Check the answers as a class.

1. Who is Mark Green?
2. Where does Mark think selfies look good?
3. Should you point the camera up or down for a good selfie?
4. What is a photobomber? **CD 1 Track 23** ⏱ 5–10 min

D 🔁 Strike your typical selfie pose. What face would you make to photobomb someone's picture? Show a partner. ⏱ 5 min

Go over the directions and have students explain what *photobomb* means. Then assign them to pairs to share their selfie poses and photobomb faces. Have students who feel comfortable share their poses with the class.

Find a selfie online that you like and bring it to class. Who took the picture and where are they? What do you like about it?

Students can find a selfie during class or for homework depending on time and access to technology. Have them share and talk about the selfies they chose in small groups.

Instructor's Notes

_____

_____

_____

_____

_____

_____

_____

_____

_____

4 SPEAKING

WARM UP Ask students their opinions about getting a tattoo. If possible, bring some photographs of tattoos into the class. If appropriate for your class, encourage students to show their tattoos or share stories about tattoos. ⏱ 5 min

A 🔊 Listen to and read Chris and Tyler's conversation. Why does Chris want a tattoo? How does he feel and why does he feel that way? How does Tyler feel? **CD 1 Track 24** ⏱ 5–10 min

If you would like students to get more listening practice, they should close their books before you play the audio. Write the questions on the board and ask them to answer only from listening. Play the audio more than once if necessary. Tell students to write their answers to the questions. When they have finished, check the answers with the class. Answer questions about vocabulary as needed.

B 📋 Brainstorm reasons for and against getting a tattoo. Then practice the conversation with a partner. ⏱ 5–10 min

Brainstorm ideas as a class, making a list on the board. Pair students to practice the conversation. Students should replace the last four lines of the dialog with the new ideas that they have brainstormed. You may wish to play and repeat the audio so that students can practice pronunciation and intonation of the dialog.

EXTRA! Writing prompt
Students can write a paragraph about something they have done or a story they have heard about a person who did something that their parents did not approve of. What did they do? How did the parents react? ⏱ 10–15 min

SPEAKING STRATEGY

C 📋 Student A is planning to make a change in his or her appearance. Choose one of the ideas below (or one of your own). Role-play the situation. Then switch roles. ⏱ 10–15 min

(See Student Book page 53 for complete instructions.)

Direct students' attention to the Useful Expressions box. Read each expression with students repeating after you. Ask students for ideas of what expressions could follow the ellipses (...). Direct students to look at the four pictures. Tell students that to use the Useful Expressions, they need to add new content to the sentences where the ellipses occur. Tell students to role-play the situation with a partner. Monitor and offer correction as needed.

LANGUAGE TIP: Disagreeing politely
Help students learn to disagree politely in English with these instructions. Sometimes you want to disagree with another person in English, but you don't want to be rude or to have a confrontation. There are several things you can do to soften your disagreement. One is to acknowledge the other person's point of view and then to say *but...* and explain your own thinking. Another method is not to finish your sentence. Instead of giving a reason, you say *but...* and don't give a reason. This expresses your skepticism or disagreement. Perhaps the most important thing is your intonation pattern. Your expression should have a questioning and uncertain tone with upward intonation, rather than a strong, definite, downward intonation, which might be perceived as rude.

TEACHING TIP: Reflection
After finishing an exercise, give the students one minute to write about what they learned during the class and what they still have questions about. This silent and individual exercise allows students to focus their thoughts and can provide you with feedback on what the students do not understand. Collect the papers and answer some of the questions during the next class. Doing this regularly helps students get into the habit of reflecting on their learning, as well as identifying what they have learned and any difficulties they have.

LARGE CLASS OPTION
The teaching tip above works well in situations where it is difficult to judge all of the students' comprehension (due to large class size and lack of individual attention). Have students reflect and hand in their reflections from time to time so you can see what students understand or need to review.

EXTRA! I disagree...
Remind students of the Useful Expressions for disagreeing politely on page 53. Tell students to make statements to each other and then to disagree. If needed, brainstorm a list of statements with the students. You might include statements like the following:

- *I think learning English is important.*
- *The coffee in the cafeteria is terrible.*
- *There will never be another band as great as the Beatles.*
- *Chocolate ice cream is the best food in the world.*
- *No one will ever make a movie as good as Star Wars.*

Tell students to stand up and move around the classroom interviewing classmates. Each student should make a statement and their partner should disagree politely. ⏱ 20 min

4 SPEAKING

A 🔊 Listen to and read Chris and Tyler's conversation. Why does Chris want a tattoo? How does he feel and why does he feel that way? How does Tyler feel? **CD 1 Track 24**

CHRIS: Guess what? I'm getting a tattoo... right here on my right arm!

TYLER: Really? Are you sure?

CHRIS: Yeah. My best friend has one. It's really cool. Now I want one.

TYLER: But what do your parents think? Did they say anything?

CHRIS: They're not too happy... but I know it's going to look great!

TYLER: I see what you're saying, but...

CHRIS: And I found a really good tattoo artist.

TYLER: But what about the cost? Isn't it expensive?

CHRIS: No, it's not too bad—and I can pay half now and the rest later.

TYLER: Yeah, but what if you don't like it?

CHRIS: Don't worry.... It's going to look great!

B 🔄 Brainstorm reasons for and against getting a tattoo. Then practice the conversation with a partner.

SPEAKING STRATEGY

Useful Expressions: Disagreeing politely	
I agree up to a point.	I'm not sure it's / that's (such) a good idea. Are you sure?
Yes, but... / I know, but...	I see what you're saying, but...
I'm not sure. / I don't know.	I see what you mean, but...
But what about...?	I see where you're coming from, but...

C 🔄 Student A is planning to make a change in his or her appearance. Choose one of the ideas below (or one of your own). Role-play the situation. Then switch roles.

Student A: Tell your partner about your change. Give reasons why you want to do it.

Student B: Listen to your partner. Politely disagree. Use the Useful Expressions to help you.

shave your head

dye your hair

get your ears pierced

get plastic surgery

> Guess what? I'm getting my ears pierced.

> Really?

> Yeah. I think it'll look cool.

> But what about your parents? What are they going to say?

5 GRAMMAR

A Turn to page 199. Complete the exercises. Then do **B–D** below.

	With questions	**With affirmative verbs**	**With negative verbs**
Adverbs Used with the Present Perfect			
ever	Have you **ever** worn makeup?		I haven't **ever** worn makeup.
never		I've **never** worn makeup (before).	
yet	Have you taken a shower **yet**?		I haven't taken a shower **yet**.
still			I **still** haven't taken a shower.
already	Have you **already** taken a shower? Have you taken a shower **already**?	I've **already** taken a shower. I've taken a shower **already**.	
just		I've **just** finished shaving.	

B Arisa is planning her wedding. Read her comments below. Add the adverbs in parentheses to the correct place in the sentences.

1. (ever) Wedding planning is difficult because I haven't done it before.
2. (already) We've made the guest list.
3. (yet) We haven't sent out the invitations.
4. (still) I haven't bought my wedding dress.
5. (never) I've hired a photographer before. I'm not sure what to do.
6. (just) We've booked the venue.

Many people spend ten hours or more a week planning their wedding!

C Imagine you are planning a party for your friends. Add one of your own ideas to the checklist below. Then check (✓) off four things you have already done.

☐ decide on the menu   ☐ make a guest list
☐ buy the food   ☐ send out invitations
☐ choose a venue   ☐ decorate the room
☐ come up with a playlist   ☐ other_____

D ⚡ Work with a partner. Ask and answer questions about your party planning.

> I've decided on the menu, but I still haven't bought any food for the party.

> Have you chosen a venue yet?

> Not yet. But I'm thinking of holding the party outside.

5 GRAMMAR
Adverbs used with the present perfect

WARM UP Ask students about engagement and wedding customs that they are familiar with. What are typical ways of becoming engaged? Are rings exchanged at the engagement and the wedding, or not at all? What kinds of preparations are needed to plan a wedding? ⏱ 5 min

CULTURE TIP: Weddings
In many European and Latin American countries (especially those with Christian populations), the tradition used to be for the bride's family to pay a dowry to the groom's family or to pay for the wedding. In many Middle Eastern countries (especially those with Muslim populations), the groom's family had to pay a dowry to the bride's family. In these modern times, many cultures have done away with dowries, and often the couples pay for their own weddings.

A Turn to page 199. Complete the exercises. Then do **B–D** below. ◗ 20–30 min

Go over the examples in the box, pointing out the position of the adverb in each one. Ask students questions, for example, *Have you ever dyed your hair? Have you ever shaved your head? Have you already gotten your ears pierced?* Encourage them to answer using an adverb following the examples in the chart. The grammar chart on page 199 includes more examples and usage explanations, expanding on the information in the chart on page 54.

TEACHING OPTION: The flipped classroom
To open up time for in-class communicative tasks, assign the Grammar Notes on page 199 as homework. Have students complete the exercises on My World Link Online as well.

The next time class meets:
1. Review the use of adverbs with the present perfect in the Grammar Notes.
2. Go through the exercises students did for homework; present new examples and reinforce points as needed. Take questions from students.
3. Turn back to page 54 and do the communicative exercises there, starting with **B**.

B Arisa is planning her wedding. Read her comments below. Add the adverbs in parentheses to the correct place in the sentences. ⏱ 10 min

Have students look at the photo and read the caption. Go over the directions with the class, then do the first one together as an example. Have students complete the rest individually. Refer them to the chart on page 199 as necessary. Have them compare their answers with a partner's, then check answers with the class.

GRAMMAR TIP: *already, just, never, still,* and *yet*
These adverbs express the concept of completion or non-completion in a period of past time. *Already* shows completion, *just* shows recent completion, *never* shows lack of completion, *still* shows non-completion, and *yet* asks about completion. Because they do not refer to a specific point in past time, they are used with the present perfect.

C Imagine you are planning a party for your friends. Add one of your own ideas to the checklist below. Then check (✓) off four things you have already done. ⏱ 10 min

Go over the directions and the ideas on the list. Have students think about when and where their party will be, who they want to invite, what they will eat, etc., and add another idea to the list. Provide vocabulary as necessary. Then have them check the four things that they have already done for their imaginary party.

D 🔁 Work with a partner. Ask and answer questions about your party planning. ⏱ 10–15 min

Model the exercise by reading the example with a student. Have the student ask you another question about your party and provide an answer. Assign students to pairs to ask and answer questions about their parties. Monitor and provide help as necessary. Call on different students to tell the class one or two things about their partner's party.

GRAMMAR TUTORIALS
• The Present Perfect with *Already, Just, Never, Still,* and *Yet*

Additional tutorials are available for reteaching and reinforcement.

Instructor's Notes

_____

_____

_____

_____

_____

_____

_____

_____

_____

1 VOCABULARY

A 🔄 Take turns reading the story below aloud with a partner. Then match each two-word verb in **blue** with its definition (1–10).

1. _____ had a good relationship

2. _____ rejected, said *no* to an invitation

3. _asked out_ invited someone on a date

4. _____ end a romantic relationship

5. _____ became an adult

6. _____ stop thinking about someone

7. _____ go on a date

8. _____ met unexpectedly

9. _____ secretly dated another person

10. _____ started a machine

Alex liked Erin. One day he asked her out on a date. Erin was shy. At first she turned Alex down.

Alex asked Erin again, and she said *yes*. She agreed to go out with him.

They enjoyed spending time together. They got along well.

Unfortunately, Alex cheated on Erin. She saw him with another girl.

Erin was very upset. She decided to break up with Alex. They stopped dating.

Alex couldn't stop thinking about Erin. He couldn't get over her.

Erin and Alex grew up and got jobs: Erin worked as a banker, and Alex was a news reporter.

They lived in the same city but never ran into each other.

One day Erin turned on the TV and saw Alex. She decided to call him...

B 🔄 Work with a partner. Cover the sentences under the pictures. Take turns retelling Alex and Erin's story using the verbs in **A**.

C 🔄 What do you think happens next in their story? Tell a partner.

2 LISTENING

A 🔊 **Understand relationships.** Alex and Karen are talking about Gabe. Listen and write down the relationships. Use the words in the box. One word is extra. **CD 1 Track 25**

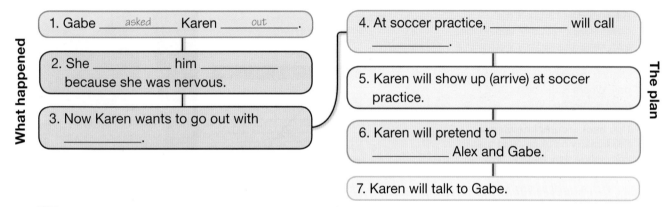

1. _____

Karen

3. _____

Alex

2. _____

Gabe

| brothers |
| friends |
| classmates |
| teammates |

B 🔊 **Complete a chart; Listen for details.** Listen. Complete the flow chart with the missing words. **CD 1 Track 26**

What happened

1. Gabe ___*asked*___ Karen ___*out*___.

2. She _____ him _____ because she was nervous.

3. Now Karen wants to go out with _____.

The plan

4. At soccer practice, _____ will call _____.

5. Karen will show up (arrive) at soccer practice.

6. Karen will pretend to _____ _____ Alex and Gabe.

7. Karen will talk to Gabe.

C 💬 Try to answer the questions with a partner. Don't look back at your answers in **A** and **B**.

1. How do Alex, Karen, and Gabe know each other?

2. What happened to Karen?

3. What is her plan now? Do you think it will work? Why or why not?

D 👥 You want to ask someone out on a date, but you're too shy. What do you do? Think of one or two ideas. Then get in a group and follow the directions below.

Speaker: Tell the group your ideas in **D**.

Listeners: For each idea a person says, use a sentence (a or b) to explain what you think.

a. The person may agree to go out with you because...

b. The person might turn you down because...

3 READING

STRATEGIES: Use background knowledge; Read for details; Infer information

WARM UP Ask students where they would take someone for a first date. What is their ideal date? ⏱ 5 min

A 🔄 **Use background knowledge.** Answer the questions about dating. Share your answers with a partner. ⏱ 5–10 min

Have students answer the questions individually, adding their own ideas before they work with a partner. When pairs have finished sharing their answers, take a class poll: Where is the best place to meet someone? Why?

Use background knowledge. Students bring to any text the knowledge they already have about life and the world in general, as well as any knowledge they have about the specific topic of the text. Students need to know that they should draw on this knowledge to help them understand what they are reading.

B **Read for details.** Read each person's response to **Question 1** in the reading. Did he or she go out on a date? Check (✓) *Yes*, *No*, or *NM* (not mentioned). ⏱ 15–20 min

Explain the format of the reading. There are two questions that were asked of the four people. Read the introduction and then give students five to ten minutes to read the article. Read the directions in **B** to the class, then give students another two to three minutes to answer the questions by completing the chart.

Read for details. Remind students that reading for details means reading a text more slowly and in depth. When they read for details they should pay attention to unfamiliar words, but try to guess their meaning from the context before they look them up.

---

3 READING

A 🔄 **Use background knowledge.** Answer the questions about dating. Share your answers with a partner.

1. Where is the best place to meet someone?
   - ☐ at school   ☐ at a party
   - ☐ your idea: _____

2. What is the best way to meet someone?
   - ☐ have a friend introduce you
   - ☐ wait to be approached by the person
   - ☐ your idea: _____

B **Read for details.** Read each person's response to **Question 1** in the reading. Did he or she go out on a date? Check (✓) *Yes*, *No*, or *NM* (not mentioned).

	Yes	No	NM
1. Mahesh			
2. Nina			
3. Kaleo			
4. Fumiko			

C **Infer information.** Read the responses to **Question 2**. Which person do you think would say each statement below? Write his or her name. There is one extra statement.

1. I can be shy, so dating one-on-one is hard. _____
2. I'm more of a dreamer than a realist. _____
3. I don't think looks are the most important thing. _____
4. I'm open to meeting someone my mom and dad know. _____
5. I want to meet someone who enjoys what I like to do. _____

D 🔄 Would you try any of the dating methods mentioned? Why or why not? Tell a partner.

58 UNIT 4 • Men and women

A couple embraces in the city center of Rome, Italy.

CULTURE TIP: Dating services

In North America, some people like to try special ways to meet a new person for love and romance. In addition to meeting someone at school or through a friend or mutual interest, people try the following:

- Matchmaking services—some wealthier people pay a person or organization to locate a suitable person for them to date.

- Internet dating services—people subscribe to an online service and post a photo or video of themselves in their account profile. Then they look at the profiles of others who look interesting to them.

- Speed dating—like Mahesh in the reading, people attend an event where they speak with many different people for just a few minutes. If they like someone, then they arrange to spend more time with them.

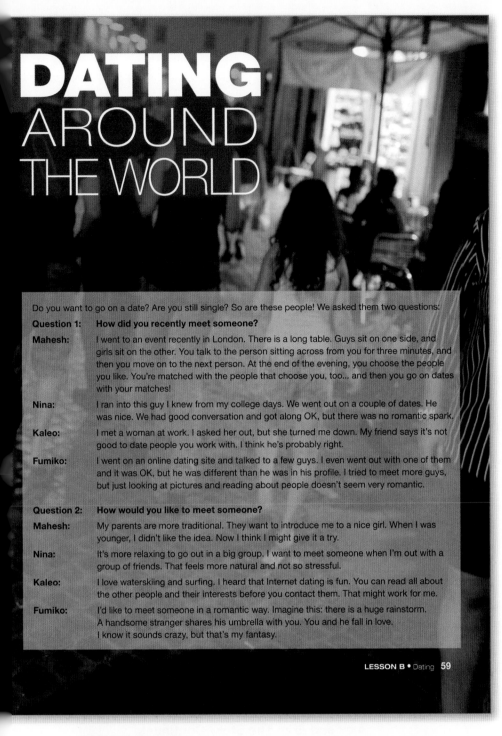

DATING
AROUND
THE WORLD

Do you want to go on a date? Are you still single? So are these people! We asked them two questions:

Question 1:   **How did you recently meet someone?**

Mahesh: I went to an event recently in London. There is a long table. Guys sit on one side, and girls sit on the other. You talk to the person sitting across from you for three minutes, and then you move on to the next person. At the end of the evening, you choose the people you like. You're matched with the people that choose you, too... and then you go on dates with your matches!

Nina: I ran into this guy I knew from my college days. We went out on a couple of dates. He was nice. We had good conversation and got along OK, but there was no romantic spark.

Kaleo: I met a woman at work. I asked her out, but she turned me down. My friend says it's not good to date people you work with. I think he's probably right.

Fumiko: I went on an online dating site and talked to a few guys. I even went out with one of them and it was OK, but he was different than he was in his profile. I tried to meet more guys, but just looking at pictures and reading about people doesn't seem very romantic.

Question 2:   **How would you like to meet someone?**

Mahesh: My parents are more traditional. They want to introduce me to a nice girl. When I was younger, I didn't like the idea. Now I think I might give it a try.

Nina: It's more relaxing to go out in a big group. I want to meet someone when I'm out with a group of friends. That feels more natural and not so stressful.

Kaleo: I love waterskiing and surfing. I heard that Internet dating is fun. You can read all about the other people and their interests before you contact them. That might work for me.

Fumiko: I'd like to meet someone in a romantic way. Imagine this: there is a huge rainstorm. A handsome stranger shares his umbrella with you. You and he fall in love. I know it sounds crazy, but that's my fantasy.

LESSON B • Dating **59**

C **Infer information.** Read the responses to **Question 2**. Which person do you think would say each statement below? Write his or her name. There is one extra statement. ⏱ 10–15 min

Give students time to read the passage again. Ask them to underline the place in the reading where they located each answer. Students can check their answers with a partner's before you check answers with the class.

Infer information. Remind students that inferring information means using the information they have in the text and background knowledge to work out something that isn't stated explicitly in the text. They can infer what someone might say from other things they say in the text.

D 🗣 Would you try any of the dating methods mentioned? Why or why not? Tell a partner. ⏱ 10–15 min

Go over the questions with the class, then have students think about their answer and reasons. Assign students to pairs to discuss the questions. Monitor and help with vocabulary as necessary. Call on different students to tell the class their partner's opinion.

Instructor's Notes

_____

_____

_____

_____

_____

_____

_____

_____

EXTRA! Post-reading

If your students are sufficiently mature, have them design a role play in which they meet someone at a speed-dating event. How would they describe themselves? What questions would they ask of their partners? In pairs, students should write the role play and then perform it for the class.
⏺ 30–60 min

EXTRA! Writing prompt

Ask students to think of how they would like to meet someone. Tell them to write two paragraphs describing how they would like to meet. If students are already in a relationship, they can describe how they met. ⏱ 15–20 min

4 GRAMMAR

A Turn to page 200. Complete the exercises. Then do **B–D** below.

Phrasal Verbs	
Separable phrasal verbs	Please **turn on** <u>the TV</u>. Please **turn** <u>the TV</u> / <u>it</u> **on**. ~~Please **turn on** it.~~
Inseparable phrasal verbs	Erin **ran into** <u>Alex</u> / <u>him</u> yesterday.
Asking questions	Did he **ask** you **out**? When did they **break up**?

B 🔊 **Pronunciation: Coarticulation.** Read the information. Then listen and say the phrasal verbs. Draw a link to connect the words. **CD 1 Track 28**

> In each phrasal verb below, the verb ends in a consonant sound. The second word starts with a vowel. In spoken English, these two sounds link together, and the two words sound like one word.

1. ask out
2. break up
3. cheat on
4. give up
5. get along
6. get over
7. run into
8. turn on
9. make up

C 🔊 **Pronunciation: Coarticulation.** Listen to and repeat the sentences. Notice how different words link together. **CD 1 Track 29**

1. Alex cheated on Erin.
2. Turn on a light, please.
3. Don't worry. You'll get over it.
4. He asked her out.

D 👥 Work in a small group. Follow the steps below.

1. On nine small pieces of paper, write the numbers 1–9. Put them face down on the desk.
2. Take turns. Pick a number. Make a sentence or question using the phrasal verb from **B** that matches that number. Then put the number back. If you make a correct sentence or question, you get a point. <u>Do not use example sentences from this page</u>.
3. Play for 15 minutes. Who got the most points?
4. Repeat steps 1–3 with a new group and play again.

5 WRITING

A Read the short summary of Alex and Erin's story from page 56. What do you think happened next to the couple? Write another paragraph telling their story. Use at least three phrasal verbs from this lesson.

> ### Alex and Erin: The Story Continues
> Alex and Erin were high school sweethearts, but Alex cheated on Erin, and the couple broke up. Their story didn't end there, though. After high school, Erin went to college and later got a job in banking in a large city. Alex went to a different school, and in time, he became a news reporter in the same large city as Erin. The pair lived separate lives and never ran into each other. Then one day, Erin turned on the TV and saw Alex on the local news. "He's still so handsome," she thought, "but has he changed?" Erin decided to call him…

4 GRAMMAR
Phrasal verbs

WARM UP Make two columns on the board. In the left-hand column, write the verbs *pick*, *put*, *turn*, *take*, and *make*. In the right-hand column, write the prepositions *up*, *down*, *out*, and *over*. Work with the class to see how many correct combinations can be made from the verbs on the left and the prepositions on the right. Have students tell you what the phrase means, not just guess at combinations. ⏱ 5 min

A Turn to page 200. Complete the exercises. Then do **B–D** below. ◐ 20–30 min

Go over the examples in the chart, explaining that the two words together give the phrasal verbs their meaning. Point out that some are separable and some are not, and that for separable verbs if the object is a pronoun (*turn it on*), the phrasal verb has to be separated. Look at the examples from the Warm Up and help students work out which ones are separable and which ones are not. The grammar chart on page 200 includes further examples of separable and inseparable phrasal verbs, expanding on the information in the chart on page 60.

TEACHING OPTION: The flipped classroom

To open up time for in-class communicative tasks, assign the Grammar Notes on page 200 as homework. Have students complete the exercises on My World Link Online as well.

The next time class meets:

1. Review the phrasal verbs in the Grammar Notes.

2. Go through the exercises students did for homework; present new examples and reinforce points as needed. Take questions from students.

3. Turn back to page 60 and do the communicative exercises there, starting with **B**. Tell students that practicing the pronunciation will help them ask questions with phrasal verbs more naturally.

GRAMMAR TIP: Phrasal verbs

Many English verbs can be followed by prepositions. The meaning of these two-part or two-word verbs is often very different from the two parts taken separately. In normal conversation, prepositions are not stressed. However, the prepositions in two-word verbs do receive stress. A good learner's dictionary is helpful for students, because unlike a regular dictionary for native speakers, a learner's dictionary will often list phrasal verbs.

Some phrasal verbs are intransitive (don't take an object) while others are transitive (do take an object.) If the verb is transitive and the object is a noun, the verb can usually be separated by the object. Either *hung up the phone* or *I hung the phone up* are acceptable.

B 🔊 **Pronunciation: Coarticulation.** Read the information. Then listen and say the phrasal verbs. Draw a link to connect the words. **CD 1 Track 28** ⏱ 5–10 min

Say the first one as an example and help students see how the consonant sound at the end of *ask* joins the vowel sound at the beginning of *out* and the two words sound like one. Point out that when that happens, the words are not only linked, but the sounds themselves are changed, with the linked sounds influencing each other.

Have students read the information, then play the audio and draw the link between the two words of each phrasal verb. Play the audio again and have students repeat each phrasal verb.

C 🔊 **Pronunciation: Coarticulation.** Listen to and repeat the sentences. Notice how different words link together. **CD 1 Track 29** ⏱ 5–10 min

Have students read the sentences out loud, then play the audio for students to listen and repeat. Focus students' attention on the words that are linked together. In cases where the first linked word ends in an *n*, the coarticulation can be especially noticeable. A word that ends in *n* can make the following vowel sound nasalized, with more air coming out of the nose.

D 🔳 Work in a small group. Follow the steps below. ⏱ 20 min

(See Student Book page 60 for full instructions.)

Go over the steps with the class. Assign students to small groups and have them prepare their pieces of paper. Model the exercise by taking a piece of paper from one group and saying a sentence with the corresponding phrasal verb. Have students play the game in their groups. Monitor and provide help checking if their sentences and questions are correct. After 10 to 15 minutes, have students form new groups and play again. Have students share some of their sentences and write an example for each phrasal verb on the board. For separable phrasal verbs, have students use them both ways in their example.

🌀 GRAMMAR TUTORIALS
• Separable Phrasal Verbs

Additional tutorials are available for reteaching and reinforcement.

5 WRITING

WARM UP Write on the board *Erin* and *Alex* and have students recall their story. Write key words on the board. ⏱ 5 min

A Read the short summary of Alex and Erin's story from page 56. What do you think happened next to the couple? Write another paragraph telling their story. Use at least three phrasal verbs from this lesson. ⏱ 15–20 min

5 WRITING (Continued)

Go over the directions with the class. Have students read the summary of the story. Then brainstorm ideas with the class about what happened next. Write their ideas on the board. Then have students help you begin writing another paragraph to continue the story on the board. Elicit phrasal verbs and tell students to use them in the sentences they dictate to you. Write the first two or three sentences of a paragraph, then have students write their own paragraph. Remind students to use phrasal verbs and refer them back to the charts on page 60 and 200 to help them.

PROCESS WRITING: Brainstorming
Brainstorming before planning and writing is an important stage in the writing process. Brainstorming produces a variety of ideas and activates language, both of which will help students when they begin the planning stage.

B Exchange papers with a partner. ⏱ 10–15 min

(See Student Book page 61 for complete instructions.)

Assign students to pairs and have them exchange papers and identify any mistakes in their partner's paragraph. Tell them to focus on the use of the simple past and phrasal verbs. Then have them answer the question about whether the story ends happily or not. Encourage students to talk about their paragraphs together, *What was clear? What was confusing? What could be better?* Remind them that the objective is to help each other improve their writing by reviewing each other's work. Then have students rewrite their paragraph making the corrections and taking into account their partner's comments on how to improve it. Monitor and provide help as necessary. Assign students to new partners and have them read each other their stories. Call on different students to tell the class whether their partner's story ends happily or not.

6 COMMUNICATION

WARM UP Ask students if they have ever completed a magazine survey or quiz. What questions were asked? How did they answer? ⏱ 5–10 min

A Complete the dating survey. Then write one question of your own about dating. ⏱ 10–15 min

Have students look at the photo at the bottom of the page and answer the question. How many people would like to go somewhere like that on a date? Ask students to complete the survey individually. Explain that they can write their own answers in e if they don't agree with the choices that are given. Make sure they add a question of their own in 6.

B 👥 Work in a small group. Take turns explaining your answers to each question in **A**. At the end, ask your question. ⏱ 10 min

Assign students to groups of three or four to compare their answers. Make sure they are explaining their reasons. After they have discussed their answers to questions 1 to 5, they should ask each other their question 6. Nominate a spokesperson for each group to tell the class which answers they had the same and which were different.

LARGE CLASS OPTION
For large classes, first have students complete the dating survey and compare their answers with a partner's. Then poll the entire class to see how many students answered each question. Are there any clear trends in your students' responses?

EXTRA! Writing prompt
Ask students to write advice for a shy friend who is having trouble meeting people. In the letter, students should offer suggestions on how the friend can meet new people and not be so shy. ⏱ 15–20 min

Instructor's Notes

_____

_____

_____

_____

_____

_____

_____

_____

_____

_____

_____

B 🔁 Exchange papers with a partner.

1. Circle mistakes in your partner's story. Does your partner's story end happily?

2. Return the paper to your partner. Make corrections to your own story.

3. Read your final story to a new partner.

6 COMMUNICATION

A Complete the dating survey. Then write one question of your own about dating.

Dating Survey

1. What *first* attracts you to a person?
   a. looks
   b. personality
   c. intelligence
   d. common interests
   e. your idea: _____

2. Your boyfriend or girlfriend has cheated on you. What do you do?
   a. break up
   b. ignore it
   c. talk to him or her and make up
   d. wait for him or her to talk to me
   e. your idea: _____

3. What should you definitely do on a first date?
   a. bring a gift
   b. talk a lot
   c. offer to split the bill
   d. have *an exit plan* (a way to escape if the date is boring)
   e. your idea: _____

4. How would you break up with someone?
   a. over the telephone
   b. by email or text
   c. face-to-face
   d. by ignoring the person
   e. your idea: _____

5. Which is the *worst* dating situation?
   a. Your date arrives an hour late.
   b. Your date runs into an old girlfriend or boyfriend.
   c. Your date doesn't have enough money.
   d. Your date doesn't dress well.
   e. your idea: _____

6. Your question: _____
   _____

B 🔼 Work in a small group. Take turns explaining your answers to each question in **A**. At the end, ask your question.

Would you like to go on a date in a place like this?

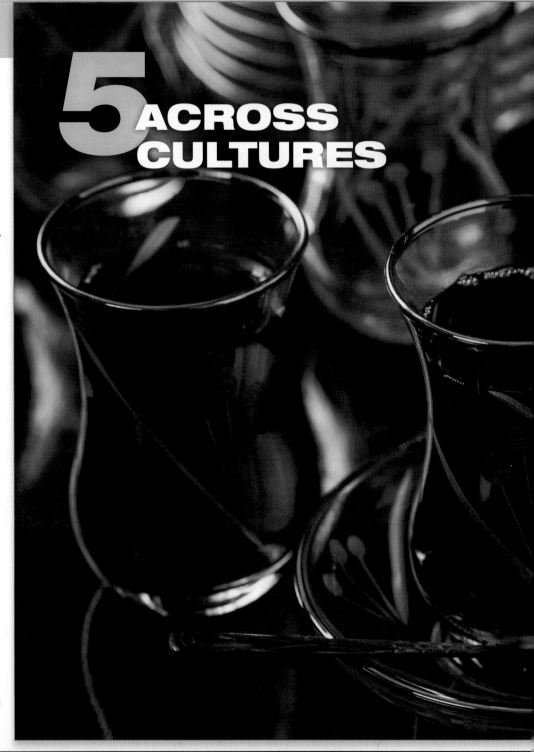

5 ACROSS CULTURES

ABOUT THE PHOTO

This photo shows tea poured from a *samovar* into beautiful glasses, a welcoming gesture in Turkish culture. When you visit someone's home in Turkey, you will be offered tea or coffee, sometimes with sweet pastries to accompany it. The Turks consider themselves very hospitable people and even in shops and stores you may be offered tea or coffee. Tea is also the principal drink offered to visitors in many homes in Ireland, the UK, and Russia. In the UK and Ireland, it will usually be served in a cup with a saucer, or in a mug, and poured from a teapot, while in Russia, it will be served in a glass and poured from a samovar, similar to the ones used in Turkey.

Did you know?

- There are four main types of tea: black, white, green, and oolong.
- Ireland has the highest per capita consumption of tea in the world: 75 percent of the population drink an average of six cups a day.
- In the UK, 165 million cups are drunk every day.

INTRODUCE THE THEME

- In this unit, students will explore the concept of cultural differences. The language in the two lessons will help students communicate on this theme, including describing behavior, asking about culturally appropriate behavior, comparing customs, and giving advice on traveling to different countries.

	Video	Vocabulary	Listening	Grammar
LESSON A Mind your manners p. 64	Smartphone Addiction p. 64	Showing respect p. 65 *appropriate, considerate, polite*	Rules at a special workplace p. 66 Build background knowledge Listen for gist Make and check predictions Listen to paraphrase	*It + be* + adjective + infinitive / Gerund + *be* + adjective pp. 68, 201
LESSON B Adjusting to a new place p. 70		Communicate across cultures p. 70 *eye contact, language barrier, body language*	Ways to communicate p. 71 Listen for gist Take notes on key details	Present and future time clauses with *before, after, when, as soon as / once* pp. 74, 202

For students: My World Link Online has personalized instruction, practice, audio, and video.

Look at the photo. Answer the questions.

1 What custom is being shown in the photo?

2 When visitors come to your home, what do you customarily do?

3 What's an important custom in your country that visitors should know about?

UNIT GOALS

1 Describe good and bad behavior

2 Ask about culturally appropriate behavior

3 Compare customs in your country with those in other countries

4 Give advice on traveling abroad

Welcoming guests with a cup of tea is a custom in Turkey.

- In Lesson A, students watch a video which talks about smartphone addiction among young people. Students will then learn to describe different kinds of behavior. They will also practice the listening strategies of building background knowledge, listening for gist, making and checking predictions, and paraphrasing. They will then learn how to ask about culturally appropriate behavior. Finally, they will learn how to talk about appropriate behavior in a public place.

- In Lesson B, students will learn to talk about adjusting to living in a different country. They will read about living in Bogotá, Colombia, practicing the reading strategies of using background knowledge and understanding purpose. They will also create and give a presentation related to dealing with a travel situation.

WARM UP

Look at the photo. Answer the questions.

- Call on students to describe what they see in the photo.

- Have students answer the questions individually or in pairs, then compare answers with the class.

- Point out the unit goals and explain what students will learn. Elicit any key vocabulary students already know (words to describe customs and behavior, expressions used to give advice, words related to travel, etc.), and write it on the board. Explain any unfamiliar phrases in the unit goals.

Pronunciation	Speaking	Reading	Writing	Communication
Linking the same sounds p. 66	Asking about culturally appropriate behavior p. 67	Welcome to Bogotá p. 72 Use background knowledge Understand purpose	Prepare a "how-to" presentation p. 75	Designing a poster to improve public behavior p. 69 Explaining how to do something p. 75

People use their phones to take pictures outside of a movie premier.

1 VIDEO Smartphone Addiction

A How much time do you spend on your phone every day? Discuss with a partner.

B Read the sentences and guess the missing words. Then watch and check your answers. The three people say they are *addicted* to their smartphones. What do you think that means?

1. "The first thing I do when I _____ up is grab for my phone."

2. Thirty-two-year-old Matthew Barrett is never _____ from his smartphone.

3. Matthew isn't the only one living his life almost completely _____.

4. "If I don't have my phone, I can't really do _____."

5. "I can't really go a _____ without it."

C Watch again. What do the experts say about smartphone addiction? Circle *True* or *False*.

1. Psychologists say smartphone users are dangerous.	True	False
2. As we connect more on our phones, we connect more in person.	True	False
3. Smartphone withdrawal can also cause physical problems.	True	False

D Discuss these questions with a partner.

1. What do you think of smartphone addiction? Do you agree with the experts?

2. When is it impolite or inappropriate to be on your smartphone?

1 VIDEO
Smartphone Addiction

WARM UP Have students look at the photo and describe the scene. Who are the people? Where are they? What are they doing? Write their ideas on the board. ⏱ 5 min

ABOUT THE VIDEO
In this video, several young people talk about their smartphone use and how they feel when they don't have their smartphone with them. The video considers how smartphones are allowing us to be more connected virtually, while also making us less connected with our reality, with the people we are with at that moment, and with the place we are in. In addition, an addiction specialist presents both the mental and physical health risks of smartphone addiction. However, it is pointed out in the video that even knowing these risks, young people are unlikely to stop using their smartphones. Giving up anything that we are addicted to is hard, and smartphone addiction is no different. Nevertheless, talking about the issue and reflecting on our own smartphone use is clearly an important thing to be doing.

TEACHING TIP: Using English videos
Another way of working with video is to assign students to pairs and have them sit face-to-face so that one student cannot see the video. Play the video, then have students who watched explain what was happening to their partner, who will ask them questions to clarify what they understood from just listening.

A 🔁 How much time do you spend on your phone every day? Discuss with a partner. ⏱ 5–10 min

Have students read the question and think about their answer. Then assign them to pairs to compare and discuss their answers. Call on different students to tell the class about their partner's daily phone use. As a class, discuss how much time students spend on their phones, what they do on their phones, and when they use their phones.

B ▶ Read the sentences and guess the missing words. Then watch and check your answers. The three people say they are *addicted* to their smartphones. What do you think that means? ⏱ 10 min

Go over the sentences and answer vocabulary questions. Have students make their guesses. Remind them to read the whole sentence so they understand the context, and to think about the kind of word needed in each space. For example, in 1 after *I*, they need a verb. Play the video twice, then have students compare their answers with a partner's. Play the video again and check answers with the class. Then have students explain what *addicted* means. Write a definition on the board.

C ▶ Watch again. What do the experts say about smartphone addiction? Circle *True* or *False*. ⏱ 5–10 min

Go over the items with the class and have them answer any they think they already know. Play the video again. Have students confirm or complete their answers, then tell them to compare them with a partner's. Play the video again to check answers with the class, pausing and repeating the parts where the answers are as necessary.

D 🔁 Discuss these questions with a partner. ⏱ 10 min

Go over the questions with the class and have students think about their answers. Encourage them to write a few notes to help them when they are speaking. Then assign students to pairs to answer the questions. Monitor and provide help as necessary. Compare and discuss the answers as a class.

EXTRA! Post-viewing
In small groups, have students think of advice to help people try to use their smartphones less, for example, *Don't have your phone at the table when you are eating*. Have groups share their advice with the class and explain how they think it would help people be less dependent on their phones. ⏱ 10 min

Extra video vocabulary	
anxiety	mental health
biological health	outweigh
cortisol (stress hormone)	physical symptoms
depression	psychologist
go psycho	(have) withdrawal
grab	vice
insomnia	

2 VOCABULARY

WARM UP Ask students what behavior of others bothers them. Write their ideas on the board. If they have trouble thinking of ideas, you might write *talking loudly on cell phones*, *borrowing things and not returning them*, or *spreading gossip*. What behavior would students prefer to see? 🕐 5 min

A 　 Read sentences 1–8. Pay attention to the words in **blue**. What does each word mean? Tell a partner.
🕐 10 min

Go over the opposites in the Word Bank and have students repeat them. Remind students of the use of prefixes to show opposite meanings, but don't explain the words yet. Assign students to pairs to read the sentences together and explain the meaning of each word in blue. Read the sentences with the class and call on different students to explain the meaning of the new vocabulary. Call on students to give further examples to illustrate the new words as possible.

B Do you agree or disagree with the opinions in **A**? Write *A* or *D* next to each one. 🕐 5 min

Have students read the statements again individually and decide whether they agree or disagree.

TEACHING TIP: Word stress
Unlike many other languages, English does not have one set pattern for which syllable receives stress in a word. Students need to learn the correct stress for each new vocabulary item they acquire. Negative prefixes can change the stress, so students may need practice to say the opposites in this lesson the right way.

LANGUAGE TIP: Negative prefixes
Point out to students that sometimes the meanings of negative prefixes can help them to understand new words. However, these prefixes cannot be added randomly. It is important to learn which one is used with which word. For example, we say *impolite,* not *unpolite.*

C 　 Explain your answers in **B** to your partner. 🕐 10–15 min

Model the example with a student. Encourage the student to respond by saying if he or she agrees or disagrees with you. Model again by saying whether you agree or disagree with another statement, giving your reason. Elicit another example from a student. Then assign students to pairs to compare and explain their opinions in **B**. Monitor and provide help as necessary. Call on different students to tell the class one of their partner's opinions.

2 VOCABULARY

In most cultures, being respectful and considerate to one's elders is expected.

A Read sentences 1–8. Pay attention to the words in blue. What does each word mean? Tell a partner.

1. You should always be **pleasant** to other people, even when you're angry about something.

2. There are some situations when it's OK to be **impolite**.

3. An **honest** person always succeeds in the end. Tell the truth and you will, too.

4. It's not always easy to tell when someone is being **insincere**.

5. Being **disrespectful** is the worst thing you can do to your grandparents.

6. When you have a disagreement, the **mature** thing to do is walk away.

7. You should always be **considerate** of other people's feelings, even when they don't think about yours.

8. It's always **appropriate** to ask a question if you don't understand something.

Word Bank
Opposites
appropriate ↔ inappropriate
considerate ↔ inconsiderate
honest ↔ dishonest
kind ↔ unkind
mature ↔ immature
pleasant ↔ unpleasant
polite ↔ impolite / rude
respectful ↔ disrespectful
responsible ↔ irresponsible
sincere ↔ insincere

B Do you agree or disagree with the opinions in **A**? Write *A* or *D* next to each one.

C Explain your answers in **B** to your partner.

> I agree that it's important to be respectful to other people.

3 LISTENING

A 🔄 **Build background knowledge.** Think of a school field trip you went on. Where did you go? What is one thing you were not allowed to do on the trip? Tell a partner.

B 🔊 **Listen for gist.** Listen. Complete the sentences.
CD 1 Track 30

1. The speaker is talking to a group of _____.

2. They are at a _____.

C **Make predictions.** Look at your answer for number 2 in **B**. This place has many different rules that visitors must follow. Can you guess what some of these rules are? Write them on a piece of paper.

D 🔊 **Check predictions; Listen to paraphrase.** Read the sentences. Then listen to the rules. Choose the best paraphrase for each rule that you hear. **CD 1 Track 31**

1. a. You must stay on the green and red paths.
   b. Always stay on the red path. You can leave the green path.

2. a. You cannot watch the staff feeding the animals.
   b. Feeding time is open to the public.

3. a. Running or making noise is not allowed anywhere.
   b. Running or making noise is only permitted in certain areas.

4. a. Birds walk freely around some areas. Please don't touch them.
   b. Birds walk freely around some areas. It's OK to touch them.

5. a. You're not allowed to eat lunch inside this place.
   b. You can enjoy lunch inside this place.

6. a. If you don't know what's recyclable, just ask.
   b. Everything goes into the recycling containers.

E 🔄 Would you like to visit this place? Why or why not? Tell a partner.

F 🔊 **Pronunciation: Linking the same sounds.** Listen and repeat the words. **CD 1 Track 32**

1. don't touch   2. want to   3. steak came   4. left twenty   5. all loved   6. Tom might

G 🔄 **Pronunciation: Linking the same sounds.** With a partner, take turns reading aloud about Mari's dinner. Notice the underlined consonant sounds.

> Tom, Sue, and I ha**d** **d**inner together. The waiter was polite and considerate. I had the most delicious **s**oup. Tom's stea**k** **c**ame out quickly, and it was perfectly cooked. We al**l** **l**oved the place. We lef**t** **t**wenty dollars for a tip. I woul**d** **d**efinitely eat there again. In fact, To**m** **m**ight go there again tonight!

ℹ️ Say each pair of underlined consonants as one long sound. You don't need to say each sound twice.

H 🔊 🔄 **Pronunciation: Linking the same sounds.** Now listen to the story in **G** and practice saying it with a partner. Pay attention to the linked consonant sounds. **CD 1 Track 33**

3 LISTENING

STRATEGIES: Build background knowledge; Listen for gist; Make predictions; Check predictions; Listen to paraphrase

WARM UP Ask students if they have ever been to a museum. Ask for examples of what is considered appropriate and inappropriate behavior in a museum. ⏱ 5 min

A 🔁 **Build background knowledge.** Think of a school field trip you went on. Where did you go? What is one thing you were not allowed to do on the trip? Tell a partner. ⏱ 5–10 min

Go over the directions with the class and give examples of school field trips (to a museum, to a local event) then assign students to pairs to talk about a school trip and what they weren't allowed to do. Provide vocabulary as necessary. Call on different students to share with the class what their partner told them.

Build background knowledge. Students bring to any text the knowledge they already have about life and the world in general, as well as any knowledge they have about the specific topic. Activating this knowledge prior to listening will help them be more prepared.

B 🔊 **Listen for gist.** Listen. Complete the sentences. **CD 1 Track 30** ⏱ 5 min

Tell students to read the two sentences. Then play the audio. Play the audio again to check the answers.

Listen for gist. Remind students that when listening for gist, they don't need to worry about understanding everything they hear; the purpose is to understand the general idea.

C **Make predictions.** Look at your answer for number 2 in **B**. This place has many different rules that visitors must follow. Can you guess what some of these rules are? Write them on a piece of paper. ⏱ 5–10 min

Have students brainstorm possible rules at the zoo and write a list on a piece of paper. Then have them compare their list with a partner's. Write a class list on the board. Answers will vary, but might include not feeding or otherwise disturbing the animals.

Make predictions. Remind students that making predictions before they listen helps them be more prepared for what they are going to hear because they will have activated prior knowledge of the topic and language related to it.

D 🔊 **Check predictions; Listen to paraphrase.** Read the sentences. Then listen to the rules. Choose the best paraphrase for each rule that you hear. **CD 1 Track 31** ⏱ 10 min

Explain to students that a *paraphrase* is a different way of saying the same thing. Read or call on volunteers to read each of the sentences in 1–6. Then play the audio. Check the answers as a class.

Check predictions. It is important to always go back to the predictions students made and help them see what they guessed correctly, and talk about why incorrect guesses were wrong.

Listen to paraphrase. Explain to students that paraphrasing means to express what they heard in different words. Doing this pushes students to understand at a deeper level; being able to express an idea in their own words demonstrates understanding.

🔊 **EXTRA! More listening comprehension**
Write these questions on the board. Then play the audio again. Check answers as a class. **CD 1 Track 31** ⏱ 10 min

1. What is the first and most important rule? (Do not climb over any fences or walls.)

2. What is one of the things that the woman *does* want the children to do? (Ask a lot of questions.)

E 🔁 Would you like to visit this place? Why or why not? Tell a partner. ⏱ 10 min

Go over the questions with the class and have students think about their answers. Tell them to write notes to help them when they are speaking. Model the exercise by saying, *I would(n't) like to visit the zoo because...* and giving your opinion. Assign students to pairs to answer the questions. Compare and discuss their answers as a class. Do students have different opinions?

F 🔊 **Pronunciation: Linking the same sounds.** Listen and repeat the words. **CD 1 Track 32** ⏱ 5 min

Read the pairs of words, then play the audio and have students repeat. Help them notice how the two sounds that are the same (at the end of the first word and at the beginning of the second) are linked.

PRONUNCIATION TIP: Linking the same sounds
Students need to notice that if the sound at the end of one word is the same as the sound beginning the next word, the sound is not repeated. The two sounds are joined.

G 🔁 **Pronunciation: Linking the same sounds.** With a partner, take turns reading aloud about Mari's dinner. Notice the underlined consonant sounds. ⏱ 10 min

Remind students to pronounce the two sounds printed in blue on the page as one sound.

H 🔊 🔁 **Pronunciation: Linking the same sounds.** Now listen to the story in **G** and practice saying it with a partner. Pay attention to the linked consonant sounds. **CD 1 Track 33** ⏱ 10 min

Point out any words that you heard them have difficulty pronouncing in **G**. Tell partners to read the story aloud, focusing on the linked consonant sounds.

4 SPEAKING

WARM UP Tell students to imagine they have been invited to dinner at a friend's house. What are some things that they should or shouldn't do in order to be polite and show good manners? Write students' answers on the board and discuss as a class. ⏱ 5 min

A 🔊 Read and listen to Ahmed and Inez's conversation. Why are people going to Ahmed's house? What custom is Inez unsure about? **CD 1 Track 34** ⏱ 10 min

Give students time to read the conversation. Then play the audio while they read. Discuss the answers as a class.

B 🔁 Practice the conversation with a partner. ⏱ 5–10 min

Play the audio line by line and have students repeat after each line. Then place students in pairs to practice the conversation. Remind students to look up from the page and to speak in a conversational tone, rather than using a "reading" tone of voice.

EXTRA! Writing prompt
Students can write a paragraph giving advice on how to behave correctly when invited to dinner in their country. What should the guest do? What should the host do?
⏱ 15–20 min

SPEAKING STRATEGY

C Read the Useful Expressions. Which responses are positive? Which are negative? ⏱ 10 min

Put students in pairs. Read the Useful Expressions to the class. Tell students to work together to figure out the answers, and then write their answers next to the box. Check the answers as a class. Explain any examples that are confusing for students.

LANGUAGE TIP: Saying no politely
Note that in the Useful Expressions box, there are several expressions that are very polite and tactful ways of saying *no*. When a person asks a question, it is sometimes more polite not to say *no* directly. So when the speaker says, *Actually, it's probably better to use a fork.* or *Normally, people use a fork.* or *Actually, it's best to remove your shoes,* the speaker is really saying, *No, don't do that,* in a very polite way.

D 🔁 Read the rules for the two situations below. Role-play one of the situations with a partner. One person asks about the culturally appropriate behavior. The other person explains them. Then switch roles and role-play another situation. ⏱ 15 min

Direct students' attention to the Useful Expressions box. Practice the expressions by reading them aloud and asking students to repeat after you. Then ask if any students have been to a mosque or had a formal Japanese dinner. What were their experiences? Read the rules for both situations, and explain vocabulary as needed. Explain *help yourself to something* and give students some examples of this phrase in sentences.

On the board, write *What should I do if I go to....* Model the exercise with a student in front of the class. Say, *What should I do if I go to a formal Japanese meal? Is it appropriate to ask for a knife and fork? I can't use chopsticks.* Have the student reply using an expression from the box. As students work on their role plays, walk around listening for the Useful Expressions. Tell students to switch roles so that each student has the chance to be the one who asks. If time allows, ask students to think of their own cultural situation, and ask about it or explain it to others.

LARGE CLASS OPTION
Divide the class into groups of eight to ten students. If possible, make sure that there is an even number of students in each group. Divide each group in half—there will be one inside group and one outside group. Tell all of the students to stand up. Each inside group should form a circle facing outward. Each person in the outside group should find a partner from someone in the inside group and begin asking and answering the questions in **D**. When you clap your hands, the students on the outside should rotate to the right and begin a conversation with a new student. Continue until each student has had the opportunity to talk with each of the students in the other group.

Instructor's Notes

_____

_____

_____

_____

_____

_____

_____

4 SPEAKING

A 🔊 Read and listen to Ahmed and Inez's conversation. Why are people going to Ahmed's house? What custom is Inez unsure about? **CD 1 Track 34**

INEZ: Wow! Everything smells delicious, Ahmed. How long did it take you to cook all this?

AHMED: A few hours. But don't worry—I like to cook for my friends. And I like to have dinner parties. Please, sit down.

INEZ: Um, can I sit anywhere?

AHMED: Sure. You're the first guest to arrive. Make yourself comfortable.

INEZ: You know, I've never had Turkish food before.

AHMED: Don't worry. I'll explain everything... Uh, here, try this.

INEZ: Um, is it OK if I use my fingers?

AHMED: Sure, go right ahead. So, what do you think?

INEZ: Mmm. It's delicious.

B 🤝 Practice the conversation with a partner.

SPEAKING STRATEGY

C Read the Useful Expressions. Which responses are positive? Which are negative?

Useful Expressions: Asking about culturally appropriate behavior	
Is it OK / appropriate to use my fingers?	Is it all right to wear shoes inside?
Is it OK if I use my fingers?	Is it all right if I wear shoes inside?
Please, go right ahead. / Absolutely.	Sure, no problem. / Yeah, it's fine.
Actually, it's probably better to use a fork.	Actually, it's best to remove your shoes.
Normally, people use a fork.	No, you really should take off your shoes.

D 🤝 Read the rules for the two situations below. Role-play one of the situations with a partner. One person asks about the culturally appropriate behavior. The other explains them. Then switch roles and role-play another situation.

Rules for visiting a mosque	
wear shoes inside	☹
wear shorts	☹
cover your head	☺
sit in a mixed group of men and women	☹

Rules for a formal Japanese dinner	
help yourself to a drink	☹
make special food requests	☹
ask for a knife and fork	☺
leave a tip	☹

> Is it appropriate to ask for a knife and fork? I can't use chopsticks.

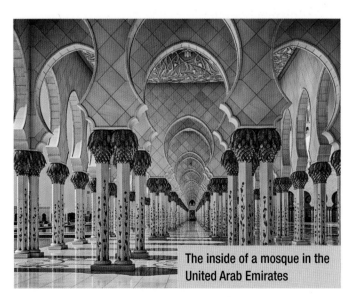

The inside of a mosque in the United Arab Emirates

5 GRAMMAR

A Turn to page 201. Complete the exercises. Then do **B–D** below.

It + be + Adjective + Infinitive; Gerund + be + Adjective						
It	*be*	**Adjective**	*(for)*	**(pronoun)**	**Infinitive**	
It	**was**(n't)	hard	(for)	(me)	to pass	the test.
It's (not)		normal	(for)	(us)	to eat	with chopsticks.

Gerund		*be*	**Adjective**	*(for)*	**(pronoun)**
Passing	the test	**was**(n't)	hard	(for)	(me).
Eating	with chopsticks	**is**(n't)	normal	(for)	(us).

B Use the key words to write two sentences about learning English.

1. English / study / fun

   It's fun _____

   Studying _____

2. impossible / master / for anyone / English grammar

   _____

   _____

3. for language students / English / speak / unnecessary / perfectly

   _____

   _____

4. practice conversation with / important / a native speaker / find

   _____

   _____

C 🔁 Look at the statements in **B**. Do you agree or disagree with each one? Discuss your answers with a partner.

> I think studying English is sometimes fun.

> Really? It's never fun for me!

D 🔁 What would you do in these situations? Discuss your ideas with a partner.

1. There is an empty seat next to you on the train. Is it OK to put your bag there? Why or why not?

2. You are in a crowded elevator, and your phone rings. Is it OK to answer the call? Why or why not?

> I think it's inconsiderate for you to put your bag on the seat. It takes up too much space.

> It depends. If the train is mostly empty, putting your bag on the seat seems appropriate.

5 GRAMMAR
It + be + adjective + infinitive /
Gerund + be + adjective

WARM UP Ask students, *What rude behavior have you seen foreigners do in your country? What mistakes have you made while traveling?* Let students share their funny stories. If students haven't traveled, but heard a funny story, let them share that. Share stories of your experiences as well. ⏱ 5 min

A Turn to page 201. Complete the exercises. Then do **B–D** below. ◑ 20–30 min

Go over the examples in the chart. Write some additional examples of the structure on the board: *It isn't nice to interrupt people. Interrupting people isn't nice. It's rude to leave without thanking your host. Leaving without thanking your host is rude.* Read the on-the-board sentences with students repeating. Underline the target structures on the board. Have students go back to the rules for visiting a mosque and going to a formal Japanese dinner on page 67 and make sentences using the structures. Write them on the board. The grammar chart on page 201 includes more examples, expanding on the information in the chart on page 68.

B Use the key words to write two sentences about learning English. ⏱ 10 min

Go over the directions with the class, then do the first one together as an example. Have students complete the rest individually. Refer them to the chart on page 201 as necessary. Have them compare their answers with a partner's, then check answers with the class.

C 🔁 Look at the statements in **B**. Do you agree or disagree with each one? Discuss your answers with a partner. ⏱ 10 min

Model the exercise by reading the example with a student. Continue the conversation by asking the student, *Why or why not?* Model again with a different student using a different statement. Assign students to pairs to discuss the statements. Monitor and provide help as necessary, encourage students to explain their reasons.

D 🔁 What would you do in these situations? Discuss your ideas with a partner. ⏱ 10–15 min

Go over the situations with the class, then have students review the opposites in the Word Bank on page 65. Model the exercise by reading the example with a student. Give students a moment to think about their opinions, and answer any vocabulary questions while they prepare their answers. Assign students to pairs to discuss the situations. Monitor and provide help as necessary. As a class, discuss what is appropriate in each situation and why. Discuss any differences of opinion.

CULTURE TIP: Sharing a glass
In Paraguay, drinks are frequently shared in social settings. That is, a glass is poured, one person takes a drink, and passes it to the next person. This is an extension of the communal culture of drinking mate (a hot, caffeinated beverage made from steeped leaves and herbs) in some parts of South America. In some other cultures, this would be frowned upon because of hygiene concerns. How do your students feel about this communal drinking?

🔁 **GRAMMAR TUTORIALS**

• *Be* + Adjective + Infinitive
• Gerunds as Subjects

Additional tutorials are available for reteaching and reinforcement.

Instructor's Notes

_____

_____

_____

_____

_____

_____

_____

_____

_____

_____

_____

_____

_____

_____

6 COMMUNICATION

WARM UP Lead a discussion with the class about customs relating to space and touch. How close together should people stand when they are talking? When is it appropriate for one person to touch another person? Do the students know of other cultures' personal space issues? ⏱ 5 min

TEACHING TIP: Realia

To help students experience a new language and culture, bring *realia*, or real objects, into the classroom. Realia can be simple objects used in daily life, such as different kinds of food or clothing. Or realia can be examples of language as it is actually used, such as brochures, newspapers, or menus. Tourism offices of English-speaking countries may be able to supply you with items you can use in your classroom. Be sure to suit the type of realia to your class objectives. For this lesson, realia about public transportation would be suitable. Search online to find a nearby city with a subway. Download a map of the subway system and information about fares and frequency of service. Share these with your students.

A ⚡ Study the people in the subway scene below. What are they doing? Use the words in the box and make sentences about their behavior. Share them with a partner. ⏱ 10–15 min

Have students look at the picture and elicit vocabulary to describe it. Write their ideas on the board. Help students with any vocabulary that they may not know, such as *skateboard*, *cane*, and *headphones*. Note that a subway may be called by another name, such as *underground* or *metro*. Model the exercise by reading the example and completing it with your own idea. Go over the words in the box and have students repeat them in both the positive and negative form. Have students make their sentences. Then assign students to pairs to share their ideas. Call on different students to share one of their sentences.

B 🔅 You are going to design a poster. Read the information below and look at the examples. Work as a group to plan your poster. Then draw it on a piece of paper. ⏱ 20–30 min

Bring in large pieces of paper or poster board and pens, pencils, and markers. Assign students to groups of three or four. Tell students not to begin working on the poster until they have brainstormed ideas and agreed on the general design. As an alternative, you may wish to assign this for homework and permit students to add photos or other materials from outside the classroom. Be sure to help students stay focused on their task.

C 🔅 Put up your posters around the room. Vote for the best one. ⏱ 10 min

Bring to class some tape, pins, or other means of putting up the posters. On the board, brainstorm with students the criteria for evaluating the poster. How will students decide which one is the best? You may wish to suggest criteria such as including a clear message and art and design that reinforce the message. Permit students to vote for a first, second, and third choice using colored dots or markers. Bring small prizes for the winning teams if appropriate.

TEACHING OPTION: Walkaround

To help students get a chance to see as many posters as possible, conduct a "walkaround." Choose one member of each group to stay with their poster. This person is responsible for explaining the poster. The other members of the group will walk around and look at the other posters and ask questions and offer comments. After a few minutes, the group members explaining the posters can be replaced by other members. This way each student will have a chance to see as many posters as possible.

LARGE CLASS OPTION

Have students work in larger groups of four to six. Each group presents their poster to the whole class, so everyone can see it without walking around. Students can vote on the presentation of the poster as well as the poster itself. You may want to hang the posters in the room after class so they are there when students return to the next session.

EXTRA! Writing prompt

Tell students to prepare a one-page information sheet describing polite behavior in a country of their choice. This should be a guide for foreigners to help them live successfully in the culture. Include local customs, good manners, and unspoken assumptions about behavior. Students can research online to find out information if necessary. This can be done in or out of class depending on time and access to the Internet. ⏱ 20 min

Instructor's Notes

_____

_____

_____

_____

_____

6 COMMUNICATION

A 🔊 Study the people in the subway scene below. What are they doing? Use the words in the box and make sentences about their behavior. Share them with a partner.

> One woman is eating ice cream on the subway. I think it's inappropriate because...

| (im)polite | (in)appropriate | (in)considerate | (un)kind |

B 👥 You are going to design a poster. Read the information below and look at the examples. Work as a group to plan your poster. Then draw it on a piece of paper.

- The city is starting a public awareness campaign for buses and subways.
- Officials are asking riders to design a poster for the campaign.
- The winners will each receive a free one-year bus and subway pass!

C 👥 Put up your posters around the room. Vote for the best one.

Giving up your seat on the subway is the polite thing to do!

MTSDC

Hey, you! Slow down!
I know you're in a hurry but...

Remember! Running in the subway station is dangerous. It can result in serious injury.

MTSDC

Body language can be an important way of communicating with other people.

1 VOCABULARY

A Match the words in groups A and B to make common English expressions. Then match the expressions to their definitions below. Use the underlined words as clues to help you.

A				B			
body	eye	jet	personal	~~barrier~~	expression	~~lag~~	space
eating	facial	~~language~~	~~small~~	contact	habits	language	talk

1. <u>words</u> that <u>prevent you from understanding</u> another person   _language_   _barrier_
2. feeling <u>tired</u> after a long <u>airplane</u> trip   _____   _lag_
3. describing <u>how or when</u> people <u>eat</u>   _____   _____
4. the <u>look</u> on a person's <u>face</u> (for example, a smile)   _____   _____
5. <u>conversation</u> about <u>unimportant or everyday</u> things   _small_   _____
6. <u>looking directly at</u> another person's <u>eyes</u>   _____   _____
7. the <u>area</u> around each <u>person</u>   _____   _____
8. <u>communication</u> through how we move our <u>bodies</u>   _____   _____

B Think of a country you would like to visit. Imagine you are going there for three months. Complete the questionnaire on the top of the next page. Write your answers on a separate piece of paper.

1 VOCABULARY

WARM UP Ask students if any of them have traveled internationally. Where did they go? What were their experiences? If no one has been abroad, what encounters have they had with people from other countries visiting their country? Remind students that going to neighboring countries is traveling internationally, too! ⏱ 5–10 min

A Match the words in groups A and B to make common English expressions. Then match the expressions to their definitions below. Use the underlined words as clues to help you. ⏱ 10 min

Students can complete the exercise individually. If necessary, give the following hint: if students look at the second of the two underlined expressions, they can then find a related word in column A. For instance, in number 7, the second underlined word is *person*, and the word being sought is *personal space*. Note that of the vocabulary terms, *eating habits* is always plural. The terms *language barrier(s)* and *facial expression(s)* can be singular or plural. The other terms are usually singular.

B Think of a country you would like to visit. Imagine you are going there for three months. Complete the questionnaire on the top of the next page. Write your answers on a separate piece of paper. ⏱ 10 min

Go over the directions with the class and have students think of a country. Call on a few people to share the country they are thinking of. Make sure they understand that they are not going for a vacation but rather to live in the country for a few months. Then have students complete the questionnaire individually. Point out the information in the Word Bank to help them. Answer questions about other vocabulary as necessary.

CULTURE TIP: Small Talk
In English-speaking countries, the weather is a very common and safe topic for "small talk"—friendly conversation with people you don't know very well. Conversation can be started with a comment like, *It's really hot today.* or *What a beautiful day!* This is a useful strategy for students to learn in order to strike up conversations with native speakers.

CULTURE TIP: Nonverbal behavior
In most Western cultures, smiling is an indication that something is humorous. In other cultures, such as Japan, smiling may sometimes signal embarrassment. Personal space also differs from one culture to another. In most Western cultures, eye contact is considered a sign of respect and trustworthiness. If you fail to look at people directly, others may think that you are ashamed or trying to hide something.

Cultural differences	
culture shock	group
customary	indirect
direct	individual
formal	informal
gesture	nonverbal communication

Instructor's Notes

_____

_____

_____

_____

_____

_____

_____

_____

_____

_____

_____

STRATEGIES: Use background knowledge; Understand purpose

WARM UP Find out if any students have ever lived away from home. What was their experience like? What are the reasons that people live away from home for periods of time? (School, camp, living with relatives, etc.) ⏱ 5 min

A 🔄 **Use background knowledge.** Read the title of the article. What do you know about this city or the country it's in? Tell a partner. ⏱ 5 min

Have students talk about what they know about Bogotá and Colombia with a partner. For example, where Colombia is, what language people there speak, what the weather is like, what products are from there, etc. Call on different pairs to share ideas and write them on the board.

Use background knowledge. Students bring to any text the knowledge they already have about life and the world in general, as well as any knowledge they have about the specific topic of the text. Students should draw on this knowledge to help them understand the reading passage.

B **Understand purpose.** Read the passage. Then complete the sentence below. ⏱ 10 min

Have students read the sentence and the options and then read the text. Remind them to underline any words they don't know and try to work out the meaning from the context. Have students choose their answer then compare it with a partner's. Check the answer with the class, having students explain what helped them figure out the purpose.

Understand purpose. Explain to students that whenever they read, they should think about what the objective of the text is: Is it to explain something, to inform the reader about something, to persuade the reader, or to tell a story? Identifying the purpose of the text will help students understand it better.

---

3 READING

A ⚡ **Use background knowledge.** Read the title of the article. What do you know about this city or the country it's in? Tell a partner.

B **Understand purpose.** Read the passage. Then complete the sentence below.

The main purpose of this reading is to _____ in Bogotá.

a. teach tourists about famous sites
b. help foreign students adjust to life
c. explain how to do business

C Complete the sentences with the words from the article.

exhausted	cues
presentable	discouraged

1. I didn't sleep on the flight, so I was _____ when we landed.

2. I watched for _____ from my friend, so I knew how to act around his family.

3. She didn't get _____ when she did poorly on the test. She studied harder and did well on the next one.

4. It is important to be _____. You should dress well in public.

D ⚡ What would be the hardest thing for you to adjust to in Bogotá? Tell a partner.

 WORLD LINK

Research another city. Write tips like the ones in the article about this city. Share your tips with the class.

72 **UNIT 5** • Across cultures

WELCOME TO BOGOTÁ

CULTURE TIP: Culture shock

When people live abroad, they often experience culture shock, which is a series of phases and feelings that a person goes through when living in another culture. When people first arrive, they enjoy the new culture, and it seems exciting. But after a while they begin to feel uncertain and less positive about the new culture. They miss home and their own way of doing things. Eventually, they adjust to life in the new country. It is during the second phase of culture shock that people feel the worst—and often they are unaware of why they feel the way they do. Students are more likely to have a positive experience if they can develop an active interest in the new culture and try to stay engaged with the people who live there.

Bogotá, Colombia, is a well-known city. Every year, thousands of students from all over the world visit it to learn Spanish and travel to other places around Colombia. Now that you've arrived, here are some things to keep in mind.

1. Jet lag. If you traveled a long way, you'll probably be exhausted for the first few days. When you feel sleepy, the best thing to do is stay awake. If you fall asleep during the day, you'll wake up at night, and it will take days to get on a normal schedule!

2. Greeting people. When you meet people, it's polite to make eye contact. Many people will also make small talk. Be ready to talk about your health, your family, and of course, your trip! Another thing to keep in mind is that people in many parts of Colombia can be more reserved than in other Latin American countries. You should always start off a conversation by being very respectful. From there, you can follow the cues[1] of the other people in the conversation.

3. Learning the language. Learning a new language is hard, and being frustrated is part of the process. But don't get discouraged! Pay attention to body language, facial expressions, gestures, and context, and your language abilities will get stronger over time. Colombia is one of the fastest-growing countries for students

[1]If you follow someone else's *cue*, you copy their behavior.

from other countries who want to learn Spanish. There are a large number of language schools and private teachers to help you.

4. Lifestyle changes. As you start to make new friends here, you'll notice people are very active. When people go out, dancing is very popular. You should learn how to do it. Smoking is uncommon, and it is illegal to do it in public places. Finally, it's important to look presentable in public at all times, so don't wear sweatpants if you're going out. This is a great place to break some of your bad habits and get healthier!

5. Homesickness. You will miss your home, family, and friends. This might make you feel sad, which is completely normal. To feel better, try keeping a few things from home around, like pictures or a favorite food. Don't overdo it, though. You should also connect to your new city. Go sightseeing with a classmate, or try new activities, like playing a sport. The more you socialize, the better you'll feel.

Most of all, remember that studying abroad is a life-changing event. You're going to learn a lot about a new country and about yourself, too. All of this takes time, but in the end, you will make friends and memories that will last for many years!

LESSON B • Adjusting to a new place **73**

EXTRA! Discussion
With the class, talk about the idea of homesickness. Have any students experienced this? Ask students to discuss their ideas in small groups. ⏱ 15 min

EXTRA! Post-reading
Introduce the idea of culture shock. Tell students to research the topic. They can use resources in the school library or look for online sources. Ask them to identify the different phases, list common symptoms, and offer suggestions for overcoming it. After students have gathered their research, ask them to present their information to the class. ⏱ 60 min

EXTRA! Writing prompt
Ask students to write about a time when they lived in a different country or when they overcame a difficult or challenging situation. ⏱ 15–20 min

---

C Complete the sentences with the words from the article. ⏱ 5–10 min

Have students read the text again and find the words in the box. Then have them read and complete the sentences. Check answers with the class.

D 🔄 What would be the hardest thing for you to adjust to in Bogotá? Tell a partner. ⏱ 10–15 min

Go over the question with the class, then have students think about their answer and reasons. Assign students to pairs to discuss the question. Model the exercise by saying, *The hardest thing for me to adjust to would be...* and sharing your answer. Write the start of the sentence on the board to help students. Call on different students to tell the class their partner's answer. As a class, discuss what aspects of the country you are in are hard for foreigners to adjust to.

EXTRA! Comprehension questions
Have pairs write questions about living in Bogotá based on information from the text. For example:

Why do students go to Bogotá?

Why is it a good idea to stay awake when you feel sleepy?

Elicit question words and review question structures as necessary, then have pairs write their questions. Monitor pairs and check that the questions are correct. Then have pairs discuss each other's questions.

WORLD LINK

Research another city. Write tips like the ones in the article about this city. Share your tips with the class.

Go over the directions with the students. Students can do their research individually or with a partner (in or out of class depending on time and resources). You can have them present their tips in poster form. They can then present their poster to the class or in small groups, depending on class size.

4 GRAMMAR

A Turn to page 202. Complete the exercises. Then do **B** and **C** below.

Present and Future Time Clauses with *before, after, when, as soon as / once*	
Main clause	**Time clause**
In Spain, people often <u>kiss</u> each other	**when** they <u>meet</u>.
Please <u>remove</u> your shoes	**before** you <u>enter</u> the temple.
We<u>'re going to go</u> to the park	**after** we <u>eat</u> lunch.
I<u>'ll call</u> you	**as soon as** / **once** we <u>arrive</u>.
Time clause	**Main clause**
Before you enter the temple,	please remove your shoes.

B Read about the four people's problems living abroad. What should each person do? Match each person with a piece of advice (a–h).

a. Skype your family.

b. Watch TV shows with subtitles.

c. Take a cooking class.

d. Spend time with friends.

e. Join a club.

f. Ask your teacher or host family for help.

g. Go on a short trip.

h. My idea: _____

"At home I'm very outgoing, but I don't know anyone here, so I'm kind of shy."

—Jin Soo in Europe

"People here are nice, but I'm homesick. I want to quit school and go home."

—Clara in North America

"I feel discouraged. I studied before I came here, but I can't communicate with anyone very well. I want to improve my language skills."

—Julia in Africa

"I like the food here, but I can only order two or three dishes, so I'm always eating the same thing!"

—Yusef in Asia

C ⟳ Work with a partner. Follow the steps below.

1. **Student A:** Take the role of one person above. Explain your problem.

   Student B: Give the person some advice using *Before / When / After / As soon as / Once you...*

2. Change roles and repeat step 1.

3. Repeat steps 1 and 2.

> Clara, I know you're homesick. Before you quit and go home, spend time with friends here. Once you do this, maybe you'll feel better.

4 GRAMMAR

Present and future time clauses with *before*, *after*, *when*, *as soon as / once*

WARM UP Ask students to write a timeline about the class on the board. What events happened before other events? Try to formulate sentences in the form of *First this happened* and *Then that happened*. Then ask the class to think about the future. Write another timeline. What will be happening in the future? In what order? What will happen first? ⏱ 5 min

A Turn to page 202. Complete the exercises. Then do **B** and **C** below. ◐ 20–30 min

Go over the examples in the chart and have students identify the tenses in each clause (simple present with simple present, or a future tense with the simple present). Point out that the main clause can come second and elicit from students how the punctuation changes in this case (a comma is needed after the time clause). Look at the class future timeline from the Warm Up and help students make sentences using time clauses, for example: *As soon as we finish the course, we're going to have a party. We'll study before we do the final exam.* The grammar chart on page 202 includes further examples and usage explanations, expanding on the information in the chart on page 74.

TEACHING OPTION: The flipped classroom
To open up time for in-class communicative tasks, assign the Grammar Notes on page 202 as homework. Have students complete the exercises on My World Link Online as well.

The next time class meets:
1. Review the present and future time clauses in the Grammar Notes.
2. Go through the exercises students did for homework; present new examples and reinforce points as needed. Take questions from students.
3. Turn back to page 74 and do the communicative exercises there, starting with **B**.

GRAMMAR TIP: Main clauses and dependent clauses
In the examples on this page, the time clause is *dependent* on the main clause. The main clause can be used independently, but the dependent clause cannot stand alone. Teach your students to recognize the dependent clause markers, such as *before*, *after*, *once*, *when*, and *as soon as*. If you use them, you need to add an independent clause. Tell students that if they have a dependent clause marker, they need to be able to identify a subject and verb in the main clause and a subject and verb in the dependent clause.

B Read about the four people's problems living abroad. What should each person do? Match each person with a piece of advice (a–h). ⏱ 5–10 min

Have students look at the chart again. Ask these questions:

- Which sentences in the chart are about facts or information in the present? the future? Which verb tenses are used in the two clauses?
- In sentence 1, which event happens first, OR do the two events happen at almost the same time?
- In sentence 2, which event happens first?
- In sentence 3, which event happens first?
- In sentence 4, which event happens first?

Go over the pieces of advice with the class. Then have students read about each person and choose the best advice for each one, adding one piece of advice of their own for one of the people. Have students compare their answers with a partner's. Compare answers with the class.

C 🔁 Work with a partner. Follow the steps below. ⏱ 15 min

(See Student Book page 74 for complete instructions.)

Go over the steps with the class. Then model the example with a student. Have the student read what Clara says in **B**, give the advice, then have the student respond to your advice. Elicit ways of responding to advice and suggestions and write them on the board, for example, *You're right, that's a good idea. Thanks, I'll try that.* Assign students to pairs and have them role-play the situations. Monitor and provide help as necessary. Encourage students to continue the conversation whenever they can by asking another question or giving more advice. Have students repeat the exercise so that they practice both roles. If time allows, students can change partners and do another role play. Have one or two pairs perform one of their role plays for the class.

CULTURE TIP: Giving advice
The expressions taught in this section are fairly direct and are suitable for giving advice to people on a basis of equality with the speaker (for example, friends, coworkers, or family members). In speaking with someone in a position of authority (such as one's boss), a native speaker would use more indirect expressions, such as *You might want to take a cab.*, or *It might be a good idea to call him.*

🎧 GRAMMAR TUTORIALS
- Future Time Clauses

Additional tutorials are available for reteaching and reinforcement.

5 WRITING

WARM UP Write on the board, *How-to presentation* and elicit from students what it refers to. If necessary, give examples, *How to cook chicken, How to change a tire*. Ask students if they have seen any presentations like this or watched videos on the Internet to learn how to do something. Have students share ideas and as a class talk about what makes a *How-to...* presentation effective. Write their ideas on the board. ⏱ 5 min

A 🔁 A student has prepared a short presentation. Read the slides and answer the questions with a partner. ⏱ 10 min

Go over the directions and the questions with the class. Then have students read the slides and answer the questions with a partner. Check answers with the class. Have students underline the time clauses.

PROCESS WRITING: Presentations
The steps of the writing process can be applied effectively to creating presentations. Brainstorming ideas will help students get ideas for their presentation, and they should plan which specific points from the brainstorming they will include and how they will be organized. Students should then write the first draft of their slides, then edit this first draft. Editing can be self, peer, or from the instructor. They should then write their final version.

B Choose an idea from the list of travel topics and prepare a short presentation about it. Organize your presentation like the example, with a title and three tips. Remember to use time clauses. ⏱ 15–20 min

Go over the list of *How to...* travel topics and have students add an idea of their own. Choose one of the topics from the list and write it on the board. With the class, brainstorm ideas for tips to give for this topic and write them on the board in note form. Then have the class help you create the presentation using the slides in **A** as a model. First, have the class decide which three tips to include from brainstorming, then begin the slides. If you can, do the presentation electronically and project it; if not, use poster paper for each slide, or just use the board. Do the four slides with the class, making sure time clauses are included. Then have students choose their own topic from the list and individually brainstorm tips. After brainstorming, have them choose the three tips to use and create their presentations following the model in **A**. If technological resources are available, have students do their presentations electronically. Monitor and provide help as necessary. Make sure they include the time clauses and refer them back to pages 74 and 202 as necessary. As students finish, pair them and have them share their slides and help each other make corrections and improvements. Then have students finalize their slides.

6 COMMUNICATION

WARM UP Elicit tips for giving a good presentation and write them on the board. For example, eye contact, volume and speed, etc. ⏱ 5 min

A 🔗 Work in a small group. Follow the directions. Repeat until each student has a chance to give his or her presentation. ⏱ 30–40 min

(See Student Book page 75 for full instructions.)

Go over the phrases in the Word Bank, saying them for students to repeat. Then go over the directions and the steps with the class. Point out the example. Then, if possible, model the exercise by giving the presentation the class helped you create. Have students answer the questions in Writing **A** about your presentation.

Give students a few moments to integrate the language from the Word Bank into their presentation, and to practice their presentations. Then have students present to the class. Remind students that when they are listening to each presentation, they need to answer the questions in Writing **A**. Have students draw a table to make it easier to record their answers for each presentation as they listen. When all students have presented, talk as a class about which presentations were the most effective and why. Based on this, students can add any more tips on giving a good presentation to the list from the Warm Up.

EXTRA! Writing prompt
Imagine that your friend is studying overseas. She writes to you to talk about the problems she is having adjusting to her new life. Write a letter in which you offer advice and encouragement in overcoming the difficulties of adjusting to living in another country. ⏱ 10 min

LARGE GROUP OPTION
In large groups, students can give their presentations in groups of 6 to 8 students with the students sitting near them. This will avoid a lot of moving around.

Instructor's Notes

_____

_____

_____

_____

_____

_____

5 WRITING

| **How to Make Small Talk at a Party** (when you don't speak the language well) | **1. Be prepared.** Before you go to the party, think of two or three things to talk about. ***Popular topics:*** sports, music, things in the news | **2. Ask a question.** Once you make eye contact with someone at the party, say *hi*, and introduce yourself. Then ask a simple question to get the conversation started: *Where are you from?* | **3. Keep things light.** After you start talking, remember to keep things light. It's easier to talk about simple topics. |

A   A student has prepared a short presentation. Read the slides and answer the questions with a partner.

1.   What is the topic of his *how-to* presentation?

2.   What are his three suggestions? Explain each in your own words.

3.   Are these good ideas? Can you think of one more suggestion to add?

B   Choose an idea from the list of travel topics and prepare a short presentation about it. Organize your presentation like the example, with a title and three tips. Remember to use time clauses.

> **Travel topics: How to...**
> • feel better when you're homesick.
> • pack for your trip.
> • overcome a language barrier.
> • stay safe when you travel.
> • my idea: _____

6 COMMUNICATION

A   Work in a small group. Follow the directions. Repeat until each student has a chance to give his or her presentation.

Speaker: Give your presentation from Writing using your slides. Remember to explain the point on each slide in more detail. Use the language below to organize your talk.

Listeners: Answer questions 1–3 in **A** in Writing about the speaker's ideas.

> Today, I'm going to talk about how to make small talk. The first thing you should do is...

Word Bank
Explaining how to do something
Today, I'm going to talk about how to...
The first thing you should do is...
A second thing to do is...
And finally...
Thanks for listening. Do you have any questions?

6 BUSINESS AND MARKETING

ABOUT THE PHOTO

This photo shows the Akihabara district in central Tokyo, an area famous for its electronics shops. In the middle of the 20th century, it became known as Akihabara Electric Town because it was the area to buy electronic goods. However, the district has evolved into a center for video games, anime, manga, and computer goods. It is also the center of Japan's otaku culture (people with obsessive hobbies; commonly used to describe fans of anime and manga). Otaku culture is seen in the style and atmosphere of Akihabara; advertising using anime and manga icons covers the buildings and shops, and many cosplayers (people in costume) can be seen walking in the streets. It is always full of shoppers and gamers of all ages, and not surprisingly, it is hard to find anyone who is not using some kind of electronic device.

Did you know?

In Akihabara, and throughout Tokyo, you can find *mangakissa*, manga cafes which have large selections of anime comics for fans to read. Manga and anime are big business in Japan.

INTRODUCE THE THEME

- In this unit, students will explore the concepts of business and marketing. The language in the two lessons will help students be able to communicate on these themes, including describing companies, emphasizing key points, and expressing opinions about ads and products.

- In Lesson A, students will watch a video about a sauce

	Video	Vocabulary	Listening	Grammar
LESSON A Success stories p. 78	Sriracha p. 78	Talking business p. 79 *advertise, employ, promote*	Fear of missing out p. 80 Listen for the main idea Listen for details Identify a speaker	The passive voice: simple present and simple past pp. 82, 203
LESSON B Advertising p. 84		Economics p. 84 *in a slump, recover, increase dramatically*	Analyze commercials p. 85 Take notes Listen for specific information Listen for gist	Connecting ideas with *because, so, although / even though* pp. 88, 204

For students: My World Link Online has personalized instruction, practice, audio, and video.

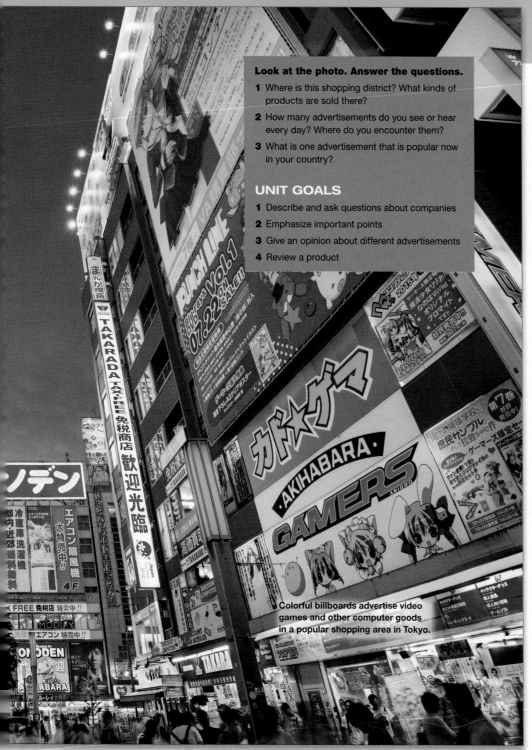

Look at the photo. Answer the questions.

1 Where is this shopping district? What kinds of products are sold there?

2 How many advertisements do you see or hear every day? Where do you encounter them?

3 What is one advertisement that is popular now in your country?

UNIT GOALS

1 Describe and ask questions about companies

2 Emphasize important points

3 Give an opinion about different advertisements

4 Review a product

Colorful billboards advertise video games and other computer goods in a popular shopping area in Tokyo.

company's success story. Students will then learn to describe things companies do. They will practice the listening strategies of listening for the main idea and for details, and identifying a speaker. They will then learn how to ask questions about what a company does, and to emphasize important points when describing something. Finally, they will learn how to describe a place in terms of business aspects.

• In Lesson B, students will learn how to understand and describe graphs and trends. They will read about a city that has reduced the number of ads on its streets, practicing the reading strategies of identifying a point of view, drawing conclusions, and scanning for details. They will also describe and review a product, and then create a commercial.

WARM UP

Look at the photo. Answer the questions.

• Call on students to describe what they see in the photo.

• Have students answer the questions individually or in pairs, then compare answers with the class. Ask students to think about where and when they see ads in their own lives.

• Point out the unit goals and explain what students will learn. Elicit any key vocabulary students already know (questions to ask about a company, expressions to give an opinion, etc.), and write it on the board. Explain any unfamiliar phrases.

Pronunciation	Speaking	Reading	Writing	Communication
Stress on nouns and verbs with the same spelling p. 80	Asking about companies / Emphasizing important points p. 81	Life without ads? p. 86 Identify a point of view Draw conclusions Scan for details	Write a product review p. 88	Presenting facts about your city or region p. 83 Creating a commercial p. 89

Bottles of Sriracha sauce

1 VIDEO Sriracha

A 🔄 Do you like spicy food? If so, what are your favorite dishes? If not, why not? Tell a partner.

B ▶ You are going to watch a video about spicy Sriracha sauce. Complete each sentence with a number from the box.

20	30	50	70	200,000
25	40	60	4,000	250,000

1. They make Sriracha sauce in a $ _____ million plant.

2. They produce _____ bottles of the sauce each day.

3. The main ingredient, jalapeno peppers, comes from a farm _____ miles away.

4. Farmer Craig Underwood has worked with David Tran for _____ years.

5. Tran started with just _____ acres (202,000 square meters) of land.

6. Next year he will have _____ acres (16.2 square kilometers).

7. There are more than _____ barrels in the warehouse.

8. Last year the company sold $ _____ million in sauce.

9. It's growing _____ % each year.

10. David Tran has worked on his product for more than _____ years.

C 🔄 What is the most interesting or surprising thing about David's story? Tell a partner.

WORLD LINK

Go online and read more about Sriracha sauce. What new information did you learn? Report back to the class.

1 VIDEO
Sriracha

WARM UP Have students look at the photo. Ask, *What is the product? Where is it from? Would you like to try it? What would you eat it with?* ⏱ 5 min

ABOUT THE VIDEO
David Tran came to the United States as a refugee after the Vietnam War. He first started making his chili sauce by mixing it in barrels on the street in Los Angeles, where he had customers in the city's growing Asian population. This video shows how that small start has become a huge business success story with Tran opening a $40 million dollar plant in 2014, which produces 200,000 bottles of sauce a day during peak periods. Sriracha sauce is no longer bought only by the Asian population, it is a favorite among many Americans. In a year, $60 million dollars' worth of the sauce are sold, and now there are even annual Sriracha festivals held in various cities in California. At the festivals, you can try dishes, including desserts and beverages, made with Sriracha chili sauce. One festivalgoer describes the sauce as having magic!

TEACHING TIP: Using English videos
Remind students that note-taking while they listen is a useful strategy to help them remember what they heard, and consequently improve their understanding. Tell students to write down key words and numbers. Remind them that spelling is not important in their notes.

A 🔲 Do you like spicy food? If so, what are your favorite dishes? If not, why not? Tell a partner. ⏱ 5–10 min

Have students read the questions and think about their answers. Then assign them to pairs to compare and discuss their answers. Call on different students to tell the class about their partner's answers. In general, is spicy food popular in the class or not?

B ▶ You are going to watch a video about spicy Sriracha sauce. Complete each sentence with a number from the box. ⏱ 10–15 min

Pre-teach the following words: *acre*, *barrel*, *feet* (measurement), *ingredient*, *jalapeno*, (manufacturing) *plant*, *product*, *warehouse*. Go over the sentences and say the numbers in the box for students to repeat. Play the video twice, then have students compare their answers with a partner's. Play the video again and check answers with the class, pausing on the parts where the numbers are given.

C 🔲 What is the most interesting or surprising thing about David's story? Tell a partner. ⏱ 10 min

Have students think about their answer to the question, then assign them to pairs to discuss answers. Call on different pairs to share their ideas with the class and write them on the board. Ask students if they know of any other similar success stories that they can share with the class.

EXTRA! Post-viewing
Have students choose one of the following options:
1. Find recipes using Sriracha sauce on the Internet and choose one to share with the class. Students should explain why they chose the recipe.
2. Research more about David Tran and his company Huy Fong Foods. Present a short summary of the company and its development to the class. ⏱ 10 min

Extra video vocabulary	
astrological sign	in hot water
brand new	in your wildest dreams
choke	lawsuit
crush	peak production
freighter	pick
grind (ground)	revenue
headquarters	

Go online and read more about Sriracha sauce. What new information did you learn? Report back to the class.

Have students research Sriracha sauce online. This can be done in or out of class depending on access to the Internet. Students can share the new information they found with the class or in small groups.

Instructor's Notes

_____

_____

_____

2 VOCABULARY

WARM UP Ask students to name some large companies they know. On the board, make a chart showing the names of the companies on the left and the products or services that they offer on the right. Which companies are well known internationally? Which companies are well known locally? ⏱ 5 min

A 🔄 Read the sentences. How many of the words in **blue** do you know? What do they mean? Use your dictionary to help you. Compare your answers with a partner's. ⏱ 10 min

Students should read the sentences, and work alone to look up words they don't know. Then they should compare their answers with a partner's and discuss any differences. Pairs should then share the meanings with a class. This way, each student will get all of the definitions. Poll the class to find out how many words are new. If students are unfamiliar with many of the terms, review the meanings with the class.

TEACHING TIP: Learner's dictionary
At this level, students can make good use of a monolingual intermediate-level learner's dictionary. Learner's dictionaries visually highlight high-frequency words and include labels such as *formal*, *informal*, and *written* to guide students' usage of the word. Most learner dictionaries include example sentences taken from a corpus, which is a huge database of millions of authentic examples of language from sources such as newspapers, books, the Internet, spoken language, etc. These authentic examples of words in context are useful for learners.

LANGUAGE TIP: Pronunciation and vocabulary
When students learn new words, be sure that they learn to put the accent or stress on the correct syllable for words of two or more syllables.

TEACHING TIP: Learning word forms
When students learn new words, they can increase their vocabulary knowledge quickly by learning related word forms. In other words, if they learn the verb *consume*, it also makes sense to learn the nouns *consumer* and *consumption*. Encourage students to look for word families in their dictionaries when they look up the meaning of new vocabulary words. This applies in **B**.

B Complete the chart with the noun forms of the verbs. Be careful of the spelling! Check your answers in a dictionary. ⏱ 10 min

If students need more space to write, they can copy the chart on a piece of paper or in their notebooks before they complete it. After they have finished, point out that the nouns that have a *–tion* ending need to drop the silent *e* before adding the suffix.

C 🔄 Make four questions using the words in **A** and **B**. Take turns asking the questions with a partner. ⏱ 10–15 min

Elicit question words from students and write a list on the board. Model the first example with a student, then have another student ask you the question in the second example. Have students review the words in **A** and **B** and elicit other possible questions from the class. Write a few prompts on the board to help students. Have students write their questions individually. Monitor and check that the questions are correct. Then assign students to pairs to ask and answer their questions. Call on students to say one of their questions and have another student answer each question.

-er suffix
The verbs in **B** also have a noun form with the suffix *–er* for the person who does the action:
advertiser
developer
employer*
manager
shipper
consumer
producer
promoter
Note the exception:
investor
*employee: the person who works *for* an employer

Instructor's Notes

_____

_____

_____

_____

_____

_____

_____

_____

_____

_____

2 VOCABULARY

A Read the sentences. How many of the words in blue do you know? What do they mean? Use your dictionary to help you. Compare your answers with a partner's.

1. They plan to **advertise** their new product on TV and online.

2. If you **consume** too many calories, you'll gain weight.

3. Since our sales plan isn't working, we'll have to **develop** a new one.

4. Their company is pretty small. It only **employs** 20 people.

5. They are looking for someone to **invest** $2 million in the project.

6. Ms. Park is the head of that department. She **manages** ten people.

7. A: What does your company make?
   B: It **produces** batteries for phones.

8. My doctor **promotes** walking as a way to lose weight.

9. Do you want to buy something? To **purchase** an item, please click on the *Buy now* button.

10. Once we receive your money, we'll **ship** your order to you.

B Complete the chart with the noun forms of the verbs. Be careful of the spelling! Check your answers in a dictionary.

Nouns ending in *-ment*				Nouns ending in *-tion*	
advertise	advertisement	invest		consume	consumption
develop		manage		produce	
employ		ship		promote	

C Make four questions using the words in **A** and **B**. Take turns asking the questions with a partner.

What have you purchased online recently?

I downloaded a couple of songs from iTunes.

How many people does Samsung employ?

I don't know, but since it's a large international company it's probably a large number.

Companies develop and test new products in special labs.

4 SPEAKING

WARM UP Ask students if they have ever studied English using mobile devices or tablets. What were their experiences? If no one has used these devices, ask about experiences learning English online. ⏱ 5 min

A 🔊 Complete the interview by filling in the missing questions. Write the correct numbers in the blanks. Then listen and check your answers. **CD 1 Track 40** ⏱ 10 min

Have students read the questions. Answer any vocabulary questions, then have students read the interview and decide where the questions go. Point out the definition of *perks* at the bottom of the interview. Play the audio and check the answers with the class. In preparation for **B** you may need to pre-teach some vocabulary, such as *CEO* (an acronym for *Chief Executive Officer*), *convenient*, *audio book*, and *bottom line*.

B 🔄 Now cover the conversation in **A** and complete the company profile of Sound Smart with a partner. ⏱ 5–10 min

To make this exercise more challenging, do not let students look at **A**. If the exercise is too difficult, jot down some of the key points on the board. Check the answers with the class.

EXTRA! Writing prompt
Tell students to imagine that they own a company where they want to put *people first*. What policies or plans would they put in place to make this happen? Tell them to write two paragraphs about their ideas. ⏱ 20–25 min

SPEAKING STRATEGY

C 🔄 Work with a partner to create your own company. On a piece of paper, make a company profile. ⏱ 10–15 min

Brainstorm ideas for products and services that students use and/or enjoy. Students can use these in their company profiles.

D 🔄 You're going to tell another pair of students about your company. Prepare a short presentation with your partner. Use the Useful Expressions to help you emphasize certain points. ⏱ 15 min

Direct students' attention to the Useful Expressions box. Read each expression with students repeating. Ask students for ideas of what other expressions could follow the ellipses. Presentations should be no longer than two minutes, and students should focus on emphasizing their company's attractive, important, and interesting points.

E 👥 Take turns presenting to another pair. The students who are listening should ask questions similar to those in **A**. Would you like to work for the company you heard about? Why or why not? ⏱ 15 min

Situate each group of four with as much distance between the other groups as possible. Choose one pair in each group to begin and tell them they will have five minutes for their presentation. Use a timer and tell them when their time is up. Before the first pair gives their presentation, the other pair should be prepared to take notes and think about the questions they will ask. While pairs are presenting, walk around the room listening, helping, and making sure that everyone has a chance to speak. If necessary, remind students to use the Useful Expressions for emphasizing important points.

TEACHING TIP: Presentation skills
When students are presenting to one another, suggest to them the following:
- Have a strong beginning, clear main points, and a strong conclusion.
- Narrow your main points—be brief and clear.
- Speak loudly and clearly, especially if your voice is quiet or you are in a large room.
- Do not read. Make eye contact with your listeners.

LARGE CLASS OPTION
You may wish to call on selected students to present their company to the class. Have the other students take notes and ask questions after each presentation.

Instructor's Notes

_____

_____

_____

_____

_____

_____

_____

_____

_____

4 SPEAKING

A 🔊 Complete the interview by filling in the missing questions. Write the correct numbers in the blanks. Then listen and check your answers.
CD 1 Track 40

1. Can I get one of your audiobooks?
2. How exactly do you do that—put people first?
3. Maybe you've seen one of our advertisements online?
4. So, my first question is, what *does* Sound Smart do exactly?
5. What is the main focus of your company?
6. Where can I get an application?

HOST: I'd like to welcome Beverly Smith, the CEO for Sound Smart Inc., to our show today. Welcome, Beverly! _____

BEVERLY: Well, as you know, a lot of people are studying English. And many of them want to be able to study anywhere, so we produce audiobooks... _____

HOST: Yes, I have. What a great idea—how convenient! _____

BEVERLY: Sure. After you make a purchase, you can download the book online. It's simple.

HOST: _____

BEVERLY: Well, we really believe in our employees. The bottom line is that happy employees make a good product. So our company slogan is *People First!*

HOST: _____

BEVERLY: Well, for one thing, we have a lot of perks.* Our company has its own gym in the building. Also, each of our 100 employees gets the day off on his or her birthday.

HOST: Nice! _____

*perks = extra things you receive because of your job (for example, extra holidays, etc.)

B 🔄 Now cover the conversation in **A** and complete the company profile of Sound Smart with a partner.

Name of company: *Sound Smart*

Product / Service: _____

Company slogan: _____

Perks: _____

Other: _____

Useful Expressions
Asking about companies
What does your company do exactly?
What is the main focus of your company?
How do you...?
Emphasizing important points
I'd like to emphasize that...
Never forget that...
This is a key point.
The bottom line is...

SPEAKING STRATEGY

C 🔄 Work with a partner to create your own company. On a piece of paper, make a company profile.

D 🔄 You're going to tell another pair of students about your company. Prepare a short presentation with your partner. Use the Useful Expressions to help you emphasize certain points.

E 👥 Take turns presenting to another pair. The students who are listening should ask questions similar to those in **A**. Would you like to work for the company you heard about? Why or why not?

1 VOCABULARY (Continued)

C Read about the graphs. Then use the words in the box to complete sentences about them. You will use one of the words twice. Compare answers with a partner's. ⏱ 10 min

You can help students by grouping the vocabulary words in the box based on whether they indicate something going up or going down. Note that more than one answer is possible to many of the questions. Accept any answer that makes sense in the context of the exercise and the discussion. Check the answers with the class.

2 LISTENING

STRATEGIES: Take notes; Listen for specific information; Listen for gist

WARM UP Ask students to think of a celebrity spokesperson—a famous person who advertises a product. Who is the person? What do they advertise? Does the famous person make students want to buy the product? Why or why not? ⏱ 5 min

A What is a commercial that you can remember? What do you remember most about it (the words, a character, a song)? Tell a partner. ⏱ 5–10 min

For this exercise, the focus is on television, video, or radio commercials. English speakers usually use the word *commercial* to describe an advertisement on radio or television. They also use the word *ad* for these. *Advertisement* or *ad* describes a printed advertisement. Students should talk about the commericals in pairs and then volunteers may share a few of their memorable commercials with the class.

B **Take notes; Listen for specific information.** Listen to three commercials. What kind of product is advertised in each one? Write down key words you hear. **CD 1 Track 41** ⏱ 5–10 min

Point out the information in the Word Bank before students listen. Play the audio for the students at least twice. The third time, stop and discuss the correct answers with the students. Remember that you can also read from the audio script if students find it challenging to understand the audio recording. The audio scripts are found on pages T220–T237. Explain vocabulary as needed. What key words did students identify? How could they tell these words were key words?

Take notes. Taking notes helps students identify main ideas and be able to clarify what they heard afterwards. Taking notes as they listen is a skill that can help them in other classes as well as when listening to English in and out of class.

Listen for specific information. Remind students that listening for specific information means to focus their attention on key words or concepts. Students should identify before they listen what words they should be listening for, in this case *selfie* as part of a title.

C **Listen for gist.** How did each ad try to make you buy the product? Circle the correct answer. Then explain your answers to a partner. **CD 1 Track 41** ⏱ 5–10 min

Repeat the audio for the students. Ask them to indicate when they hear an answer to one of the questions by raising their hands. When checking answers, replay the relevant portion of the audio or read it from the audio script. The audio scripts are found on pages T220–T237.

Listen for gist. Remind students that when listening for gist, they don't need to worry about understanding everything they hear, the purpose is to understand the general idea.

TEACHING OPTION: Support
Replay the audio phrase by phrase. Ask the students to repeat each phrase aloud to practice pronunciation. Listen and correct pronunciation as needed.

D Would you buy or use any of these products? Discuss with a partner. ⏱ 10–15 min

Go over the question with the class, then have students think about their answer and reasons. Assign students to pairs to discuss the question. Model the exercise by saying, *I would buy the (photo software) because...* and sharing your answer. Write the start of the sentence on the board to help students. Monitor and help with vocabulary as necessary. Call on different students to tell the class their partner's answer. Which product was the most popular with the class?

CULTURE TIP: Advertising in the United States
Americans may see more advertising in their daily lives than anyone else in the world. Advertising appears on park benches, supermarket carts, pens and pencils, and even on the doors of public toilets. Some supermarkets and large chain stores now have TV screens that show only advertising.

Instructor's Notes

_____

_____

_____

_____

_____

C Read about the graphs. Then use the words in the box to complete sentences about them. You will use one of the words twice. Compare your answers with a partner's.

| decrease | gradual | rose | a slump |
| down | increase | slightly | up |

1. We've seen a(n) _____ _____ in unemployment, but numbers are still _____.

2. New car sales are in _____. Recently they _____ _____.

3. The number of students studying English is _____ and _____down_____, but overall there has been a(n) _____.

2 LISTENING

A What is a commercial that you can remember? What do you remember most about it (the words, a character, a song)? Tell a partner.

B **Take notes; Listen for specific information.** Listen to three commercials. What kind of product is advertised in each one? Write down key words you hear. **CD 1 Track 41**

1. Product: _____

   Key words: _____

2. Product: _____

   Key words: _____

3. Product: _____

   Key words: _____

Word Bank
catchy = fun and easy to remember
clever = funny or interesting in a smart way
slogan = a short, easy-to-remember phrase used in an ad to sell a product

C **Listen for gist.** Listen again. How did each ad try to make you buy the product? Circle the correct answer. Then explain your answers to a partner. **CD 1 Track 41**

Ad 1: a. It told a moving story.

      b. It made a personal connection.

Ad 2: a. It talked about an innovative product.

      b. It had a catchy slogan.

Ad 3: a. It targeted specific people.

      b. It had a jingle.

D Would you buy or use any of these products? Discuss with a partner.

STRATEGIES: Identify a point of view; Draw conclusions; Scan for details

WARM UP Have students look at the picture and describe it. Is it an ad? ⏱ 5 min

A ⚡ Do you think advertising is necessary to sell products? Why or why not? Tell a partner. ⏱ 5–10 min

Go over the question with the class then give students a moment to think about their answer. Assign students to pairs to share their opinions. Discuss the question as a class.

B ⚡ **Identify a point of view; Draw conclusions.** Read the article. How would the author of the article answer the question in **A**? Use information from the article to explain your answer to a partner. ⏱ 10–15 min

Go over the directions with the class. Tell students to read the article, thinking about what the author's opinion is as they read. Point out the definitions in the footnotes and remind students not to worry about words they don't know. Tell them to underline parts of the text that help them understand the author's opinion. When they have finished reading, they should answer the question with a partner, using information in the text to support their answers. Check the answer with the class.

Identify a point of view. Explain to students that whenever they read, they should think about the author's point of view, or the point of view of someone in the text. Identifying this opinion will help students understand the text better as it can help them understand or infer information.

Draw conclusions. Explain to students that coming to, and expressing, conclusions about what they have read is a good way to check their understanding of the content of a text. In order to draw conclusions, students have to analyze and synthesize the information, and it will push them to infer anything that isn't directly stated.

---

3 **READING**

A ⚡ Do you think advertising is necessary to sell products? Why or why not? Tell a partner.

B ⚡ **Identify a point of view; Draw conclusions.** Read the article. How would the author of the article answer the question in **A**? Use information from the article to explain your answer to a partner.

C **Scan for details.** Complete the sentences with the correct information.

1. Many people think that ads are a _____ influence.

2. The law in São Paulo took down over _____ billboards.

3. The ads in São Paulo covered _____ and _____ that needed to be cleaned.

4. The ads were replaced by _____.

5. One of the best ways to learn about new products is by _____ - _____ - _____, that is, from family and friends.

6. _____ reviews are a modern version of word-of-mouth.

D ⚡ Answer the questions with a partner.

1. Do you think it's a good idea to limit ads in public places, like they did in São Paulo?

2. Do you think that there are too many ads in your city?

3. Has an ad ever persuaded you to buy or do something?

4. Have you ever read online reviews of a product? Do you trust them? Why or why not?

86 UNIT 6 • Business and marketing

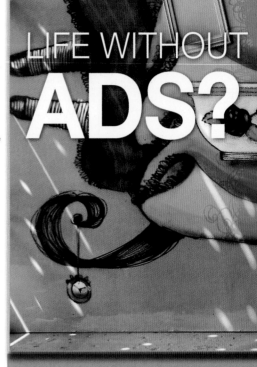

LIFE WITHOUT ADS?

Is advertising really necessary? Billions of dollars are spent on it every year, so it must be important. After all, it's a busy world. You have to advertise to get people's attention to sell products!

But there is a downside to this. Researchers say that ads can negatively influence people to make them feel like they should be someone else. They argue that the ads are deceptive[1] and create a false sense of reality. Research has even shown that many children can't tell the difference between an ad and real life!

Others believe there are too many ads and that they make cities look unattractive. Some cities are taking action. In 2006, a law was passed in São Paulo, Brazil, that prohibited ads such as outdoor posters and billboards.[2] Over 15,000 billboards were taken down. This has caused people to look at their city in a new way. Before, their attention was constantly drawn to the large number of ads on

---

EXTRA! Comprehension questions

Have students answer the following questions, individually or in pairs:

1. What is the problem with children and advertising?

2. What did they need to do in São Paolo when the billboards came down?

3. What other cities are reducing the number of advertisements on their streets?

4. Why do you have to be careful with online reviews?

EXTRA! Discussion

Students can list the advertising techniques that they think are effective or not. Discuss what students agree and disagree on. What would be the perfect advertising campaign? ⏱ 10–15 min

the streets. But now, people are able to clearly view and enjoy the beauty of the old buildings and modern structures.

In addition, problems that existed in the city for years are now getting fixed. For example, some neighborhoods needed to be cleaned and buildings needed to be repaired, but ads covered those areas and made them easy to ignore. When the billboards came down, people noticed the problems and started to fix them. Now these buildings are covered in beautiful art. São Paulo was one of the first major cities to pass a law like this, but now other cities, such as Paris, Tehran, and New York, have taken steps to reduce the number of advertisements on the streets.

So, how do people hear about new products now? One of the oldest, and best, ways is still word-of-mouth. People trust friends, family, and people they talk to more than they trust billboards. This makes word-of-mouth very persuasive![3] Word-of-mouth advertising has other advantages, too. It's cost-effective (after all, it's free), and a company doesn't have to create a complex business plan to do it.

Many people also use the Internet to review and share products. This is similar to word-of-mouth because people discuss opinions and personal experiences, but many more people can be part of the conversation. You have to be careful about online reviews, though. Unlike a suggestion from a friend or family member, you don't always know who is posting a review online!

[1]If something is *deceptive*, it makes you believe something that is not true.
[2]A *billboard* is a large ad on a sign.
[3]If something is *persuasive*, it makes someone believe something.

LESSON B Advertising 87

LESSON B Advertising **87**

CULTURE TIP: The new word-of-mouth
The new word-of-mouth advertising is the online world. In the past, companies relied on people to have conversations in person, but they now hope that people will talk about them online. This includes posting news or becoming fans on social networks, talking about their products on blogs, or mentioning or using them in videos on YouTube.

EXTRA! Post-reading
Bring in (or have students bring in) old magazines in English or in the students' language. Students can look through them, or look online, and choose an ad that they especially like or don't like. Give them time to prepare an explanation. Then students take turns showing their ad and explaining why they like or don't like it. ⏱ 20 min

C Scan for details. Complete the sentences with the correct information. ⏱ 5–10 min

Have students quickly read the text again and find the information to complete the sentences (note that in 1, they will need to change the form of the word *negatively* to *negative*). Have students compare answers with a partner, then check answers with the class.

Scan for details. Remind students that scanning means looking over a text quickly in order to find specific information. Students shouldn't read in detail until they find the information they are looking for, and then read that sentence carefully.

D ✦ Answer the questions with a partner. ⏱ 10–15 min

Go over the questions with the class, then have students think about their answers. Model the exercise by having a student ask you the first question, then ask the student his or her opinion, *What about you, do you think it's a good idea?* Assign students to pairs to discuss the questions. Monitor and help with vocabulary as necessary. For each question, call on several students to tell the class their partner's answer.

TEACHING TIP: Working with errors in spoken English
Immediate correction during group and pair work is often not very effective. The following are some alternatives.

- Make notes on errors frequently heard during the exercise and give a mini-lesson after the exercise.

- Listen to different groups in rotation, write down important errors, and give the list to the groups to correct.

- Write down sentences with errors during the exercise and project them on a screen, make photocopies, or write them on the board. Together, the class identifies and corrects the errors.

- Give a quiz by writing down sentences with errors and having students correct them.

LESSON PLANNER • Unit 6, Lesson B 87a

2 SEE IT AND SAY IT

WARM UP Ask students to come up with as many phrasal verbs as they can. Ask two or three students to be the secretaries and write the verbs on the board for the class. Review the meaning of any words that students have forgotten. Practice pronunciation, reminding students that in phrasal verbs the preposition or particle receives stronger stress than usual. ⏱ 10 min

A 🔄 Look at these pictures of Julia and Dan and answer the questions. Use some of the verbs from the box in your answers. Work with a partner. ⏱ 5–10 min

Note that when the word *work out* is a phrasal verb, the primary stress is on the second word: *work OUT*. However, when the same two words function as a compound noun, the stress comes on the first word: *WORKout*.

Working out at the gym
classes: yoga, dance, aerobics, spinning, zumba
exercise, stretch, cross fit training
jogging
treadmill, elliptical, exercise bike
warm up, cool down
weights, weight machine
weight-lifting

LANGUAGE TIP: Athletics
In American English, the word *athletics* is used in discussions of all sports in a general way. Most high schools and colleges have an athletics department whose purpose is to oversee the sports at the institution. In British English, the word *athletics* refers only to one particular sport that requires running, jumping, and throwing. In the United States, that sport is called *track and field*. The running events are called the track events. The jumping and throwing events are called the field events. A person who participates in sports is called an *athlete*.

B 🔄 Write a conversation for each situation on a separate piece of paper. Practice the conversations with your partner. ⏱ 10–15 min

Place students in pairs. Clarify any questions about vocabulary or pronunciation. Tell students to include as much detail as possible about the conversations. Remind students to use the words from the box at the top. You can also tell them to use the words that the group came up with in the Warm Up. Follow the teaching tips on page T90 to provide a variety of ways for students to practice their conversations.

C 👥 Get together with another pair. Take turns acting out your conversations. ⏱ 10–15 min

Join pairs to form groups of four and have them take turns acting out their conversations. Monitor and take notes of any common problems to address at the end of the actvity. Call on volunteers to perform one of their conversations for the class.

EXTRA! Classroom dramatics
Stage a performance of student conversations and/or role plays. Be sure that all students have memorized their lines. Coach students to speak with confidence and expression. Invite guests from other classes or areas of your school to come and watch. If time allows, students can create and print a program listing the "acts" and performers. One student can act as the master of ceremonies (MC) and introduce the other acts. At the end, bring all of the actors onstage to bow. ⏱ 30–45 min

EXTRA! Writing prompt
Assign students to write a paragraph about what happens in the future between Julia and Dan. Does their relationship continue? Is there a happy ending? Or do they find that they don't get along and break off their relationship? ⏱ 15 min

Instructor's Notes

_____

_____

_____

_____

_____

_____

_____

_____

_____

Look at the photo. Answer the questions.

1 What is the person in the photo doing?

2 In your opinion, is this activity good for your health? Do you ever do it?

3 What are some things you do to stay healthy?

UNIT GOALS

1 Describe symptoms when you don't feel well

2 Give, accept, and reject serious health advice

3 Talk about modern health problems

4 Describe health tips you've been given

A jogger goes for a run on a cool autumn day in Berlin, Germany.

modern health issues, and explaining health tips.

- In Lesson A, students will watch a video which considers the safest way to say hello: shaking hands or bumping fists. Students will then learn how to describe symptoms of being unwell. They will also practice the listening strategies of making and checking predictions, listening for details, and inferring information. Finally, they will learn how to give health advice, as well as accept and reject it.

- In Lesson B, students will learn how to describe difficult situations involving work and school. They will read about modern heath issues, practicing the reading strategies of scanning for information, making and checking predictions, reading for details, and inferring meaning. They will also write and talk about tips for living healthily.

WARM UP

Look at the photo. Answer the questions.

- Call on students to describe what they see in the photo.

- Have students answer the questions individually or in pairs, then compare answers with the class.

- Point out the unit goals and explain what students will learn. Elicit any key vocabulary students already know and write it on the board. Explain any unfamiliar phrases to the students.

Grammar	Pronunciation	Speaking	Reading	Writing	Communication
Describing symptoms pp. 100, 206	The schwa sound p. 100	Giving, accepting, and refusing serious advice p. 99	Modern health problems p. 104 Scan for information Make predictions Check predictions Read for details Infer meaning	Write about a healthy change p. 106	Suggesting an alternative treatment p. 101
Reported speech: commands and requests pp. 106, 207					Giving tips for a healthy life p. 107

Two friends fist-bump

1 VIDEO Is it Better to Shake (Hands) or (Fist) Bump?

A 🔁 Look up these words in your dictionary: *bacteria*, *germs*, *transmit*, *disease*. Then read the title of the video. What do you think this video is going to be about? Tell a partner.

B ▶ Watch the beginning of the video. Complete the questions. How would you answer them?

Is handshaking the _____ or _____ way of saying hello? Could there be another _____? What about the _____ _____?

C ▶ Watch the entire video. You are going to hear about a doctor named Tom McClellan. He did a study about handshaking and fist-bumping. Listen and complete the outline.

1. The situation
   A. In the _____, we shake hands all day.
   B. You can _____ diseases when you shake hands.

2. The study
   A. We shook hands with _____ different workers.
   B. We checked to see how many _____ we'd collected.
   C. We repeated the process with fist-bumping.

3. The results
   A. There was _____ times the amount of bacteria on hand shakers.

D 🔁 What do you think of Dr. McClellan's study? After watching the video, are you going to change your behavior in any way? Tell a partner.

1 VIDEO
Is it Better to Shake (Hands) or (Fist) Bump?

WARM UP Have students look at the photo, ask, *What are they doing? How do you greet a friend? Do you shake hands? kiss? hug? What about someone you don't know so well?* ⏱ 5 min

ABOUT THE VIDEO

This video presents an animation of a study on which is the most hygienic way to say hello—shaking hands or bumping fists. Fist-bumping has typically been considered the way younger, "cooler" people greet each other, but it is now becoming more popular in mainstream society. Dr. Tom McClellan, a surgeon and therefore someone who knows clean hands are very important, carried out a study in his hospital to see which way of greeting led to more germs being spread. McClellan and his team of researchers greeted 20 different health workers throughout the hospital, first shaking hands, then fist-bumping. After each greeting, they collected the germs on their hands to find out which method is the cleanest.

TEACHING TIP: Using English videos

This video is an animation, so students may find it harder to understand because they can't see the person speaking. Explain to them that animations can actually support their understanding because they show visually what is being said. It is therefore important for them to pay attention to what they see to help them understand new words. For example, the word *door handle* is used, which students may not be familiar with, but as it is mentioned an image of a door handle appears on the screen.

A 🔗 Look up these words in your dictionary: *bacteria, germs, transmit, disease.* Then read the title of the video. What do you think this video is going to be about? Tell a partner. ⏱ 5–10 min

Say the words and have students repeat them. Then have them look them up and write down definitions or examples. Assign students to pairs to read the title and answer the question. Go over the meaning of the words with the class, having students provide definitions or examples. Then share predictions about what the video is going to be about.

B ▶ Watch the beginning of the video. Complete the questions. How would you answer them? ⏱ 10 min

Go over the questions and encourage students to guess what the missing words could be. Play the beginning of the video (to :30) twice, giving students time to write their answers. Have students compare their answers with a partner's, then play the video again and check the answers. Call on students to share their answers to the questions.

C ▶ Watch the entire video. You are going to hear about a doctor named Tom McClellan. He did a study about handshaking and fist-bumping. Listen and complete the outline. ⏱ 10 min

Go over the outline with students and make sure they understand that it represents the main ideas from the study. Play the entire video, then give students time to finish writing before playing it again. Have students compare their answers with a partner's. Play the video again. Check answers with the class, playing the video again and pausing on the answers if necessary.

D 🔗 What do you think of Dr. McClellan's study? After watching the video, are you going to change your behavior in any way? Tell a partner. ⏱ 10 min

Have students think about their answers to the questions, then assign them to pairs to discuss. Call on different pairs to share their ideas with the class. How many students are planning on changing their behavior?

EXTRA! Post-viewing

Have students go online and search for more information about Dr. McClellan and his study, using the search terms: *shake or bump Tom McClellan video.* Students can either watch a different video about the safest way to greet someone, or read an article about Dr. McClellan and his study. Remind students they don't need to understand everything in the article they read, just the main ideas or key points. The objective is to be exposed to authentic English and a broader vocabulary, but through a topic they are already familiar with. Have students take notes on the new information they find out and share it with the class, or in small groups. ⏱ 10 min

Extra video vocabulary	
amount	offering of peace
be confronted by	promotion
entire	reduce
mutual agreement	spread (germs)

2 VOCABULARY

WARM UP Direct students' attention to the unit theme. Ask, *Do you have a healthy lifestyle, or an unhealthy lifestyle?* Students should explain their answers and give examples. ⏱ 5 min

A Read part of a story below. What do the words in **blue** mean? ⏱ 10 min

Tell students to look at the picture. Have students describe the scene. Where is the person? What is he doing? After reading, instruct students to match the words with their meanings. Check answers with the class. Answer any remaining vocabulary questions.

B 🔄 Now answer the questions about the story in **A** on a separate piece of paper. Compare your answers with a partner's. ⏱ 10 min

For these questions, there are clear and obvious answers for items 1 and 2. However, there is no correct or obvious answer for items 3 and 4. Any of the answers to number 3 are possible, but students should give reasons for their answers. The expression *turn back* is a phrasal verb, which means to stop what you are doing and return the way that you came from. After students have compared their answers with a partner's, discuss answers as a class.

C Here are some more words about health. (You might hear these sentences in a doctor's office.) Can you match each word in **blue** with one or more parts of the body on the right? ⏱ 10 min

Ask a student to read the words in the box, while you point to these parts of your body. Then ask students if they can recall any sentences commonly said by doctors, whether from their own visits to the doctor or from TV shows set in hospitals. Students can complete this exercise individually then compare their answers with a partner's. Remind them that more than one body part may be correct for a question. Check answers with the class.

Health and wellness
blood pressure
blood test
injection, shot, vaccination
insurance card
physical condition
physical exam
prescription

EXTRA! Simon Says

A good way to review body parts is this game. Students should follow your directions, but only if you first say *Simon says*. Tell the class to stand up. Touch your head and say, *Simon says touch your head.* All should touch their heads. You should touch your back and say *Simon says touch your back.* All should touch their backs. Touch your foot and say *Touch your foot.* They should not do the action because you didn't say *Simon says.* Anyone who touched their foot must sit down! Continue giving directions at a quick pace, using the vocabulary from the lesson and other items. The last student standing is the winner, who can give directions for the next round of the game. ⏱ 10–20 min

Instructor's Notes

_____

_____

_____

_____

_____

_____

_____

_____

_____

_____

_____

_____

_____

_____

_____

_____

_____

2 VOCABULARY

A Read part of a story below. What do the words in blue mean?

Adventure on a Mountain by Michael Yamato

There were more than 20 climbers on the mountain that day. We had been climbing for hours. My partner, Ed, and I were trying to reach the top before noon.

It was freezing, and the winds were strong. We were both wet and cold. Worst of all, a big storm was approaching.

That's when the trouble began. Ed started to get **drowsy**. He kept saying, "I just want to sleep." He was talking, but I couldn't understand him clearly—he wasn't **making sense**. The air was very thin, and I felt **dizzy**, too, but Ed was *really* confused. His steps were heavy. He was obviously **exhausted**.

Ed's body was very cold. Then he started to **shiver** uncontrollably. His **breathing** was slowing down. I was getting scared. I **felt weak**, too, but suddenly my own weakness disappeared. I had a lot of energy and knew that I needed to help Ed. It was then that I remembered the dry clothes and warm drinks in my backpack...

Match the words with their meanings.

1. drowsy _e_
2. make sense ____
3. dizzy ____
4. exhausted ____
5. shiver ____
6. breathe ____
7. weak ____

a. not strong	d. very tired
b. to shake because of the cold	~~e. sleepy~~
c. to be clear or understandable	f. to take air into your body
	g. unable to balance

B Now answer the questions about the story in **A** on a separate piece of paper. Compare your answers with a partner's.

1. Where were Michael and Ed? How did they feel at first?
2. What happened to Ed next?
3. What do you think they should have done? (Give a reason to support your answer.)
   ☐ continued to the top   ☐ waited for help   ☐ turned back
4. How do you think the story ended?

C Here are some more words about health. (You might hear these sentences in a doctor's office.) Can you match each word in blue with one or more parts of the body on the right?

1. Don't **chew** the medicine—just **swallow** it with some water. _____, _____	chest eyes mouth
2. Look straight ahead. Try not to **blink**. _____	nose
3. Please relax and just **breathe** normally. _____	teeth
4. Please cover your mouth when you **cough**. _____	throat

3 LISTENING

A 🔁 **Make predictions.** Which word do you think makes the statement true? Discuss with a partner.

Word Bank
symptom = something wrong with your body

1. _____ too much is bad for your health.

    a. Sitting   b. Standing   c. Running

B 🔊 **Check predictions.** Listen to the conversation. What did Lea learn? Circle the correct answer in **A**. **CD 2 Track 2**

C 🔊 **Listen for details.** Listen again. Choose the correct answer for each question. For some items, more than one answer is correct. **CD 2 Track 2**

1. How did Lea describe her symptoms?

    a. Her back was hurting.   b. She felt dizzy.   c. She had neck pain.

2. What did the doctor do?

    a. He sent her to the hospital.   b. He asked her a question.   c. He did some tests.

3. How many total hours a day was Lea sitting?

    a. 9–10   b. 11–12   c. 14–15

4. How can sitting be bad for your health?

    a. It can make it hard to go to sleep.   c. It can make your muscles hurt.

    b. It can affect your energy.   d. It can give you headaches.

D 🔊 **Infer information.** Listen to these lines from the audio. Choose the correct answer for each item. **CD 2 Track 3**

1. Why did Lea say "no kidding" to Cooper?

    a. She was saying, "I'm surprised."

    b. She was saying, "I agree with you."

2. Why did the doctor ask Lea the strange question?

    a. He couldn't find anything else wrong with her.

    b. He didn't believe her symptoms.

3. Why did Lea say "you got it" to Cooper?

    a. To tell Cooper that he understood correctly.

    b. To tell Cooper that he might be sick, too.

Studies show that people who spend time each day outside feel healthier and more energized.

E 🔁 It's important to be active. What are one or two simple things you can do to sit less and be more active during the day? Share your answers with a partner.

3 LISTENING

STRATEGIES: Make predictions; Check predictions; Listen for details; Infer information

WARM UP Ask students *What do you do to stay healthy?* Find out students' ideas about avoiding illness, especially during extremely cold or extremely hot weather. ⏱ 5 min

A **Make predictions.** Which word do you think makes the statement true? Discuss with a partner. ⏱ 5 min

Assign students to pairs to read the statement and decide which word to use to complete it. Compare answers as a class and have students explain their reasons.

Make predictions. Remind students that predicting before they listen helps them be more prepared for what they are going to hear because they will have activated prior knowledge of the topic and language related to it.

B **Check predictions.** Listen to the conversation. What did Lea learn? Circle the correct answer in **A**. **CD 2 Track 2** ⏱ 5–10 min

Play the audio for students to check their prediction in **A**. Check the answer with the class.

Check predictions. It is important to always go back to the predictions students made and help them see what they guessed correctly, and talk about why incorrect guesses were wrong.

C **Listen for details.** Listen again. Choose the correct answer for each question. For some items, more than one answer is correct. **CD 2 Track 2** ⏱ 10–15 min

Go over the questions and the options with the students. Encourage them to answer any they think they know. Play the audio again. Give students time to complete their answers then compare them with a partner's. Play the audio again. Check answers with the class, playing the audio again and pausing as necessary.

Listen for details. Remind students that they do not need to hear and understand everything in order to understand specific details. Encourage them to get into the habit of identifying key words to listen for before they listen.

D **Infer information.** Listen to these lines from the audio. Choose the correct answer for each item. **CD 2 Track 3** ⏱ 10 min

Go over the questions and options with the class. Make sure students understand that they're just going to listen to three specific parts of the conversation this time. Encourage students to answer any they think they already know. Play the audio, pausing after each part. Have students compare their answers with a partner's; then play the audio again. Check answers with the class.

Infer information. Remind students that inferring information means using the information they have, the context, and their background knowledge to work out something that isn't stated or explained explicitly.

E It's important to be active. What are one or two simple things you can do to sit less and be more active during the day? Share your answers with a partner. ⏱ 10 min

Go over the directions with the class, then give students a moment to think about their ideas. Assign students to pairs to share their ideas. Monitor and encourage students to ask follow-up questions to keep the conversation going. Call on different pairs to share their ideas with the class and write a list on the board.

Instructor's Notes

_____

_____

_____

_____

_____

_____

_____

_____

_____

_____

_____

_____

4 SPEAKING

WARM UP Ask students, *How do you feel today?* You can teach them expressions like *great*, *so-so*, and *not so hot*. Ask them to explain their responses. ⏱ 5 min

A 🔊 Ming wants to join the school swim team. Before she can do that, she has to get a checkup from her doctor. Listen to and read the conversation. Then answer the questions below. **CD 2 Track 4** ⏱ 5–10 min

Read the questions with the class. Then play the audio while students listen and read the conversation. If your students need more practice with listening, tell them to close their books while they listen to the conversation. Students can compare their answers with a partner's before you check answers as a class.

B 🔄 Practice the conversation with a partner. ⏱ 5–10 min

Play or read the conversation for the class to repeat. Pair students to practice the conversation. Remind them to look at their partner while speaking and to deliver their lines like an actor, with emotion.

TEACHING TIP: Language functions
Often instructors think of language in terms of parts of speech, such as nouns, verbs, adjectives, and adverbs. Or they look at language skills, such as listening, speaking, reading, and writing. Another way to think about language is in terms of *functions*. Functions answer the question, *What are we trying to DO with the language?* In this conversation, the key function is giving advice. The expressions *I always advise my patients to...* and *In my opinion, I think you should...,* are two different ways of expressing the function of advice. There are many other functions in this conversation such as expressing agreement, expressing doubt, wishing someone luck, giving explanations, and helping someone feel better.

LARGE CLASS OPTION
On the board, write down the beginning of several ways of giving advice, such as *I think you should...*; *maybe you ought to...*; *have you thought about...*; *why don't you...*; *perhaps you could...*; *you really ought to....* Then, brainstorm with students some situations where a person would need advice, such as not doing well in school, having been in a car accident, needing to lose weight, being concerned about a friend's smoking, etc. Tell the students to stand and turn to the person next to them. One student should indicate a problem and the other should offer advice. Then they switch roles. After each student has had a turn, he or she can turn to another student beside, behind, or in front of them to continue asking and giving advice.

EXTRA! Writing prompt
Present the class with a person who needs advice, such as someone trying to be more organized or trying to meet new friends. Tell students to write a paragraph offering advice on how best to solve their problem. ⏱ 15–20 min

SPEAKING STRATEGY

C 🔄 Look at the two photos to the right. Work with a partner and answer these questions. ⏱ 5–10 min

Assign students to pairs to answer the questions. Tell students to emphasize question 2, *How does each person feel? What would make that person feel better?* Call on different pairs to say what has happened in each photo. Write key vocabulary on the board.

D 🔄 Choose one of the situations in **C** and write a conversation. Work with your partner. Use the Useful Expressions to help you. ⏱ 10–15 min

(See Student Book page 99 for complete instructions.)

Introduce the Useful Expressions, and point out how they can be used. Tell students to choose one of the pictures and write a conversation using some of the Useful Expressions. Pairs should practice the conversation and switch roles. Then each pair should make a new conversation about a different problem. Practice the conversation and switch roles for the second conversation. As students are practicing, walk around helping with vocabulary and expressions.

E 🔵 Perform your conversation for the class. ⏱ 10–15 min

Pairs can perform their conversations for the class. Point out to the class places in the conversations when someone uses some of the Useful Expressions particularly well. Make a note of common errors to discuss later.

CULTURE TIP: Giving advice
The imperative mood includes forms of commands. For giving advice, native speakers use it only in addressing someone in a lower position, as in doctor to patient (*Get more sleep.*), instructor to student (*Learn 10 new words every day.*), or parent to child (*Eat more vegetables.*). In other types of relationships, native speakers "soften" the advice by using other expressions:

You should get more sleep.
If I were you, I would get more sleep.
You might want to think about getting more sleep.

4 SPEAKING

A 🔊 Ming wants to join the school swim team. Before she can do that, she has to get a checkup from her doctor. Listen to and read the conversation. Then answer the questions below. **CD 2 Track 4**

1. What expressions does the doctor use to give advice? Underline them.

2. Do you think the language is formal or informal?

DR. PENA: OK, Ming, we're finished. As far as I can tell, you're completely healthy!

MING: Great!

DR. PENA: But I do want to talk to you about one thing.

MING: Uh-oh. This doesn't sound good.

DR. PENA: No, it's nothing scary. It's just that winter is coming. You need to prepare. I always advise my patients to get a flu shot.

MING: Hmm... I could never do that. I'm afraid of needles!

DR. PENA: Don't worry, Ming. The shot doesn't hurt at all.

MING: Really? Well, maybe...

DR. PENA: It will protect you from the flu. You'll be able to swim all year without getting sick. In my opinion, I think you should do it.

MING: Well, OK. Maybe I'll give it a try.

DR. PENA: Good! I'll tell the nurse to come in and see you. Take care and good luck on the swim team this year!

B 🔁 Practice the conversation with a partner.

SPEAKING STRATEGY

C 🔁 Look at the two photos to the right. Work with a partner and answer these questions.

1. What's happened in each photo?

2. How does each person feel?

D 🔁 Choose one of the situations in **C** and write a conversation. Work with your partner. Use the Useful Expressions to help you.

Student A: You are a helpful person.

Student B: You have the problem.

A: Excuse me. Are you all right?

B: I'm not sure.

A: What happened?

B: I fell off my bike.

A: Are you dizzy? I think you should call a doctor.

E ⬡ Perform your conversation for the class.

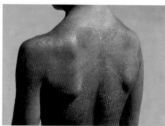

Useful Expressions	
Giving serious advice	
In my opinion, you should...	I think the best idea (for you) is to...
I always advise people to...	If I were you, I'd...
Accepting advice	**Refusing advice**
You're right. Thanks for the advice.	I'm not sure that would work for me.
That makes (a lot of) sense. I'll give it a try.	That doesn't (really) make sense to me.
I'll try it and get back to you.	I could never do that.

5 GRAMMAR

A Turn to page 206. Complete the exercises. Then do **B–E** below.

Describing Symptoms						
	have	Noun		Possessive adjective	Noun	*hurt*
I	have	a headache,	and	my	throat	hurts.
	feel / be	Adjective			*can't stop*	*-ing* verb
I	feel / am	tired,	and	I	can't stop	shivering.

Other common vocabulary

have + noun: I have (a stomachache / an earache / a backache / a toothache / a cut / a sore throat / a fever / a temperature / a cold / <u>the</u> flu).

possessive adjective + noun + hurt: My (arm / finger / back / stomach) hurts. My (legs) hurt.

feel / be + adjective: I feel / am (dizzy / nauseous / drowsy / exhausted / faint / weak / sick).

can't stop + -ing verb: I can't stop (coughing / scratching / sneezing).

B 🔊 **Pronunciation: The schwa sound.** Listen and repeat. Underline the vowels that use a schwa sound. **CD 2 Track 5**

1. I have a cold.
2. I was coughing all the time.
3. I think I have the flu.
4. And my stomach hurts.

C Think of a time when you or someone you know was sick. On a piece of paper, write four sentences about the symptoms.

> I didn't feel well.
>
> I couldn't stop coughing.
>
> My chest was hurting.
>
> I couldn't swallow food.

D 🔁 Role-play with a partner. One student is the patient, and the other student is the doctor.

Patient: Imagine you are sick now. Describe your symptoms to the doctor.

Doctor: Listen to the symptoms. Give the patient some advice.

> Doctor, I don't feel well at all. I think I may have a fever, too.

> Well, let's see. You do have a temperature. What other symptoms do you have?

> My chest hurts, and I can't stop coughing. It's impossible for me to sleep at night.

E 🔁 Switch roles and do the role play again.

5 GRAMMAR
Describing symptoms

WARM UP Either bring in a photo of a sick person or clearly overact the role of a sick person. Tell the class, *I have a cold. I don't feel very good today.* Ask for their advice and suggestions on how you can feel better. ⏱ 5 min

A Turn to page 206. Complete the exercises. Then do **B–E** below. 🕐 20–30 min

Elicit ways of describing how you feel when you feel unwell. Write students' ideas on the board. Then go through the symptoms in the chart and the examples below. Clarify vocabulary as necessary. Say different symptoms and have students act them out. The grammar chart on page 206 includes further examples and more common vocabulary used for describing symptoms, expanding on the information in the chart on page 100.

TEACHING OPTION: The flipped classroom
To open up time for in-class communicative tasks, assign the Grammar Notes on page 206 as homework. Have students complete the exercises on My World Link Online as well.

The next time class meets:

1. Review describing symptoms in the Grammar Notes.

2. Go through the exercises students did for homework; present new examples and reinforce points as needed. Take questions from students.

3. Turn back to page 100 and do the communicative exercises there, starting with **B**.

B 🔊 **Pronunciation: The schwa sound.** Listen and repeat. Underline the vowels that use a schwa sound. **CD 2 Track 5** 🕐 5–10 min

Remind students of the schwa sound (/ə/) in English for unstressed vowels. As an example, write on the board, *I have a fever.* Say it and have students focus on how the article *a* sounds (it is unstressed and therefore the sound is schwa, /ə/). Play the audio and have students repeat the sentences. Play it again and have them underline the vowels that have a schwa sound. Check answers with the class, then play the audio again and have students repeat each sentence.

C Think of a time when you or someone you know was sick. On a piece of paper, write four sentences about the symptoms. 🕐 5–10 min

Point out the example sentences, then have students write their sentences about a time when they were sick. Provide help with vocabulary as necessary and write any new words on the board for others to use. Remind students to use past tense forms. Call on different students to share the symptoms they had with the class.

D 🔄 Role-play with a partner. One student is the patient, and the other student is the doctor. 🕐 10 min

(See Student Book page 100 for complete instructions.)

Have students look at the photo and say what is happening. Then model the example with a student. Tell students to imagine they are sick now and decide what their symptoms are. Assign students to pairs to role-play the situation. Monitor and provide help as necessary and note down common problems to discuss at the end of the exercise.

E 🔄 Switch roles and do the role play again. 🕐 10 min

Have students change roles so the students who were doctors in **D** are now patients.

EXTRA! At the doctor's
Write the following scenarios on the board:

A patient gets some unusual advice from the doctor.
A patient goes to the doctor, but he doesn't like the doctor's advice.
A patient goes to the doctor with an unusual problem.

Match students with a partner and tell them to choose one scenario to role-play. Give them time to prepare and practice. When all pairs are ready, they can present their role plays to the class. 🕐 15–20 min

🔊 GRAMMAR TUTORIALS
• Verb + Noun / Adjective / Verb (*-ing*); Use of *Hurt*

Additional tutorials are available for reteaching and reinforcement.

Instructor's Notes

_____

_____

_____

_____

_____

_____

_____

_____

6 COMMUNICATION

WARM UP Ask the class, *Where do people get health information? Where did you learn about healthy and unhealthy things—in school? online? from newspapers or magazines? on TV? Where is the best place to get health information?* ⏱ 5 min

A 🗣 What do you know about the treatments below? Would you ever want to try them? Tell a partner. ⏱ 5–10 min

Student familiarity with these treatments may depend on cultural backgrounds. Before pairing students, ask some general questions about these treatments to find out what students already know. Pair students who have greater familiarity with students who have lesser familiarity to promote information sharing and better conversations.

LANGUAGE TIP: Alternative medicine
The term *alternative medicine* is used to describe treatments other than those you might get from a medical doctor at a hospital. Some other alternative forms of treatment include:

acupuncture	treatment with special needles
aromatherapy	treatment with scented plant oils
herbalism	treatment using dried plants as medicine
homeopathy	treatment with very small doses of certain medicines
nutritional supplements	treatment with vitamins and minerals

B 👥 In groups of four, role-play the following situations. ⏱ 10–15 min

(See Student Book page 101 for complete instructions.)

Go over the different treatments, pointing out that all of them have both positive and negative aspects. Have each student complete the fourth box about another treatment of their choice. If necessary, elicit other alternative treatments or share the information in the Teaching Tip above. Model the exercise with two students using the example dialog. Remind students to also mention the negative points of the treatment, and that the terms *but* and *however* may be useful when describing the drawbacks. Assign students to groups of four and assign one student to be student A for the first role play in each group.

C 👥 Student A chooses the treatment he or she prefers and explains why. Then switch roles and perform the role play again. Repeat until everyone has had a chance to play Student A. ⏱ 15–20 min

Give students a clear countdown of the time remaining to be sure that each student has an opportunity to play Student A. This is an excellent exercise to have students practice speaking without looking at the book. Walk around the room, listening and noting common errors for discussion later. Choose one or two groups to do their role play for the class.

LARGE CLASS OPTION
After students have had time to prepare their role plays, ask three groups of students to come to the front of the room and perform. Critique the performances so that students have a clear idea of your expectations for this exercise.

EXTRA! Writing prompt
A friend of yours is complaining that he or she is tired and that his or her back and other muscles are in pain. Write a paragraph giving advice about how he or she should treat the condition. ⏱ 15–20 min

TEACHING TIP: Error quiz
This is a very targeted way to review grammar. Over the course of the unit, collect 8–10 sentences containing errors with the target structure from students' oral and written work. Make a copy for each student. (Do not indicate the names of the students who made the errors.) Have students work individually or in pairs to correct the sentences. When all students have finished, go over the sentences as a class, making sure that all students have marked the corrections on their papers.

Instructor's Notes

_____

_____

_____

_____

_____

_____

_____

_____

_____

_____

_____

_____

_____

6 COMMUNICATION

A What do you know about the treatments below? Would you ever try them? Tell a partner.

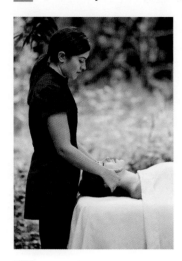

B In groups of four, role-play the following situations.

Student A: Think of a health problem. Tell your partners at least three of your symptoms.

Students B–D: Give Student A advice about the problem. Each student should recommend a different treatment: massage, yoga, meditation, or some other treatment. You can use the notes and example below to help you.

Massage	Meditation
+ used to treat aches and pains	+ helps with relaxation
+ increases your flexibility	+ has been done for thousands of years
+ can help with your mood	+ can be done alone or in a group
− can be expensive	− can be frustrating or boring
Yoga	**A treatment of your choice:**
+ a good way to exercise	+
+ emphasizes breath control	+
+ no special equipment necessary	+
− can be physically challenging	−

A: I'm having trouble sleeping.

B: In my opinion, you should try meditation.

A: Really? Have you tried it?

B: Absolutely. It really helps with relaxation.

A: I'm not sure that would work for me. It sounds kind of boring.

C: If I were you, I'd try yoga because…

C Student A chooses the treatment he or she prefers and explains why. Then switch roles and perform the role play again. Repeat until everyone has had a chance to play Student A.

1 VOCABULARY

A  Work with a partner. Look at the Word Bank. Then do the following.

1. Each person should take one person's comment below and read it aloud with feeling.

2. Then explain the person's situation in your own words. Your partner will give you some advice.

Word Bank
Word partnerships with *sick*
be / feel sick = be / feel ill
be sick of (something) = be tired of (something)
be worried sick = be very worried
call in sick = call your work to say you are ill
sick days = days you can take off from work when you are ill

CAROLINA: My favorite band is playing on Saturday night, but I have class until 6:00, and then I have to work. I'm thinking about **cutting class** and **calling in sick** to work so I can go to the concert. I'm doing well in my class, and I have a lot of **sick days** left, so I don't have to worry.

JILL: I'm **sick of** my parents **bossing** me **around**. I'm supposed to be at home right after school, but yesterday I came home late. My mother said she was **worried sick** about me. Now she's **grounded** me—I can't go out with my friends for a week. My parents **treat** me like a baby even though I'm 16 years old! I can **take care** of myself!

B Read the pieces of advice below. Who does each one apply to: Carolina or Jill? Write the name.

1. Try to follow the rules. Your parents worry because they **care about** you. _____

2. You have a **well paid** job. You don't want to lose it. I think you should go to work. _____

3. You **might as well** listen to your parents. If you don't, they'll just get upset. _____

4. If you're a good student, talk to your instructor. He might understand. _____

C  Ask and answer the questions with a partner.

1. Have you (or someone you know) ever cut class? called in sick to work? been worried sick about something? been grounded? Why?

2. What's something you're sick of?

3. Do your parents or older siblings ever boss you around or treat you like a baby?

CHOICES AND CONSEQUENCES

1 VOCABULARY

WARM UP Write on the board, *giving advice*, and elicit the different expressions used to give advice that students already know: *I think you should...*; *maybe you ought to...*; *have you thought about...*; *why don't you...*; *perhaps you could...*; *you really ought to...* ⏱ 5 min

A 🔁 Work with a partner. Look at the Word Bank. Then do the following. ⏱ 10–15 min

(See Student Book page 102 for complete instructions.)

Go over the directions with the class and say the expressions in the Word Bank for students to repeat. Make sure students understand the two stages: first they read the person's comments as though they were the person, then they explain the situation to their partner using the third person (*Jill feels…*). Their partner will then give advice. Assign students to pairs and tell them to each choose a person. Monitor and provide help as necessary. After students have given advice for each situation, go over the words and phrases in blue and have students explain their meaning, then call on different students to share the advice their partner suggested.

TEACHING OPTION: Support / challenge

Instead of using the first person (*I feel...*), tell students to use the third person (*Ben feels...*) to explain the situation of the person in the book. This gives students extra practice with the more challenging third-person verb endings.

B Read the pieces of advice below. Who does each one apply to: Carolina or Jill? Write the name. ⏱ 10 min

Point out that the expressions *may as well* and *might as well* are interchangeable. Have students complete the exercise individually; then check answers with the class.

EXTRA! Dictation

Tell students to take out a piece of paper or their notebooks. Read the four sentences from **B**. Read each sentence three times. The first time, students should listen only. The second time, they should write down exactly what you say. The third time, they should check their own writing. To check the answers, ask several students to write their sentences on the board. ⏱ 15 min

C 🔁 Ask and answer the questions with a partner. ⏱ 10 min

Go over the questions with the class and give students a moment to think about their answers and write a few notes. Then assign students to new pairs to ask and answer the questions. Monitor and ask follow-up questions to encourage students to talk more. Call on several students to share one of their partner's answers with the class.

TEACHING TIP: Word associations

This short exercise provides a quick, general review of vocabulary. Work as a whole class. Begin by giving a word associated with the current unit, such as *headache*. The first student says a word that is associated with *headache*: for example, *aspirin*. Write it on the board. The second student says a word associated with *aspirin*: for example, *medicine*. The third might say *drug store*, the fourth might say *sick*. Continue around the class until all students have contributed a word. Review interesting words, and discuss the links between them.

LANGUAGE TIP: Other types of *sickness*

Altitude sickness—can happen when people climb mountains or even visit cities located at high altitudes. Common symptoms are dizziness and fatigue.

Decompression sickness—is caused by a rapid decrease in pressure after a person has been in a compressed atmosphere. This very dangerous condition can affect divers, miners, and people in some types of aircraft. Symptoms include joint pain and difficulty breathing.

Motion sickness—is a sick feeling some people get from traveling in a moving vehicle. Types of motion sickness include car sickness, sea sickness, and air sickness. Common symptoms are dizziness, fatigue, and nausea.

Morning sickness—is the nausea and vomiting some women experience (often in the morning) during the first few months of pregnancy.

Instructor's Notes

_____

_____

_____

2 LISTENING

STRATEGIES: Infer information; Listen for feeling; Listen for details

WARM UP With the class, talk about the challenges of beginning life in a new school. What difficulties have students had when they first began studying in a new place? 5 min

A **Infer information.** Read the question below. Then listen and answer it. **CD 2 Track 6** 5–10 min

Go over the question and answer options with the class. Remind students that they need to infer; the information won't be stated directly. Play the audio, then give students time to choose their answers. Have them compare their answers with a partner's, then play the audio again. Check answers with the class and have students explain what helped them infer the information.

Infer information. Remind students that inferring information means to use the information they have, the context, and their background knowledge to work out something that isn't stated or explained explicitly.

B **Listen for feeling.** Listen. How does Ben feel about the three topics below? Write the correct letter next to each topic. (One item is extra.) **CD 2 Track 6** 5 min

Play the audio only once, and tell students to write their answers. Move on to **C** before checking the answers. Then go back and check the answers to both **B** and **C** together.

Listen for feeling. Explain to students that listening for feeling means trying to understand how people feel based on what they say, and how they say it. This can help students work out meanings of new concepts and words because how the person feels will give them an idea if the meaning is something positive or negative. Point out that the speaker's tone of voice and the words he or she uses can help students understand how he or she feels.

C **Listen for details.** Listen again. Which words describe Ben? someone else? If you checked *someone else*, who is being described in each case? **CD 2 Track 6** 10–15 min

Be sure to emphasize that not all of the words describe Ben. Students should listen carefully not only for the vocabulary but also for the name of the person being described. Check the answers by playing the audio again. Following the audio script, stop after each answer and check it with the class. Check answers to **B**.

Listen for details. Remind students that they do not need to hear and understand everything in order to understand specific details. Encourage them to get into the habit of identifying key words to listen for before they listen.

TEACHING OPTION: Support / challenge
Dictate the following words to students. Then play the audio again. Tell students to raise a hand when they hear each expression. Help the class try to figure out the meaning of the expression from the context.

can't stand it	don't like or enjoy it
give up	stop trying
show him around	take someone to see places that are new for them
what's going on	what is happening
try-outs	a competition to join a team or group
check it out	to go to learn more about
I figure	I think; I guess
give it a try	try or attempt something to see what it is like

D Think about a time you were in a new situation. Describe how you felt to a partner. 10–15 min

Go over the directions with the class, then have students think about a situation. Tell them to think about when, where, who, and how they felt. Help with vocabulary as necessary. Assign students to pairs to explain their situations and feelings at the time. Model the exercise by sharing an experience of your own. Ask a few comprehension questions about your experience, for example, *What happened? When? Where was I? How did I feel?* Monitor and ask follow-up questions to prompt more conversation. Call on volunteers to share their experience with the class.

Instructor's Notes

_____

_____

_____

_____

_____

_____

_____

_____

2 LISTENING

A 🔊 **Infer information.** Read the question below. Then listen and answer it. **CD 2 Track 6**

Which two things are probably true about Ben? Circle them.

    a. He lives at home with his parents.
    b. He studies at a school in another city.
    c. He is getting ready to graduate from college.
    d. He just started college recently.

B 🔊 **Listen for feeling.** Listen. How does Ben feel about the three topics below? Write the correct letter next to each topic. (One item is extra.) **CD 2 Track 6**

    1. math class _____
    2. roommate _____
    3. the soccer team _____

    a. He likes it / him.
    b. He doesn't like it / him.
    c. He's not sure about it / him.
    d. He used to like it / him.

C 🔊 **Listen for details.** Listen again. Which words describe Ben? someone else? If you checked *someone else*, who is being described in each case? **CD 2 Track 6**

	Ben	Someone else	Person described
1. an early riser	☐	☑	Ben's mother
2. homesick	☐	☐	
3. well behaved	☐	☐	
4. not feeling well	☐	☐	
5. at home after 8:00	☐	☐	

D 🔄 Think about a time you were in a new situation. Describe how you felt to a partner.

3 READING

STRATEGIES: Scan for information; Make predictions; Check predictions; Read for details; Infer meaning

WARM UP Introduce the word *syndrome*: a medical condition that is characterized by a particular group of signs and symptoms. Ask students if they have heard this word before. What syndromes are they familiar with? Contrast with the word *symptom*: something wrong with your mind or body that is a sign of an illness. ◯ 5 min

A 🔁 Can modern life make you sick? If yes, how? Tell a partner. ◯ 5–10 min

Assign students to pairs to share their opinions. Discuss the question as a class.

B 🔁 **Scan for information; Make predictions.** Copy the chart below on a piece of paper. Then scan the article. What are the names of the five medical conditions mentioned? Write the answers in the chart under *Syndrome*. When you have this problem, what do you think happens? Tell a partner. ◯ 5–10 min

Remind students that scanning means to read quickly for specific information. For this exercise they should not write down the descriptions and solutions but only the names of the syndromes. Once they have the names, they should talk to a partner about what they think happens in each syndrome.

Scan for information. Remind students that scanning means looking over a text quickly in order to find specific information. Students shouldn't read in detail until they find the information they are looking for.

Make predictions. Remind students that predicting before they read helps them be more prepared for the text because they will have activated prior knowledge of the topic and language related to it.

---

3 READING

A 🔁 Can modern life make you sick? If yes, how? Tell a partner.

B 🔁 **Scan for information; Make predictions.** Copy the chart below on a piece of paper. Then scan the article. What are the names of the five medical conditions mentioned? Write the answers in the chart under *Syndrome*. When you have this problem, what do you think happens? Tell a partner.

Syndrome	Description	Possible solution
1. CHAOS	You feel embarrassed because your house is messy.	
2.		
3.		
4.		
5.		

C **Check predictions; Read for details.** Now read the article. Complete the chart above with the description and possible solution for each syndrome. If a solution is not mentioned, write *NM*.

D 🔁 **Infer meaning.** What do the words below mean? Find them in the passage. Then work with a partner to guess the definitions. Check a dictionary for the answers.

1st paragraph: *tidy* _____
2nd paragraph: *fatigue* _____
3rd paragraph: *rushing* _____
5th paragraph: *gentle* _____

E 👥 Look at where you wrote *NM* in the chart in **B**. Can you suggest some possible solutions?

Which syndrome is the worst? Why? Take a vote as a class.

MODERN HEALTH PROBLEMS

Margaret's friend is taking a new job in a faraway city. Margaret wants to have a goodbye dinner party at her home. But she can't. Margaret suffers from *CHAOS (Can't Have Anyone Over Syndrome)*. Her apartment is messy, and she's embarrassed by it. "I've never been a tidy person," she says. "My best friend gave me some good advice. He told me to get a house cleaner."

These days we get and receive so much information every day. People call, text, and email us all day long, and they expect quick responses from us. It can be very demanding—and it's making some people sick. They have *information fatigue syndrome*. There is so much information, they become paralyzed[1] and can't think clearly. "I can't

[1]If you are *paralyzed*, you cannot move.

sleep at night because I worry," says Bahman, a college senior. "I'm sick of it."

Do you sometimes engage in *deskfast* (eating breakfast at your desk at work)? If your answer is *yes*, then you may suffer from hurry sickness. *Hurry sickness* is a straightforward name for another syndrome of modern life. "I'm always rushing. And I'm tired all the time. Just last week I had to call in sick because I was so stressed," says Mari, a company employee. "I'm worried about using all of my sick days."

We've all complained about having too much work to do. Well, how about not having enough work? *Underload syndrome* is caused by having little or nothing to do at the office. Steven works

as a project manager. "I can finish my work in about four hours, but I'm afraid to say anything about it. I don't want to be assigned too much work!" So what does he do? Steven pretends to be busy. "I'm thinking about getting a part-time job in the evening. That's one possible idea."

Chances are you've experienced *text neck* before. Another name for it would be *pain in the neck*, because that's what people with this condition experience. Looking down at your phone and texting for a long time causes *text neck*. How can you take care of it? Getting a gentle neck massage—nothing too hard—will help you relax and feel better.

C **Check predictions; Read for details.** Now read the article. Complete the chart above with the description and possible solution for each syndrome. If a solution is not mentioned, write *NM*. 🕐 10–15 min

Give students time to reread the article and complete their charts. Tell students to underline the places in the reading that give them the answers. Check answers as a class.

Check predictions. It is important to always go back to the predictions students made and help them see what they guessed correctly, and talk about why incorrect guesses were wrong.

Read for details. Remind students that reading for details means reading a text more slowly and in depth. When they read for details they should pay attention to unfamiliar words, and try to guess their meaning from the context before they look them up.

D 🔄 **Infer meaning.** What do the words below mean? Find them in the passage. Then work with a partner to guess the definitions. Check a dictionary for the answers. 🕐 10 min

Check answers with the class, having students explain the meanings and give more examples if possible.

Infer meaning. Remind students that it is often possible to find the meaning of a new word from how it is used in the text. They should look at the whole sentence, not just the word, and try to decide what kind of word it is (verb, noun, etc.). This will help them guess its meaning. They should also use the context the word is being used in to help them infer meaning.

E 🔗 Look at where you wrote *NM* in the chart. Can you suggest some possible solutions? 🕐 10–15 min

Assign students to small groups to discuss solutions. Monitor and provide help as necessary, ask questions to prompt further discussion where possible.

TEACHING TIP: Tone of a reading
Fluent readers of English can pick up on an author's tone: the author's purpose and writing style. Some articles are serious or are trying to convince you of something important. Others are humorous or clever. There are many serious syndromes, such as AIDS: Acquired Immune Deficiency Syndrome. But in this article, the author is writing about non-life-threatening problems. The syndromes described should not be taken very seriously and are intended to be humorous.

EXTRA! Writing prompt
Students write about the challenges and stresses of living in the modern world. What are the factors that make modern life difficult? How can we address those challenges? 🕐 15–20 min

4 GRAMMAR

A   Turn to page 207. Complete the exercises. Then do **B–D** below.

Reported Speech: Commands and Requests		
	Quoted speech	**Reported speech**
Command	The doctor said, "Get some rest." The doctor said, "Don't smoke."	The doctor **told** <u>me</u> **to get** some rest. The doctor **told** <u>him</u> **not to smoke**.
Request	Jon said, "Please turn off <u>your</u> phone." Maria asked, "Can <u>you</u> help <u>me</u>?"	Jon **asked** <u>me</u> **to turn off** <u>my</u> phone. Maria **asked** <u>us</u> **to help** <u>her</u>.

B   Take three small pieces of paper. Do the following.

- On one piece of paper, write a command in quoted speech.

- On a second piece of paper, write a second command in quoted speech. It should use *not*.

- On a third piece of paper, write a request in quoted speech.

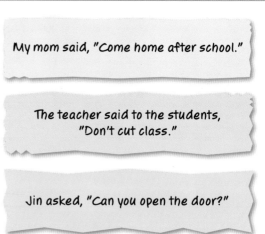

My mom said, "Come home after school."

The teacher said to the students, "Don't cut class."

Jin asked, "Can you open the door?"

C   👥 Work in a small group. Follow the steps below.

1. Put all your papers together and mix them. Put them face down on the desk in a pile.

2. One person begins. Turn over a paper. You have 15 seconds to make a reported speech statement using the sentence on the paper.

My mom told me to come home after school.

3. If you make a correct reported statement, you get a point. Then put the paper aside. If you can't make a correct statement, put the paper at the bottom of the pile.

4. Then the next person goes. Play until you use all the papers. Who has the most points?

D   👥 Take your three sentences and get together with a new group. Repeat **C**.

5 WRITING

When I was in high school, my dad always told me to exercise and eat healthy food. He did these things, but I didn't. I was too busy with my studies, and I didn't have time to exercise. I ate a lot of junk food and didn't treat my body well, so I gained weight. Six months ago, I started college, and I decided to make a change. First, I joined a gym. Then I asked a trainer to help me with a diet and exercise plan. I started eating better and exercising more. Today, I'm doing well. I'm five kilos lighter, and I have more energy. Too bad I didn't listen to my dad's advice in high school. He was right!

4 GRAMMAR
Reported speech: commands and requests

WARM UP Write on the board: *Commands* and *Requests*. Elicit classroom examples of both and write them on the board, for example, *Open your books. Can I borrow your dictionary?* Etc. ⏱ 5 min

A Turn to page 207. Complete the exercises. Then do **B–D** below. ◑ 20–30 min

Go over the examples in the chart and have students identify the differences between quoted speech and reported speech. They should notice the change from *said* to *told* in commands and from *said* to *asked* in requests, the use of the object pronouns, and the use of *to* + base form. Go back to the commands and requests students suggested in the Warm Up and have students transform them to reported speech. The grammar chart on page 207 includes further examples, expanding on the information in the chart on page 106.

B Take three small pieces of paper. Do the following. ⏱ 5–10 min

(See Student Book page 106 for complete instructions.)

Go over the directions with the class and read the examples. Then have students write their commands and requests. Monitor and help with corrections as necessary.

C 👥 Work in a small group. Follow the steps below. ⏱ 10–15 min

(See Student Book page 106 for complete instructions.)

Go over the steps with the class, then assign students to groups of three or four. Have each student put their papers down on the desk. Then model the exercise by taking a paper from one group's desk and saying the command or request in reported speech. Have students take a paper and do the same. Remind them that they should keep time; each student only has 15 seconds to make their reported speech statement. Monitor as groups work and help with doubts as necessary.

D 👥 Take your three sentences and get together with a new group. Repeat **C**. ⏱ 10 min

Assign students to new groups of three or four and have them repeat the exercise.

EXTRA! Additional sentences
Students can complete the following sentences with information that is true for them. Then share their sentences with a partner. ⏱ 10–15 min

1. Once my friend told me to...

2. A complete stranger asked me...

3. I always like it when someone tells me...

4. My mother likes it when I...

GRAMMAR TUTORIALS
• Reported Speech: Requests and Commands

Additional tutorials are available for reteaching and reinforcement.

Instructor's Notes

5 WRITING 🔊

WARM UP With the class, brainstorm a list of modern-day sicknesses and syndromes. Focus on illnesses that probably did not exist 50 years ago. ⏱ 5 min

A 🔄 Read the paragraph on page 106. Answer the questions with a partner. ⏱ 10 min

Go over the questions with the class. Then have students read the paragraph and answer the questions with a partner. Check answers with the class.

B Think of health advice you've gotten for living a happy and healthy life. It could be from a person (like a parent or doctor) or from another source (like a magazine). Answer questions 1–3 in **A**. Then use your notes and the example to help you write a paragraph of your own. ⏱ 20–25 min

Write *health advice* in the middle of the board. Tell the class about health tips you've gotten, and who or where you got them from. Around *health advice* on the board, draw a mind map with the specific advice you got, who gave it you, and other details. Then have the class help you write your paragraph using the one in **A** as a model. Make sure students suggest examples with reported speech when they tell you what to write. Then have students think of advice they've been given and individually do a mind map with the details of the advice, who gave it to them, and other details. After doing their mind map, have them write their paragraph following the model in **A**. Monitor and provide help as necessary. Make sure they include some reported speech and refer them back to pages 106 and 207 as necessary.

C 🔄 Exchange your writing with a partner. Read his or her paragraph. ⏱ 10–15 min

(See Student Book page 107 for complete instructions.)

Assign students to pairs and have them exchange papers and identify any mistakes in their partner's paragraph. Tell them to focus on the use of reported speech and vocabulary related to healthy living. Then have students answer the questions in **A** about their partner's paragraph. Encourage students to talk about their paragraphs together, *What was clear? What was confusing? What could be better?* Then have students rewrite their paragraphs, making the corrections and taking into account their partner's comments on how to improve it. Provide help as necessary. Collect the paragraphs to give them feedback if possible.

PROCESS WRITING: Graphic organizers
Using graphic organizers (such as the mind map suggested in **B**) to brainstorm and plan before they write can help students be more focused and organized, and consequently write more effectively.

6 COMMUNICATION

WARM UP Write this common expression on the board: *An apple a day keeps the doctor away*. Ask students what other folk wisdom they know about for keeping healthy. ⏱ 5 min

A Look at the tips for leading a healthy and happy life. Add four more tips to the list. ⏱ 5–10 min

Tell students to brainstorm silently and write down their tips individually. The term *hang out* is a phrasal verb and idiom that means *to spend time with someone*.

B 🔗 Ask three different classmates: "What is important for a healthy and happy life?" Write their names and answers in the chart. ⏱ 10–15 min

Tell all of the students to stand and mingle in a "cocktail party" format. They should give and receive an answer from one student and then move on to the next one. Remind students of the useful expressions for giving and receiving advice on page 99.

C 🔗 Get into small groups. Take turns reporting what your classmates said. Do you agree with their advice? Why or why not? ⏱ 10 min

Remind students of the different ways of reporting speech, as shown on page 106. Model the exercise by reading the example with a student. Remind students to discuss whether they agree with the advice or not. Model and prompt with questions as necessary.

D 🔗 Review all the advice you got in **B**. Together, choose the three best tips and share your answers with the class. ⏱ 10–15 min

Ask the groups to choose their three best tips. Then finish with a whole-class discussion of the best ideas for leading a healthy and happy life.

LARGE CLASS OPTION
Rather than have a whole-class discussion of the best ideas for leading a healthy and happy life, choose a few representatives of the class. Ask them to come to the front of the room and seat themselves facing the rest of the class. They will be a panel of experts. Give them each a minute or two to state what they think are the best ideas. Then permit students in the class to ask questions of the panelists.

A 🔁 Read the paragraph on page 106. Answer the questions with a partner.

1. What health advice did the writer get and from whom?

2. Did the writer follow that advice? Why or why not?

3. Does the writer think it was good advice? Why or why not?

B Think of health advice you've gotten for living a happy and healthy life. It could be from a person (like a parent or doctor) or from another source (like a magazine). Answer questions 1–3 in **A**. Then use your notes and the example to help you write a paragraph of your own.

C 🔁 Exchange your writing with a partner. Read his or her paragraph.

1. Are there any mistakes? If yes, circle them.

2. Answer questions 1–3 in **A** about your partner's writing.

3. Return the paper to your partner. Make corrections to your own paragraph.

6 COMMUNICATION

A Look at the tips for leading a healthy and happy life. Add four more tips to the list.

Tips for leading a healthy and happy life			
Get plenty of rest.	Eat healthy foods.		
Spend time with good friends.	Don't hang out with negative people.		

B 👥 Ask three different classmates: "What is important for a healthy and happy life?" Write their names and answers in the chart.

Name	Answer
1.	
2.	
3.	

C 👥 Get into small groups. Take turns reporting what your classmates said. Do you agree with their advice? Why or why not?

> Pablo told me to eat a big breakfast every morning.

> Yuki told me not to worry about my exams too much.

D 👥 Review all the advice you got in **B**. Together, choose the three best tips and share your answers with the class.

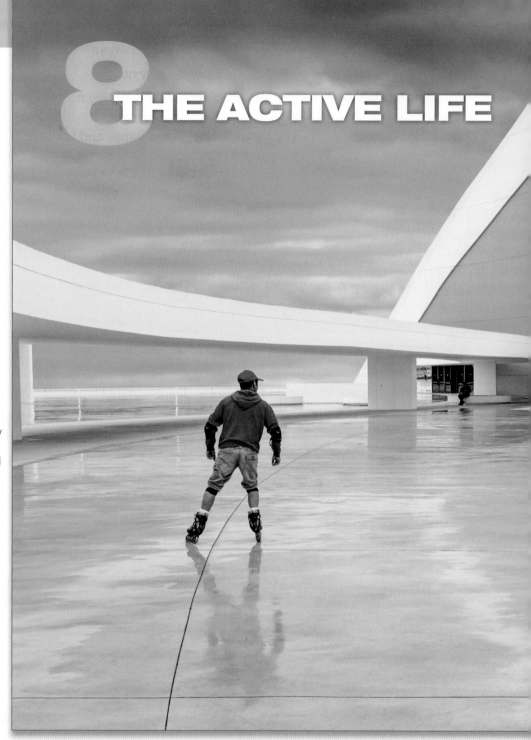

8 THE ACTIVE LIFE

ABOUT THE PHOTO

The Oscar Niemeyer International Cultural Center in Aviles, Spain, was designed by Brazilian architect Oscar Niemeyer. The building is part of a major urban renewal project to redevelop the industrial areas of the city. Located in the industrial port area, the Niemeyer Center is based on three fundamental concepts: education, culture, and peace. It aims to integrate the arts and education, and therefore has spaces for exhibitions, music, theatre, dance, film, and lectures. The center also includes a restaurant, conference and meeting rooms, and a play area. This photo shows the open square, a large outdoor space between the different buildings that make up the center, which reflects Niemeyer's idea of a "square open to the world." We can assume that the man taking advantage of the space to skate freely is something that the architect would have approved of because he wanted the space to be for everybody.

INTRODUCE THE THEME

- In this unit, students will explore the concept of living an active life. The language in the two lessons will help students communicate about being active, including talking about ways to stay active, explaining the organization and rules of a game, talking about how long they've done an activity, and describing a favorite activity.

	Video	Vocabulary	Listening
LESSON A Leisure time p. 110	Rock Climbing in Oman p. 110	Being involved p. 111 *take part in, active, participate in*	Staying active p. 112 Listen for details Infer information
LESSON B Daring activities p. 116		An epic journey p. 116 *prepare for, pay for, believe in*	A parkour trip p. 117 Listen for gist Listen for details

For students: My World Link Online has personalized instruction, practice, audio, and video.

Look at the photo. Answer the questions.

1 What is this person doing? Have you ever done this activity?

2 What do you do to stay active?

3 What is one popular leisure time activity in your country?

UNIT GOALS

1 Talk about things you do to stay active

2 Explain the set-up and rules of a game

3 Talk about how long you've done certain activities

4 Describe a favorite activity in detail

A man in-line skates at the Oscar Niemeyer
International Cultural Center in Aviles, Spain.

- In Lesson A, students watch a video about three professional rock climbers. Students will then learn how to talk about being involved in an activity. They will also practice the listening strategies of listening for details and inferring information. Then they will learn how to explain a game and how to play it. Finally, they will learn how to express how long they've been doing an activity.

- In Lesson B, students will learn how to describe different kinds of physical activities. They will read about the X Games, practicing the reading strategies of using background knowledge, scanning for information, and reading for details. They will also write and talk about one of their hobbies.

WARM UP

Look at the photo. Answer the questions.

- Call on students to describe what they see in the photo.

- Have students answer the questions individually or in pairs, then compare answers with the class.

- Point out the unit goals and explain what students will learn. Elicit any key vocabulary students already know, and write it on the board. Explain any unfamiliar phrases in the unit goals to the students.

Grammar	Pronunciation	Speaking	Reading	Writing	Communication
The present perfect vs. the present perfect continuous pp. 114, 208 Review: The simple past vs. the present perfect vs. the present perfect continuous pp. 120, 209	Stress in compound nouns p. 112	Explaining the set-up and rules of a game p. 113	A star in the X Games p. 118 Use background knowledge Scan for information Read for details	Write about a hobby p. 121	Talking about a new skill p. 115 Interviewing classmates about hobbies p. 121

2 VOCABULARY

WARM UP Ask the class, *What do you do in your free time?* Write a list of students' responses on the board. ⏱ 5 min

A Read about the person below. Do you know anybody like this? ⏱ 10 min

Have students look at the picture and explain what the people are doing. Remind students about collocations, words that are often used together, and go over the information in the Word Bank with the class. Have students read the text, paying attention to the words in blue. When students have finished reading, ask some comprehension questions, for example:

How many hours a week does the person play online video games?
Why does he watch videos of other players?
What do gamers share online?

Then have students answer the question. How many of them know someone like this?

B 🔁 Circle T for *True* or F for *False*. Explain your answers to a partner. ⏱ 5–10 min

Go over the statements with the class, then have them choose *true* or *false* according to their behavior or what they believe. Assign students to pairs to explain and discuss their points of view. Monitor and provide help as possible, making sure students explain their reasons. Call on different students to explain one of their partner's answers.

C 🔁 Answer the questions with your partner. ⏱ 10 min

Have students think about their answers to the questions, then assign them to pairs to talk about their answers. Monitor and provide help as necessary. Ask follow-up questions to encourage more conversation. Survey the class to find out what activities students do.

EXTRA! Class poll
Divide the class into groups with an equal number of members (for example, five groups of four members). Have each group think of two questions about sports and activities (*Do you like soccer? How often do you go swimming?*). Each group member should write down the questions. Form new groups with one member of each group. (For example, if you started with five groups of four members, assign each student a letter A–B–C–D, and say, *All A's sit here, B's sit there, C's sit there, D's sit there*.) Each student should ask the questions and record the responses of everyone in the new group. Then students should return to their original groups to compile the answers. Finally, each group presents their results to the class. (*Five students love soccer. Two students like it a little*, etc.) ⏱ 15–20 min

Sports		
basketball	karate	skateboarding
football	tae kwon do	running, jogging
ice hockey	skiing	wrestling
surfing	lacrosse	boxing
windsurfing	soccer	horse riding, racing
rowing	sailing	car racing
diving	swimming	

Instructor's Notes

2 VOCABULARY

A Read about the person below. Do you know anybody like this?

Some parents worry that their children spend too much time playing games online.

Word Bank
activity
be involved in an / participate in an / take part in an ~
spare / leisure time ~
physical, mental, outdoor, extracurricular, classroom ~
active
stay / remain ~
highly / extremely / very ~
fairly, increasingly ~
mentally, physically ~
athlete
amateur, professional, serious ~

This is my friend. He's really **into** playing video games online. In his spare time, he plays games ten hours a day, seven days a week. He **takes part in** competitions every couple of months and has even won money playing!

He started out playing only on weekends, but became more **active** as his skill level increased. He even watches videos of other players to remain as up-to-date as possible. He knows a lot of other gamers, and they share tips online.

The game requires a lot of mental activity, but his mother worries he isn't **physically active**. She would also like to see him **participate in** some **extracurricular activities** at school, not just be on his computer all the time. He argues that he is **fairly active**, and the game gives him a chance to **be involved in** a team.

B 🔄 Circle T for *True* or F for *False*. Explain your answers to a partner.

1. I take part in an online community.	T	F
2. I think it's OK to spend a lot of time online.	T	F
3. It's strange to make money from playing video games.	T	F
4. Video games can keep you mentally active.	T	F
5. It's important to spend some time outdoors every day.	T	F

C 🔄 Answer the questions with your partner.

1. What do you do to stay active?

2. What things do you like to do in your spare time?

3 LISTENING

A 🔊 **Pronunciation: Stress in compound nouns.** A compound noun is a phrase or word made up of more than one noun. Listen and repeat. **CD 2 Track 8**

1. BOARD game   2. BASKETball   3. COMPUTER game

B 🔊 💬 **Pronunciation: Stress in compound nouns.** Look at the underlined compound nouns. Circle the stressed word in each one. Then listen and practice saying the sentences with a partner. **CD 2 Track 9**

1. Sergei is the national <u>table tennis</u> champion.
2. I want to stay active, so I got a <u>gym membership</u>.
3. How many <u>comic books</u> does he have?
4. I need to practice to get my <u>driver's license</u> in my spare time.
5. I've put the best photos in my <u>photo album</u>.
6. She's good at <u>baseball</u>.

C Read the two definitions for *renew*. Then match each definition (1 or 2) with a sentence (a or b).

> 1. You can **renew** (= begin again) an activity or relationship.
> 2. You can also **renew** (= extend the time period of) documents.

     a. Members can renew their museum membership online.

     b. I saw him for the first time in 20 years, and we renewed our friendship.

D 🔊 **Listen for details; Infer information.** You will hear a couple of conversations between two people. Read the items below. Then listen and select the best response to each question. **CD 2 Track 10**

Conversation 1

1. What is Andy calling Lucia about?
   a. her gym membership
   b. a new gym
   c. a workout plan

2. How much is Andy offering?
   a. 40 percent off
   b. 20 percent off
   c. 20 dollars off

3. What can be inferred?
   a. Lucia exercises too much.
   b. Lucia paid already.
   c. Lucia hasn't met Andy before.

Conversation 2

1. What does Deo want to do?
   a. drive more on the weekends
   b. get rid of his car
   c. take his car to work

2. What can be inferred?
   a. It's easy to shop in Deo's neighborhood.
   b. Deo's car is popular.
   c. Deo doesn't pay for parking.

3. What will Deo probably not do?
   a. sell his car
   b. renew his license
   c. get a new car

E 💬 Check your answers in **D** with a partner. Then think about one of the decisions from the conversations. What do you think of the decision? Tell your partner.

3 LISTENING

STRATEGIES: Listen for details; Infer information

WARM UP Ask students to think of one thing that they used to do but that they don't do anymore. Then ask them to think of something that they stopped doing but have started doing again. ⏱ 5 min

A 🔊 **Pronunciation: Stress in compound nouns.** A compound noun is a phrase or word made up of more than one noun. Listen and repeat. **CD 2 Track 8** ⏱ 5–10 min

After the students have had a chance to listen to the audio a couple of times, play the audio again and ask students to repeat the pronunciation aloud.

LANGUAGE TIP: Compound nouns
In compound nouns, the first noun modifies or describes the second. So a *doghouse* is a house that is for a dog. A *housecat* is a cat that lives inside a house.

B 🔊 ♻ **Pronunciation: Stress in compound nouns.** Look at the underlined compound nouns. Circle the stressed word in each one. Then listen and practice saying the sentences with a partner. **CD 2 Track 9** ⏱ 5–10 min

Tell students to read the sentences aloud, with the stress they think is correct. Have students circle the stressed word, then play the audio for them to check their answers. Play the audio again for students to repeat each sentence. Then have them practice saying the sentences with a partner.

C Read the two definitions for *renew*. Then match each definition (1 or 2) with a sentence (a or b). ⏱ 10 min

Read the definitions with the students. After students have finished matching the definitions, check the answers with the class.

D 🔊 **Listen for details; Infer information.** You will hear a couple of conversations between two people. Read the items below. Then listen and select the best response to each question. **CD 2 Track 10** ⏱ 10 min

Give students time to read the questions and answer choices for Conversation 1. Play the audio one or more times, and check answers with the class. Then repeat with Conversation 2. If necessary, explain *expire*, *you're kidding*, *casual drives*, *within walking distance*, *it's killing me*.

Listen for details. Remind students that they do not need to hear and understand everything in order to understand specific details. Teach them to get into the habit of identifying key words to listen for before they listen.

Infer information. Remind students that inferring information means to use the information they have, the context, and their background knowledge to work out something that isn't stated or explained explicitly.

TEACHING TIP: Listening for inference
To *infer* something is to understand it from the context of the situation even though it isn't stated directly. For example, if your friend says, *I'd love a hamburger*, you can infer that your friend is hungry, even if she didn't directly say, *I'm hungry*. Inference can be tricky because it is not stated directly. Inference questions are common on standardized tests such as the TOEFL©, TOEIC©, and IELTS©.

E ♻ Check your answers in **D** with a partner. Then think about one of the decisions from the conversations. What do you think of the decision? Tell your partner. ⏱ 10 min

After checking answers with their partner, have students discuss the decisions made and what they think of them. Then check answers to **D** with the class, having students explain how they were able to infer the answers to item 3 in each conversation. Then, as a class, discuss the two decisions.

Instructor's Notes

_____

_____

_____

_____

_____

_____

_____

_____

_____

_____

_____

_____

_____

4 SPEAKING

WARM UP Ask if anyone in the class has ever played or watched an unusual sport. What did they do/watch? Where was it? How did they participate? Also, ask if anyone has been to a sporting event in another country. How was it different from going to the same sport in their own country?
⏱ 5 min

A 🔊 🔄 Rohan is telling Ana about cricket, a game that he likes to play. Listen to and practice the conversation with a partner. Then complete the sentences below.
CD 2 Track 11 ⏱ 10–15 min

First, students should listen to the conversation with books closed. Ask, *What sports did they talk about?* Then students can open their books. Play the conversation again, and tell students to read along. Then have students practice the conversation in pairs. Students can complete the sentences individually. Check answers with the class. If necessary, explain the word *oval*.

CULTURE TIP: Talking about sports
In English-speaking cultures, one common form of small talk is to talk about sports. Some *sports fans* spend many hours watching sports on television and are eager to talk about the games in great detail. In some places, people gather in *sports bars* to watch important games or matches.

EXTRA! Writing prompt
Tell students to write about a sports event they have watched or participated in. Ask, *Where was the event? Can you describe how it was played and the atmosphere?*
◑ 20–30 min

SPEAKING STRATEGY

B 🔲 Look at the photo and read about the game of bocce. With a partner, write a conversation similar to the one in **A**. Use the Useful Expressions to help you. Perform your conversation for another pair. ◑ 15–20 min

Direct students' attention first to the photo, then to the Useful Expressions box. Review the expressions with the class. Say each one with students repeating after you. Give clear examples of the grammatical patterns that follow the expressions that end with ellipses. (for example, *-ing* after *by*, subject + verb after *when*: *One team starts by kicking the ball. The game begins when one team kicks the ball.*) Give students time to read about the game, then put them in pairs to write their conversations. Give students time to practice their conversations before performing for another group. Listen and offer help and correction as needed. Call on pairs to present their conversations without looking at their papers.

TEACHING OPTION: Support / challenge
Tell students to think of a sport or game and to write a conversation about it. However, instead of using the name of the sport, they should substitute an invented nonsense word. When they perform their conversation for another group, that group tries to guess the game.

LARGE CLASS OPTION
Pairs can present their conversations in groups of four or six.

EXTRA! Talking about sports
Tell students they are going to tell a partner about a sports event they watched or participated in. Students should make notes and prepare to talk about the event, giving as many details as possible. Then match students with a partner to take turns talking about the events. Their partner should ask questions about the events. Finish with a whole-class discussion of the most interesting or exciting sports events. ⏱ 10–15 min

EXTRA! Writing prompt
If one sport is a particular favorite with most of your students, teach them some vocabulary for the game. For example:

baseball: base, pitch, catch, run, ball, strike, home run, foul, inning, etc.

soccer: goal, goal post, midfielder, header, referee, run, offside, striker, throw in, kick, penalty, etc.

Then assign them to write two or three paragraphs explaining how to play the game. ◑ 20–25 min

CULTURE TIP: Popular sports
Some of the most popular sports in the world are soccer (called football in many countries), cricket, basketball, baseball, rugby, field hockey, volleyball, ice hockey, and American football.

Instructor's Notes

_____

_____

_____

_____

_____

_____

4 SPEAKING

A 🔊 🔁 Rohan is telling Ana about cricket, a game that he likes to play. Listen to and practice the conversation with a partner. Then complete the sentences below. **CD 2 Track 11**

ROHAN: Cricket is a great game. I love it!

ANA: I've never heard of it.

ROHAN: Oh, it's really popular, especially in England, India, and some other countries in Asia.

ANA: Well, how do you play?

ROHAN: It's played with a bat and a ball. Oh, and you need gloves, too. You start by pitching the ball to the striker.[1]

ANA: It sounds like baseball to me.

ROHAN: They're similar. But in cricket, there are 11 players on a team. And you play on an oval field.

ANA: How do you win?

ROHAN: The object of the game is to get more runs than the other team, and... Hey, what time is it?

ANA: Four o'clock. Why?

ROHAN: I have to go. I'm late for cricket practice!

[1]*the striker* = the hitter

1. Cricket is similar to _____.

2. Each team has _____ players.

3. The team with the most _____ wins.

4. You need a _____, a _____, and _____ to play.

SPEAKING STRATEGY

B 👥 Look at the photo and read about the game of bocce. With a partner, write a conversation similar to the one in **A**. Use the Useful Expressions to help you. Perform your conversation for another pair.

What you need:

- a small ball
- several bigger balls
- two teams of 1–4 people each

How to play:

- First, throw the small ball down the field.
- Each team then rolls the bigger balls down the field.
- Score a point for the big ball that is closest to the small ball.
- The team with the most points wins!

Useful Expressions: Explaining the set-up and rules of a game	
Equipment	It's played with... / You don't need any special equipment.
People	There are 11 players on each team. / You compete against each other.
Playing the game	One team starts by... / The game begins when...
How to win	The team with the most points wins. / The object is to score the most runs.
Location	It's played on a field. / It's played all over the world.

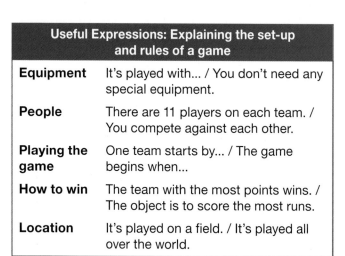

5 GRAMMAR

A Turn to page 208. Complete the exercises. Then do **B** and **C** below.

The Present Perfect vs. the Present Perfect Continuous
I've played cricket <u>since I was a child</u>. = **I've been playing** cricket <u>since I was a child</u>.
I've read a book about long-distance running. It was excellent. (The action is completed.)   ≠   **I've been reading** a book about long-distance running. I'm enjoying it. (The action is ongoing.)
I've been going to the gym a lot <u>lately</u>.   <u>Recently</u> **I've been working out** more.
~~**I've been owning** that car for ten years.~~   **I've owned** that car for ten years.
~~**I've been taking** this test three times already.~~   **I've taken** this test three times already.

B On a piece of paper, answer the questions using the present perfect or present perfect continuous tense.

1. What is one extracurricular activity you've participated in this year?
2. What is one you've been participating in recently?

3. Name someone who has moved recently.
4. Name someone who has been living in the same place for a long time.

5. What celebrity has received a lot of attention from the media?
6. What celebrity have people been talking about lately?

7. What is one helpful thing you've learned in school?
8. What is something you've been studying for a long time, but don't really like?

9. What is one classroom activity you've disliked?
10. What is one you've been enjoying recently?

C 🔄 Now ask a partner the questions in **B**. Ask follow-up questions to get more information.

> What is one extracurricular activity you've participated in this year?

> I've been a member of the drama club. It's a lot of fun.

> What do you like about it?

5 GRAMMAR
The present perfect vs. the present perfect continuous

WARM UP Write true sentences about yourself using the present perfect and present perfect continuous. For example, *I have been riding horses since 1995* or *I have lived in Santiago for five years*. Ask students to each give a true sentence about themselves using one of the same tenses.
⏱ 5 min

A Turn to page 208. Complete the exercises. Then do **B** and **C** below. ◗ 20–30 min

Have students look at the first pair of examples and ask, *Does he still play cricket?* (Yes.) Then have students look at the second pair of examples, help them see the difference between the finished action with present perfect and the ongoing activity with present perfect continuous. Go over the next pair of examples, pointing out the words *lately* and *recently*, which are often used with the present perfect continuous. Compare the examples in the chart with your examples on the board from the Warm Up. Then go over the final two pairs of examples and help students see how they cannot be continuous because they are not ongoing actions (*own* is a state, and an exam is taken once each time and finished).

Remind students about stative verbs, verbs which describe mental states and senses (for example: *know*, *understand*, *believe*, *taste*, *smell*) rather than actions and so aren't usually used in continuous tenses. The grammar chart on page 208 includes further examples, negatives, and detailed use explanations, expanding on the information in the chart on page 114.

GRAMMAR TIP: Present perfect and present perfect continuous

The present perfect continuous is used to emphasize the ongoing aspect of an activity that began in the past and still continues. With certain verbs, such as *live* and *work,* the present perfect can also be used with the same meaning. For example, *I've worked here for 10 years* has the same meaning as *I've been working here for 10 years*. The second sentence leaves the listener believing that the speaker will most likely continue to work here. The first sentence could be interpreted as the person is quitting the job or could mean the person will continue to work here.

The continuous tenses are not used with stative verbs. It is not correct to say **I have been knowing him since I was young.*

B On a piece of paper, answer the questions using the present perfect or present perfect continuous tense. ◗ 10–15 min

Have students read and answer the questions individually. Monitor and help as necessary, referring students back to the charts on this page and on page 208 to help them.

C 🔁 Now ask a partner the questions in **B**. Ask follow-up questions to get more information. ◗ 10–15 min

Have students look at the photo and say what is happening. Then model the example with a student. Point out the follow-up question. *What do you like about it?* Model again by having a student ask you one of the questions and providing an answer of your own. Encourage the student to ask you another follow-up question. Assign students to pairs to ask and answer questions. Monitor and prompt students to ask follow-up questions and keep the conversation going as necessary.

EXTRA! Discussion
Write these questions on the board for students to discuss in pairs or groups.
1. What is a television program or series that you have been watching for a long time? How long have you been watching it?
2. How long have you been living where you live now?
3. For how many years have you been studying English?
⏱ 10–15 min

🎵 **GRAMMAR TUTORIALS**
• Present Perfect vs. Present Perfect Continuous

Additional tutorials are available for reteaching and reinforcement.

Instructor's Notes

_____

_____

_____

_____

_____

_____

_____

_____

_____

_____

6 COMMUNICATION

WARM UP Ask, *Have you ever told a white lie?* Call on students to tell the class about their experiences. A white lie is when you say something that isn't true in order to not hurt someone's feelings or because it isn't convenient to tell the truth. A white lie is sometimes considered OK because it isn't usually harmful to other people. ⏱ 5 min

A Write about two things you started doing in the past and still do today. ⏱ 5 min

Read the example with the class, then have students write their own examples. To help students think of ideas, brainstorm a list of possible categories with the class. For example: hobbies, sports, musical or artistic interests, academic interests, travel plans, interests in certain authors, or types of books or movies. Provide vocabulary as necessary. Monitor and check that students are using the tenses correctly.

B 🔾 Get into a group of three people. Follow the steps below. ⏱ 10 min

(See Student Book page 115 for complete instructions.)

Go over the directions and the steps with the students. Make sure they understand that they will share their sentences from **A** with their group, but that the group will only choose one of the activities to ask questions about. Assign students to groups of three to carry out the exercise. Monitor and check that all groups have understood the directions. Provide help as necessary. Remind them to ask as many questions as possible about the activity so that they all know a lot of details. This will allow them to do **C** successfully.

C 🔾 Take turns playing a guessing game as a class. Follow the steps below. ⏱ 20–25 min

(See Student Book page 115 for complete instructions.)

Go over the directions and the steps with the students. Make sure they understand that in each group, they are **all** going to answer questions about the activity they talked about in **B**. The class is going to guess which student has really been doing that activity, so they need to be convincing. Have one group of three come to the front and model the exercise with the class, using the example. Have groups take turns coming to the front. Remember to allow only two minutes for questions before the class has to guess who they think is telling the truth. Finish the exercise by asking which activity they thought was the most interesting, which one they would like to try, and which one they would like to know more about.

LARGE CLASS OPTION

This game can work well in a large classroom by having both the student group and a panel of questioners come to the front of the class. The panel of three students should be on one side of the room. On the other side, put a panel of three students who will ask them questions. At the end, the panel should give their votes for who is telling the truth and the rest of the student audience should vote as well.

EXTRA! Dictation

Follow the instructions in the Teaching Tip below to dictate the following paragraph: *My family has been coming to the beach here every summer since 2013. My son has been learning how to scuba dive and water ski. My wife has gone swimming almost every day while I have been sitting on the beach and reading. We hope to come back again next year.* ⏱ 10–15 min

TEACHING TIP: Dictogloss

This is a form of dictation that can be used to practice a grammar point. Before class, prepare a short text (such as a single long paragraph) that contains a number of examples of the language you want to teach. Put students in groups of three or four. Introduce the topic of the text, and discuss what they know about it to activate background knowledge. Tell students that you will read the text only once, and they should note down as many words and phrases as they can. Emphasize that they are NOT expected to copy down the entire text. Then read the text without pausing, at a normal rate or slightly slower. Give students time to finish writing. Then tell them to work with their group members to put together the entire text. Walk around helping as needed, reminding them of what they know about the target structure. When all groups have finished, compare versions as a class, sentence by sentence, and compile a single correct paragraph on the board. Finish by reading the complete paragraph again, at normal speed.

Instructor's Notes

_____

_____

_____

_____

_____

_____

6 COMMUNICATION

A Write about two things you started doing in the past and still do today.

> I've been making model airplanes since I was a little kid.

> I've been learning how to cook French food for the past year.

1. _____

2. _____

B 🔾 Get into a group of three people. Follow the steps below.

1. Look at the sentences each student wrote in **A**. Choose one sentence to talk about.

2. Ask the student who wrote the sentence as many questions as possible about the sentence. You will have two minutes to learn everything you can.

C 🔾 Take turns playing a guessing game as a class. Follow the steps below.

1. Now the group of three students stands in front of the class. All three students say the sentence they chose in **B**. Two students lie, but they want the class to believe that they are the ones who have had the experience.

> I've been learning how to cook French food for the past year.

2. The other students in the class ask the members of the group questions. They have two minutes to find out which student is telling the truth, and which two are lying.

> Dmitri, what's your favorite French food?

> Carmen, what's one dish you've learned to make?

> Kumiko, who has taught you how to cook French food?

2 LISTENING

STRATEGIES: Listen for gist; Listen for details

WARM UP Have students look at the picture and say where the person is and what they think he is doing and why. ⏱ 5 min

A 💬 Is there an activity that you've always wanted to try? What is it? Tell a partner. ⏱ 5 min

Go over the question with the class and have them think about their answer and their reasons for wanting to try the activity. Provide vocabulary as necessary. Then assign them to pairs to talk about the activity. Call on different students to tell the class what activity their partner would like to try and why. Write a list on the board.

B 🔊 **Listen for gist.** Listen to the beginning of the conversation. What activities are part of parkour?
CD2 Track 12 ⏱ 5 min

Go over the five options then play the audio. Check answers with the class.

Listen for gist. Remind students that when listening for gist, they don't need to worry about understanding everything they hear, the purpose is to understand the general idea.

C 🔊 **Listen for details.** Listen to the conversation. Circle the correct sentence (a or b). **CD 2 Track 13** ⏱ 10 min

Go over the sentences, then play the audio. Have students compare their answers with a partner's, then play the audio again. Check answers with the class, playing the audio again and pausing as necessary.

Listen for details. Remind students that they do not need to hear and understand everything in order to understand specific details. Encourage them to get into the habit of identifying key words to listen for before they listen.

D 💬 Would you like to try this activity? Why or why not? Tell a partner. ⏱ 10 min

Have students think about their answer to the question and their reasons, then assign them to pairs. Monitor and provide help, asking questions to prompt further conversation. Call on different students to say whether their partner would like to try parkour or not, and why.

Now that students know about parkour, tell them to look again at the photo at the top of the page. Ask them to describe what the man is doing. What would the next two or three images show if this were a film or a series of photos?

CULTURE TIP: Parkour
Parkour is a training regimen in which a person moves through their surroundings as if on an obstacle course. The person uses a variety of movements, such as running, jumping, vaulting, and climbing, depending on the location. The person practicing parkour is supposed to see the area in terms of how to pass over, under, around, and through objects or structures. It is usually practiced in urban settings.

Instructor's Notes

_____

_____

_____

_____

_____

_____

_____

_____

_____

_____

_____

_____

_____

_____

_____

_____

2 LISTENING

A 🔄 Is there an activity that you've always wanted to try? What is it? Tell a partner.

B 🔊 **Listen for gist.** Listen to the beginning of the conversation. What activities are part of parkour?
CD 2 Track 12

running   mountain biking   swimming   jumping   climbing

C 🔊 **Listen for details.** Listen to the conversation. Circle the correct sentence (a or b).
CD 2 Track 13

1. a. The man will run, jump, and climb in cities and parks.

   b. The man will run, jump, and climb in stadiums.

2. a. The man is careful and studies an area before he starts.

   b. The man starts and deals with challenges when he sees them.

3. a. There is a paramedic nearby if something bad happens.

   b. His friend has a first-aid kit and phone if something bad happens.

4. a. The purpose of the trip is to accomplish a goal and show people a way to be active.

   b. The purpose of the trip is to get from one place to another.

D 🔄 Would you like to try this activity? Why or why not? Tell a partner.

3 READING

3 READING

STRATEGIES: Use background knowledge; Scan for information; Read for details

WARM UP Are there any sports that you would consider dangerous or scary? What are those sports? Do you think you would like to try them? Some possible answers: snowboarding, parachuting, ski jumping, rock climbing. ⏱ 5 min

A 🔁 **Use background knowledge.** Look at the title of the article and the photo. Ask and answer these questions with a partner. ⏱ 5–10 min

In this exercise, students should read and focus only on the title of the reading and the photo. Tell students to NOT read the article, and to only look at the title and photo, then answer the questions with a partner.

Use background knowledge. Students bring to any text the knowledge they already have about life and the world in general, as well as any knowledge they have about the specific topic of the text. Students need to know that they should draw on this knowledge to help them understand what they are reading.

B **Scan for information.** Look quickly at the article. Add at least two examples to each item in the chart below. ⏱ 5–10 min

Remind students to read quickly. Tell them to close their books when they have finished—make a note of which students finish first. After checking answers, ask the fastest, as well as the most accurate, students how they did this.

Scan for information. Remind students that scanning means looking over a text quickly in order to find specific information. Students shouldn't read in detail until they find the information they are looking for.

A 🔁 **Use background knowledge.** Look at the title of the article and the photo. Ask and answer these questions with a partner.

1. Have you ever heard of the X Games?
2. Can you name any sports that are played at these games?

B **Scan for information.** Look quickly at the article. Add at least two examples to each item in the chart below.

Item	Examples
1. summer sports	
2. winter sports	
3. regional teams in the global championships	
4. categories of in-line skating	

C **Read for details.** Read the statements about Fabiola. Then find a sentence in the reading that supports each statement.

1. Fabiola's mom didn't make a lot of money. _____
2. Fabiola wins against women. _____
3. Fabiola wins against men. _____
4. Fabiola is well known outside her own country. _____
5. Fabiola has her own sense of style. _____

D 🔁 Who are some popular female athletes you know? What sports do they play? Which would you rather see, the Olympics or the X Games? Why? Discuss with a partner.

118 UNIT 8 ● The active life

A STAR IN THE X GAMES

When the X Games first started out, they were not well known. Only a few people watched and competed in them. However, the Games had an attitude and style that reflected things many young people cared about, and in time, they became popular around the world.

In different areas of the world, athletes train and compete in their own versions of the X Games. The best athletes can advance to the global championship. At the championship, teams from six regions (Asia, Australia, Canada, Europe, South America, and the United States) face each other. There are summer sports (in-line skating, biking, and skateboarding) and winter ones (skiing and snowboarding). The sports are so popular that some are even in the Olympics now!

There are many champions in the X Games, but one woman, Fabiola da Silva, has always stood

---

EXTRA! Comprehension questions

Have students answer further questions about the article:
Were the X Games always popular? Why or why not?
How would you describe Fabiola's style of clothing?
Was it easy for Fabiola to become a skater as a child?
Does Fabiola think of herself as a celebrity?
⏱ 5–10 min

EXTRA! Writing prompt

Write a paragraph about a favorite athlete, and why you admire him or her.
⏱ 10–15 min

out from the crowd. She's an in-line skater from Brazil, and she's easily recognizable with her tank top and nose ring.

There are two different in-line skating categories: *park* and *vert*. In the park event, skaters compete on a course that has ledges, handrails, and other obstacles. In the vert event, skaters do tricks on a half-pipe[1]. They try to fly high in the air and spin. Fabiola competes in both events and has won six gold medals in the vert event, her specialty. She has been skating for years and has dominated[2] the women's events.

Fabiola is a pioneer. She was one of the first women to get very famous from the X Games, but she's not afraid of the guys. Ever since she received her first pair of skates at the age of 12, she's played with boys. Now she skates in competitions with them, and she beats many of them.

Fabiola's mother was a housekeeper and life was hard, but she saved her money to buy Fabiola's skates. It was a good investment. Fabiola has traveled abroad for events and has become famous in the international skating world.

Success hasn't gone to her head[3], though. She's still a typical young woman: she has a boyfriend, likes to listen to rock music, and prefers healthy foods. And she doesn't seem to care much about the attention she gets.

[1]A *half-pipe* is a curved structure with high sides, used for doing tricks.
[2]If you *dominate*, you are powerful and successful.
[3]If something *goes to your head*, it makes you think you are very important.

TEACHING TIP: Scanning
Scanning is an important real-life reading skill for students to practice. Students may feel that to read "properly" they need to read and understand every word in a text. Point out to them that when reading in their native language, they read many different ways—sometimes slowly and carefully, and other times more quickly, just to find the information they need. Point out that this is the same in any language.

EXTRA! Discussion questions
1. Is there an athlete that you like and admire? Who is it? What sport does he or she compete in? Why is he or she well known?

2. What sport would you compete in if you were a famous athlete?

3. Are there any sports that are too dangerous to try? What are they? 🕐 10–25 min

C Read for details. Read the statements about Fabiola. Then find a sentence in the reading that supports each statement. 🕐 10–15 min

Tell students that they will now look back through the article and read it more slowly and carefully. Point out the definitions in the footnotes. Tell them to circle any vocabulary they don't understand. Tell them to underline the sentences in the story that support each statement and to write them down.

Read for details. Remind students that reading for details means reading a text more slowly and in depth. When they read for details they should pay attention to unfamiliar words, but try to guess their meaning from the context before they look them up.

D 🔁 Who are some popular female athletes you know? What sports do they play? Which would you rather see, the Olympics or the X Games? Why? Discuss with a partner. 🕐 10–15 min

Go over the questions with the class, then assign students to pairs to discuss them. Tell pairs to make a list of well-known female athletes and the sports they play. Monitor as students discuss the questions and prompt with follow-up questions as necessary. Call on pairs to share their lists and write a class list on the board. Take a poll of the class: How many would rather see the Olympics? The X Games?

TEACHING TIP: Schema building
Research has shown that students can understand what they read better if they already have knowledge to fit the new information into. The existing background information is called *schema*. To help students with comprehension, spend time before the reading doing *schema-building exercises*. These exercises include helping students think about what they already know about a topic and looking at pictures in the reading. It is also helpful for students to look at titles and headings.

4 GRAMMAR

A Turn to page 209. Complete the exercises. Then do **B–D** below.

Review: The Simple Past vs. the Present Perfect vs. the Present Perfect Continuous		
	Completed past action	**Actions started in the past continuing up to now**
Simple past	I **visited** South Africa <u>in 2010</u>.	
Present perfect	I**'ve visited** South Africa once.	Fabiola **has skated** for years.
Present perfect continuous		Fabiola **has been skating** for years.

B With a partner, complete the chart with the names of famous people you know something about.

Actors	
Singers	
Athletes	
Others (your idea)	

C With the same partner, choose one of the famous people in **B**. Complete the sentences about him or her. Then write the questions you would ask to get that information.

Sentences	Questions
1. I was born in _____.	When / Where were you born?
2. I became famous because _____.	
3. I've _____ since _____. I've been _____ for _____.	
4. I got interested in _____ when I _____.	
5. I've recently been in the news because _____.	

D Join another pair. Use the questions in **C** to interview the other pair. You might need to change some questions. Can you guess their famous person's name?

> How long have you been playing baseball professionally?

> I've been playing for five years.

4 GRAMMAR
Review: The simple past vs. the present perfect vs. the present perfect continuous

WARM UP Review the present perfect by asking the class questions like, *How long have you lived here? Have you ever been to (Spain)?* After one student answers, have another student repeat the answer in the third person. Student A: *I've lived here for three years.* Student B: *She's lived here for three years.* ⏱ 5 min

A Turn to page 209. Complete the exercises. Then do **B–D** below. ◑ 20–30 min

Go over the examples in the chart and focus students' attention on the time expressions used in each one. Remind students that although both present perfect and simple past can be used to talk about completed actions in the past, with specific times in the past (*in 2010*, *last year*, *on Monday*, etc.), the simple past must be used. The grammar chart on page 209 includes further examples and use explanations, expanding on the information in the chart on page 120.

GRAMMAR TIP: Simple past vs. present perfect
Remember that the simple past is used when the listener knows or the speaker says when the action took place. The present perfect is used when the speaker is not specifying when the action took place. *I went to Spain last year* instead of *I've been to Spain* (at some undetermined time in the past).

B With a partner, complete the chart with the names of famous people you know something about. ⏱ 5 min

Go over the directions with the class, pointing out that they should only write the names of people that they know a little bit about. Have them complete the chart with a partner.

C With the same partner, choose one of the famous people in **B**. Complete the sentences about him or her. Then write the questions you would ask to get that information. ⏱ 10–15 min

Go over the directions and the chart with the class. Point out the first question as an example. Then have students complete the information about the famous person they have chosen and write the questions. Refer them back to the chart on this page and on page 209 as necessary. Monitor and provide help as necessary. Make sure students have the questions completed correctly because they will need them for **D**. If necessary, and if there is access to the Internet, allow students to search for information about their person.

D Join another pair. Use the questions in **C** to interview the other pair. You might need to change some questions. Can you guess their famous person's name? 🕐 10–15 min

Have pairs join to make groups of four students. Model the example with a student. Point out to students that they will need to change their questions depending on the other pair's person; for example, they may need to say *How long have you been acting?* instead of *How long have you been playing baseball?* They should take turns interviewing each other to guess who the famous person is.

TEACHING TIP: Students explaining grammar
It is important that students be able to explain why they choose the answers they do while completing exercises in class. Students who are just lucky with guessing will not be as successful language users as those who can explain why they do what they do. It is useful to have students explain why they gave the answers they did.

For further practice, write incorrect sentences on the board and have good students come to the front of the class and correct them, while explaining why they made the changes.

GRAMMAR TUTORIALS
• The Simple Past Tense vs. the Perfect Tenses

Additional tutorials are available for reteaching and reinforcement.

Instructor's Notes

_____

_____

_____

_____

_____

_____

_____

_____

_____

5 WRITING

WARM UP Have students look at the photo and say what the young woman is doing. Ask, *Do you think she is a professional or is it a hobby?* ⏱ 5 min

A 🔄 Read the paragraphs. Answer the questions with a partner. ⏱ 10 min

Go over the questions with the class. Then have students read the paragraphs and answer the questions with a partner. Check answers with the class.

B What is your hobby? Answer the questions in **A**. Then use your notes and the example to help you write three paragraphs of your own. ◑ 20–25 min

Tell the class about your hobby. Be sure to include the information needed to answer the questions in **A**. Write the topics of the four questions on the board as headers for an outline, for example:

My hobby:	
How long:	
At first? Now?	
Why I like it:	

Ask the class the questions in **A** about your hobby and, with their answers, write notes in the chart. Then have the class help you begin writing your paragraphs using the ones in **A** as a model, and your notes in the chart as an outline. Make sure students suggest examples with the present perfect when they tell you what to write in the first paragraph. Then have students decide the hobby they are going to write about and do an outline. After doing their outline, have them write their paragraphs following the model in **A**. Monitor and provide help as necessary. Make sure they use the present perfect tenses and the simple past. Refer them back to pages 120 and 209 as necessary.

C 🔄 Exchange your writing with a partner. Read his or her paragraphs. ◑ 10–15 min

(See Student Book page 121 for complete instructions.)

Assign students to pairs and have them exchange papers and identify any mistakes in their partner's paragraphs. Tell them to focus on the use of the simple past and present perfect tenses and vocabulary related to describing an activity. Then have students answer the questions in **A** about their partner's paragraphs. Encourage students to talk about their paragraphs together: *What was clear? What was confusing? What could be better?* Then have students rewrite their paragraphs, making the corrections and taking into account their partner's comments on how to improve them. Provide help as necessary. Collect the paragraphs to give feedback if possible.

PROCESS WRITING: Outlining

A useful way for students to learn to structure their writing is through outlining. When making an outline, students break their subject down into smaller parts. In this case students can use the questions in **A** as the main topics in their outline. Underneath these main topics they can jot down supporting ideas. Students often want to rush directly into writing. It is a good practice to help them slow down and plan their writing before they plunge in.

6 COMMUNICATION

WARM UP Ask students what they think the most popular hobbies are around the world. ⏱ 5 min

A Write the four questions from Writing **A** so they are in the second person (*you*) form. ⏱ 5–10 min

Point out the first question in Writing **A** and how it is has been changed here. Then have students write the rest of the questions. Have students compare their questions with a partner's. Check the questions with the class to make sure everyone has them done correctly.

B 🔄 Interview six classmates using the questions in **A**. Take notes on their answers. ◑ 10–15 min

Go over the directions, reminding students to take notes because they will need them for **C**. Model the exercise by asking a student the first two questions and writing notes of his or her answers. Have students interview their classmates.

C 🔄 Work with a partner. Answer the questions. ⏱ 10 min

Go over the questions with the class, then assign students to pairs to answer them. When they have finished discussing, call on different pairs to share their answers. Do they all agree on each question? What differences in opinion are there?

Instructor's Notes

_____

_____

_____

_____

_____

_____

_____

5 WRITING

A 🔁 Read the paragraphs. Answer the questions with a partner.

1. What is the writer's hobby?

2. How long has she been doing it?

3. Was she good at the activity at first? Is she good at it now?

4. Why does she like the activity?

> My hobby is rock climbing. I've been doing it for a year. In the beginning, I wasn't very good, but I've gotten better.
>
> I started rock climbing in high school. I went to an indoor place with my friends. On the first day, I was really nervous, so I only climbed low rocks. It was hard, but fun. I kept working, and now I can climb very fast. I even climb outside now.
>
> I like rock climbing because it helps me stay in shape. It's also a good way to make friends. I've met a lot of people. We climb, but we also hang out and spend time doing other things now.

B What is your hobby? Answer the questions in **A**. Then use your notes and the example to help you write three paragraphs of your own.

C 🔁 Exchange your writing with a partner. Read his or her paragraphs.

1. Are there any mistakes? If yes, circle them.

2. Answer the questions in **A** about your partner's writing.

3. Return the paper to your partner. Make corrections to your own paragraphs.

6 COMMUNICATION

A Write the four questions from Writing **A** so they are in the second person (*you*) form.

1. What is your hobby?

2. _____

3. _____

4. _____

B 👥 Interview six classmates using the questions in **A**. Take notes on their answers.

C 🔁 Work with a partner. Answer the questions.

In your class…

1. which hobbies are the most popular?

2. which hobby is the most interesting or unusual?

3. who's been doing his or her hobby the longest?

> How long have you been doing it?

> Since last year.

9 SOCIAL ISSUES

ABOUT THE PHOTO

The reality of life in downtown Bangkok, Thailand's capital and largest city, is one of heavy traffic, crowds, and high levels of energy consumption. This photo shows CentralWorld, the largest shopping complex in Thailand. CentralWorld has about 500 stores, 100 restaurants and cafes, movie theaters, a hotel, and an ice-skating rink. Such urban growth and development is not without its issues. The rising demand for electricity in Thailand, and other countries, can lead to ecological problems. The Mekong River, which flows through Thailand, Cambodia, Laos, Vietnam, China, and Myanmar, is being dammed to provide Southeast Asia with electricity. The electricity is clean, but the dams have caused increased flooding and a decline in fish populations, both of which adversely affect life along the Mekong. Finding solutions that work for everyone is an important objective for the 21st century.

Did you know?

With a metropolitan area population of nearly 15 million, Bangkok is considered one of the world's megacities.

INTRODUCE THE THEME

- In this unit, students will explore the concept of social issues. Students will communicate about social and environmental problems, including being able to give a presentation on an issue, discussing problems,

	Video	Vocabulary	Listening
LESSON A In my community p. 124	Seven Billion p. 124	Political campaigns p. 125 *making progress, candidate, vote for*	A campaign speech p. 126 Use background knowledge Listen for gist Listen for context Listen for main ideas
LESSON B Modern challenges p. 130		Urban sprawl p. 130 *development, waste, improve*	Urban and suburban issues p. 131 Listen for details Infer information Listen for reasons

 **For students:** My World Link Online has personalized instruction, practice, audio, and video.

Look at the photo. Answer the questions.

1 What problems do you see in the photo?

2 Do these things happen where you live?

3 What is an important social issue (problem) where you live?

UNIT GOALS

1 Give a short formal presentation

2 State the purpose and important points of your presentation

3 Discuss environmental and social problems

4 Make predictions and talk about consequences

Traffic in downtown Bangkok, Thailand

making predictions, and talking about consequences.

- In Lesson A, students watch a video which presents statistics about the world's population. Students will then learn how to talk about elections. They will also practice the listening strategies of using background knowledge, listening for gist, listening for context, and listening for main ideas. Then they will learn how to give a short, formal presentation.

- In Lesson B, students will learn how to describe problems in urban areas. They will also read about a program where young children spend time with senior citizens, practicing the reading strategies of using background knowledge, making predictions, inferring information and meaning, reading for details, and drawing conclusions. They will also give predictions and explain consequences, as well as discuss problems and suggest solutions.

WARM UP

Look at the photo. Answer the questions.

- Call on students to describe what they see in the photo.

- Have students answer the questions individually or in pairs, then compare answers with the class.

- Point out the unit goals and explain what students will learn. Elicit any key vocabulary students already know, and write it on the board. Explain any unfamiliar phrases in the unit goals to the students.

Grammar	Pronunciation	Speaking	Reading	Writing	Communication
Too and *enough* pp. 128, 210	Using pauses in public speaking p. 127	Language for presentations p. 127	People of all ages p. 132 Use background knowledge Make predictions Infer information Infer meaning Read for details Draw conclusions	State your opinion about a future event p. 134	Completing and talking about a lifestyle survey p. 129
Future real conditionals pp. 134, 211					Giving a speech about a solution to a problem p. 135

Apartment buildings in Hong Kong, one of the *megacities* of the world.

1 VIDEO Seven Billion

A Currently, over 7 billion people live on Earth, and the number is increasing. Do you think this is a problem? Why or why not? Discuss with a partner.

B ▶ Work with a partner. Read the questions and guess the answers. Then watch the video to check your guesses.

1. It would take 2 / 20 / 200 years just to count to 7 billion out loud.

2. In 2045, the world's population could be 9 / 12 / 15 billion.

3. In 2010, the average person lived 53 / 61 / 69 years.

4. In 1960, the average person lived 53 / 61 / 69 years.

5. In 1975, the world's three megacities were New York City, Tokyo, and Mexico City / Rome / Sydney.

6. Right now there are 7 / 14 / 21 megacities in the world.

7. By 2050, 50 / 70 / 90% of us will be living in cities.

8. Seven billion people, speaking 7,000 languages, living in 19 / 94 / 194 countries.

C Read these statistics from the end of the video. Which one is the biggest problem and why? Discuss with a partner.

5% of the population consumes 23% of the world's energy.

13% of the people in the world don't have clean drinking water.

38% of the world's population lacks adequate sanitation.

WORLD LINK

Go online and find one other problem that population growth is causing in the world. Report back to the class.

1 VIDEO
Seven Billion

WARM UP Have students look at the photo and describe what they see. How many students live in a large city like this? How many would like to? Why or why not? Write on the board any key vocabulary that comes up related to large cities. ⏱ 5 min

ABOUT THE VIDEO
On October 31st, 2011, the world's population became seven billion. To coincide with this, *National Geographic* magazine did a year-long series on world population. This video is part of that series and presents interesting facts and figures related to population growth. It also shows us what seven billion people looks like, and what the future possibly holds for us in terms of continued population growth. The video ends with a focus on the need to achieve balance. At the moment, we live in a very unbalanced world, with 5% of the population consuming 23% of the world's energy. Being one of seven billion is something for us all to think about; a population of seven billion and rising has a big impact on the Earth and its resources, as well as how those resources are used. We need to become responsible users of the resources, working together to solve the problems we face.

TEACHING TIP: Using English videos
It can be helpful to pre-teach some of the key vocabulary that is new to students before they watch a video. If there are key words or phrases that they don't know, but which are essential to understanding the main idea, provide them and have students look them up before watching, or provide definitions and examples. For example, in this video, it would help for students to know *urban / rural areas*, *increase*, *average*, *balance*, *consume*, and *lack* before they listen.

A 🎬 Currently, over 7 billion people live on Earth, and the number is increasing. Do you think this is a problem? Why or why not? Discuss with a partner. ⏱ 5–10 min

Assign students to pairs to discuss the question. Compare opinions as a class. Write key vocabulary on the board.

B ▶ 🎬 Work with a partner. Read the questions and guess the answers. Then watch the video to check your guesses. ⏱ 10 min

Go over the statements with the class and say the numbers and years for students to repeat. Before watching, assign students to pairs to guess the correct option to complete each statement. Have students share their guesses, then play the video.

C 🎬 Read these statistics from the end of the video. Which one is the biggest problem and why? Discuss with a partner. ⏱ 10 min

Have students read the statistics and think about their answer to the question, then assign them to pairs to share their answer and explain why. Monitor and provide help as necessary. Ask follow-up questions to encourage more conversation. Survey the class to find out which one they think is the biggest problem, and why.

EXTRA! Post-viewing
In pairs, have students research one of the world's megacities and give a short presentation about it. Pairs can present their information to another pair or in small groups (try to group pairs who have chosen different cities). ⏱ 10 min

Extra video vocabulary
average person
balance
consume
increase
lack (adequate sanitation)
rural areas
urban areas

WORLD LINK

Go online and find one other problem that population growth is causing in the world. Report back to the class.

Have students research problems related to population growth and report back to the class. They can share their problem with the class or in small groups depending on class size.

2 VOCABULARY

WARM UP Write the titles of elected officials on the board. You might include: *mayor, governor, president, representative, senator, councilor,* or other titles that apply in your location. Ask students how many of their elected officials they can name. Ask what issues people are concerned about locally. ⏱ 5 min

A Doris Chavez and Amelia Smith are running for mayor. Read their ads. Then answer the questions by checking the correct box(es) with a partner. ⏱ 5–10 min

Tell students that these are posters for two candidates for mayor. Assign students to pairs to read the posters and work together to figure out the meaning of any words they don't know. At this point do not explain any words because students will have more time to work on figuring them out in **B**. When they finish reading, they should work together to answer the questions.

CULTURE TIP: The language of politics
The advertisements for Doris Chavez and Amelia Smith provide excellent examples of language that is often used in political campaigns in many countries. Doris Chavez is currently mayor. She says, *We're making progress...,* and *Why change now?* Amelia Smith wants the mayor's job. She suggests, *No more politics as usual,* and *It's time for change...* Point out that the messages are very direct and that the tone is forceful, but inclusive. Note also the emphasis on three common concerns: education, taxes, and public safety.

B Look at the information in **A**. Write the word(s) in blue next to their definitions. ⏱ 10–15 min

Give students time to fill in the blanks. Call on students to tell you their answers, and discuss the answers with the class. Ask students what new words they learned and write them on the board. Then explain any words that are still unclear. Note that the word *fixed* in number 3 has multiple meanings. Here it means *settled, determined, unchanging,* or *agreed-upon.*

C Discuss the questions with a partner. ⏱ 10 min

Go over the questions with the class. Have students think about their answers to the questions, then assign them to pairs to talk about their answers. Monitor and provide help as necessary. Ask follow-up questions to encourage more conversation. Survey the class to find out how politicians campaign in different places.

CULTURE TIP: Elections
Voting and elections differ around the world, but there are many common features. Often the candidates belong to political parties, which present different points of view, both liberal and conservative. How to spend taxpayers' money is usually an issue. The established candidates point to what they have already accomplished, while their challengers assert that a change would be better.

EXTRA! Campaign
Divide the class into three groups of equal size for a role play and debate. One group will organize the mayoral campaign of Doris Chavez from **A**.

The second group will organize the campaign of Amelia Smith from **A**. The third group will be the voters. They will vote on who should win the election. The campaigning groups should:

- select one member to be the candidate.
- write a speech for the candidate to deliver, stating her positions.
- come up with new advertising slogans for the candidate.

Meanwhile, the voters should prepare questions to ask the candidates. When everyone is finished, each candidate should give her speech. After this, the voters ask questions. Finally, the voters vote by secret ballot. The candidate with the most votes wins the election. ⏱ 20 min

Instructor's Notes

_____

_____

_____

_____

_____

_____

_____

_____

_____

_____

_____

_____

_____

2 VOCABULARY

A 🔁 Doris Chavez and Amelia Smith are running for mayor. Read their ads. Then answer the questions by checking the correct box(es) with a partner.

DORIS CHAVEZ for mayor!

"We're making progress in many areas. Why change now? Reelect Doris Chavez!"

In her first term, Mayor Chavez:
• launched a new school lunch program for elementary school students.
• taxed large companies to raise extra money.
• worked enthusiastically to improve life for everyone—crime is down 30%.

There is no better candidate than Doris Chavez for mayor!

AMELIA SMITH for mayor! ★ ★ ★ ★ ★

"No more politics as usual. It's time for change in our city! Vote for Amelia Smith!"

Amelia Smith vows:
• to expand the school lunch program to include older students.
• not to raise taxes on corporations.
• to work hard for all citizens to keep our city streets safe.

Amelia Smith is the clear choice for mayor!

	Doris	Amelia
1. Who is currently the mayor?	☐	☐
2. Who doesn't want to increase taxes?	☐	☐
3. Who is interested in the school lunch program?	☐	☐
4. Who mentions crime and safety?	☐	☐

B Look at the information in **A**. Write the word(s) in **blue** next to their definitions.

1. doing (something) the same way: ___as usual___
2. eagerly, with great energy: _____
3. a fixed period of time: _____
4. increase in size: _____
5. large companies: _____
6. started: _____
7. promises: _____
8. moving forward: _____
9. obvious: _____
10. a person who is competing for a position: _____
11. members of a city or country: _____
12. made someone pay money to the government: _____

C 🔁 Discuss the questions with a partner.

1. Do you ever see ads like the ones in **A**? How else do politicians campaign where you live?

2. Think of a person who was up for reelection recently. Did people vote for or against him or her? Why?

3 LISTENING

A **Use background knowledge.** Read the sentences below. What does the word in bold mean? When do election campaigns typically happen?

There are two candidates running for mayor. The **campaign** will begin on February 1st, and the election will be on March 15th.

B 🔊 **Listen for gist.** Listen to the beginning of speeches given by Doris and Amelia. Choose the best answer to complete each sentence. (One answer is extra.) **CD 2 Track 15**

1. Doris is giving her speech because _____

2. Amelia is giving her speech because _____

    a. she is going to run for mayor.

    b. she has been elected mayor.

    c. she has lost the race for mayor.

C 🔊 **Listen for context.** Listen again. Choose the best answers. **CD 2 Track 15**

1. When Doris says *never in my wildest dreams*, she means...

    a. she was pretty sure.

    b. she couldn't imagine it.

2. When Doris says *I gave it my best shot*, she means...

    a. she was very disappointed.

    b. she worked really hard.

3. When Amelia says *Doris and I were running neck and neck*, she means...

    a. they had almost the same number of votes.

    b. there was a clear winner.

4. When Amelia says *we saw a record turnout*, she means...

    a. a large number of people voted.

    b. a small number of people voted.

D 🔊 💬 **Listen for main ideas.** Now listen to the rest of Amelia's speech. Check (✓) the topics she refers to in her speech. What key words in the listening helped you choose your answers? Tell a partner. **CD 2 Track 16**

☐ the economy   ☐ public transportation   ☐ crime   ☐ pollution   ☐ education

E 💬 Look at the topics in **D**. Which one do you think is the biggest problem where you live? Why? Tell a partner.

Pollution is a major problem for many cities.

3 LISTENING

STRATEGIES: Use background knowledge; Listen for gist; Listen for context; Listen for main ideas

WARM UP Have students look at the photo at the bottom of the page and describe the problem. What other problems do cities have? Make a list on the board. ⏱ 5 min

A Use background knowledge. Read the sentences below. What does the word in bold mean? When do election campaigns typically happen? ⏱ 5 min

The answer to the question *When do election campaigns typically happen?* will vary, depending on your location. A *campaign* is the period before the election when candidates try to persuade citizens to vote for them. The timing depends on when the election takes place.

Use background knowledge. Students bring to any text the knowledge they already have about life and the world in general, as well as any knowledge they have about the specific topic of the text. Students need to know that they should draw on this knowledge to help them understand what they are going to listen to.

B 🔊 Listen for gist. Listen to the beginning of speeches given by Doris and Amelia. Choose the best answer to complete each sentence. (One answer is extra.) **CD 2 Track 15** ⏱ 5 min

Play the audio twice. Tell students to write their answers individually. Also tell them to write down the key words that support their answer choice. Check the answers with the class. Key sentences for item 1: *Today just wasn't our day. I have already called Amanda Smith to congratulate her on winning the election.* Item 2: *I am so honored.... We pulled ahead and won!*

Listen for gist. Remind students that when listening for gist, they don't need to worry about understanding everything they hear, the purpose is to understand the general idea.

C 🔊 Listen for context. Listen again. Choose the best answers. **CD 2 Track 15** ⏱ 10 min

Play the audio of Doris's speech so that students can answer questions 1 and 2. Pause, and then play the audio of Amelia's speech so that students can answer questions 3 and 4. Discuss the answers as a class. If necessary, explain the following vocabulary words and expressions from the speech: *never in my wildest dreams* = I really never thought that this would happen; *give it my best shot* = to try my hardest to do this; *running neck and neck* = to be tied with, or to have the same level of support (this is taken from horse racing); *pull ahead* = to move in front of someone, especially in a race; *a record turnout* = more people than ever before have attended or participated. Play the whole audio track again so students can check their answers.

Listen for context. Remind students that when they listen they should always try to work out what the context is: who is speaking, to whom, where, and why. Understanding the context will help them infer information and meaning.

D 🔊 💬 Listen for main ideas. Now listen to the rest of Amelia's speech. Check (✓) the topics she refers to in her speech. What key words in the listening helped you choose your answers? Tell a partner. **CD 2 Track 16** ⏱ 10–15 min

Play the speech through once while students mark their answers. Then play the speech again. Play the speech a third time and ask students to raise their hands to stop you when Amelia mentions the topics.

Listen for main ideas. Remind students that listening for main ideas means to focus on the general ideas of what they are listening to, without worrying about details. Understanding main ideas will then help them be able to work out the details more easily even if they don't recognize all the words used.

E 💬 Look at the topics in **D**. Which one do you think is the biggest problem where you live? Why? Tell a partner. ⏱ 10 min

Go over the directions with the class. Have students think about their answers to the questions, then assign them to pairs to discuss which one they think is the biggest problem in their area. Monitor and provide help as necessary. Ask follow-up questions to encourage more conversation. Call on different pairs to tell the class what they discussed. Can the class agree on which is the most serious problem?

Instructor's Notes

_____

_____

_____

_____

_____

_____

_____

4 SPEAKING

WARM UP Ask students to describe the traffic in your area. Is it crowded? Are there often traffic jams? What causes this problem? ⏱ 5 min

A 🔊 Listen to and read the speech below. What is the problem? What is one thing causing it? Can you think of other causes? **CD 2 Track 17** ⏱ 10 min

Tell students to look at the picture and talk about what is happening in it. Tell students they are going to hear a speech about traffic. If necessary, explain that a speech is when someone presents a topic. Play the audio while the students listen and read the speech. Review answers to the questions with the whole class. For further practice, you can play the audio or read the conversation out loud for the class to repeat for accuracy of pronunciation.

LARGE CLASS OPTION
Place students in groups of four to eight students. Tell them to discuss the causes of the problem in **A**. Then tell them to brainstorm possible solutions. If desired, they can write a list of solutions to hand in so you can check their work.

B 🔊 **Pronunciation: Using pauses in public speaking.** Read the sentences below. Guess where the speaker will pause. Write a slash mark (/) for each pause. Then listen and check your answers. **CD 2 Track 18** ⏱ 10 min

Have students read the first part of the speech and identify where they think the pauses are. Have them compare their answers with a partner's, then play the audio for them to check. Have students practice reading the introduction in pairs. Remind them to focus on pausing in the right places. Tell them that the pauses help the listeners follow.

C 🔊 🔄 Listen again to the speech in **A** and take turns saying it aloud with a partner. Pay attention to pausing. **CD 2 Track 17** ⏱ 5–10 min

Play the whole speech again, then assign students to pairs to practice it. Monitor and make sure students are pausing appropriately. Have a volunteer say the speech to the class.

EXTRA! Writing prompt
Direct students to write a paragraph about crowding, congestion, and traffic. First they should describe the problem. Then they should offer solutions. ⏱ 15–20 min

SPEAKING STRATEGY

D Match each word on the left with one on the right to make a list of common city problems. Write them on a piece of paper. Can you add to the list? ⏱ 5 min

Students can work on their lists individually. To check answers, call on a student to name a combination. Confirm the combination, then ask for a show of hands for who else had this combination. Which combinations did the fewest students list? Write those on the board and review them. Note the stress patterns of the compound constructions: *unaffordable HOUsing, high unemPLOYment, dirty STREETS, NOISE pollution.*

E 🔄 Choose one of the city problems in **D** or one of your own. Work with a partner and complete the information below. ⏱ 10 min

The purpose of exercise **E** is to provide students with material to discuss in exercise **F**. Students should complete this exercise with a partner. Be sure that students are clear about the difference between the problem and the cause of the problem. There is no need to check the answers for this exercise but you may wish to walk around the room making sure that students are following the proper general idea.

F 🔄 Join another pair and follow the instructions. Then switch roles and repeat. ⏱ 15 min

(See Student Book page 127 for complete instructions.)

Direct students' attention to the Useful Expressions box. Read each expression with students repeating after you. Ask students for ideas of what other words or ideas could follow the expressions. Remind students to use the expressions from the Useful Expressions box in their presentations. Be sure that listeners are paying attention, and call on them to offer possible suggestions on how to solve the problems.

EXTRA! Class presentation
Giving presentations is an important skill in classrooms and in business. Ask students to polish their speeches and present them in front of the class. If you have a small class, this can take one class period. If you have a large class, have 2–3 students give a presentation at the beginning of every class until everyone has had a turn. When students present, they should only use an index card with notes, NOT a written out speech. ⏱ 30–45 min

TEACHING TIP: Ensuring that students listen to presenters
To keep non-presenters accountable, the presenter should also prepare a short quiz, asking questions about what he or she presented. For example, *1. What are the three main causes of traffic?* Students not presenting must take notes. After the presenter speaks, he or she should give the quiz to the class. Students may use their notes to answer the quiz questions.

4 SPEAKING

A 🔊 Listen to and read the speech below. What is the problem? What is one thing causing it? Can you think of other causes? **CD 2 Track 17**

Today I'd like to talk to you about rush hour traffic. I'll begin by telling you about the problem. Then I'll list the three things I think are causing this problem.

So, let's start by talking about rush hour traffic in this city. We've all experienced it, and in recent years it's gotten worse. Ten years ago, it used to take about 45 minutes to drive across town. Now it takes two hours. One of the main causes of this problem is too many cars on the road. More cars means more traffic and, of course, more traffic accidents. Another cause of rush hour traffic is...

B 🔊 **Pronunciation: Using pauses in public speaking.** Read the sentences below. Guess where the speaker will pause. Write a slash mark (/) for each pause. Then listen and check your answers. **CD 2 Track 18**

What is one of the biggest problems facing our city today? It's rush hour traffic.

Today we're going to talk about this important problem. I'll begin by telling you about the problem. Then I'll list three things...

C 🔊 🔁 Listen again to the speech in **A** and take turns saying it aloud with a partner. Pay attention to pausing. **CD 2 Track 17**

SPEAKING STRATEGY

D Match each word on the left with one on the right to make a list of common city problems. Write them on a piece of paper. Can you add to the list?

unaffordable	high		streets	unemployment
dirty	noise		housing	pollution

E 🔁 Choose one of the city problems in **D** or one of your own. Work with a partner and complete the information below.

Problem: _____

Causes of the problem:

1. _____

2. _____

3. _____

> **Useful Expressions:**
> **Language for presentations**
>
> **Stating the purpose**
>
> Today, I'd like to talk to you about...
>
> I'll begin by (talking about the issue). / I'll provide an overview of (the issue).
>
> Then I'll list the (two / three / four)...
>
> **Stating important points**
>
> Let's talk first about... / Let's start by talking about...
>
> One of the main causes of (traffic) is...
>
> Another / A second cause of (traffic) is...
>
> And finally...

F 👥 Join another pair and follow the instructions. Then switch roles and repeat.

Presenters: Use the Useful Expressions to explain your problem in **E** clearly. One person should introduce the talk. The second person should explain the causes of the problem.

Listeners: Take notes. After the presentation, give suggestions for how to solve the problem.

A Turn to page 210. Complete the exercises. Then do **B–D** below.

Too + Adjective / Adverb; *too much* / *too many* + Noun				
	too	**Adjective / adverb**	**(Infinitive)**	
You're 17. You're	**too**	young	to vote.	
I can't understand him. He speaks	**too**	quickly.		
	too much / too many	**Noun**	**(Infinitive)**	
	Too much	pollution		is bad for your lungs.
Our city has	**too many**	problems	to solve	in one day.

Adjective / Adverb + *enough*; *enough* + Noun				
	Adjective / adverb	*enough*	**(Infinitive)**	
I'm 21. I'm	old	**enough**	to vote.	
These are good seats. I can hear	well	**enough**.		
	enough	**Noun**	**(Infinitive)**	
We have	**enough**	water	to get by	for now.
They have	**enough**	police officers		on the street.

B Complete the statements about school life with *too*, *too much*, *too many*, and *enough*.

School Life	Agree	Disagree
1. There are _____ rules in this school.	☐	☐
2. There is _____ emphasis on memorization.	☐	☐
3. We don't have _____ time for extracurricular activities.	☐	☐
4. Classes are not interesting _____.	☐	☐
5. _____ students study only to pass the test.	☐	☐
6. We don't have _____ opportunities to practice English conversation.	☐	☐
7. There's _____ homework.	☐	☐
8. The school day is _____ long.	☐	☐

C Now check (✓) *Agree* or *Disagree* for each statement in **B**.

D 🔁 Share your answers with a partner. Give examples and discuss solutions for the statements you agreed with.

> I think there are too many rules in this school. For example, we shouldn't have to wear school uniforms all the time.

> I agree. I think you can look neat enough in a pair of jeans and a nice shirt.

5 GRAMMAR
Too and *enough*

WARM UP On the board, write two columns. At the top of one column, write *too much* and at the top of the other column, write *not enough*. Ask students how they are enjoying your course so far. Ask them to list what things they think you do too much of in class and what things they think you don't do enough of. Write their list on the board. Then tell students that you will consider what to change as a result of their suggestions. ⏱ 5 min

A Turn to page 210. Complete the exercises. Then do **B–D** below. ◐ 20–30 min

Go over the examples in the first chart, pointing out the use of an adjective or an adverb after *too*, and the use of a noun after *too many / too much*. Remind students about count and noncount nouns and elicit more nouns. Have students say whether the nouns go with *too many* or *too much*. Make sure students understand that *too* is used negatively, to say there is an excess of something. Then go over the second chart, pointing out the use of an adjective or an adverb before *enough*, and the use of a noun (count or noncount) after *enough*. Elicit more examples from the class and write them on the board, for example: *There are enough chairs in the classroom (everyone has a chair). We have too much homework (we don't have time to do it all)*. The grammar chart on page 210 includes further examples and usage explanations, expanding on the information in the chart on page 128.

TEACHING OPTION: The flipped classroom
To open up time for in-class communicative tasks, assign the Grammar Notes on page 210 as homework. Have students complete the exercises on My World Link Online as well.

The next time class meets:
1. Review using *too* and *enough* in the Grammar Notes.
2. Go through the exercises students did for homework; present new examples and reinforce points as needed. Take questions from students.
3. Turn back to page 128 and do the communicative exercises there, starting with **B**.

LANGUAGE TIP: *Too* vs. *very*
Too is used when there is a negative judgment about something. *Very* is used when the person feels favorably or neutral about something. If a person likes hot weather, they can comment that *it is very hot today*. If a person doesn't like heat, they will complain *it is too hot*. The temperature is the same, but the feelings of the speaker are distinguished through the use of these adverbs.

B Complete the statements about school life with *too*, *too much*, *too many*, and *enough*. ◐ 10 min

Do the first item with the class as an example, then have students complete the rest of the statements individually. Have them compare their answers with a partner's. Refer them back to the charts on this page and on page 210 as necessary to check any they disagree on. Check answers with the class. Clarify the meaning of each statement making sure students understand that *too* is used to show excess of something, in a negative sense.

C Now check (✓) *Agree* or *Disagree* for each statement in **B**. ⏱ 5 min

Have students decide if they agree or disagree with each statement.

GRAMMAR TIP: Adjective + *enough* / *too* + adjective + infinitive
An adjective + *enough* is sometimes followed by an infinitive form like this: *It is bright enough to see* or *He is rich enough to buy the whole town*. As long as *be* is positive, this construction means the action CAN happen. *It is bright enough to see = I can see. (It isn't bright enough to see = I can't see.)*

A similar adjective can sometimes follow *too* + adjective: *It's too dark to see*. This means the person cannot see. *He is too poor to buy it = He can't buy it.*

D 🗣 Share your answers with a partner. Give examples and discuss solutions for the statements you agreed with. ◑ 10–15 min

Model the example with a student, then model again with the second statement. Assign students to pairs to discuss the statements they agreed with and possible solutions. Monitor and provide help as necessary, prompt further conversation by asking further questions. As a class, discuss which statements students agree with and what possible solutions they suggested.

GRAMMAR TUTORIALS
• *Too* and *Enough*

Additional tutorials are available for reteaching and reinforcement.

Instructor's Notes

_____

_____

_____

_____

6 COMMUNICATION

WARM UP Write the following prompts on the board: *I have too many/much _____. I have enough _____. I don't have enough _____.* Ask students to orally complete the sentence blanks with their own ideas. ⏱ 5 min

A Follow the instructions to complete the survey below. Then check (✓) *Yes* or *No*. 🕐 15 min

(See Student Book page 129 for complete instructions.)

Explain that in questions 1–6 students should write *enough*, either on the blank line before the word or on the one after the word, but not in both places. If necessary, for questions 7–12, remind students that *too* is used before adjectives and adverbs, *too many* before count nouns, and *too much* before noncount nouns. Remind students to check the box to indicate their answer to each question. Check the answers for the placement of *enough* and for the correct use of *too, too many,* and *too much.* But don't ask students at this time to indicate their *Yes / No* answers to the questions.

B 🔄 Use the questions in **A** to interview a partner. Ask follow-up questions. 🕐 10–15 min

Tell students to take at least three turns each for every question by adding follow-up questions or comments. Model the exercise and follow-up questions by reading the example with a student. Ask another follow-up question. Then have the student ask you one of the questions and then two follow-up questions. The class can help with the follow-up questions if necessary. Pair students for the interviews, and walk around to listen and offer suggestions.

TEACHING OPTION

Arrange the class in large circles of 8–12 students each. Send the questions around the circle by having one student begin and ask question 1 to the student on his or her left. The second student answers, then asks the next question of the student on his or her other side. Continue until the questions have traveled all the way around the circle. If it is not possible for students to move their seats, this exercise can be done across a row or sections of rows. If you are ambitious, try sending the questions in two directions at the same time!

LARGE CLASS OPTION

As students interview their partners, they should write the answers and hand them in. This ensures students are staying on task.

TEACHING TIP: Monitoring pair work

Pair work provides several benefits.

- Students have greater opportunities to talk than they do when the whole class is together.

- The instructor is no longer the center of attention, so the students concentrate on language.

- Students can offer ideas, help, and assistance to each other.

While students are working in pairs, the instructor can circulate around the room checking on how things are going. Some suggestions:

- Give students a little time to get started, unless someone clearly needs help. The immediate presence of the instructor can be inhibiting.

- Keep your ears open for people having problems. Some students will be reluctant to call on you for help.

- When talking with students, sit down with them or kneel or squat on the floor so that you aren't towering above them. This makes it easier to talk quietly without disturbing others and makes for better eye contact. It also makes you seem somewhat less like an authority figure.

- Be careful not to get so caught up with one pair or group that you fail to get around to the others. Try to spend your time more or less evenly with all of the pairs or groups.

TEACHING TIP: Memorizing vs. speaking

Explain to students that it can be more important to speak fluently than to memorize perfect lines. Usually students are afraid of making mistakes, so they will write out and memorize a whole speech. The problem is that during speaking exams, such as the TOEFL© or IELTS©, they will not know the topic in advance. Or if they study in an English-speaking country, they will actually *lose* grade points for having a memorized speech. Remind students to practice now by having only a few notes on cards and just keep practicing the speech again and again aloud, without memorizing actual sentences.

EXTRA! Writing prompt

Tell students to fill in the blank and then write a paragraph responding to the following writing prompt: *I think that in this school we have too much/many ____.* Tell students that they can't use the word *homework!* 🕐 20 min

Instructor's Notes

_____

_____

_____

_____

_____

_____

6 COMMUNICATION

A Follow the instructions to complete the survey below. Then check (✓) *Yes* or *No*.

- **For questions 1–6:** Write *enough* before or after each word. (Only one position is correct.)
- **For questions 7–12:** Write *too, too much,* or *too many*.

	Yes	No
1. Did you get _____ sleep _____ last night?		
2. Do you have _____ credits _____ to graduate?		
3. Is it _____ quiet _____ for you to study at home?		
4. Do you typically have _____ time _____ to finish your homework?		
5. Have you eaten _____ food _____ today?		
6. Do you get along _____ well _____ with your parents?		
7. Do you spend _____ time watching TV?		
8. Is English _____ difficult to learn?		
9. Do you sometimes eat _____ sweets?		
10. Do you have _____ problems in your life?		
11. Is it possible to earn _____ money?		
12. At 20, are people _____ young to get married?		

B Use the questions in **A** to interview a partner. Ask follow-up questions.

> Is it quiet enough for you to study at home?

> No, not really. It's pretty noisy.

> Where do you study then?

> Mostly at the library.

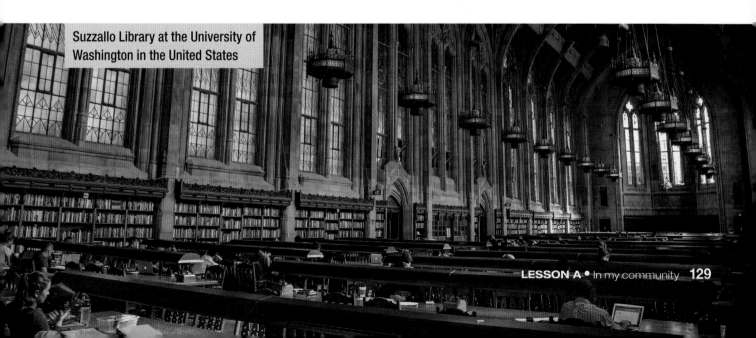

Suzzallo Library at the University of
Washington in the United States

LESSON D MODERN CHALLENGES

Sydney, Australia, has so much urban sprawl that
the city has spread almost into the ocean!

1 VOCABULARY

A Read about the problem of **sprawl**. Then tell a partner: Is sprawl a problem in your area?

- Sprawl is a problem in my city. In the past five years, there has been a lot of new **development**. As this **spreads** across the land, it **destroys** parks, farms, and open spaces.

- In many of these new neighborhoods, people live far away from public transportation, stores, and schools. This **forces** people to **rely on** their cars so they can drive longer distances. Driving a lot is a **waste** of time. It also creates more pollution.

- So what can we do? First, we should stop all new development. This will **protect** our open spaces for future generations. Then, we should **support** a law that **provides** money for public transportation and new bike paths. This will **encourage** people to leave their cars at home. If this happens, air quality will **improve**.

B Write a **blue** word from **A** next to its definition.

1. _encourage_: to persuade or get someone to do something

2. _____: to damage completely

3. _____: to keep something safe

4. _____: to move gradually outward

5. _____: to use something in a bad or careless way

6. _____: to try to help a person or idea succeed

7. _____: to offer or give something

8. _____: to make someone do something difficult

9. _____: the building of houses, stores, and other structures

10. _____: to need or depend on something

11. _____: to make better

C Answer the questions with your partner using the new words in **A**.

1. What is the problem with sprawl? What does it do?

2. What does the writer suggest doing? How will these things help?

1 VOCABULARY

WARM UP Tell students to close their eyes and use their imaginations. First, have them imagine that they are in a place with very few people. It is quiet and calm. Tell them to think about how they feel. Then tell them to imagine that they are in a place with a lot of people. It is noisy and busy. Tell them to think about how they feel. Then tell students to open their eyes. Ask them for adjectives to describe how they felt in each place and write them on the board. ⏱ 5–10 min

A 🗲 Read about the problem of **sprawl**. Then tell a partner: Is sprawl a problem in your area? ⏱ 10–15 min

Have students look at the photo and read the caption. Would they like to live there? Have students read the text. Remind them to try to guess the meanings of the words in blue. (They will focus on the meanings in **B**.) Then assign them to pairs to answer the question. Tell students that *sprawl* does not simply mean densely populated. The focus of the word is on the gradual and unplanned spread of growth. Native speakers of English have negative ideas about the word *sprawl*, even though many of them live in it. As a class, discuss places students know where sprawl is a problem.

CULTURE TIP: Avoiding sprawl
Many communities attempt to avoid sprawl by using *planning and zoning regulations*. An organized group within the town or city makes regulations about what types of buildings and businesses are permitted in specific locations. If the town or city is well organized, it can steer planned growth and development in positive ways. Find out if your city or town has such regulations, and describe them for students.

B Write a **blue** word from **A** next to its definition. ⏱ 10 min

Tell students to first read the definitions in **B** and then to look for the corresponding blue word in **A**. Call on individual students to give the correct answers.

C 🗲 Answer the questions with your partner using the new words in **A**. ⏱ 10–15 min

Go over the questions with the class, then assign students to pairs to discuss them. Monitor and encourage them to use the words in **A**. Conclude this exercise with a whole-class discussion about sprawl and its implications.

2 LISTENING

STRATEGIES: Listen for details; Infer information; Listen for reasons

WARM UP Ask the class about films they have seen. Which were set in urban areas? Which in suburban or rural areas? How did the setting influence what happened in the film? ⏱ 5 min

A 🔗 Look at the photos. Do you live in an urban or suburban area? Explain to a partner. ⏱ 5 min

Pair students to answer the question. Note that the photographs of the urban and suburban areas are both very beautiful. Ask students what aspects of life in those locations are not pictured here.

B 🔊 **Listen for details; Infer information.** You will hear three speakers. Where do they live now? Where do they want to live in the future? Write *U* for urban and *S* for suburban. Write *NM* if the information is not mentioned. **CD 2 Track 19** ⏱ 5–10 min

Play the audio for the students at least twice. The second time, pause as needed and discuss the correct answers with the students. Remember that you can also read from the audio script if students find it challenging to understand the audio. If necessary, explain vocabulary: *fast-paced* = quickly moving; *glamorous* = exciting and interesting; *predictable* = it is obvious what will happen; doesn't change; *commuting* = traveling to and from home to work; *wow* = an expression of excitement; *seniors* = elderly, retired people; *I can't wait* = I want it to happen soon.

Listen for details. Remind students that they do not need to hear and understand everything in order to understand specific details. Encourage them to get into the habit of identifying key words to listen for before they listen.

Infer information. Remind students that inferring information means to use the information they have, the context, and their background knowledge to work out something that isn't stated or explained explicitly.

C 🔊 **Listen for reasons.** Where does each person want to live? Circle the answers below. Then listen and take notes on their reasons. **CD 2 Track 20** ⏱ 10 min

Have students circle their first answers. Then play the audio. Remind them to take notes in the second part of each item as they listen. Have students compare their answers with a partner's, then play the audio again. Check answers with the class, playing the audio again, pausing as necessary.

Listen for reasons. Explain to students that being able to understand reasons people give will help them infer other information and the meaning of words they aren't familiar with in the same listening.

D 🔗 What do you think the underlined expressions mean? Which person from **B** do you think would say each sentence? Write the names. Explain your answers to a partner. ⏱ 10–15 min

Go over the sentences with the class. Individually have students think about what the expressions mean and decide who would say each one. Then assign them to pairs to compare and explain their answers. Check answers with the class.

E 🔗 Where do you want to live in the future? Why? Tell a partner. ⏱ 10 min

Have students think about their answer to the question and their reasons, and then assign them to pairs. Monitor and provide help, and ask questions to prompt further conversation. Call on different students to say where their partner would like to live in the future, and why.

TEACHING TIP: Listening tests
Being able to recognize paraphrases is a common standardized listening test item. Explain to students that the choice that *sounds* closest to what the person is saying is usually a distracter. For example, if the person says, "I am running to the train," the distracter could be "She is training for a race." But the actual paraphrase would be "She is quickly going to the railway station." Students need to focus on the meaning of words, not catching and repeating all of the actual words said. This is why vocabulary development is so important.

Instructor's Notes

_____

_____

_____

_____

_____

_____

_____

_____

_____

2 LISTENING

A Look at the photos. Do you live in an urban or suburban area? Explain to a partner.

urban

suburban

B **Listen for details; Infer information.** You will hear three speakers. Where do they live now? Where do they want to live in the future? Write *U* for urban and *S* for suburban. Write *NM* if the information is not mentioned. **CD 2 Track 19**

Bella: now: _____   Anne: now: _____   Mercedes: now: _____

　　future: _____　　　　　　 future: _____　　　　　　　 future: _____

C **Listen for reasons.** Where does each person want to live? Circle the answers below. Then listen and take notes on their reasons. **CD 2 Track 20**

1. Bella wants to live in the city / suburbs.　　Reason(s): _____

2. Anne wants to live in the city / suburbs.　　Reason(s): _____

3. Mercedes wants to live in the city / suburbs.　Reason(s): _____

D What do you think the underlined expressions mean? Which person from **B** do you think would say each sentence? Write the names. Explain your answers to a partner.

1. I hope I can move—I have to <u>wait and see</u>, I guess.　　_____

2. Now that I've <u>put down roots</u>, I probably won't move.　　_____

3. I needed <u>a change of scenery</u>, and I got it!　　_____

E Where do you want to live in the future? Why? Tell a partner.

3 READING

STRATEGIES: Use background knowledge; Make predictions; Infer information; Infer meaning; Read for details; Draw conclusions

WARM UP On the board, write: *seniors* and *children*. Brainstorm adjectives to describe each. Ask, *Do elderly people and children have anything in common?* ⏱ 5 min

A 🔁 **Use background knowledge.** This article is about a *daycare center* and a *retirement home*. What are these places? How are they similar? Discuss with a partner. ⏱ 5–10 min

Assign students to pairs to discuss the two places and their similarities. Call on different pairs to share their ideas.

Use background knowledge. Students bring to any text the knowledge they already have, as well as any knowledge they have about the specific topic of the text. Students need to know that they should draw on this knowledge to help them understand what they are reading.

B 🔁 **Make predictions; Infer information.** Look at the photo. Answer the questions with a partner. ⏱ 5–10 min

Go over the questions with the class. With the same partner, have them look at the photo and answer the questions. Compare predictions as a class.

Make predictions. Remind students that predicting before they read helps them be more prepared for the text as they will have activated prior knowledge of the topic and language related to it.

Infer information. Remind students that inferring information means to use the information they have, the context, and their background knowledge to work out something that isn't stated or explained explicitly.

3 READING

A 🔁 **Use background knowledge.** This article is about a *daycare center* and a *retirement home*. What are these places? How are they similar? Discuss with a partner.

B 🔁 **Make predictions; Infer information.** Look at the photo. Answer the questions with a partner.

1. How do you think the people in the photo know each other?

2. Look at the word *intergenerational* in the caption. What do you think it means?

C **Infer meaning.** Read the article. Then match the words (1–4) with the correct definitions (a–d).

1. at risk (line 4) _____

2. launched (line 11) _____

3. be exposed to (line 31–32) _____

4. tolerant (line 34) _____

a. started

b. in danger of something bad happening

c. be given the chance to experience something new

d. able to accept different ideas and situations

D 🔁 **Read for details; Draw conclusions.** The article talks about an intergenerational program. What are the benefits of the program? Underline them in the passage. Can you think of any challenges? Explain your ideas to a partner.

E 🔁 Why do you think many older and younger people are in retirement homes and daycare centers in the US? Is this common in your country? Do you think it's good? Why or why not? Discuss with a partner.

132 UNIT 9 ● Social issues

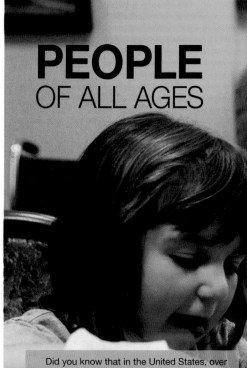

PEOPLE
OF ALL AGES

Did you know that in the United States, over 25 percent of senior citizens (people over 65) live alone? Without enough friends and family nearby, seniors are at risk for depression.[1]
5 This is a serious problem. Studies show that people with depression are more likely to have other health problems as well.

Now, many communities are trying to find a solution to this problem. Providence Mount
10 St. Vincent, a retirement home near Seattle, Washington, has recently launched an intergenerational program. Over 400 senior citizens live at Providence Mount St. Vincent, and over 40 children from a few months old
15 to age five go to daycare there. The children spend the day there with the senior citizens while workers look on.

[1]A person with *depression* feels very unhappy and unable to do anything.

EXTRA! Comprehension questions

In pairs, have students write four or five comprehension questions. Elicit question words and write them on the board. Then have the class look at the first paragraph of the article and suggest a question, for example, *How many old people live by themselves?* Have pairs write their questions. Then have pairs exchange papers and answer each other's questions. ⏱ 10–15 min

EXTRA! Writing prompt

Ask students to write a few paragraphs describing the benefits and challenges of an intergenerational program. ⏱ 15–20 min

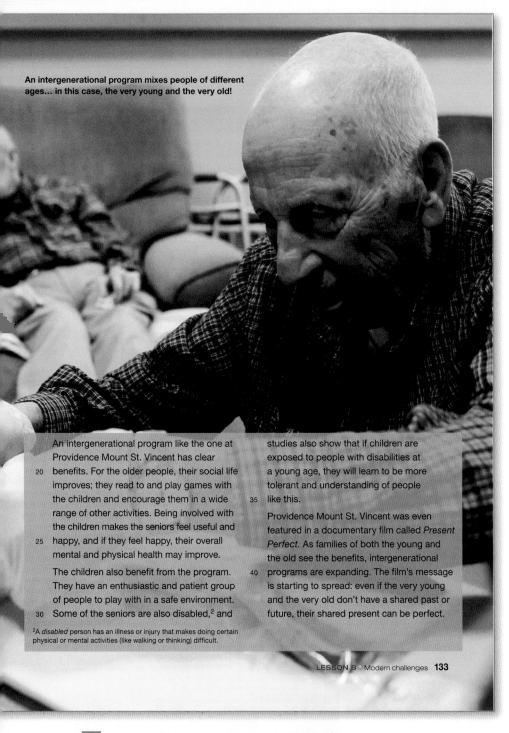

An intergenerational program mixes people of different ages... in this case, the very young and the very old!

An intergenerational program like the one at Providence Mount St. Vincent has clear
20 benefits. For the older people, their social life improves; they read to and play games with the children and encourage them in a wide range of other activities. Being involved with the children makes the seniors feel useful and
25 happy, and if they feel happy, their overall mental and physical health may improve.

The children also benefit from the program. They have an enthusiastic and patient group of people to play with in a safe environment.
30 Some of the seniors are also disabled,[2] and

studies also show that if children are exposed to people with disabilities at a young age, they will learn to be more tolerant and understanding of people
35 like this.

Providence Mount St. Vincent was even featured in a documentary film called *Present Perfect*. As families of both the young and the old see the benefits, intergenerational
40 programs are expanding. The film's message is starting to spread: even if the very young and the very old don't have a shared past or future, their shared present can be perfect.

[2]A *disabled* person has an illness or injury that makes doing certain physical or mental activities (like walking or thinking) difficult.

LESSON B ○ Modern challenges **133**

C Infer meaning. Read the article. Then match the words (1–4) with the correct definitions (a–d). ⏱ 10 min

Tell students to read the article in detail and focus on inferring the meanings of the words. Have them compare their answers with a partner's, then check answers with the class.

Infer meaning. Remind students to look at the whole sentence, not just the isolated word, and try to decide what kind of word it is (verb, noun, etc.) as this will help them guess its meaning. They can also use the context the word is being used in.

D ✂ Read for details; Draw conclusions. The article talks about an intergenerational program. What are the benefits of the program? Underline them in the passage. Can you think of any challenges? Explain your ideas to a partner. ⏱ 10 min

Go over the directions with the class and have students explain the meaning of *benefits* and *challenges*. Have them underline the benefits mentioned in the article then think of challenges. Assign students to pairs to discuss the benefits and challenges of intergenerational programs. As a class, discuss possible challenges and how they could be overcome.

Read for details. Remind students that reading for details means reading a text more slowly and in depth. When they read for details, they should pay attention to unfamiliar words, but try to guess meaning from context.

Draw conclusions. Explain to students that coming to conclusions about what they have read, and being able to express these, is a good way for them to check their understanding of the content of a text.

E ✂ Why do you think many older and younger people are in retirement homes and daycare centers in the US? Is this common in your country? Do you think it's good? Why or why not? Discuss with a partner. ⏱ 10–15 min

Go over the questions with the class, then give students a moment to think about their answers. Assign them to pairs to discuss the questions. Monitor as students discuss the questions and prompt with questions as necessary. As a class, discuss their answers.

EXTRA! Discussion
Put students into groups. Tell them to discuss the advantages and disadvantages of elderly people living in retirement homes, and of children being taken care of in daycares. ⏱ 15 min

4 GRAMMAR

A Turn to page 211. Complete the exercises. Then do **B–D** below.

Future Real Conditionals	
If clause	**Result clause**
If a woman **works**,	(then) a family **will have** more money.*
If we **don't protect** our open spaces,	(then) future generations **won't have** places to relax.
Result clause	**If clause**
A family **will have** more money	if a woman **works**.

*If you aren't certain, you can use *might (not)* or *may (not)* in a result clause:
*If a woman works, a family **may / might have** more money.*

B 🗭 Complete the sentences with a partner. How many sentences can you make? Make follow-up sentences for each one.

> If people have smaller families,...

> If you eat too many sweets,...

> If you eat too many sweets, you'll probably get sick.

> And if you get sick, you might miss class.

C Take out five small pieces of paper. On each piece, write an *if* clause like the examples in **B**.

D 🗭 Work in a small group. Follow the steps below.

1. Put all your papers together and mix them. Put them face down on the desk in a pile.

2. One person begins. Turn over a paper. You have 15 seconds to complete the sentence.
   - If you make a correct sentence, you get a point. Then put the paper aside.
   - If you don't make a correct sentence, put the paper at the bottom of the pile.

3. Then the next person goes. Play until you use all the papers. Who got the most points?

5 WRITING

A Read the paragraph. What is the writer predicting? Under the paragraph, circle your opinion.

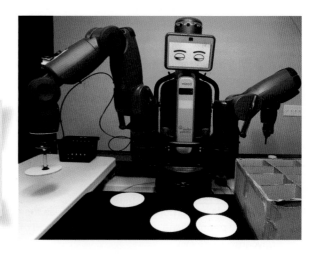

> In the future, robots will do more of our jobs. Robots already work in some places today, like factories and restaurants. In five to ten years, you may see them in hospitals and schools. They'll even drive cars. Will this improve our lives?

In my opinion, it will / won't.

4 GRAMMAR
Future real conditionals

WARM UP Ask students to list things that will probably happen in the future and things that will probably not happen. Which are possible? Which are probably not possible? Which might happen? Which will probably not happen? For example: *I will probably study engineering. It's unlikely that I will go to the moon.* ⏱ 5 min

A Turn to page 211. Complete the exercises. Then do **B–D** below. ◑ 20–30 min

Go over the examples in the chart and have students identify the tense used in each clause (*if* clause: simple present; result clause: future with *will*). Point out that the result clause can come first, and no comma is used in these cases. Elicit examples related to students' lives, for example: *If I pass this course, I'll...; I'll go to the movies tonight if I....* Point out the use of *might* and *may* when you are less certain about the result. The grammar chart on page 211 includes further examples, usage explanations, and formal rules, expanding on the information in the chart on page 120.

GRAMMAR TIP: Real conditionals
English has three types of conditional sentences with *if*:

- Real situations in the present or future (sometimes called the first conditional): *If I study hard, I will get a good grade.*

- Unreal situations (sometimes called the second conditional): *If I studied hard, I would get better grades.*

- Unreal situations in the past (sometimes called the third conditional): *If I had studied hard, I would have gotten a better grade.*

This section introduces conditional sentences for future real situations, the first conditional.

B 🔁 Complete the sentences with a partner. How many sentences can you make? Make follow-up sentences for each one. ⏱ 10 min

Model the example with a student. Point out how each time they say a sentence they can then change it to become a follow-up sentence by making the consequence the *if* clause of the follow-up sentence. Add another follow-up sentence to the example and write both sentences on the board so students can see how to make the chain of consequences. Assign students to pairs to make sentence chains from the two prompts. Monitor and provide help and ideas as necessary. Call on volunteers to say their chain of sentences.

C Take out five small pieces of paper. On each piece, write an *if* clause like the examples in **B**. ⏱ 5–10 min

Provide ideas and help as necessary as students write their *if* clauses. Remind them they don't need to write the whole sentences, only the *if* part. Refer them to the chart as necessary.

D ⚃ Work in a small group. Follow the steps below. ⏱ 10–15 min

(See Student Book page 134 for complete instructions.)

Go over the directions and the steps. Assign students to groups of three or four students and have them place their papers face down on the desk. Model the exercise by taking one of the papers and completing the sentence. Nominate a timekeeper and a scorekeeper in each group. Have students play the game. Monitor and help clarify doubts about whether sentences are correct or not.

GRAMMAR TUTORIALS
- Future Real Conditionals with *Be Going To* and *Will*

Additional tutorials are available for reteaching and reinforcement.

5 WRITING

WARM UP Have students look at the photo and describe what is happening. Ask, *What will robots be able to do in the future?* Then have students make a follow-up sentence from their answer; for example, *Robots will be able to do operations. If robots do operations, we won't need so many doctors.* Etc. ⏱ 5 min

A Read the paragraph. What is the writer predicting? Under the paragraph, circle your opinion. ⏱ 10 min

Go over the directions with the class. Then have students read the paragraph and answer the question with a partner. Check answers with the class and compare opinions.

TEACHING TIP: *I learned* statements
From time to time during your course, it is helpful to hear from your students about what they are learning. Write three or four open-ended sentences on the board such as: *I learned that _____. I'm surprised that _____. I'm happy about _____. I wish we could do more _____. I want to know more about _____.* Tell students to reflect on the class so far, then have them write down and complete the sentences. In small groups students can read their sentences in turn. Students can skip by saying *pass.* Allow time for groups to discuss interesting sentences they heard.

Instructor's Notes

_____

_____

_____

1 STORYBOARD

A Mr. Stevens and his son, Ian, are waiting in the doctor's office. Look at the pictures and complete the conversations. More than one answer is possible for each blank.

B 🐝 Practice the conversations in groups of four. Then change roles and practice again.

C 🔗 With a partner, create and perform your own conversation between a doctor and a patient.

1 STORYBOARD

WARM UP Ask the class what they studied in the past three units. See if they can remember the names of the units without looking in their books. Draw a chart on the board with three sections, one for each unit, and have students tell you as many new vocabulary and grammar items as they can remember from each topic. ⏱ 10 min

A Mr. Stevens and his son, Ian, are waiting in the doctor's office. Look at the pictures and complete the conversations. More than one answer is possible for each blank. ⏱ 10–15 min

Give students two minutes to look at the pictures and review the story. Answer any questions about vocabulary. Explain that students must provide words for the blanks. Tell them that some of the lines require more than one word. When students are finished, check the answers by calling on individuals to share their answers with the class.

TEACHING TIP: Encouraging use of English
Here are some approaches to consider when helping students to speak more English in class.

- Explain the rationale for using English in class. Tell students, *We learn to speak English by speaking English.*

- Use only English for instructions and classroom management. If necessary, review expressions like *Please repeat that* and *Sorry, I don't understand.*

- Be very clear about your position on speaking other languages in class. Students need to know when it is okay to use their own language and when they are expected to be using only Engllsh.

B 👥 Practice the conversations in groups of four. Then change roles and practice again. ⏱ 10–15 min

When students have finished **A**, they can practice the conversations in groups of four to six. Tell them to be "actors" while speaking—they shouldn't just read the sentences from the page. They should show emotion. In order to do this, tell them to think about how each person feels. As students practice, remind them to read, look up, and speak to the others in their group. Call on groups to present one exchange to the class.

TEACHING OPTION: Support / challenge
Focus students' attention on the intonation and stress patterns of the sentences in the conversation. Write the sentences on the board or write them out ahead of time, and make copies for students. Tell the class to mark the stress and intonation patterns of each sentence. Read them aloud so that students can check their answers. Then read the sentences and direct students to repeat after you in chorus. If necessary, exaggerate the intonation and stress patterns to help students pronounce accurately.

CULTURE TIP: Talking to doctors
In almost all parts of the world, medical doctors are treated with great respect. In most English-speaking countries, patients are encouraged to ask questions and to speak plainly to the doctor if they don't understand something. Try the following if you need to go to the doctor's office or to the hospital.

- Ask the assistants, doctors, and nurses to speak slowly and clearly.

- Stop and ask people to repeat if you don't understand them.

- Repeat your diagnosis to the doctor to be sure that you have understood it.

- Bring along a picture dictionary with pictures of the inside and outside of the body.

- Bring a bilingual dictionary, electronic translator, or translating app on your phone or tablet to help you. Or bring along another person who can help translate for you.

- Don't allow yourself to be rushed or intimidated. Ask questions if you need to.

- Be polite and courteous to nurses and doctors.

C 🔄 With a partner, create and perform your own conversation between a doctor and a patient. ⏱ 10 min

Point out to students that the conversation in **A** shows only the beginning and the end of the discussion. Students should include the middle part of the conversation as well. The student playing the role of the patient needs to think of symptoms of their illness. The doctor needs to ask questions to figure out what is wrong.

2 SEE IT AND SAY IT

WARM UP Ask students to name the participants in a recent election. Who were the candidates? What were the issues? What was the outcome? Some students may feel passionately about these issues, so make sure students are respectful of each other's ideas. ⏱ 10 min

A 🔊 Look at the picture. Use the words in the box to talk about it. Then answer the questions with a partner. ⏱ 10–15 min

Read the words in the box out loud with students repeating after you. Emphasize pronunciation. In pairs, students should take turns describing the picture to each other and then answer the questions. If necessary, review the meaning of *election* as opposed to *campaign*, which is the period leading up to the election when candidates try to persuade voters to support them.

TEACHING OPTION: Support / challenge
One student in each pair should close his or her book and turn so that he or she can't see their partner's book. The partner with the book describes the picture in as much detail as he or she can. The other student draws the picture as it is described. After a few minutes, permit the student who is drawing to see the picture in the book again. How accurate is the drawing? Ask students if there was anything that they couldn't describe because of vocabulary that they don't know.

LANGUAGE TIP: Politics
A person who runs for elected office is called a *politician*. The practice of running for office, getting elected, and then holding power is called *politics*. Both the person and the activity can be described as being *political*. Voters are generally opposed to *politics as usual*, in which a small number of people make self-interested decisions for everyone. *Politicians* are often the people who establish *policy*.

B 👥 Work with a partner. Write a brief speech for Mike Gold. Perform your speech for another pair. ⏱ 10–15 min

Brainstorm with the class a list of things that might be said in a political speech, and write them on the board. Your list might include promises to do things, promises to eliminate things, personal qualities of the candidate, or previous accomplishments. Point out the language and tone of campaign speeches and the posters in the picture. (You can review the posters in Unit 9 page 125 if desired.) Pair students to write their speeches. Then join pairs to present their speeches to each other. Students should stand to deliver their speeches to each other. If possible, move them a short distance away from each other to remind them to project their voices and speak clearly. Remind students to look up from their text while speaking.

C 👥 Work with a partner. Write a brief speech for a candidate running against Mike Gold. Perform your speech for another pair. ⏱ 10–15 min

Point out the things Mike Gold wants and tell students that someone running against him might be against those things. Put pairs in groups to perform their speeches.

TEACHING OPTION: Support / challenge
Hold an election for class president. Students can nominate their peers and form parties. Candidates and their advisers can form platforms (positions on issues). Have each candidate give a speech to the class. Then hold a secret ballot and elect the president.

EXTRA! Dictation
Dictate the following paragraph to students. They should write down your words exactly. First read the paragraph all the way through. Next read each sentence twice, pausing each time so that students have a chance to write. Then read the entire paragraph again. ⏱ 15 min

Today the campaign for mayor continues. Mike Gold is speaking to the crowd. He is promising that there will be no new taxes. But he also wants there to be more schools and highways. How will he pay for his new ideas? People are listening and carrying signs. I wonder who will win the election?

Check the answers by having individual students write sentences on the board.

EXTRA! Speech contest
Tell your students that you will hold a competition to decide who can give the best speech. Set a general topic for the speech that allows students to use different supporting ideas, and come up with different points of view. You can choose the topic yourself or let students help. Give students a day or two to prepare their speeches outside of class. Evaluate the speeches for content, language, and delivery. You can award the prize or let the students vote for the best speaker.

You can also have students give each other feedback on their speeches. Students should have enough small pieces of paper to have one for each member of the class. On the papers, have them write:

Name:

Topic:

I liked:

You could improve:

They should complete one for each speaker and give them to him or her at the end of the speech. ⏱ 60 min

2 SEE IT AND SAY IT

A  Look at the picture. Use the words in the box to talk about it. Then answer the questions with a partner.

campaign	election	speech
candidate	enthusiastic	term
citizens	running for (a political office)	

- Is this Mr. Gold's first political campaign?
- Look at the banner. Which of these ideas does Mr. Gold support?

  building more schools   encouraging public transportation

  raising taxes   stopping business development

- Who do you think will vote for Mike Gold? Who is going to vote against him?

B Work with a partner. Write a brief speech for Mike Gold. Perform your speech for another pair.

C Work with a partner. Write a brief speech for a candidate running against Mike Gold. Perform your speech for another pair.

3 I'M EXHAUSTED BECAUSE...

A Match Camille's behaviors on the left with the causes on the right. Compare your answers with a partner's.

1. Camille is stressed out.
2. She's dizzy and hungry.
3. She's breathing hard.
4. She's shivering.
5. She's just swallowed two aspirin.

a. She's been playing tennis for two hours.
b. She forgot to bring her coat.
c. She works too much.
d. She skipped breakfast and lunch.
e. She has a headache.

B In two to three minutes, add as many items as you can to each category.

Things that make you...

1. cough: _cigarette smoke,_ _____

2. feel exhausted: _____

3. feel dizzy: _____

4. shiver: _____

C Ask a partner questions beginning with *What makes you...?* for each category in **B**.

4 TERRY'S DIARY

A Use the words in the box to complete Terry's diary entry about living in the city. (Three words are extra.)

action	opportunities
active	pollution
activity	taxes
affordable	traffic
dirty	transportation
in	with

Last night I went out with some old friends. They're all married and live in the suburbs. I'm single and still live in the city. They wanted to know why I still live here.

It's true—living in the city can be annoying sometimes. We have a problem with (1.) _____ streets. Plus, there's a lack of (2.) _____ housing. Everything is so expensive! The air (3.) _____ is pretty bad, too. You have to deal (4.) _____ a lot of these kinds of hassles every day.

On the other hand, the city is pretty great! First of all, there are a lot of job (5.) _____ here. I certainly have a well-paying job! The (6.) _____ can be pretty bad, but I avoid it. I take public (7.) _____ everywhere. I also stay (8.) _____ by walking all over the city.

The city is where all the (9.) _____ is, and I love it here!

B What kind of hassles (difficult or frustrating situations) do you have to deal with in your city or town? Make a list with a partner.

3 I'M EXHAUSTED BECAUSE ...

WARM UP Write the word *exhausted* on the board. Ask students to share examples of times when they felt exhausted. What had they done to become so tired? ⏱ 5 min

A 🔁 Match Camille's behaviors on the left with the causes on the right. Compare your answers with a partner's. ⏱ 10 min

Do item 1 as a class. Then pair students. Students can draw a line from the behavior on the left to the cause on the right, or they can write the letter of the cause next to the number of the behavior. Check the answers as a class.

B In two to three minutes, add as many items as you can to each category. ⏱ 5–10 min

Review the vocabulary in the exercise. Then tell students to brainstorm ideas in each category. Remind them to think of ideas beyond illnesses; for example, smoke makes you cough. Tell students to think of at least five words in each category. Write each of the categories on the board, then add all of the words that the students thought of. Explain new words as needed and help students understand why certain words or ideas don't quite belong.

TEACHING TIP: Brainstorming

Whether for a class exercise or for a writing assignment, students are often asked to engage in *brainstorming*. The idea of brainstorming is to think of as many ideas as possible in a short period of time. The key to successful brainstorming is to not judge or evaluate the ideas as they come up. If you or the students stop in the middle to criticize a word or idea as being impractical or inappropriate, it stops the flow of creative thinking. Remind students not to judge. Just push them to come up with as many ideas as possible in a short period of time: There are no bad ideas. There will be time to judge and evaluate the quality of the suggestions after the brainstorming period.

C 🔁 Ask a partner questions beginning with *What makes you...?* for each category in **B**. ⏱ 5–10 min

Assign partners. The first partner should ask *What makes you (cough)?* and fill in the blank with one of the categories from **B**. The second partner explains, then repeats the question for their partner to answer. Pairs alternate asking and answering questions. If necessary, assist students by writing possible answer forms on the board: *Smoke makes me cough*, or *I shiver when I suddenly become afraid*.

EXTRA! Writing practice

Assign students to groups to write a paragraph about one of the topics in **B**. They should describe a time when they experienced coughing, exhaustion, dizziness, or shivering. What was the cause? How did they feel? How long did it last? How did they finally stop it? Students can exchange their paragraphs and give each other feedback. Encourage students to write a second draft based on this feedback. Collect these for grading. ⏱ 30 min

4 TERRY'S DIARY

WARM UP Write the words *diary* and *journal* on the board. Ask students if any of them keep a diary or journal to write down thoughts, ideas, and experiences. Point out to students the difference between the word *diary* and the word *dairy*—which describes products that come from milk, including milk, cream, cheese, and butter. Note: In British English, the word *diary* has a similar meaning to the American terms *schedule* or *daily calendar*, especially in written form. ⏱ 5 min

A Use the words in the box to complete Terry's diary entry about living in the city. (Three words are extra.) ⏱ 10–15 min

Tell students to complete this exercise individually. Do not review the vocabulary in advance—see if students can complete the diary entry on their own. Check the answers by reading the diary entry aloud with the correct answers. If there is vocabulary that students don't remember, ask the class for help with the explanations.

B 🔁 What kind of hassles (difficult or frustrating situations) do you have to deal with in your city or town? Make a list with a partner. ⏱ 15 min

First tell students to brainstorm a list of difficult or frustrating situations. Then ask them to choose their top three. Tell them to spend five minutes thinking of how to best deal with these problems. What solutions can they think of? Ask students to share their best solution with the class.

Instructor's Notes

_____

_____

_____

_____

_____

5 POKER TIPS

WARM UP Poll the class to find out their views on gambling. Do students find the idea interesting and exciting, or does the idea of gambling seem foolish and wasteful to them? Have any students been to locations that are famous for gambling? What were their experiences? Note: If talking about gambling would offend your students, do not do this exercise. Use your judgment. 5–10 min

A Read the advice given by a professional about how to play poker well. Rewrite each tip in reported speech, using the verb in parentheses. 10 min

Tell students to turn in their books to page 106. Review the language used for reported speech. In **A**, point out the words in parentheses that students must use. Do item 1 together. Then, students can complete the exercise individually. Check the answers by asking for students to volunteer their answers and write them on the board.

B Now think of a sport or game that you know how to play. Complete the sentences below. Don't show anyone! 10 min

Tell students to think of a sport or game, but not to say it out loud. They should write their sentences on a separate piece of paper. Provide vocabulary as necessary. Remind them to not show any other students their completed sentences. If necessary, explain that *the object of the game* means the purpose or goal of the game.

C With a partner, take turns asking and answering questions about each other's sport or game. Can you guess what it is? 10–15 min

Model this exercise by thinking of a sport or activity but not telling students what it is. They should ask you questions about it. With the class, brainstorm possible questions, and write them on the board. Pair students to ask and answer each other's questions. Instead of alternating asking and answering, let one student ask and one student answer until the game or sport has been guessed. Then partners can change roles.

EXTRA! Two-minute presentations
Tell students to choose a sport, game, or activity to explain to the class. Give students time to prepare their presentation, perhaps as homework. When presenting, students have only two minutes in which to explain the basic idea of the game and a few of the rules. Appoint one student as the timer and be sure that he or she is strict about the time limit. 30–45 min

6 LISTENING

A You are going to hear a lecture. Complete the notes. Write no more than two words for each answer. Then answer the question below. **CD 1 Track 22** 10–15 min

Tell students to read through the notes before you play the audio. For this exercise, play the audio entirely, without pausing, and let students write down notes. Give students time to finish writing, then repeat the audio. Remind them to check a box to answer the question. Have students compare their answers with a partner's, then play the audio again. The third time through, stop after each paragraph (you can follow along on the audio script) and check the answers with the class. If necessary, explain that *to sweat* means to lose water from the body through the skin.

TEACHING OPTION: Support / challenge
Challenge students by having them take real notes. Students can read the notes on page 139. Then have them close their books and listen to the audio two or three times. They should take outline notes of the lecture. As a class, compare what they wrote to what was in the book. What did they miss that was important? What did they write that isn't in the book? What information do they think was not important to include?

Instructor's Notes

_____

_____

_____

_____

_____

_____

_____

_____

_____

5 POKER TIPS

A Read the advice given by a professional about how to play poker well. Rewrite each tip in reported speech, using the verb in parentheses.

1. Learn the different kinds of cards. (tell)

   _____

2. Don't bet too much money. (ask)

   _____

3. Study the other players' facial expressions. (ask)

   _____

4. Don't take unnecessary risks. (tell)

   _____

B Now think of a sport or game that you know how to play. Complete the sentences below. Don't show anyone!

People: There are... people on each team. / You play by yourself.

Equipment: The game is played with...

Location: It's played in / on...

Playing the game: The game starts when...

How to win: The object of the game is...

C 🔁 With a partner, take turns asking and answering questions about each other's sport or game. Can you guess what it is?

> Is it a sport?

> No. It's a card game.

> How many people play it?

> Four to six people play it. There aren't any teams—you play by yourself.

6 LISTENING

A 🔊 You are going to hear a lecture. Complete the notes. Write no more than two words for each answer. Then answer the question below.
CD 2 Track 22

In which class would you probably hear this lecture?

☐ science

☐ math

☐ business

I. Dehydration: defined

A. Most of your body's weight is due to _____ —about _____%.

B. Dehydration occurs when the amount of water _____ the body is greater than the amount _____.

   1. "I'm dehydrated" means _____.

II. Causes

A. You can become dehydrated when you _____ a lot or are _____ on a hot day.

III. Symptoms

A. Include a _____ and getting _____.

   1. If you remain dehydrated, you may have to go to the _____.

UNIT 10

10 MONEY

ABOUT THE PHOTO

Shopping is considered one of the highlights of Ho Chi Minh City, Vietnam. For the truly fashion conscious, the boutique fashion stores in Ho Chi Minh City are a must because they offer something for all styles and budgets. Finding bargains on international, high-end brands is part of the excitement of shopping in Ho Chi Minh City. The Vincom Center is the city's largest and most luxurious shopping mall, with more than 250 stores. The mall occupies two sites, one in a colonial building, and the other across the street in a modern, glass skyscraper. This division reflects the contrasts of shopping in Ho Chi Minh City; the traditional Ben Thanh market is as popular for shopping as the fancy boutiques and malls. Offering everything from fresh produce to fashion to food stalls, the market is busy all day and night.

Did you know?
Ho Chi Minh City, also called Saigon, has an interesting mix of traditional Vietnamese temples, modern buildings, and French colonial architecture.

INTRODUCE THE THEME

• In this unit, students explore the concept of money. The language in the two lessons will help students communicate about ideas related to money, including being able to describe their saving and spending habits, making and accepting apologies, expressing hopes and regrets, and talking about money.

	Video	Vocabulary	Listening
LESSON A Saving and spending p. 142	Take the Money… and Run? p. 142	Money p. 143 *pay back, afford, borrow*	People's needs p. 144 Use background knowledge Listen for details Take notes Summarize
LESSON B Striking it rich p. 148		Big winner p. 148 *donate, invest, squander*	How millionaires live p. 149 Use background knowledge Make and check predictions Listen for details

 For students: My World Link Online has personalized instruction, practice, audio, and video.

Look at the photo. Answer the questions.

1 What store were the women shopping in?

2 How much do you think it costs to shop there?

3 Where do you like to spend money?

UNIT GOALS

1 Describe your saving and spending habits

2 Make and accept apologies

3 Express hopes and regrets using *wish*

4 Talk about things you do with money

Women in a shopping area in
Ho Chi Minh City, Vietnam

• In Lesson A, students watch a video which presents a social experiment: If people are offered free money, will they take it? Students will then learn how to describe their money habits. They will also practice the listening strategies of using background knowledge, listening for details, taking notes, and summarizing. Then they will learn how to make and accept apologies. Finally, they will learn how to talk about hopes and regrets.

• In Lesson B, students will learn how to describe other things we do with money, such as donate it or invest it. They will also read about unusual ways of making money, practicing the reading strategies of making predictions, reading for details, inferring meaning, and comparing and evaluating. They will also learn how to express impossibility, ability, necessity, and advice, and review stating opinions and explaining reasons.

WARM UP

Look at the photo. Answer the questions.

• Call on students to describe what they see in the photo.

• Have students answer the questions individually or in pairs, then compare answers with the class.

• Point out the unit goals and explain what students will learn. Elicit any key vocabulary students already know, and write it on the board. Explain any unfamiliar phrases in the unit goals to students.

Grammar	Pronunciation	Speaking	Reading	Writing	Communication
Wish statements pp. 146, 212	Word final /t/ and /d/ p. 152	Apologizing and accepting an apology p. 145	Money from unusual sources p. 150 Make predictions Read for details Infer meaning Compare and evaluate	Give an opinion on the best way to donate money p. 153	Renting an apartment p. 147
Negative modals pp. 152, 213					Persuading someone to donate money p. 153

If you saw someone in a city like this giving away an item for free, what would you do? Would you trust them?

1 VIDEO Take the Money... and Run?

A ▶ 🔁 Watch the first 45 seconds of the video. Fill in the blanks. Explain the experiment to a partner.

1. They set up a _____.

2. They are offering free _____.

3. People can _____ as much or as little as they want.

4. Hidden _____ are everywhere.

5. What will people do? Will they take any _____?

B 🔁 What do you think the people in the experiment will do? Why do you think that? Tell a partner.

C ▶ Now watch the full video. Right before each person makes a decision, make your prediction. Then watch and check your answer.

Will the person take it? If your answer is *yes*, how much will he or she take (a little or a lot)?

1. first young woman ☐ no ☐ yes │ ☐ a little ☐ a lot

2. older man ☐ no ☐ yes │ ☐ a little ☐ a lot

3. young man ☐ no ☐ yes │ ☐ a little ☐ a lot

D ▶ 🔴 Watch the end of the video. What do you think happens when they remove the man from the booth? How will the results of the experiment change? Discuss in a small group.

1 VIDEO
Take the Money... and Run?

WARM UP Have students look at the photo and describe what they see. Read the caption and, as a class, discuss their answers to the question. Explain that this waterfront is the location of the video they are about to watch. Do we usually trust people or not in that kind of situation? Why or why not? ⏱ 5 min

ABOUT THE VIDEO
This video poses an interesting question: Will people take money if it's being offered for free? Part of the National Geographic Channel's Emmy-nominated series, *Brain Games*, this video shows a hidden camera experiment carried out by the *Brain Games* team to try to answer the question. We're brought up to believe that "There's no such thing as a free lunch," and that things can be "too good to be true," so we can be distrustful. We're always looking for the catch when a situation seems too good to be true. The *Brain Games* team want to find out whether people's built-in distrust will keep them from taking advantage of an offer that really doesn't have any strings attached, and has no catch, so they set up a booth in a busy pedestrian area with a sign saying *Free Money*. As people pass by, they are offered money. How will people react? Will they be convinced? This experiment will provide the answer.

TEACHING TIP: Using English videos
Remind students to look at what is happening in the video: where the person is, what objects or other people there are, what the other people are doing, etc. Noticing these aspects will help students understand the context of what they are listening to, and therefore help them understand what is being said. It will also help them infer the meaning of words they are not familiar with. For example, in this case, the phrases *set up a booth*, *hidden cameras*, and *pinky promise* are easy to understand if students pay attention to what is happening as the narrator speaks.

A ▶ 🔁 Watch the first 45 seconds of the video. Fill in the blanks. Explain the experiment to a partner. ⏱ 5–10 min

Explain to students that they are going to watch a video about an experiment to see what people will do when they are offered something for free. Have them read the items. Remind students they don't need to understand everything they hear in order to understand what is happening. Play the first part of the video twice for students to complete the blanks. Have students explain the experiment to a partner. Check answers with the class.

B 🔁 What do you think the people in the experiment will do? Why do you think that? Tell a partner. ⏱ 10 min

With the same partner, have students say what they think people will do and why. Will they take the money or not? Have students share their opinions. Ask what they would do.

C ▶ Now watch the full video. Right before each person makes a decision, make your prediction. Then watch and check your answer. ⏱ 10 min

Go over the directions with the class and make sure students understand that they need to predict what each person will do: take some money or not, and if yes, how much will they take. Play the video, pausing before each person so students can make their predictions. Check answers with the class.

D ▶ 🔢 Watch the end of the video. What do you think happens when they remove the man from the booth? How will the results of the experiment change? Discuss in a small group.

Play the last part of the video again, then assign students to groups of three or four to discuss the questions. Monitor and encourage students to explain their reasons. Compare predictions as a class, having students explain their reasons.

EXTRA! Post-viewing
Have students find and watch another *Brain Games* episode online and take notes so they can explain the experiment or idea to another student. Have students explain the episodes in pairs or small groups, then as a class discuss the most interesting ones, or ones with the most surprising results. ⏱ 10 min

Extra video vocabulary
(the) catch
distrust / trust
guaranteed win situation
hesitate
no strings attached
practical joke
trick
trust detectors go off

2 VOCABULARY

Money and banking
ATM, bank machine
buy, pay for
cash, coins, bills
save

A Read the money quiz and review the items in **blue**. Then take the quiz. ○ 10 min

Go over the words in the Word Bank with the class. Have students read through the quiz and work out the meaning of the words in blue. Tell them they can look them up if they need to, but to first try to work them out by reading the complete context. Then go over the words, having students explain their meaning. Students should then answer the quiz.

CULTURE TIP: Talking about money
Attitudes and ideas about money vary across cultures. In some parts of the world, people are curious about and interested in money. In China, for instance, it is not uncommon for a stranger to ask you how much money you make. In some English-speaking countries, such as the United States and Canada, it is considered impolite to ask a person about their salary. This is considered to be private information. It is also generally impolite to ask a person how much they paid for something—unless they volunteer the information because they are proud of having made a good deal.

B 🔄 Share your answers with a partner. Ask and answer follow-up questions. ○ 10–15 min

Read the speech bubbles with a student to model the exercise. With a partner, students should alternate asking and answering the questions. Tell them to extend the conversation by asking follow-up questions, such as, *Why is that?* or *Why do you think that?* Finish the exercise with a whole-class discussion.

EXTRA! The whisper game
Divide the class into circles of eight to ten students. Tell them that they are going to pass information around the circle, whispering so that others can't hear. Listeners are not allowed to ask questions—they should just repeat what they hear. Have the first student in each circle write down one of his or her answers from the discussion in **B** and hold on to it. Then have the student whisper his or her sentence to the person on their right. Students should pass the sentence on by whispering, until it makes it back to the person next to the original speaker. Then that person should also write down what he or she hears. Compare the two statements. Are they the same? Repeat the exercise with other students, using different answers from their discussion in **B**. For smaller classes, this can be done with the whole class. ○ 10–15 min

Instructor's Notes

2 VOCABULARY

A Read the money quiz and review the items in **blue**. Then take the quiz.

1. a. I **make a budget** and **stick to it**.
   b. I don't **have a budget**, but I want to try to make one.
   c. Budget? What budget?

2. a. I should **save** more **money**, but I never seem to do it.
   b. I sometimes save a little, but then I always spend it.
   c. Saving money is easy for me because I have a goal in mind.

3. a. I try not to **borrow money** because it's always hard to **pay** it **back**.
   b. I sometimes borrow money even though I don't like to **go into debt**.
   c. I borrow money when I need to.

4. a. When I **lend money**, I don't worry about people **owing** me.
   b. People don't usually ask me for money.
   c. I can't **afford** to lend anyone money. I'm too **broke**.

5. a. I can **get by** on very little money. I'm used to it.
   b. When I'm **short on cash**, I don't go shopping or out to eat.
   c. I need a certain amount of money to live well.

Word Bank
Things we do with money
stick to / **make** / **have** a budget
save ↔ **spend** money
borrow ↔ **lend** money

B 💬 Share your answers with a partner. Ask and answer follow-up questions.

> Saving money is easy for me because I have a goal in mind.

> Really? What goal is that?

Many countries put images that are important to them on their money. South Africa's money has images of the country's famous wildlife.

1 VOCABULARY

A  Have you, or someone you know, ever won anything in the lottery? Tell a partner.

B Read the question and answers in the box. Write each item in **blue** next to its definition.

1. give to charity: _____

2. make a lot of money suddenly: _____

3. save: _____

4. money you've made: _____

5. waste: _____

6. use money to make more money: _____

C  Answer the question in the box. Explain your answer(s) to a partner.

> I would set aside some of the money. It's always good to save money. Then I'd buy a car!

*Imagine you **strike it rich** in the lottery. What would you do with the money?*

a. I'd **donate** some to a charity (an organization that helps others).

b. I'd **invest** some in a house.

c. I'd **set aside** some of the **earnings** for the future.

d. I'd probably **squander** the money on things like expensive cars and vacations.

Word Bank
Word partnerships with *money*
donate
earn / make
invest
set aside / save ↔ spend
squander / waste

STRIKING IT RICH

1 VOCABULARY

WARM UP Have students look at the photo and say what the balls are for. What are the numbers on the balls for? Is their a national lottery in the students' country? ⏱ 5 min

A 🔁 Have you, or someone you know, ever won anything in the lottery? Tell a partner. ⏱ 5 min

Assign students to pairs to discuss their experiences with the lottery. Call on students who have won, or who know someone who has won, to share their experience with the class.

CULTURE TIP: Jackpots
In a lottery, the prize is often called a *jackpot*. The largest jackpot ever was US$1.6 billion, and that was in 2016 in the United States. In Europe, the largest jackpot amount, €190, has been won twice, first in 2012 and then again in 2014. Asia's largest jackpot, US$87 million, was won in China in 2012. Also in 2009, South America's largest prize of R$145 million was won in Brazil.

B Read the question and answers in the box. Write each item in **blue** next to its definition. ⏱ 10 min

Point out the collocations in the Word Bank and say them for students to repeat. Don't answer questions about meaning yet. Have students read the information, and then work out the meanings. Have students compare their answers with a partner's, then check answers with the class.

C 🔁 Answer the question in the box. Explain your answer(s) to a partner. ⏱ 10–15 min

Read the situation and the question in the box and tell students your answer, prompting them to ask you a follow-up question. Then tell them something else you would do and have them ask you a question. Assign students to pairs to discuss their answers. Call on different students to tell the class what their partner would do if he or she won the lottery.

EXTRA! A special prize
Tell students to imagine they have won $10,000 (or a similar sum) in a lottery. However, the prize has a special rule: the winner can use the money only to buy things for other people—family, friends, or people they don't know (such as for a charity). Tell students to write down what they would buy, for whom, and why. When all students are ready, put them in groups of four to six to compare answers. Then discuss the answers with the whole class. Who had an unusual plan? ⏱ 5 min

Instructor's Notes

2 LISTENING

STRATEGIES: Use background knowledge; Make predictions; Check predictions; Listen for details

WARM UP Ask students if they know of people who are very wealthy. Who are they? How did they come to be so rich? You may wish to prepare by going online and finding a list of the wealthiest people in the world or in your students' country. ⏱ 5 min

A **Use background knowledge.** Name a famous millionaire. How did the person make his or her money? Discuss with a partner. ⏱ 5–10 min

Assign students to pairs to discuss famous millionaires. Provide vocabulary as necessary. Call on different pairs to tell the class about one of the people they talked about. Write a list of millionaires and how they made their money on the board.

Use background knowledge. Students bring to any text the knowledge they already have about life and the world in general, as well as any knowledge they have about the specific topic of the text. Activating this knowledge prior to listening will help them be more prepared when they listen.

B **Make predictions.** Read the information below and then guess the answers to 1–3. ⏱ 5–10 min

Have students read the information and then make their predictions. Share predictions as a class. If students have different answers, have them explain why they made the predictions they made.

Make predictions. Remind students that predicting before they listen helps them be more prepared for the text as they will have activated prior knowledge of the topic and language related to it.

C **Check predictions.** Listen to the interview, and check your answers in **B**. Correct the false statements.
CD 2 Track 26 ⏱ 10 min

Play the audio for students to check their predictions. Have students compare their answers with a partner's, then play the audio again. Have students correct the false statements.

Point out the Information box. Tell students to listen for how these phrases are used in the audio. Play the audio. Ask for volunteers to explain the usage in their own words.

Check predictions. It is important to always go back to the predictions students made and help them see what they guessed correctly, and talk about why incorrect guesses were wrong.

D **Listen for details.** What do you remember? Complete the sentences. Then listen and check your answers.
CD 2 Track 26 ⏱ 10 min

Have students read the sentences and complete them from what they remember. Play the audio again for them to check and complete their answers. Check answers with the class.

Listen for details. Remind students that they do not need to hear and understand everything in order to understand specific details. Encourage them to get into the habit of identifying key words to listen for before they listen.

E **Answer the questions with a partner.** ⏱ 10–15 min

Have students think about their answers to the questions, then assign them to pairs. Monitor and provide help as necessary, and ask questions to prompt further conversation. As a class, discuss whether they were surprised by what most millionaires do and don't do.

Instructor's Notes

_____

_____

_____

_____

_____

_____

_____

_____

_____

_____

_____

_____

2 LISTENING

A 🗣 **Use background knowledge.** Name a famous millionaire. How did the person make his or her money? Discuss with a partner.

B **Make predictions.** Read the information below and then guess the answers to 1–3.

> Two researchers studied wealthy people. They wrote about their findings in a book called *The Millionaire Next Door.* Here are some things they learned.

Most millionaires…

1. wear expensive clothes.	True	False
2. drive expensive cars.	True	False
3. donate some of their money.	True	False

Word Bank
affordable = not expensive
millionaire = a person with at least a million dollars
wealthy = rich

C 🔊 **Check predictions.** Listen to the interview and check your answers in **B**. Correct the false statements. **CD 2 Track 26**

D 🔊 **Listen for details.** What do you remember? Complete the sentences. Then listen and check your answers. **CD 2 Track 26**

> ℹ️ Notice how the man speaking uses *(but) actually* and *but in fact* to show the opposite of what people think.

Most millionaires…

1. don't squander their money on expensive _____ or _____.

2. _____ their earnings in things like property.

3. make an annual _____ and don't _____ more money than they _____.

4. _____ some of their money for the future.

E 🗣 Answer the questions with a partner.

1. How did your idea of a typical millionaire in **B** compare to the speaker's?

2. Do you do any of the things in **D**? Which ones?

> I thought most millionaires…, but actually, they…

3 READING

STRATEGIES: Make predictions; Read for details; Infer meaning; Compare and evaluate

WARM UP Ask students if they can name any unusual or interesting jobs or ways to make money. Make a list on the board. ⏱ 5 min

A **Make predictions.** Look at the pictures and the title of the article. How do you think these two groups have made money? Tell a partner. ⏱ 5–10 min

Assign students to pairs to predict how the two groups of people are making money. Share predictions and write them on the board.

Make predictions. Remind students that predicting before they read helps them be more prepared for the text as they will have activated prior knowledge of the topic and language related to it.

B **Read for details.** Read and answer the questions about your people only. Write your answers on a piece of paper. ⏱ 5–10 min

Go over the directions and the questions with the class. Assign students to A-B pairs and make sure they know who is reading which text. Remind them to focus on the details they're looking for. Have them write the answers to the questions so they have them for **C**.

Read for details. Remind students that reading for details means reading a text more slowly and in depth. When they read for details they should pay attention to unfamiliar words, but try to guess their meaning from the context before they look them up.

C Ask your partner the questions in **B** about his or her people. Take notes. Then read the other profile to check your partner's answers. ⏱ 10 min

3 READING

A **Make predictions.** Look at the pictures and the title of the article. How do you think these two groups have made money? Tell a partner.

B **Read for details.** Read and answer the questions about your people only. Write your answers on a piece of paper.

Student A: Read about the San.

Student B: Read about the monks.

1. Where do they live?
2. How do they make their money (or how will they in the future)?
3. How do they spend their money (or how will they in the future)?

C Ask your partner the questions in **B** about his or her people. Take notes. Then read the other profile to check your partner's answers.

D **Infer meaning.** Find the words in **bold** in the reading. Complete each sentence with the correct word(s).

1. If something is *worth money*, it is / isn't valuable.
2. You get *easy money* by working hard / without working at all.
3. If money *pours in*, it comes to you quickly / slowly.
4. If you *accept* something, you take it from / give it to another person.

E **Compare and evaluate.** Answer the questions with a partner. Use your notes to help you.

1. Are the San and the monks similar in any way?
2. Think about the ways the San and the monks are making money. Do you think it is good for them to earn money this way? Why or why not?

150 UNIT 10 Money

MONEY
FROM UNUSUAL SOURCES

TEACHING TIP: Unfamiliar vocabulary in reading texts

After reading, allow students a limited number of "free" vocabulary explanations. First guide them through guessing as many words as possible. At that point, write their remaining vocabulary requests on the board. Let students vote on which ones you'll explain. Tell them to add their individual choices of interesting or useful words to their vocabulary notebooks.

EXTRA! Discussion

Ask students whether they think one of the ways of making money in the article is more appropriate. Have them debate this, justifying their opinions. ⏱ 15 min

EXTRA! Writing prompt

Students can research and write a short composition on a group that raises money in an interesting way to help others. ⏱ 15–20 min

Greek monks

When you think of a monk, you might think of a quiet man living in a place far away from others. The "free monks" of Greece do live far from others, but they are anything but quiet. In fact, they sing. They have been recording songs and selling many albums in Greece.

People of all ages love them. Their songs are recorded in different styles (digital keyboard and rock, for example) and are not only religious. The monks also sing about problems like drugs and globalization.

The cash from music sales isn't **pouring in**, but the monks are earning some money. A few people don't like this; they think monks shouldn't sing for money. But the monks happily **accept** the money. They set it aside for summer camps for teenagers. The monks also donate some of the money to social programs that help many people.

The San people have lived in Southern Africa for almost 40,000 years, hunting[1] animals and gathering plants. But recently, many San people lost their land. Some tried to move to large cities, but it was hard to get jobs. Broke, they returned home and watched as their culture and traditions began to die.

But all this may be changing. The San have struck it rich. They recently signed an agreement with a large drug company. The San have traditional knowledge about plants that is **worth** a lot of **money**. The drug company is especially interested in a particular plant and how the San use it.

In the past, the San went on long hunting trips. While away from home, they ate a special plant to slow their hunger. Using the San's knowledge, the drug company wants to make a new medicine from this plant. For people around the world who have weight problems, this drug could really help.

The San are being careful with this "**easy money**." They plan to use it to create jobs for their people. They also want to focus on education. Through education, they hope to save their culture and language for future generations.

[1] If you *hunt* an animal, you follow and kill it for food.

Southern Africa's San people

LESSON B • Striking it rich **151**

Have students ask their partner about the people he or she read about and answer the questions. Once they have the answers for both groups, they should read the text they didn't read and check the answers. Check answers with the class.

D Infer meaning. Find the words in **bold** in the reading. Complete each sentence with the correct word(s). ⏱ 10 min

Students should complete the sentences independently and then compare their answers with a partner's. Tell them to go back to the text and check the context if they disagree on any. Then check answers with the class.

Infer meaning. Remind students that it is often possible to work out the meaning of a new word from how it is used in the text. They should look at the whole sentence, not just the isolated word, and try to decide what kind of word it is (verb, noun, etc.). This will help them guess its meaning. They should also use the context the word is being used in to help them infer its meaning.

E 🔄 **Compare and evaluate.** Answer the questions with a partner. Use your notes to help you. ⏱ 10–15 min

Go over the questions with the class, then give students time to look at their notes from **B** and **C** and think about their answers. Assign them to pairs to discuss the questions. Monitor and prompt pairs with questions as necessary. As a class, discuss answers.

Compare and evaluate. Comparing and then evaluating what they have read helps students to clarify their understanding. By comparing two concepts or situations from a text in order to evaluate them, students are pushed to question what they think they understood, and confirm or modify this understanding to compare and evaluate effectively.

TEACHING TIP: Extensive reading
You may wish to use additional reading materials with your class. Research shows that student abilities are improved by doing extensive reading—that is, to read longer passages at a level of difficulty that is not too challenging for them.

EXTRA! Post-reading
Students can work with a partner to prepare a report about a famous person, how he or she achieved success, and how he or she contributes to society by supporting organizations working with social issues. What can we learn from his or her career? ⏺ 60 min

4 GRAMMAR

A Turn to page 213 and complete the exercises. Then do **B–D** below.

Negative Modals	
Impossibility	You **can't** have the winning lottery ticket. I have it!
Ability	Sorry, but I **can't** lend you any money. I'm broke.
Necessity	You **don't have to** / **don't need to** be rich to travel.
Advice	You **shouldn't** waste money on expensive cars.
Strong advice	You**'d better not** lose this ring. It's very valuable.

B 🔊 **Pronunciation: Word final /t/ and /d/.** Listen and repeat. Pay attention to the final /t/ and /d/ sounds. **CD 2 Track 28**

1. can'**t**   You can'**t** have the winning ticket.
2. don'**t**   You don'**t** have to be rich.
3. shouldn'**t**   You shouldn'**t** waste money.
4. You'**d** better no**t**   You'**d** better no**t** lose this ring.

C Complete the sentences with the negative form of each modal.

1. Money (can) _____ buy happiness.
2. You (should) _____ borrow money from friends.
3. You (have to) _____ go to college to get a good job.
4. You (had better) _____ show your wallet on the subway. Someone might steal it.
5. You (need to) _____ work for a large company to earn good money.
6. You (should) _____ pay for most things with a credit card.
7. You (can) _____ get married until you have a good job.

D 🔁 Say each sentence in **C** aloud. Pay attention to your pronunciation. Do you agree or disagree with each statement? Why? Tell a partner.

> You shouldn't pay for most things with a credit card.

> I agree. It's easy to spend too much money and go broke.

4 GRAMMAR
Negative modals

WARM UP Ask students to name things that a) they are unable to do, and b) that it is not a good idea to do. Write the list on the board and practice using negative modals such as *can't* and *shouldn't.* ⏱ 5 min

A Turn to page 213 and complete the exercises. Then do **B–D** below. ◖ 20–30 min

Go over the examples in the chart and elicit further examples for each one. Remind students that after modals, the verb is always in the base form, it doesn't change no matter what the subject is. The grammar chart on page 213 includes further examples and usage explanations, expanding on the information in the chart on page 152.

TEACHING OPTION: The flipped classroom

To open up time for in-class communicative tasks, assign the Grammar Notes on page 213 as homework. Have students complete the exercises on My World Link Online as well.

The next time class meets:

1. Review negative modals in the Grammar Notes.

2. Go through the exercises students did for homework; present new examples and reinforce points as needed. Take questions from students.

3. Turn back to page 152 and do the communicative exercises there, starting with **B**.

GRAMMAR TIP: Negative modals

The key difference in the use of these modals is in the meaning they convey.

can't expresses inability to do something or impossibiity of something.

don't have to / don't need to express a lack of obligation = it isn't necessary to do something.

shouldn't expresses advice. It's better if you don't do this thing.

had better not expresses stronger advice. You mustn't do this thing.

B 🔊 **Pronunciation: Word final /t/ and /d/.** Listen and repeat. Pay attention to the final /t/ and /d/ sounds. **CD 2 Track 28** ⏱ 5 min

Say the two sounds for students to repeat. Help them notice the difference between them: the /t/ is voiceless and the /d/ is voiced. If students place their fingers on their throat and say each sound, they should feel the vocal chords move or vibrate for /d/ but not for /t/. Play the audio and have students repeat.

PRONUNCIATION TIP: Word final /t/ and /d/

Note that at the end of a syllable there is no aspirated /d/ sound.

Also note that the coarticulation of /n/ and /t/ makes the end of *can* and *can't* sound similar because the /n/ weakens the sound of the the /t/ in *can't*. When this happens, you can still tell the two apart because the /æ/ is shorter in *can't.*

C Complete the sentences with the negative form of each modal. ⏱ 5–10 min

Have students complete the sentences individually then compare their sentences with a partner's. Check answers with the class.

D 🔄 Say each sentence in **C** aloud. Pay attention to your pronunciation. Do you agree or disagree with each statement? Why? Tell a partner. ◖ 10–15 min

Assign students to pairs to talk about whether they agree or disagree with the statements in **C** and explain their reasons. Model the example with a student. Remind them to say each one aloud first to practice the pronunciation of the /t/ and /d/ sounds. Monitor and prompt with further questions as necessary. As a class, discuss the statements.

GRAMMAR TUTORIALS

• Negative Modals

Additional tutorials are available for reteaching and reinforcement.

Instructor's Notes

_____

_____

_____

_____

_____

_____

_____

_____

_____

_____

5 WRITING

WARM UP Have students brainstorm the kinds of organizations and institutes millionaires should donate money to. Write a list on the board. ⏱ 5 min

A 🔁 Read the question below and one person's reply on the right. What reason does the writer give for his opinion? Can you think of one more reason? Tell a partner. ⏱ 10 min

Go over the directions with the class. Then have students read the questions and the reply and answer the questions with a partner. Tell them to underline the reason the writer gives to support his opinion. Check the answer with the class and share other reasons students thought of. Point out the use of the connectors *for one thing* and *in addition* to introduce the reasons.

B What do you think? Outline your ideas and then write a paragraph. Think of two reasons one group should get the money and the others shouldn't. Explain each reason in a sentence or two as shown in the example. ⏱ 15–20 min

Go over the directions and have students decide which group they think should get the donation. Model an outline on the board. First write who the money should go to, then your reasons. Then have students write an outline. Remind them to organize their ideas into sections and to fill in those sections with notes, not complete sentences. Then have students help you begin writing your paragraph using the paragraph in **A** and the outline to guide them. Make sure they suggest sentences with negative modals. Finally, have students write their own paragraphs using their outline. Monitor and provide help as necessary. Make sure they use negative modals to express their opinion and their reasons, refer them back to pages 152 and 213 as necessary.

C 🔁 Exchange your writing with a partner. Circle any mistakes. Then return the paper to your partner. Make corrections to your own paragraph. ⏱ 10–15 min

Assign students to pairs and have them exchange papers and identify any mistakes in their partner's paragraph. Tell them to focus on the use of negative modals and the connectors to introduce their reasons. Then have students identify their partner's opinion and the reasons given to support the opinion. Encourage students to talk about their paragraphs together, *What was clear? What was confusing? What could be better?* Then have students rewrite their paragraphs, making the corrections and taking into account their partner's comments on how to improve it. Provide help as necessary. Collect the paragraphs to give students feedback.

PROCESS WRITING: Free writing
Free writing can also be used to generate ideas and as a good way to get ideas down on paper without outside influence or criticism. Try telling students to write for a brief period, maybe three minutes, without stopping. Tell them to not lift their pen from the paper as they write. They should just keep writing. You can use free writing during the planning stage to help students generate ideas for a first draft.

6 COMMUNICATION

WARM UP Write on the board, *debate*. Have students explain what a debate involves. Ask, *What kind of language should you use in a debate?* (formal, clear, strong, persuasive). ⏱ 5–10 min

A 🔵 Work in a group of four. Each person should take a role. Students A, B, and C should think of two reasons he or she should get the money. Student D should think of questions to ask the others. ⏱ 10–15 min

Go over the directions with the class and assign students to groups of four. Students can choose their roles or you can assign them. Have them work individually on preparing their ideas. Monitor and provide ideas and vocabulary as necessary. Write useful vocabulary on the board.

B 🔵 Have a debate. ⏱ 15–20 min

(See Student Book page 153 for complete instructions.)

Go over the directions and the steps. Make sure students understand how a debate works, that each speaker has two opportunities to speak; first to present his or her arguments, and then to argue against the other speakers' ideas. Read the examples and have students say which is the first speech and which is the second. Make sure the millionaire understands where he or she participates, and has his or her questions ready. Have groups carry out the debate simultaneously. Monitor and provide help as necessary. Note down any language difficulties you notice to explain afterwards. When groups have finished, survey them to see which organizations got the money and why.

EXTRA! Writing prompt
Tell students to imagine that it is 10 years into the future. They have become millionaires! Students should imagine the house they live in and their daily routine. They should also think about how they became a millionaire. Tell them to write the story of how they became rich. They should also write about what organizations they support and why. ⏱ 25–30 min

Instructor's Notes

_____

_____

_____

_____

_____

_____

5 WRITING

A 🔁 Read the question below and one person's reply on the right. What reason does the writer give for his opinion? Can you think of one more reason? Tell a partner.

> A millionaire in your community plans to donate money to one group below. Which one should get the money and why? Give two reasons.
>
> - A charity: It helps poor teenagers go to college.
> - A museum: It needs the money or it will close.
> - A hospital: It helps people with cancer.

> In my opinion, the millionaire should donate money to the hospital for two important reasons. **For one thing**, everyone needs a hospital. People don't have to go to museums, and they don't need to go to college. But a person with cancer has to go to a hospital. With the money, the hospital can help more people. **In addition**…

B What do you think? Outline your ideas and then write a paragraph. Think of two reasons one group should get the money and the others shouldn't. Explain each reason in a sentence or two as shown in the example.

In my opinion, the millionaire should donate money to the

_____.

For one thing, _____.

In addition, _____.

For these reasons, I believe the millionaire should donate money to the

_____.

C 🔁 Exchange your writing with a partner. Circle any mistakes. Then return the paper to your partner. Make corrections to your own paragraph.

6 COMMUNICATION

A 👥 Work in a group of four. Each person should take a role. Students A, B, and C should think of two reasons he or she should get the money. Student D should think of questions to ask the others.

Student A: You work for the charity.   **Student C:** You work for the hospital.

Student B: You work for the museum.   **Student D:** You're the millionaire.

B 👥 Have a debate.

1. Each student (A, B, C) speaks for one minute. The others take notes.

2. At the end of each student's talk, Student D can ask questions.

3. After all three students have spoken, each student (A, B, C) has one minute to speak and argue against the other ideas.

4. At the end, Student D decides who gets the money and explains why.

> I work for the hospital. It does cancer research. We should get the money for two reasons. For one thing…

> You said "teenagers don't have to go to college." But a person has to go to college to get a good job!

11 HONESTY

ABOUT THE PHOTO

This photo shows two men sitting on a bench outside of a store in a town in the Lombardy region of northern Italy. They appear to be sitting deliberately at either end of the bench, with their backs to each other. What does this gesture show? Are they angry with each other? Has there been some kind of disagreement? Physical gestures, such as turning your back to somebody, as well as words, can be used to express emotions. We reveal feelings through our posture, gestures, and facial expressions. This unit looks at being truthful and trustworthy. Can we tell from body language and facial expressions if someone's telling the truth? If not, can we trust them?

Did you know?

Children learn to lie by as young as two years old. Researchers found that more than 70% of young children who lied revealed the lie when asked a follow-up question. However, as they get older, children become more convincing. According to the research, only 50% of six- and seven-year-olds revealed the lie when asked a follow-up question.

INTRODUCE THE THEME

• In this unit, students will explore the concept of honesty. The lessons teach students to communicate about honesty and trust, including speculating about imagined events, giving advice, expressing opposing or unexpected information, and reporting what someone said.

	Video	Vocabulary	Listening
LESSON A Telling the truth p. 156	Are You a Good Liar? p. 156	Honesty p. 157 *exception, tell the truth, circumstances*	A résumé p. 158 Use background knowledge Listen for details
LESSON B Who do you trust? p. 162		Trusting someone p. 162 *counting on, keep my word, have confidence in*	Reasons to lie? p. 163 Identify key details Infer meaning Listen for gist Listen for details

For students: My World Link Online has personalized instruction, practice, audio, and video.

Look at the photo. Answer the questions.

1 How do these two people feel?

2 What do you think happened before the photo was taken?

3 Have you ever been *lied to*? How did you feel?

UNIT GOALS

1 Speculate about imagined events

2 Give strong advice

3 Introduce surprising or opposing information

4 Report what someone else has said

Two men turn their backs to each other in Lombardy, Italy.

- In Lesson A, students watch a video showing a test to find out if someone is likely to be a good liar or not. Students then learn to talk about being honest. They will also practice the listening strategies of using background knowledge and listening for details. Then they will learn how to give strong advice. Finally, they will learn how to talk about unreal or imagined events and say how they would react in certain situations.

- In Lesson B, students will describe the characteristics of a trustworthy person. They will also read about a situation where a couple were rescued by some trustworthy people, practicing the reading strategies of making connections, making predictions, sequencing events, and inferring meaning. They will also learn how to report what someone said, and finally they will write about a situation where they told a lie.

WARM UP

Look at the photo. Answer the questions.

- Call on students to describe what they see in the photo.

- Have students answer the questions individually or in pairs, then compare answers with the class.

- Point out the unit goals and explain what students will learn. Elicit any vocabulary students already know, and write it on the board. Explain any unfamiliar phrases in the unit goals to students.

Grammar	Pronunciation	Speaking	Reading	Writing	Communication
Present unreal conditionals pp. 160, 214	Repeating with rising intonation to show surprise p. 158	Giving strong advice p. 159	The kindness of strangers p. 164 Make connections Make predictions Sequence events Infer meaning	Describe a lie p. 166	Talking about dishonest actions p. 161
Reported statements with *say* and *tell* pp. 166, 215					Explaining your actions p. 167

1 **VIDEO** Are You a Good Liar?

A You are going to do a simple test to see if you are a good liar or not. Follow the steps below.

1. Hold a small piece of paper to your forehead.

2. Take five seconds and write the capital letter *Q* on the paper.

3. Find a partner and compare your letters.

B Watch the video. Fill in the missing words.

Some people (1.) _____ the *Q* in a way that could be read by somebody (2.) _____ them, with the tail on the (3.) _____ side of their forehead. If you did that, then you tend to be aware of how other people (4.) _____ you. You are (5.) _____ being the center of attention and you are a (6.) _____ liar.

Other people (7.) _____ the *Q* so that they themselves can read it, with the tail on the (8.) _____ hand side of their forehead. If you did that, then you tend to be more of an introvert and (9.) _____ very good at lying.

C Discuss these questions with a partner.

1. What do you think of the results from the video? How did you draw your letter *Q*?

2. Do you think it's easy to spot a "good liar"? If so, how do you do it? If not, why not?

VIDEO
Are You a Good Liar?

WARM UP Have students look at the photo and describe what they can see. Point out the lesson title and ask, *How does this picture relate to telling the truth?* Have students say whether they think they are good at telling lies or not.
⏱ 5 min

ABOUT THE VIDEO
The presenter of this video has a series of videos in which he explains something in 59 seconds. In this one, he explains a simple test that involves drawing a capital Q on your forehead. According to the presenter, how a person draws the Q reveals whether they are introverted or extroverted, and whether they are likely to be a good liar or not.

TEACHING TIP: Using English videos
Remind students that as with any audio or video, the first time they watch they shouldn't worry about understanding every detail. They should focus on understanding the gist of the video. Realizing they can understand the main ideas in a video in authentic English will help build their confidence. Encourage students to build on this confidence by watching short videos in English on the Internet about topics they're interested in outside of class.

A You are going to do a simple test to see if you are a good liar or not. Follow the steps below. ⏱ 5–10 min

(See Student Book page 156 for complete instructions.)

Have each student get a small piece of paper ready, then follow steps 1 and 2 as a class. Count 5 seconds as students draw their Q. Then have students do step 3 and compare their Q with a partner's. Have they done it the same or is it different? Don't answer questions about the significance of their Q's yet. Tell them they will find out when they watch the video.

B Watch the video. Fill in the missing words. ⏱ 10 min

Go over the text and tell students they should try to complete the missing information as they watch. Play the video twice, then have students compare their answers with a partner's. Play the video again, pausing as necessary, and check answers with the class.

C Discuss these questions with a partner.

Go over the questions with the class, then assign students to pairs to discuss them. Monitor and ask follow-up questions to encourage further discussion. Discuss the questions as a class. According to the presenter's theory, how many students are introverted and how many are extroverted? Do students agree? How do students spot liars? Write their ideas on the board.

EXTRA! Post-viewing
Students can either:

Find and watch another *59 Seconds* presentation and share what they learned with the class.

Or:

Research other ways of knowing if people are lying, or good liars, and share what they find with the class.
⏱ 10 min

Extra video vocabulary
be aware of (something)
dominant hand
gain an insight into (somebody or something)
introvert
trace

Instructor's Notes

_____

_____

_____

_____

_____

_____

_____

_____

2 VOCABULARY

Ask students if they think it is ever OK to lie. If so, under what circumstances? ⏱ 5 min

A 🔁 Look at the picture. Who are the people in it and what just happened? Do you think the boy is telling the truth? Why or why not? Tell a partner. ⏱ 5–10 min

Assign students to pairs to look at the situation and discuss the questions. Call on several students to share their opinions. It seems likely from the illustration that the boy is responsible for breaking the window but doesn't want to "admit it" or say that it is his fault. Perhaps he is afraid that the woman (his mother?) will be angry and punish him.

VOCABULARY TIP: *The* truth, *a* lie
Point out to students that the word *truth* takes the definite article *the*, but that the word *lie* takes the indefinite article *a*. *Lie* is a count noun. *Truth* is a noncount noun. The word *honest* can also be used independently as in the sentence: *I'm honest*. The opposite of *honest* is *dishonest*.

B Read the statements below. Notice the words in **blue**. Look up any expressions you don't know. Then check (✓) the boxes that are true for you. ⏱ 10–15 min

Explain the column headings if necessary. Go over the words and expressions in the Word Bank and have students repeat them. Be sure to give students time to look up any words that they don't know before they check the boxes in the columns.

TEACHING TIP: Looking up expressions
In **B**, students are told to look up the expressions they don't know. In many cases, a regular monolingual dictionary won't supply a full phrase. A learner's dictionary provides words in context. In this case, the dictionary should have "against the law" as one of the examples under the entry "against." "Hurt someone's feelings" and "depends on the circumstances" are listed as word partnerships or collocations in this kind of dictionary.

If your students cannot find expressions in a dictionary, they can try looking them up online, or ask a native speaker or instructor.

C 🔁 Discuss your answers with a partner. ⏱ 10 min

Clarify the meaning of any of the words in blue as necessary before beginning **C**. Give your students the language they need for this exercise by writing on the board: *I strongly agree that...*; *I agree that...*; *I disagree that...*; and *I strongly disagree that...*. Model the conversation by reading the speech bubbles with a student. Elicit a follow-up question for the second speech bubble, for example, *When do you think it is okay to lie?* Students can do this exercise in pairs or in a small group. Tell students to ask follow-up questions in their conversations.

CULTURE TIP: Honesty
Honesty is highly-valued in American culture. Two of the most famous US presidents have stories about their honesty—though it isn't clear if these events actually happened. The first US president, George Washington, supposedly cut down a cherry tree when he was a small boy. When asked by his mother if he had done it, he is said to have answered: "I cannot tell a lie. I chopped down the cherry tree." Another famous president, Abraham Lincoln, was known as Honest Abe. Lincoln is said to have walked several miles in order to return a small amount of change to another man when he was quite young.

EXTRA! Two truths and a lie
Divide the class into small groups of five to eight students. Students take turns giving three sentences about themselves. Two of the sentences should be true, and one of them should be a lie. It is the job of the other students in the group to guess which of the three statements is false. The game works better if the true statements and the lies are not too obviously true or false. ⏱ 10–15 min

Instructor's Notes

_____

_____

_____

_____

_____

_____

_____

_____

_____

_____

_____

2 VOCABULARY

A  Look at the picture. Who are the people in it and what just happened? Do you think the boy is telling the truth? Why or why not? Tell a partner.

Word Bank
an honest person ↔ a liar
(depend on the) circumstances
exception
hurt (someone's feelings)
obvious
reward someone ↔ punish someone (for their behavior)
tell the truth ↔ tell a lie

B Read the statements below. Notice the words in **blue**. Look up any expressions you don't know. Then check (✓) the boxes that are true for you.

	Strongly agree	Agree	Disagree	Strongly disagree
1. Honesty is always best. There are no **exceptions** to this rule.				
2. You should never lie if it's **against the law**.				
3. You shouldn't **tell the truth** if it **hurts someone's feelings**.				
4. The truth isn't always so clear—it's not really **obvious**.				
5. Sometimes I tell the truth, and sometimes I don't. It depends on the **circumstances**.				
6. You shouldn't **punish** small children too severely if they **tell a lie**.				

C  Discuss your answers with a partner.

> I strongly agree that honesty is always best. If you always tell the truth, you won't have any trouble.

> I chose *disagree* for that one. I don't think you should *always* tell the truth.

3 LISTENING

A 🔄 **Use background knowledge.** You are going to hear a conversation about a job résumé. When you prepare a résumé, what kind of information should be included? Make a list with a partner.

_____ _____

_____ _____

B 🔊 **Listen for details.** Listen. Check (✓) *True* or *False*. Correct the false sentences to make them true. **CD 2 Track 29**

	True	False
1. Cindy quit her job.	☐	☐
2. Denise was sick last week.	☐	☐
3. There was a problem with Cindy's résumé.	☐	☐
4. She lied about her hours.	☐	☐
5. Denise is worried about the amount of work.	☐	☐
6. Interviewing is happening today.	☐	☐

C 🔊 Listen. Complete the expressions with the missing words. **CD 2 Track 30**

1. Well, _____, I don't know the details.

2. Uh-huh. She _____ her experience.

3. I agree. I don't think her boss was very happy that she had _____ him.

4. It's too bad but, _____, I'm worried.

D 🔊 🔄 **Pronunciation: Repeating with rising intonation to show surprise.** Listen. Speaker B shows surprise by repeating what Speaker A says. Notice the rising intonation and stress. Then practice the conversations with a partner. **CD 2 Track 31**

Conversation 1

A: Cindy was fired.

B: She was fired? Why?

A: Because she lied on her résumé.

B: I can't believe it!

Conversation 2

A: Cindy got into trouble.

B: She got into trouble? How?

A: She dented her parents' car.

B: You're kidding!

E 🔄 **Pronunciation: Repeating with rising intonation to show surprise.** Work with a partner. Use the situations below to make short conversations about Cindy like the ones in **D**. Remember to repeat with rising intonation to show surprise.

1. fail her exam / cheat on it

2. get a ticket / be caught speeding

3. move out / have an argument with her roommate

3 LISTENING

STRATEGIES: Use background knowledge; Listen for details

WARM UP Ask students to think about the reasons why a person could be *fired* from their job. ⏱ 5 min

A 🔄 **Use background knowledge.** You are going to hear a conversation about a job résumé. When you prepare a résumé, what kind of information should be included? Make a list with a partner. ⏱ 10 min

Note that the word *résumé* is sometimes written with accent marks above the letter *e* (because it was originally a French word), but it can also be written without the accents. Both ways are correct.

Answers will vary here but might include information about previous jobs, including responsibilities and places of employment, as well as educational background and skills.

Use background knowledge. Students bring to any text the knowledge they already have about life and the world in general, as well as any knowledge they have about the specific topic of the text. Students need to know that they should draw on this knowledge to help them understand what they are going to listen to.

CULTURE TIP: Résumé vs CV
In American English, a paper with a person's credentials, work experience, and education is called a résumé. It is usually one page in length. A curriculum vitae (or CV) is a much longer document, which includes the same information as a résumé plus all publications, presentations, and detailed explanation of prior jobs. They are primarily used for professorships and are considered too lengthy for most job applications in the US.

British English, however, calls an American résumé a CV. When applying for a job, if it is not a teaching position, assume the employer wants the shorter, more concise version. If you are applying for a teaching position, you might want to inquire about which of the two documents the employer is really requesting.

LANGUAGE TIP: *Résumé* and *resume*
One reason to include the accents on the word *résumé* is to avoid confusion with the verb *resume*, meaning to continue to do something one has stopped doing. *Résumé* is pronounced with three syllables, with primary stress on the first syllable and secondary stress on the third syllable. *Resume* has only two syllables, with primary stress on the second. However, the accents are often left off the word *résumé*, so both spellings are considered acceptable.

B 🔊 **Listen for details.** Listen. Check (✓) *True* or *False*. Correct the false sentences to make them true. **CD 2 Track 29** ⏱ 10–15 min

Play the audio twice from beginning to end. Remind students that if the answer is false, they need to correct the sentence to make it true. Check the answers with the class by playing the audio and stopping when the answer is given.

Listen for details. Remind students that they do not need to hear and understand everything in order to understand specific details. Encourage them to get into the habit of identifying key words to listen for before they listen.

C 🔊 Listen. Complete the expressions with the missing words. **CD 2 Track 30** ⏱ 10–15 min

Play only the conversation and give students a chance to write their answer. Then repeat the conversation and check that students have written the correct answers in the blanks. Write any vocabulary that students have questions about on the board. Before explaining the words, see if another student can give the definition. Ask whether anyone was able to figure out the terms from context.

D 🔊 🔄 **Pronunciation: Repeating with rising intonation to show surprise.** Listen. Speaker B shows surprise by repeating what Speaker A says. Notice the rising intonation and stress. Then practice the conversations with a partner. **CD 2 Track 31** ⏱ 10 min

Play the audio while the students read along in their books. Explain the idea of rising intonation. Play the audio again. Read the sentences out loud, emphasizing the rising intonation, with students repeating after you. Then students can practice the conversations (using rising intonation) with a partner.

E 🔄 **Pronunciation: Repeating with rising intonation to show surprise.** Work with a partner. Use the situations to make short conversations about Cindy like the ones in **D**. Remember to repeat with rising intonation to show surprise. ⏱ 10–15 min

Do the first one with a student as a model, or make up a new example. If possible, students should work with a new partner. Tell students to follow the pattern in the conversations in **D**. They should have at least four exchanges. As partners are talking, walk around listening for correct intonation.

LANGUAGE TIP: Rising intonation
Students are often reluctant to raise the pitch of their voices sufficiently to create proper rising intonation. Writing words on the board and drawing a rising line above the words may help them to hear and reproduce the correct sound. Repeat the audio as needed for them to get it right.

4 SPEAKING

WARM UP Ask students: *Have you ever had a problem at a restaurant or store? What did you do?* ⏱ 5 min

A 🔊 Listen to and read the conversation. Where are Mr. and Mrs. Ward? What's the problem? **CD 2 Track 32**
⏱ 10–15 min

Play the audio for the students. Students can answer the questions as a class. Point out the intonation of Mr. Ward's *It's all right*, which suggest that it is, in fact, not all right. Play the audio again. Pause after each of the following phrases and ask if anyone can explain them in the context of the conversation: *send it back, I guess*.

VOCABULARY TIP: Steak cooking terms
If you order certain types of meat, such as beef, in a restaurant, the server will ask, *How would you like that done / cooked*? *Rare* indicates that the meat on the inside is red; *Well done* indicates that the meat is cooked all the way through. *Medium* is in between *rare* and *well done*.

CULTURE TIP: Service staff
In the United States, patrons at restaurants and stores generally treat the servers and staff with respect and courtesy. Unless the service is poor or the staff is rude, patrons are unlikely to complain. The value of equality in the United States means that the person being served and the person doing the serving are equals.

B 💬 What would you say to the waiter? How would you complain? Write an ending to the conversation and practice it with a partner. ⏱ 10–15 min

Answers to **B** will vary, but student responses should include the conversation between Mr. and Mrs. Ward and the waiter. Mr. Ward should explain that his steak was not cooked correctly. The waiter should offer to get him another piece of meat cooked medium rare. Useful expressions might include: *My steak is overcooked. I asked for medium rare, but this is well done. Could I please have another one?*

EXTRA! Writing prompt
Ask students to imagine that they have been to a restaurant where the food or service was poor. Direct students to write a letter or email of complaint about the incident to the owner or manager of the restaurant.
⏱ 20–25 min

SPEAKING STRATEGY

C 💬 Read about the three situations below. Choose one and write a role play with a partner. ⏱ 5–10 min

Read the Useful Expressions. Explain *insisting* if necessary. Then arrange partners in pairs. Students should read about all three incidents. They then should choose one of the three situations and prepare and practice a role play using the Useful Expressions. If time permits, students may practice role plays with the other situations.

D 🔵 Perform your dialog for the class. ⏱ 15–20 min

Bring pairs to the front of the class to perform their role plays. Take notes on students' use of expressions, delivery, grammar, vocabulary, and pronunciation. Give feedback individually in writing.

LARGE CLASS OPTION
Students can work in groups of 8–12 students. Tell students to act out their role play from **D** in front of the other students in the group. Students can offer critiques of language and style.

EXTRA! What would you do?
Tell students to write a short paragraph describing a situation in which they didn't know the right thing to do. Tell them to not put their names on their papers. Divide the class into groups of four, and appoint a secretary in each group. Give each group one paper. The group should read and discuss the situation, comparing what they would do, and the secretary should take notes. If time permits, each group can discuss several situations. Finish with one member of each group presenting the most interesting situation they discussed and group members' reactions. ⏱ 20 min

Instructor's Notes

_____

_____

_____

_____

_____

_____

_____

4 SPEAKING

A 🔊 Listen to and read the conversation. Where are Mr. and Mrs. Ward? What's the problem? **CD 2 Track 32**

MR. WARD: So, how's the chicken?

MRS. WARD: Delicious. How about your steak?

MR. WARD: It's all right...

MRS. WARD: Are you being honest? You don't sound very happy with it.

MR. WARD: Well, it's not cooked right. I asked for medium rare. This is well done.

MRS. WARD: Why don't you send it back?

MR. WARD: Oh, I don't want to bother anyone. I can eat it, I guess.

MRS. WARD: But it's expensive. I don't think you should eat it. Let's call the waiter. You won't hurt his feelings!

MR. WARD: Yeah, but...

MRS. WARD: If you don't say something, you're not going to enjoy your meal. Excuse me, waiter!

B 🔁 What would you say to the waiter? How would you complain? Write an ending to the conversation and practice it with a partner.

SPEAKING STRATEGY

C 🔁 Read about the three situations below. Choose one and write a role play with a partner.

Student A: Play the role of one of the friends or the coworker.

Student B: Warn Student A about his or her actions. Use the Useful Expressions to give strong opinions.

Useful Expressions: Giving strong advice
If you don't leave a bigger tip, the waiter **is going to** be upset.
I don't think you should spend so much time playing games on your computer.
You have to do your homework by yourself.

Your friend, who is a student in the US, often doesn't leave a big enough tip in restaurants.

Your coworker wastes a lot of time playing games on her computer.

Your friend, who doesn't like to study, often copies another friend's homework.

D 👥 Perform your dialog for the class.

5 GRAMMAR

A Turn to page 214. Complete the exercises. Then do **B–C** below.

Present Unreal Conditionals	
If clause	**Result clause**
If you **told** the truth,	(then) you **would feel** relieved.
If I **didn't have** a lot of homework,	(then) **I'd go** to the movies.
If I **found** a wallet,	(then) **I'd return** it.
Result clause	**If clause**
You**'d feel relieved**	if you **told** the truth.

Present unreal conditionals are used to talk about imagined or unreal events.
The *if* clause presents an imagined condition. It is not true right now.
The result clause presents an imagined result. It can come first or second in the sentence with no change in meaning.

B Use the correct form of the verb in parentheses to make present unreal conditional sentences.

1. If I (graduate) __graduated__ with honors, I (throw) __would throw__ a big party.

2. If today (be) _____ a holiday, I (stay) _____ at home.

3. If I (have) _____ a lot of time off, I (go) _____ to Colombia.

4. I (not / have) _____ time to see my friends if I (get) _____ a part-time job.

5. If I (not / study) _____ English, I (study) _____ German.

6. I (be) _____ good at basketball if I (be) _____ taller.

C  Get into a group of four people. Follow the steps below. See how long you can go for. Then switch roles and start again.

Student A: Start a sentence chain. Choose one of the *if* clauses in **B** and finish the sentence with your own idea.

Student B: Add a sentence to Student A's sentence.

Students C & D: Continue the game with your own sentences.

> If today were a holiday, I'd go somewhere fun.

> If I went somewhere fun, I'd buy a souvenir.

> If I bought a souvenir, I'd give it to...

> If you were in Istanbul, would you buy a lamp as a souvenir?

5 GRAMMAR
Present unreal conditionals

WARM UP With the students, review the future real conditional introduced on page 134. Emphasize that in that conditional, the future events are possible and that the verb in the *if* clause is in the simple present. Elicit some examples and write them on the board. ⏱ 5 min

A Turn to page 214. Complete the exercises. Then do **B–C** below. ⏱ 20–30 min

Go over the examples in the chart and have students identify the tense used in each clause (*if* clause: simple past; result clause: *would + base verb*). Point out that the result clause can come first, and that no comma is used in that case. Compare with the future real conditional examples from the Warm Up and help students understand that with this conditional we are talking about unreal, imagined situations (*I didn't tell the truth, so I don't feel relieved; I have a lot of homework, so I can't go to the movies,* etc.). Elicit examples related to students' lives, for example: *If I practiced more, I'd speak English more fluently. If the teacher didn't give us homework, we'd be happier.* The grammar chart on page 214 includes further examples and usage explanations, expanding on the information in the chart on page 160.

B Use the correct form of the verb in parentheses to make present unreal conditional sentences. ⏱ 10 min

Go over the example with the class, then have students complete the rest individually. Refer them to the charts on pages 160 and 214 as necessary. Have students compare their answers with a partner's, and then check answers with the class.

Note that in English, in sentences like number 1, you can say *have a party,* as well as *throw a party.* You cannot say *make a party* or *do a party.*

GRAMMAR TIP: Present unreal conditionals

When talking about present unreal conditionals, the *if* clause presents a condition that is not true right now. The result clause shows the unreal result of that condition. We use a past tense in the *if* clause, even though the meaning is present or future, and we use *would* + infinitive in the result clause of the sentence.

C 👥 Get into a group of four people. Follow the steps below. See how long you can go for. Then switch roles and start again. ⏱ 10–15 min

(See Student Book page 160 for complete instructions.)

Go over the directions and the steps with the class. Model the example with students, having them continue adding a few more sentences to the chain. Assign students to groups of four to play the game. Monitor and provide ideas and vocabulary as necessary. Make note of difficulties with the unreal conditional form to deal with afterwards.

TEACHING TIP: Form vs. meaning of grammar

Focus students' attention on the difference in meaning between the future real conditional and the present unreal conditional. What is the difference between *If I win the lottery, I will buy you a car* and *If I won the lottery, I'd buy you a car?* (The first one assumes the person bought a ticket and has expectations that their luck is good — maybe they've already matched the first four numbers. The second can mean the person hasn't even bought a ticket. They are really just dreaming about being rich but don't have any real expectation to win the lottery.) Draw students' attention to the difference between the sentences and the formation.

EXTRA! What if?

Write the following on the board. Then, in pairs, have students make up sentences in response to indicate what they would do.
What would you do if...
   you inherited a million dollars?
   you could be any animal?
   you were in an earthquake right now?
   you spoke four languages fluently?
   you didn't have to work?
   you ran your own company? ⏱ 10–15 min

🔊 GRAMMAR TUTORIALS
• Present Unreal Conditionals

Additional tutorials are available for reteaching and reinforcement.

Instructor's Notes

_____

_____

_____

_____

_____

_____

_____

_____

_____

6 COMMUNICATION

WARM UP Ask students if they have ever been in a difficult situation where they had to decide whether something was right or wrong to do. What was the situation? What did they decide? What was the outcome? ⏱ 5 min

A Look at the situations. Would you ever do any of these things? Write *yes*, *no*, or *maybe*. ⏱ 10 min

Note that not all of the suggested activities are illegal and some are not definitely wrong. However, most of them are either not polite or are of questionable honesty.

B 🗣 Discuss your answers in **A** with a partner. ⏱ 10–15 min

Point out to students the information about adverbs in the Information box and model the example answers in the speech bubbles at the bottom of the page. Tell students to use follow-up questions to extend the conversation. They should take turns asking and answering the questions. When they are finished, conclude the exercise with a whole-class discussion about these ethical questions.

ℹ️ *Definitely* and *probably* are useful adverbs to modify the verbs in the answers to these questions. If the answer is *no*, you might use the adverb *never* to modify the verb in your response.

LARGE CLASS OPTION
For each of the situations in **A**, students can write one sentence with *I would* and one with *I wouldn't*. For example: *I wouldn't keep a pair of sunglasses I found on the ground. Somebody might come back to look for them.* Divide the class into groups of six to eight and have them compare answers. Which situations did they all agree about?

EXTRA! Writing prompt
Many reality television programs challenge their participants to take part in unusual activities, such as eating live insects or doing dangerous stunts. Tell students to imagine that they are going to be on a reality TV show. What would they do? What wouldn't they do? ⏱ 20 min

6 COMMUNICATION

A Look at the situations. Would you ever do any of these things? Write *yes*, *no*, or *maybe*.

Would you ever...

1. eat a whole platter of food at a party? _____

2. keep a pair of sunglasses that you found on the ground? _____

3. use the restroom in a cafe without actually buying anything there? _____

4. stand and read an entire magazine in a store without buying it? _____

5. download music, TV shows, or movies from the Internet without paying? _____

6. take extra supplies from your office to use at home? _____

B Discuss your answers in **A** with a partner.

> Would you ever keep a pair of sunglasses that you found on the street?

> It depends on the circumstances. If they were expensive, I'd probably keep them!

> If you answered *yes*, you can use *definitely* in your answer. If you answered *maybe*, you might want to use *probably* in your answer.

2 LISTENING

STRATEGIES: Identify key details; Infer meaning; Listen for gist; Listen for details

WARM UP Ask students if they have ever been told a lie, or told a lie themselves. What was the situation? ⏱ 5 min

A 🎧 What are some reasons that people lie? Make a list of ideas in your notebook with a partner. ⏱ 5–10 min

Assign students to pairs to make their lists. Have pairs share their ideas and write a list on the board.

B 🔊 **Identify key details.** Listen to the first part of a lecture. What are reasons people lie? List the two reasons you hear. Are either of these reasons on your list from **A**? **CD 2 Track 33** ⏱ 5–10 min

Go over the directions with the class. Make sure students understand what a lecture is. Remind them to take notes as they listen. Play the audio twice. Check answers with the class. Are the two reasons on the class list from **A**?

Identify key details. Remind students that to understand details, they need to focus on key words. This exercise will help raise their awareness of how key words help them work out details when they listen.

C 🔊 **Infer meaning.** Read sentences 1–4. The speakers use the expressions in italics in the talk. Listen to the full lecture and choose the best answer. **CD 2 Track 34** ⏱ 10 min

Go over the sentences with the students. Tell them they need to infer the meaning of each expression from the context. Play the audio and have students choose their answers. Then have them compare their answers with a partner's. Play the audio again, then check answers with the class.

Infer meaning. Remind students that inferring meaning means to work out the meaning of an unknown word or phrase from how it is used. Students need to think about the context, who is using the word or phrase, when, and to whom. These elements can help them infer the meaning.

D 🔊 **Listen for gist.** Read the sentences. Then listen again. Circle T for *True* or F for *False*. **CD 2 Track 34** ⏱ 10 min

Have students read the sentences and choose their answers if they think they already know them. Play the audio again for them to check or complete their answers. Check answers with the class, playing the audio again as necessary.

Listen for gist. Remind students that when listening for gist, they don't need to worry about understanding everything they hear, the purpose is to understand the general idea.

E 🎧 **Listen for details.** Answer the questions with a partner. Use information from the lecture to explain. ⏱ 10–15 min

Have students look at the photo and answer the question in the caption. Then assign them to pairs to answer the questions using the information they heard in the lecture. Call on different pairs to share their answers with the class.

Listen for details. Students can use the details they understood from a listening to be able to answer specific questions about the topic after they've listened.

Instructor's Notes

_____

_____

_____

_____

_____

_____

_____

_____

_____

_____

_____

_____

_____

_____

_____

_____

_____

_____

_____

4 GRAMMAR
Reported statements with *say* and *tell*

WARM UP Ask students if they have ever overheard something that they weren't supposed to hear. Who said it? What did they say? ⏱ 5 min

A Turn to page 215. Complete the exercises. Then do **B** and **C** below. ◑ 20–30 min

Go over the examples in the chart one by one and elicit what the tense shift is from quoted to reported speech in each one (simple present to simple past, etc.). Point out that with both *said* and *told*, *that* is optional, but with *told* they have to use a person (tell them to ask themselves, *Told who?* Told me/him/us/the instructor/ his friend, etc.). The grammar chart on page 215 includes further examples and usage explanations, expanding on the information in the chart on page 166.

GRAMMAR TIP: Reported speech
In reported speech, verb tenses shift as follows:

    simple present → simple past

    present progressive → past progressive

    present perfect → past perfect

    past → past perfect

    past perfect tenses do not change

B 🔀 Work with a partner. Follow the steps below. ⏱ 10–15 min

(See Student Book page 166 for complete instructions.)

Go over the steps with the class and model the examples. Elicit another example from students. Then assign students to pairs to take turns reporting the things Dylan said. Remind them to use *but in reality* and *in fact*. Monitor and provide help as necessary. Refer students to the charts on this page and on page 215 as necessary. Call on students to say sentences and write them on the board, with the class helping you correct them as necessary.

C 🔀 Answer the questions with a partner. ⏱ 10–15 min

Go over the questions with the class, then model the example. Assign students to pairs to answer the questions. Monitor and ask follow-up questions to prompt more conversation. Call on different students to share with the class something their partner told them.

EXTRA! Telephone game
Have students sit in a circle of 8–10 students. The first student makes a statement and whispers it in the ear of the person on their right. The second student reports what they heard by whispering it in the ear to the person on his or her right: *She said...*, and so forth. The reported statement travels around the circle until it comes back to the first student, who checks for accuracy and reports any differences to the group. The results can be very funny. (If your students sit in rows, the message can travel across the row. The last student to hear the message can get up and walk over to report the message to the first student.) This can be a whole-class exercise in small classes. ⏱ 10–15 min

GRAMMAR TUTORIALS
- Reported Statements (with *That*)

Additional tutorials are available for reteaching and reinforcement.

Instructor's Notes

_____

_____

_____

_____

_____

_____

_____

_____

_____

_____

_____

_____

_____

_____

_____

5 WRITING

WARM UP An old excuse for schoolchildren to tell the teacher is, *The dog ate my homework*. Ask students what creative excuses they have used to avoid completing school work. ⏱ 5 min

A 🔀 Read the paragraph and finish the story with a partner. ⏱ 15 min

Have students read the paragraph and answer the questions with a partner. Then they should write the end of the story together. Check answers with the class. Select a handful of students to read their endings to the class.

PROCESS WRITING: Sequencing
The structure of this story is in chronological order—that is, in time order, or order of occurrence. To help students sequence the events, use a chart. Students can then plan their paragraph in **B** using a chart to sequence the events in their story.

B Think about a time you (or someone you know) lied about something. Answer the questions in **A**. Then use your notes and the example to help you write a paragraph of your own. ⏱ 5–20 min

Assure students that you don't intend to pass judgment on them for their lie. This is simply an exercise to practice English. Have them think of the situation they want to write about and plan by answering the questions in **A** about their situation. Tell them they only need to write notes at this point. Provide vocabulary as necessary. Once students have their notes, have them write their paragraph using the example in **A** as a model. Remind them to use time markers to help them sequence the events. Refer them to the charts on pages 166 and 215 to help them with the reported speech as necessary. Monitor and provide help as necessary.

C 🔀 Exchange your writing with a partner. Read his or her paragraph. ⏱ 10–15 min

Assign students to pairs and have them exchange papers and identify any mistakes in their partner's paragraph. Tell them to focus on the use of reported speech and sequencing words. Then have students answer the questions in **A** about their partner's paragraph. Encourage students to talk about their paragraphs together, *What was clear? What was confusing? What could be better?* Then have students rewrite their paragraphs, making the corrections and taking into account their partner's comments on how to improve it. Provide help as necessary. Collect the paragraphs to grade if possible.

6 COMMUNICATION

WARM UP Elicit what students remember about Dylan from the Grammar page. Write things they remember him saying on the board. ⏱ 5–10 min

A 🔀 Work with a partner. Choose a situation about Dylan from the previous page. Create a role play, using reported speech. ⏱ 10–15 min

Go over the directions with the class and model the example with a student. Assign students to A-B pairs. Students can choose their roles or you can assign them. Have them work in their pairs preparing and practicing their role play. Monitor and provide ideas and vocabulary as necessary. Make sure they are using reported speech. Write useful vocabulary on the board.

CULTURE TIP: White lies
A white lie is a "small" lie that you tell to avoid hurting someone's feelings. Telling a white lie is acceptable, or even polite, in English-speaking cultures if the topic is not very important. For example, a person might tell someone else, "You don't look like you've gained weight." even though their clothes have gotten tight. A grandparent might tell a child, "You play the piano beautifully!" after only two weeks of piano lessons. To avoid going to a party, a person might say that they have family obligations. White lies are less acceptable in work or school situations, though.

B 🔀 Perform your role play for another pair. After you listen to the other pair, answer this question: How did Dylan explain his behavior? What did he say? ⏱ 10–15 min

Go over the directions and the questions. Have pairs join to make groups of four and perform their role plays for each other. Remind them to answer the questions after each one. Have volunteers perform their role play for the class.

EXTRA! Writing prompt
Tell students to imagine they have been invited to an event that they don't wish to attend. They should write a letter or email of apology in which they make up a white lie to avoid attending. ⏱ 15–20 min

Instructor's Notes

_____

_____

_____

_____

5 WRITING

A  Read the paragraph and finish the story with a partner.

1. Why did the writer lie? What did she say?

2. Did the other person find out the writer was lying? What happened?

B Think about a time you (or someone you know) lied about something. Answer the questions in **A**. Then use your notes and the example to help you write a paragraph of your own.

C Exchange your writing with a partner. Read his or her paragraph.

1. Are there any mistakes? If yes, circle them.

2. Answer the questions in **A** about your partner's writing.

3. Return the paper to your partner. Make corrections to your own paragraph.

> ### CAUGHT IN A LIE
>
> Last year, I lied to a classmate of mine. He invited me to go to the movies, but I didn't want to go. I also didn't want to hurt his feelings, so I said that I couldn't go to the movies. Even though I was fine, I said that I was sick. Later that same day, I went shopping with a friend. While we were shopping, I unexpectedly…

6 COMMUNICATION

A Work with a partner. Choose a situation about Dylan from the previous page. Create a role play, using reported speech.

Student A: You find out Dylan lied to you about something. Ask him to explain.

Student B: You're Dylan. Try to explain yourself.

GIRLFRIEND: So, Dylan, I was talking to Lena yesterday.

DYLAN: Yeah? What about?

GIRLFRIEND: She said that she had a party at her house.

DYLAN: Oh, I didn't go.

GIRLFRIEND: Oh really? It's obvious that you're lying, because she said…

B Perform your role play for another pair. After you listen to the other pair, answer this question: How did Dylan explain his behavior? What did he say?

UNIT 12

12 OUR WORLD

ABOUT THE PHOTO

Humpback whales migrate from the cold waters of Alaska to spend the winter months in warm waters off the Pacific coast of Mexico, where they breed and give birth. Whale watching is a popular tourist attraction during the months the whales visit, but great emphasis is placed on respecting the whales and protecting their habitat.

This photo won the National Geographic Traveler Photo Contest in 2015. It was taken by Mexican photographer Anuar Patjane Floriuk, and shows a humpback whale and her newborn calf swimming among divers. The whales were swimming near Roca Partida Island, about 390 km (242 miles) southwest of the Baja California Peninsula. Several species of whale have been in danger of extinction recently. Photos like this help raise our awareness of these incredible animals, and remind us of the need to take care of our world, its animals, and their habitats.

Did you know?
During the breeding period, male humpback whales sing. Their songs are considered to be the most complex in the animal kingdom. The humpback song usually lasts for 30 minutes, but some whales will sing for hours. Interestingly, humpbacks from the same area sing the same song, but it changes over time.

INTRODUCE THE THEME

- In this unit, students will explore the world we live in. The language in the two lessons will help students communicate about the natural world and the human impact on it,

Divers swim with humpback whales off the coast of Mexico.

	Video	Vocabulary	Listening
LESSON A The natural world p. 170	The Steward of Ormond Beach p. 170	Habitats p. 171 *declining, environment, endangered*	Talking about animals p. 172 Use background knowledge Listen for details and numbers
LESSON B The man-made world p. 176		An architectural marvel p. 176 *construction, efficient, sustainable*	A civil engineer's job p. 177 Listen for gist Listen for details

For students: My World Link Online has personalized instruction, practice, audio, and video.

Look at the photo. Answer the questions.

1 What animals are in the photo? What do you know about them?

2 What are the people doing? Why do you think they are doing this?

3 What is one way that humans might be affecting these animals and their natural habitat?

UNIT GOALS

1 Describe rare animals and their habitats

2 Ask questions in an indirect way

3 Offer another opinion

4 Talk about man-made structures and their impact on the environment

including being able to describe animals and habitats, ask indirect questions, offer opinions, and talk about man-made structures.

- In Lesson A, students watch a video about the steward of a beach in California. Students will then talk about endangered animals. They will also practice the listening strategies of using background knowledge, listening for details, and listening for numbers. Then they will learn how to offer opinions about where to live. Finally, they will learn how to ask indirect questions.

- In Lesson B, students will describe a man-made structure. They will also read about the challenges we face with rising sea levels, practicing the reading strategies of using background knowledge, making predictions, taking notes on key details, inferring meaning, summarizing, and giving an opinion. Finally, they will express opinions about issues cities face.

WARM UP

Look at the photo. Answer the questions.

- Call on students to describe what they see in the photo.

- Have students answer the questions individually or in pairs, then compare answers with the class.

- Point out the unit goals and explain what students will learn. Elicit any key vocabulary students already know, and write it on the board. Explain unfamiliar phrases in the unit goals to students.

Grammar	Pronunciation	Speaking	Reading	Writing	Communication
Embedded questions pp. 174, 216	Negative questions to confirm information p. 177	Offering another opinion p. 173	When the seas rise p. 178 Use background knowledge Make predictions Take notes on key details Infer meaning Summarize Give opinions	Give an opinion on new construction p. 181	Taking a quiz about the world p. 175
The passive with various tenses pp. 180, 217					Choosing a civic project p. 181

Walter Fuller walks down Ormond Beach, California.

1 VIDEO The Steward of Ormond Beach

A Read the title. What is a *steward*? What do you think a steward of a beach does?

B ▶ Watch the video. Circle *True* or *False* for each item.

1. Walter Fuller is the steward for Ormond Beach.	True	False
2. His other title is "protector of sea life of Ormond."	True	False
3. For the past 15 years, Walter has been living at Ormond Beach.	True	False
4. In the beginning, Walter visited the beach on his days off.	True	False
5. There are many wetland areas on the Southern California coast.	True	False
6. Walter used to be a volunteer.	True	False
7. In high school, Walter studied the eagle family.	True	False
8. The coastline is considered to be a beautiful part of the United States.	True	False
9. Walter says that having a job motivates him.	True	False

C 🔗 Answer these questions. Share your answers with a partner.

1. What area do you know that needs a steward? _____

2. Why did you choose that area? _____

LESSON **A**
THE NATURAL WORLD

1 VIDEO
The Steward of Ormond Beach

WARM UP Have students look at the photo and describe what they can see. Where are the people? What are they doing? Write vocabulary students suggest on the board. Would they like to go to this beach? Why or why not? ⏱ 5 min

ABOUT THE VIDEO
William Fuller is the steward of Ormond Beach in Oxnard, California. Fuller began going to Ormond Beach when he worked as a janitor at the nearby naval base, but he now spends every day there as a volunteer steward taking care of the beach and its wildlife, talking to visitors, and raising awareness of the importance of protecting this wetland area. Ormond Beach is one of the last wetland areas in California, and an area of natural beauty. It is also home to many different species of birds. Without Ormond Beach, many birds would no longer have a home. Fuller is completely committed to doing his part in protecting the area as its steward; but as he states in the video, we are all stewards for this Earth.

TEACHING TIP: Using English videos
As with readings, students should try to get into the habit of predicting and activating prior knowledge about what they are going to see and hear before they watch a video in order to help them be more prepared for the content, and therefore likely to understand more. It is important to help students recognize that looking at titles, captions, and images before they watch, whenever possible, is an effective strategy to help them be more successful viewers.

A Read the title. What is a *steward*? What do you think a steward of a beach does? ⏱ 5–10 min

Have students look up *steward* and give you a definition to write on the board. Then have them explain what they think a steward of a beach does. Write their ideas on the board.

B ▶ Watch the video. Circle *True* or *False* for each item. ⏱ 10 min

Go over the statements with the class, having students explain vocabulary as necessary. Tell students they should try to choose their answers as they watch. Play the video twice, then have students compare their answers with a partner's. Play the video again, pausing as necessary, and check answers with the class.

C 🔁 Answer these questions. Share your answers with a partner.

Go over the questions with the class, then have students write their answers individually. Tell them they don't need to write full sentences. Assign students to pairs to discuss their answers. Monitor and ask follow-up questions to encourage further discussion. Call on different students to tell the class about the place their partner told them about.

EXTRA! Post-viewing
Have students create a job ad for the steward at the place they discussed in **C**. They should think about the reasons the place needs a steward, what the steward's responsibilities will be, what experience he or she needs to have, and whether it is a voluntary or paid position. ⏱ 10 min

Extra video vocabulary
artwork
become a legend
breed
confine
endangered species
keep an eye on (someone / something)
nest
(a) presence
trail

Instructor's Notes

_____

_____

_____

_____

_____

_____

2 VOCABULARY

WARM UP Write the words *endangered species* on the board. Endangered species are animals or plants that are in danger of becoming extinct. Ask students to name any endangered species that they know. Do they know of any efforts to preserve these animals in their country or elsewhere? ⏲ 5 min

A ⚡ Work with a partner. You are going to learn about two different animals. Follow the instructions below. Look up any words you don't know. ⏲ 5–10 min

(See Student Book page 171 for complete instructions.)

Go over the directions with the class, then assign students to A-B pairs. Make sure they understand that they should only read about their animal. Have them read and look up any words that they don't know.

B ⚡ Interview your partner about his or her animal. Ask questions to complete the information in the chart. ⏲ 10–15 min

Go over the chart with the class and point out the example question. Elicit a question for each of the other items, for example *habitat – Where does the snow leopard live?* etc. Have students ask their partner the questions and complete the chart. Check answers with the class, having students tell you the questions first.

C ⚡ The snow leopard and the mountain gorilla are **suffering**. Both animals are almost **extinct**. What would you do to **raise awareness** of their situations? What would you tell people? Discuss with a partner. ⏲ 10–15 min

Go over the directions with the class, then give them a few moments to think about their answers. Encourage them to write down a few notes with their ideas. Model some examples using *would*: *I would give a presentation at school. I would tell them about the animals' situation, I would explain that…*, etc. Write the prompt *I would…* on the board and have students say what comes after *would* (base verb). Assign students to pairs to discuss what they would do. Remind students to ask follow-up questions. Monitor and provide help as necessary. Have students tell the class about the partner's ideas.

EXTRA! Campaign
In pairs or small groups, have students create posters with information about one of the animals (or they can research another endangered animal). The poster should urge people to do something to support protecting animals in danger of extinction. Students can stick their posters around the class or school and present them.

TEACHING TIP: Writing on the board
Writing on the board is a good way to check answers, and it also helps students to build confidence in their English. Students feel less self-conscious when they write on the board at the same time as others. You can check an exercise by calling on a different student to write each answer on the board. Then check the answers after all students have finished writing. Students can often find and correct mistakes easily when they see them written on the board.

CULTURE TIP: Endangered species
The term *critically endangered* means the species faces an extremely high risk of extinction in the immediate future. Some examples of critically endangered species are the mountain gorilla, Arakan forest turtle, Darwin's fox, Javan rhinoceros, Brazilian merganser, gharial, Philippine eagle, and vaquita.

The term *endangered* means the species faces a very high risk of extinction in the near future. Some examples of endangered species are the dhole, blue whale, bonobo, Ethiopian wolf, giant panda, snow leopard, African wild dog, tiger, three species of albatross, Chaco eagle, orangutan, Grévy's zebra, and Tasmanian devil.

Instructor's Notes

_____

_____

_____

_____

_____

_____

_____

_____

_____

_____

4 SPEAKING

A 🔊 Gustav and Carolina are telling Bart about their summer job. Listen to and read their conversation. Where did they work and what did they do? Why can't Bart apply for the job? **CD 2 Track 37**

BART: So, what exactly did you do over the summer?

GUSTAV: We worked as volunteers at Glacier National Park.

BART: I've never been there. What's it like?

CAROLINA: It's beautiful. There are mountains and lakes... and, of course, glaciers!

BART: How was the job?

GUSTAV: We had to do a lot of physical work. It was kind of hard.

CAROLINA: That's true, but it was exciting, too! We actually saw bears!

BART: Wow! That *does* sound exciting. Maybe I should apply. I'll need a job next summer.

CAROLINA: Sorry, Bart, but you can't apply to that program. It's a special program for international students.

B 👥 Practice the conversation in groups of three.

SPEAKING STRATEGY

C 🔁 Imagine that you and your partner are looking for a place to live together as roommates. Write down some of the important things to consider.

cost, _____

_____

_____

Useful Expressions
Offering another opinion
That's true, but...
Yes, but on the other hand,...
Even so,...
But then again,...

D 🔁 Read about these two possible places to live. Add three more ideas to each list. With a partner, discuss the positive and negative aspects of each place. Use the Useful Expressions to help you.

City apartment	Suburban home
expensive	big backyard
near public transportation	need a car
small bedrooms	quiet neighborhood
big balcony with a great view	nothing to do on weekends
_____	_____
_____	_____
_____	_____

> An apartment in the city would be expensive.

> Yes, but on the other hand, living in the city is exciting. There's so much to do!

E 👥 With your partner, have a discussion and then choose one of the places to live in **D**. Tell the class which location you chose and why.

5 GRAMMAR

A Turn to page 216. Complete the exercises. Then do **B–D** below.

Embedded Questions	
What is a tapir?	Do you know **what a tapir is**? I'd like to know **what a tapir is**.
Asking for information	**Saying you don't know something**
Can / Could you tell me… Do you know… Do you remember… Do you have any idea…	I don't know / I'd like to know… I'm not sure… I can't remember… I wonder…

B Find and correct the error in each sentence.

1. Could you tell me what is the answer?

2. Can you remember me how to get there?

3. I'm not sure how to do it?

4. What's your opinion? I like to know what you think.

5. I'm not sure where is the exit.

C Turn each question on the left into an embedded question on the right.

1. Where do they live?   I'd like to _____ where _____.

2. What is their habitat?   Can you _____ me _____?

3. What challenges do they face? Do you _____ any _____ what _____?

4. How much does a capybara weigh? I'm not _____ how much _____.

5. How do sloths sleep?   I wonder _____.

6. Where do tapirs spend their time? I don't know _____.

7. Why are monkeys called "acrobats"? Do you know _____?

8. What is the name of that animal? I can't _____ what _____.

D  Think of an animal. Take turns asking a partner about his or her animal.

> Can you tell me where red pandas live?

> They're from China.

> What is their habitat?

> I'm not sure what their habitat is. Maybe they live in the mountains.

5 GRAMMAR

Embedded questions

WARM UP Ask students embedded questions about content they've learned in this unit so far. For example, *Could you tell me what the names of some endangered animals are? Do you remember what animal is on the opener spread?* etc.
⏱ 5 min

A Turn to page 216. Complete the exercises. Then do **B–D** below. ◑ 20–30 min

Go over the examples in the chart and have students identify how the word order changes in an embedded question (it is the same as in a regular statement, subject + verb). The grammar chart on page 216 includes further examples, additional forms, and usage explanations, expanding on the information in the chart on page 174.

B Find and correct the error in each sentence. ⏱ 10 min

Do the first one with the class. Write the correct version on the board. Have students complete the rest individually. Refer them to the chart on this page and on page 216 as necessary. Have students compare their answers with a partner's, then check answers with the class. Write (or have students write) them on the board so that students can check they have the answer recorded correctly.

C Turn each question on the left into an embedded question on the right. ⏱ 10–15 min

Go over the directions and do the first one with the class. Write the complete embedded question on the board. Have students complete the rest individually. Have students compare their answers with a partner's, then check answers with the class. Write (or have students write) them on the board so that students can check they have the answer recorded correctly.

D 🗨 Think of an animal. Take turns asking a partner about his or her animal. ⏱ 10–15 min

Have students look at the photo and describe the animal. Then model the conversation with a student. Give students a moment to think of an animal and write a few notes about it. Provide vocabulary as necessary. Assign them to pairs to ask and answer questions. Remind them to use the structures in the chart.

🔊 GRAMMAR TUTORIALS

• Embedded Questions

Additional tutorials are available for reteaching and reinforcement.

6 COMMUNICATION

WARM UP Ask students if they have ever traveled to an unusual place in their country or another one. Where was it? What sights did they see or visit? ⏱ 5 min

A Work alone. Take the quiz. Look up any words you don't know. ⏱ 10 min

Look at the photo and the caption with the students. Go over the quiz to check if there are any difficulties with vocabulary. If you want students to play the game in **B**, be sure not to correct the answers in **A**. That will give the game away.

B 🎮 Get into a group of four people. Imagine that you are on a quiz show. Follow the steps below. ⏱ 15–20 min

(See Student Book page 175 for complete instructions.)

Go over the steps with the class. Then model the example with a student. Remind them that they need to use the structures from the Grammar page. Assign students to groups of four. Each student should have a blank piece of paper on which to write his or her answers. Be sure that the announcer writes down the score after each round to ensure a fair result.

CULTURE TIP: The Andes

The Andes are the longest continental mountain range in the world. The Andes are more than 7,000 kilometers (4,300 miles) long. Located on the west coast of South America, the Andes cross seven different countries: Venezuela, Colombia, Ecuador, Bolivia, Peru, Chile, and Argentina. The highest peak in the Andes is called Aconcagua. It is 6,962 meters high (22,841 feet).

EXTRA! Discussion questions

Students can ask and answer these questions in their small groups: Which of the places in **A** would you most like to visit? least like to visit? Why? What do you think the place is like? ⏱ 10 min

LARGE CLASS OPTION

Large classes should be able to perform the tasks in **B** in groups of four. If you need larger groups, quantities of 8 or 10 are possible, but less desirable because students won't have as many opportunities to talk.

EXTRA! Writing prompt

Assign students to research and write one or two paragraphs about a country or destination that interests them. ⏱ 20 min

TEACHING TIP: End-of-class review

A few minutes before the end of the class period, when the board is covered with vocabulary, ask a volunteer to come to the front of the room and sit with his or her back to the board. By giving definitions and clues and asking questions, members of the class should try to get the student to say each vocabulary word on the board. As each word is said, erase it. See if the class can clear the board before the period ends.

Instructor's Notes

_____

_____

_____

_____

_____

_____

_____

_____

_____

_____

_____

_____

_____

_____

_____

_____

_____

_____

_____

_____

_____

_____

6 COMMUNICATION

A Work alone. Take the quiz. Look up any words you don't know.

A *harbor* is a protected area of water where boats are protected from storms.

What / Where is the world's...

1. busiest harbor?
   a. Singapore
   b. Pusan (South Korea)
   c. Hong Kong (China)

2. largest island?
   a. Great Britain
   b. Greenland (Denmark)
   c. Honshu (Japan)

3. highest waterfall?
   a. Tugela Falls (South Africa)
   b. Angel Falls (Venezuela)
   c. Sutherland Falls (New Zealand)

4. oldest active volcano?
   a. Kilauea (US)
   b. Yasur (Vanuatu)
   c. Etna (Italy)

5. longest mountain range?
   a. the Austrian Alps (Europe)
   b. the Andes (South America)
   c. the Urals (Europe)

6. longest cave?
   a. Mammoth Cave (US)
   b. Holloch Cave (Switzerland)
   c. Sistema Ox Bel Ha (Mexico)

7. deepest lake?
   a. Lake Superior (US / Canada)
   b. Lake Nyasa (Africa)
   c. Lake Baikal (Russia)

8. largest desert?
   a. the Sahara (North Africa)
   b. the Australian (Australia)
   c. the North American (Mexico / US)

9. longest coastline?
   a. Australia
   b. Canada
   c. Chile

B 👥 Get into a group of four people. Imagine that you are on a quiz show. Follow the steps below.

Student A: quiz show announcer

Students B–D: quiz show contestants

1. **Student A:** Read a question from the quiz in **A**.

2. **Students B–D:** Write down your answer on a piece of paper.

3. **Student A:** Ask each contestant for his or her answer. Then check page 218 and give each contestant one point for a correct answer. Continue asking questions.

4. **Students B–D:** The person with the most points at the end of the game wins.

> Maria, do you know what the largest island in the world is?

> I'm not sure what the answer is, but I chose Great Britain. Is that correct?

The Burj Khalifa, Dubai, United Arab Emirates

- This skyscraper is the tallest building in the world at 829.8 meters (2,722 feet).

- Architects **proposed** ideas for the building in 2003 and **construction** was finished in 2010.

- Architects faced many **obstacles** in building a skyscraper this big. The building needed to be very strong to **withstand** its own weight! The extreme heat of Dubai also had to be **considered**.

- Another issue was how to safely and quickly **transport** people and **goods** around the building. The builders found an **efficient** solution to **get around** this problem. The building has 57 high-speed elevators. Each can travel 600 meters a minute and **accommodate** 10–12 people.

- The building has many **sustainable** features as well. For example, it collects and reuses water from the air conditioners, saving 15 million gallons of water a year!

1 VOCABULARY

A 🔄 What do you know about the famous building in this photo? Tell a partner. Then take turns reading about it aloud.

B 🔄 Complete the sentences using the words in **blue** from above. Work with a partner.

1. Engineers need to make sure the skyscraper can ___withstand___ earthquakes before they start _____.

2. There are other _____ to think about, too. For example, where will people park?

3. To answer this question, the architect _____ an idea: build an underground parking lot. It will be able to _____ 1,500 cars.

4. From the parking lot, an elevator will _____ people and goods to the top floor in 15 seconds.

5. The team _____ the architect's idea and agreed with his suggestion.

6. There should also be a(n) _____ way of heating and cooling the building.

7. With solar panels, the building will have plenty of energy and also be _____.

C 🔄 Discuss the questions with a partner.

1. Why is the Burj Khalifa special?

2. What were some of the obstacles that architects faced when they designed it?

3. What's special about the building's elevators?

4. How is the building good for the environment?

1 VOCABULARY

WARM UP Ask students to name some great man-made structures they know in their city, country, or the world. List them on the board. Then ask students if they know the reasons why these structures were built. ⏱ 10 min

A 🗨 What do you know about the famous building in this photo? Tell a partner. Then take turns reading about it aloud.

Assign students to pairs to talk about the building and read the text to each other. Then have students close their books and ask, *Who already knew about the building? What do you now know about it*? Have them tell you what they remember without looking at the text. Write their ideas on the board.

LANGUAGE TIP: Get around

In **A**, "get around a problem" is defined as *solved*. Besides *to solve* a problem, this phrase can also mean *avoid* or *deal with* a problem.

EXTRA! More man-made structures

Name another great man-made structure. Where is it? What makes it special? Work on this exercise with the whole class. If students have trouble thinking of man-made structures, prompt them by suggesting general categories, such as bridges, dams, and buildings. Do an online search to find the newest tall buildings and long bridges. ⏱ 5 min

B 🗨 Complete the sentences using the words in **blue** from above. Work with a partner. ⏱ 10–15 min

Say the words in blue and have students repeat them. Then assign them to new pairs to complete the sentences. If students can't work out the meaning of any of the words from the context, they can look them up. Check answers with the class.

C 🗨 Discuss the questions with a partner. ⏱ 10–15 min

Go over the questions with the class, then assign students to pairs to discuss them. Monitor and ask follow-up questions to prompt further discussion. Check answers to the questions as a class.

CULTURE TIP: The world's tallest buildings

1. Burj Khalifa, Dubai	828 meters
2. Shanghai Tower, Shanghai	632 meters
3. Abraj Al-Bait Clock Tower, Mecca	601 meters
4. Ping An Finance Centre, Shenzhen	599 meters
5. Goldin Finance 117, Tianjin	597 meters
6. Lotte World Tower, Seoul	555 meters
7. One World Trade Center, New York City	541 meters
8. CTF Finance Centre, Guangzhou	530 meters
9. Taipei 101, Taipei	509 meters
10. Shanghai World Financial Center, Shanghai	492 meters

TEACHING TIP: Explaining new vocabulary

There are many approaches you can use to explain the meaning of unknown vocabulary words: Use visual aids, such as the pictures and photos in the unit, props, or drawings on the board; Demonstrate by miming; Use the word in a number of English sentences and help students work out the meaning; Explain the meaning in simpler English; Have students look it up in a dictionary. It's good to vary your approach and rely as much as possible on students' background knowledge and knowledge of English.

Instructor's Notes

2 LISTENING

STRATEGIES: Listen for gist; Listen for details

WARM UP Write the word *engineer* on the board and ask students what an engineer does. Note that there are different types of engineers, for example: *electrical engineers*, *mechanical engineers*, *industrial engineers*, and *civil engineers*. ⏱ 5 min

A Which words in the box do you know? With a partner, look up any unfamiliar words in your dictionary. ⏱ 5–10 min

If possible, pair students who have good dictionary skills with students who need to develop those skills. Help students with the pronunciation of *access* and *architect*. Call on students to explain the words.

B **Listen for gist.** Which photo shows what the woman does in her job? Listen and circle the correct one. **CD 2 Track 38** ⏱ 5–10 min

Tell students to look at the photos. Call on students to describe each photo. Note that in the photo at the far left, Jamie can be seen rappelling down the side of a building. Then play the audio once, and have students answer the question. Play the audio again, and stop and discuss the correct answer with the students. Remember that you can also read from the audio script if students find it challenging to understand the audio recording.

Listen for gist. Remind students that when listening for gist, they don't need to worry about understanding everything they hear, the purpose is to understand the general idea.

C **Listen for details.** Listen. Complete the sentences about Jamie's job. **CD 2 Track 38** ⏱ 5–10 min

Go over the sentences with the class. Play the audio again, and give students time to write their answers. Play it once again and then check answers with the class.

Listen for details. Remind students that they do not need to hear and understand everything in order to understand specific details. Encourage them to get into the habit of identifying key words to listen for before they listen.

EXTRA! More listening
For additional listening practice, tell students to close their books. Read the sentences from **C** as dictation. ⏱ 10 min

D **Pronunciation: Negative questions to confirm information.** Complete the negative questions. Then listen and check your answers. **CD 2 Track 39** ⏱ 10 min

Remind students about intonation in English and write the example on the board. Say it (or play the audio) and have students tell you whether the intonation goes up or down at the end of the question. Draw an arrow going up at the end. Point out that the questions are in the negative form and explain that we use this structure to confirm information. Have students write the questions. Check the question forms by writing them on the board as students tell you the questions. Play the audio and have students focus on the intonation. Play it again and tell them to draw an arrow on each question, as in the example on the board. Check answers with the class by adding the rising intonation arrows above the last word of each question. Say each question and have students repeat.

E Practice asking and answering questions 1–4 in **D** with a partner. Pay attention to intonation. ⏱ 5–10 min

Assign students to pairs to ask and answer the questions. Remind them to use the appropriate intonation. Call on a different pair to say each question and answer for the class.

Instructor's Notes

_____

_____

_____

_____

_____

_____

_____

_____

_____

2 LISTENING

A 🔁 Which words in the box do you know? With a partner, look up any unfamiliar words in your dictionary.

architect	edge	investigate
blueprint	get access (to a place)	leaky

B 🔊 **Listen for gist.** Which photo shows what the woman does in her job? Listen and circle the correct one. **CD 2 Track 38**

C 🔊 **Listen for details.** Listen. Complete the sentences about Jamie's job. **CD 2 Track 38**

1. Jamie works with _____ buildings.

2. She checks problems so that they don't _____ mistakes.

3. Rappelling is a way to get access to _____ places.

4. After you hook up to the top of the building, you _____ over the edge.

5 Rappelling is scary, but you can get _____.

D 🔊 **Pronunciation: Negative questions to confirm information.** Complete the negative questions. Then listen and check your answers. **CD 2 Track 39**

1. (be / you / an engineer) _Aren't you an engineer?_   That's correct. I'm a civil engineer.

2. (work / you / on the second floor) _____   No, actually I work on the third floor.

3. (be / the Burj Khalifa / in the UAE) _____   Yes, it is, in Dubai.

4. (be / the Eiffel Tower / built in 1900) _____   No. It was finished in 1889.

E 🔁 Practice asking and answering questions 1–4 in **D** with a partner. Pay attention to intonation.

3 READING

3 READING

STRATEGIES: Use background knowledge; Make predictions; Take notes on key details; Infer meaning; Summarize; Give opinions

WARM UP Ask students if they know of a place where people live on boats or houses that are above water. Why might people live on water? ⏱ 5 min

A **Use background knowledge; Make predictions.** Look at the title and the names of the two countries in the article. Do you know anything about these countries? What do you think is happening in these countries? ⏱ 5 min

Assign students to pairs to discuss the questions. Have pairs share their ideas and write key vocabulary on the board.

Use background knowledge. Students bring to any text the knowledge they already have about life and the world, as well as any knowledge they have about the specific topic of the text. Students need to know that they should draw on this knowledge to help them understand what they are going to read.

Make predictions. Remind students that predicting before they read helps them prepare for the text, as they will have activated prior knowledge of the topic and language related to it.

B **Take notes on key details.** Read the article. As you read, think about questions 1 and 2. Underline the information in the passage that answers the questions. ⏱ 10 min

Go over the questions before students read the article. Remind students to focus on key details. Have students compare their answers with a partner's. Check answers with the class.

A **Use background knowledge; Make predictions.** Look at the title and the names of the two countries in the article. Do you know anything about these countries? What do you think is happening in these countries?

B **Take notes on key details.** Read the article. As you read, think about questions 1 and 2. Underline the information in the passage that answers the questions.

1. How are rising sea levels affecting the Seychelles and the Netherlands specifically?

2. What is each country doing about these problems?

C **Infer meaning.** Match the words in bold in the reading with their definitions.

_____ a short description

_____ planned pieces of work

_____ to damage land or rock so it disappears

_____ close to the height of the ocean

_____ walls built across bodies of water to hold the water back

D ⚡ **Summarize; Give opinions.** Answer the questions with a partner.

1. Look again at the questions in **B**. Explain your answers to a partner in your own words.

2. Has global warming affected the area where you live? What do you think can be done to help?

WHEN THE SEAS RISE

A solar-powered floating house in Rotterdam, the Netherlands.

ESTRA! Discussion questions

1. How might people in the Seychelles feel about having to move from their homes?

2. Are there any negative aspects of living in a floating house? ⏱ 10–15 min

EXTRA! Post-reading

Have students research floating houses in the Netherlands and find out more about how they are built, or research the Seychelles and what people there are doing about the problem of rising sea levels. ⏱ 30–60 min

When most people think of global warming[1], they think of something that will happen in the future, something that doesn't affect their daily life. But for many people around the world, the future is now. Research shows that sea levels worldwide have been rising at a rate of 0.14 inches (3.5 millimeters) per year since the early 1990s. The trend, linked to global warming, is putting thousands of coastal cities at risk of being destroyed over time. The two countries below offer a **snapshot** of what climate change might look like for all of us.

Seychelles

This chain of islands in the Indian Ocean has been called one of the most beautiful places on Earth. There is a problem, though. Many of the country's most populated regions were constructed in **low-lying** areas, near the water. As sea levels rise, many people will lose their homes.

Already, the island's tourism industry is being hurt. Seychelles's famous beaches are being **eroded** by the rising water, as well as by storms that grow more powerful each year. In addition, the country's coral reefs (a popular tourist attraction) are suffering because of warmer water.

To fight these problems, the government of the Seychelles has been trying to relocate people living in low-lying coastal areas to higher ground. Unfortunately, there isn't enough land to accommodate many of these people. The country's citizens are also trying to bring as much attention as possible to global warming and the danger it poses. They point out that if these things happen to the Seychelles, they can happen to big countries like the United States, China, or Brazil next.

The Netherlands

For the people of the Netherlands, rising waters have been an obstacle for years. The country is close to 30 percent under sea level! A series of **dams and dikes** has protected the country from mass flooding for many years, but as sea levels continue to rise, more extreme solutions are being considered. One of them is a large increase in "floating houses." These houses are built on water or in areas that flood, and each structure is able to rise and fall with the water. Sustainable and efficient apartment buildings that can float are also being planned.

Engineers in the Netherlands are also continuing the country's tradition of doing large construction **projects** to help hold the water back. Larger dams have been built in recent years, and rivers have been rerouted so they are not as close to cities. Today, engineers from many countries visit the Netherlands to learn more about these projects. They fear that in the future, as the Earth warms and sea levels continue to rise, Dutch building techniques will have to be used all over the world.

[1]*Global warming* is an increase in the Earth's temperature, caused in part by humans' use of fossil fuels (oil, gas). As the Earth warms, ice melts, causing sea levels to rise.

LESSON B • The man-made world **179**

EXTRA! Writing prompt

Ask students to write about their ideas for solving the problem of rising seas, or another problem such as overcrowding in cities. 🕐 15–20 min

---

Take notes on key details. Taking notes on key details helps students identify main ideas and be able to clarify what they read afterwards. Taking notes as they read is a skill that can help them in other classes, as well as when reading in English in and out of class.

C Infer meaning. Match the words in bold in the reading with their definitions. 🕐 5–10 min

Have students read through the definitions, then go back to the text and find the words in bold. Have students match the words and definitions. Then check answers with the class.

Infer meaning. Remind students that it is often possible to work out the meaning of a new word from how it is used in the text. They should look at the whole sentence, not just the isolated word, and try to decide what kind of word it is (verb, noun, etc.) because this will help them guess its meaning. They should also use the context the word is being used in to help them infer its meaning.

D 🔄 Summarize; Give opinions. Answer the questions with a partner. 🕐 10–15 min

Go over the questions with the class, then give students a moment to think about their answers. Assign them to pairs to discuss the questions. Monitor as students discuss the questions and prompt with questions as necessary. As a class, discuss their answers.

Summarize. Explain to students that summarizing means explaining the main ideas and supporting details in their own words. Doing this pushes students to understand a text at a deeper level because in order to explain it in their own words they have to analyze and synthesize the information they have heard.

Give opinions. By giving an opinion about the topic and applying it to their own context, students are able to demonstrate understanding of a text and personalize the information. Personalizing also makes the new information more meaningful.

4 GRAMMAR

A Turn to page 217. Complete the exercises. Then do **B** below.

The Passive with Various Tenses		
	Active	**Passive**
Simple present	Engineers <u>build</u> skyscrapers with a steel frame structure.	Most skyscrapers **are built** with a steel frame structure.
Simple past	The Woolworth Company <u>built</u> a skyscraper in 1913.	One of the first skyscrapers **was built** in 1913.
Present perfect	Engineers <u>have built</u> the world's tallest building in Dubai.	The world's tallest building **has been built** in Dubai.
Present continuous	Engineers <u>are building</u> a lot of tall buildings in Shanghai.	A lot of tall buildings **are being built** in Shanghai.
Simple future	Someday they <u>will build</u> a skyscraper without concrete.	Someday a skyscraper without concrete **will be built**.

B Work with a partner. Follow the steps below.

1. Read the information below. Look up the underlined words in a dictionary.

2. Each person should choose a role (Student A or B).

3. Debate the issue with your partner. In your own words, explain what you want to do. Give two reasons to support your opinion. Try to agree about what to do.

4. Share your plan with another pair.

A large construction company wants to <u>tear down</u> traditional buildings in a neighborhood in your city. The buildings are beautiful, but they were built 100 years ago and aren't in good condition.

Student A: You work for the construction company. Here is your plan:

- The old buildings will be torn down, and new office and apartment buildings will be built.

- The new buildings will be safer and will be able to accommodate more people.

- Former <u>tenants</u> will be allowed to move back into a new apartment, but it will take three years for the project to be finished. For now, those people must find other housing.

Student B: You live in one of the old buildings now. You have this opinion:

- A lot of modern buildings have been built in our city. Older structures should be <u>preserved</u>.

- Many people in the buildings are elderly. They shouldn't be <u>forced</u> to leave their homes.

> The old buildings should be preserved. They connect us with our past.

> Yes, but on the other hand, these old buildings may not withstand...

4 GRAMMAR
The passive with various tenses

WARM UP Have students look at the photo at the bottom of the page. What is happening? What kinds of buildings can they see? ⏱ 5 min

A Turn to page 217. Complete the exercises. Then do **B** below. ◑ 20–30 min

Go over the examples in the chart one by one and point out the difference between the active and the passive voice in each tense. Note how the active voice focuses attention on the subject, but the passive emphasizes the action rather than the agent responsible. Focus students' attention on the way the passive is formed (the verb *be* in the appropriate tense + past participle of the main verb).

GRAMMAR TIP: The passive voice
The passive is not a tense, but a form of sentence that emphasizes the receiver of an action. As such, the passive voice can be used in any tense.

B 🎲 Work with a partner. Follow the steps below.
◑ 15–20 min

(See Student Book page 180 for complete instructions.)

Go over the steps with the class, then have students read the text, looking up the underlined words. Answer any questions students have about the information. Model the example conversation with a student. Assign students to A-B pairs to debate the problem. Give them time to prepare their reasons. Make sure students understand that they will discuss their opinions, but that they need to come to an agreement as a pair on what they are going to do. They will explain their plan to another pair when they are ready. Monitor and provide help as necessary.

When pairs are ready, have them join another pair and present their plan. Monitor and provide help and prompt with questions as necessary. Call on different pairs to tell the class about the other pair's plan. If time allows, debate the issue as a class.

TEACHING TIP: Monolingual dictionaries
At this level, students can make good use of a monolingual intermediate-level dictionary. Point out to students the advantages of a monolingual dictionary, which lets them work entirely in English. When looking up a word, remind students to look up the unknown words in the exact forms needed—for example, *apply to*, not just *apply*. If the dictionary does not have *apply to*, help students choose the correct definition of *apply* (there will be at least two) and then figure out what *apply to* means in the context. Learning to use a dictionary will help your students become independent learners and explore vocabulary that is relevant to their own interests.

EXTRA! Problem solving
With the class, brainstorm a list of problems in city life, and write them on the board. Discuss which ones could be solved by technology. ◑ 20–25 min

🌀 GRAMMAR TUTORIALS
- The Passive: Past
- Present Perfect Passive
- Future Passive

Additional tutorials are available for reteaching and reinforcement.

Instructor's Notes

_____

_____

_____

_____

_____

_____

_____

_____

_____

_____

_____

_____

_____

_____

_____

_____

_____

_____

5 WRITING

WARM UP Have students recall the issue they discussed on the Grammar page. Write what they can remember on the board in note form. ⏱ 5 min

A What do you think about the issue in Grammar **B**? In five minutes, outline your ideas below. Then, in 20 minutes, write a paragraph. Explain each reason with an extra sentence or two. ⏱ 25–30 min

Remind students about the importance of planning before they begin writing, and go over the outline with them. Then have them think about their opinion, referring them back to page 180 to read the information again as necessary. Give students five minutes to complete the outline with their reasons in note form. Provide help as needed. Then have students develop their outline into a paragraph. Encourage them to add more details if they can. Monitor and provide help as necessary. Check that students are using passive voice structures correctly.

B 🔄 Exchange your writing with a partner. Circle any mistakes in your partner's writing. Do you agree with your partner's opinion? Why or why not? Return the paper to your partner. Make corrections to your own paragraph. ⏱ 10–15 min

Assign students to pairs and have them exchange papers and identify any mistakes in their partner's paragraph. Tell them to focus on the use of passive voice. Then have pairs discuss whether they agree with each other's opinion or not, and explain why. Encourage students to talk about their paragraphs together, *What was clear? What was confusing? What could be better?* Then have students rewrite their paragraphs, making the corrections and taking into account their partner's comments on how to improve it. Provide help as necessary. Collect the paragraphs to grade if possible.

6 COMMUNICATION

WARM UP Ask students what major development problems they have seen in their city. Are opinions divided on any of the projects? Why? ⏱ 5–10 min

A 🔄 Read about Diamond City's problems. What projects have been proposed to solve problems? Use your own words to explain each situation with a partner. ⏱ 10–15 min

Have students read about the problems and the projects. Encourage students to try to guess the meaning of any new words, and only to look them up if they really need to. When they have finished reading, they should work with a partner to explain the situations in their own words. Call on a different pair to explain each situation.

B 🔄 With your partner, rank the projects in the order you would do them. Give reasons for your order. Note: A new project can be started only after the previous one has been finished. ⏱ 10–15 min

Be sure that students understand that a new project can only be started once the previous one has been finished. It may be helpful to mark out on a chart or timeline the amount of time that each project would take. Remind students about the Useful Expressions for offering another opinion in Lesson A on page 173. Quickly review these expressions. You may want to write them on the board for students to refer to when speaking with their partner. Have pairs discuss and make their decisions. Ask students how they decided on their rankings. Emphasize that both students must agree on the order.

C 👥 Explain your plan from **B** to another pair. Are your ideas similar? If not, whose plan is better? Why? ⏱ 10–15 min

Go over the directions and the questions. Have pairs join to make groups of four and present their plans to each other. After both pairs have presented their plan, have them answer the questions. Call on different groups to share with the class the plan they decided was better.

CULTURE TIP: City planning
Many cities and towns have elected officials who serve as a planning board or commission. The job of this group is to make plans for the future and to authorize important projects. Find out if your city has such a board or commission. What issues are they discussing?

EXTRA! Writing prompt
Tell students to imagine they have been given the power to change the future of their city. What changes would they recommend? How would they be sure that the changes will take place? Have them write two paragraphs. ⏱ 15–20 min

TEACHING TIP: Self-evaluation
At the end of the course, it's useful to have students spend some time reflecting on the progress they've made and their goals for future learning. One way to do this is by having them fill in a questionnaire, and then, if time permits, having a brief meeting with each student to discuss his or her answers. Here are some possible questions you could ask:

How much have you improved in these areas? Write A lot, Some, or A little:
Speaking, listening, writing, reading, vocabulary, grammar, pronunciation

Which exercises in class have helped you the most?

How can you continue to improve your English outside of class?

What are your goals for using English?

What will you do differently in your next class?

5 WRITING

A What do you think about the issue in Grammar **B**? In five minutes, outline your ideas below. Then, in 20 minutes, write a paragraph. Explain each reason with an extra sentence or two.

In my opinion, the old buildings should / shouldn't be torn down for two reasons.

For one thing, _____.

In addition, _____.

For these reasons, I believe the old buildings should / shouldn't be torn down.

B 🔁 Exchange your writing with a partner. Circle any mistakes in your partner's writing. Do you agree with your partner's opinion? Why or why not? Return the paper to your partner. Make corrections to your own paragraph.

6 COMMUNICATION

A 🔁 Read about Diamond City's problems. What projects have been proposed to solve these problems? Use your own words to explain each situation with a partner.

Problem 1: The dam was built 30 years ago, and it is weak.	**Problem 3:** The traffic is terrible, and businesses are leaving the city because of it.
Project: Repair the dam. This will take three years.	**Project:** Build a new subway line to transport people. It will take three years to finish.
Notes: The city has been hit by a huge flood every 100 years. The last flood was 20 years ago, and the downtown area was destroyed.	**Notes:** Construction will be difficult and expensive, but a new subway system is needed to transport people.
Problem 2: The baseball stadium is old.	**Problem 4:** There isn't enough office space in Diamond City.
Project: Repair the stadium. It will take two years.	**Project:** Build a new skyscraper to keep businesses in the city. It will take two years to finish.
Notes: The Diamond City Miners baseball team is a big moneymaker for the city. But if the stadium isn't fixed soon, the team may move to another city.	**Notes:** The land around the skyscraper is polluted and must be cleaned up first. This will take a year or more. Then construction can begin.

B 🔁 With your partner, rank the projects in the order you would do them. Give reasons for your order. Note: A new project can be started only after the previous one has been finished.

C 🔵 Explain your plan from **B** to another pair. Are your ideas similar? If not, whose plan is better? Why?

1 STORYBOARD

A Lisa is asking Ana about her recent vacation. Look at the pictures and complete the conversation. More than one answer may be possible for each blank.

1. Hi, Ana! How was your vacation?

_____! We went hiking in the _____ forest.

2. What was the rainforest _____?

_____ amazing! But I was also surprised by something.

What was that?

There was a lot of _____ near the rainforest.

Really?

Yeah. A lot of animals are _____. They could _____ extinct in a few years.

5. I'd _____ to _____ awareness about this

6. SAVE THE RAINFOREST

DONATE: $ _____

How will you do that?

I want to _____ a website where people can _____ money to help.

B 🔁 Practice the conversation with a partner. Then change roles and repeat.

C 🔁 What do you think of Ana's idea? What would you do to raise awareness? Tell a partner.

1 STORYBOARD

WARM UP Ask the class what they studied in the past three units. See if they can remember the names of the units without looking in their books. Draw a chart on the board with three sections, one for each unit, and have students tell you as many new vocabulary and grammar items as they can remember from each topic. ⏱ 5 min

A Lisa is asking Ana about her recent vacation. Look at the pictures and complete the conversation. More than one answer may be possible for each blank. ⏱ 10–15 min

Give students time to look at the pictures and review the story. Answer any questions about vocabulary. Explain that students must provide words for the blanks, and that some of the lines require more than one word. When students are finished, correct the answers by calling on individuals to read the conversation.

TEACHING TIP: Fluency vs. accuracy
One of the biggest challenges instructors face is balancing the competing needs of developing fluency in students and also developing accuracy. Fluency is the ease, speed, and naturalness with which students speak. Accuracy means that grammatical forms, vocabulary words, and pronunciation rules are followed correctly. Sometimes instructors lean more toward one than the other. Sometimes instructors encounter students who may be extremely fluent but not very accurate, or accurate but not very fluent. The ideal is a balance between the two. So, for an exercise such as **B**, you might try to focus on the following, but not all at the same time.

- Suggest that students read the conversation slowly and carefully, trying hard to get it right (accuracy).

- Suggest that students read quickly and smoothly without worrying too much about getting things exactly right (fluency).

- Suggest that students focus on pronunciation (accuracy).

- Suggest that students focus on rhythm and intonation (could be either).

- Tell students not to look at their books but just to make up a new conversation (fluency).

B 🔄 Practice the conversation with a partner. Then change roles and repeat. ⏱ 10 min

When students have finished **A**, they can practice the conversation with a partner. Tell them to be "actors" while practicing—they shouldn't just read the sentences from the page. As students practice, remind them to read, look up, and speak to their partners to help them remember the words and sentences. Call on pairs to present one exchange each to the class, while the other students listen.

EXTRA! Letter to the editor
One method of raising awareness about issues is to get news of the issue into the local media. A traditional method for this is writing a letter to the editor of a newspaper or a news website. Tell students to choose a cause or issue that they feel strongly about and to write a letter or email to the editor about it. Encourage them to use their best persuasive writing to make their point. Help students with persuasive language. ⏱ 15–20 min

TEACHING TIP: Graphic organizers
A graphic organizer is a chart, diagram, or other visual representation that organizes and shows relationships between ideas and information. Graphic organizers can be useful for brainstorming ideas, showing sequences of events, organizing ideas for writing or presentations, or showing how concepts fit together.

C 🔄 What do you think of Ana's idea? What would you do to raise awareness? Tell a partner. ⏱ 10 min

Student answers will vary but there are two main themes. One is to raise awareness by letting people know about the endangered animals. The other theme is to raise money for the cause so that others can continue the work. Any number of answers is possible. After students have talked about this in pairs, ask them to share any new ideas that they have with the class.

Instructor's Notes

_____

_____

_____

_____

2 SEE IT AND SAY IT

WARM UP Ask students if they have ever been on a hike or gone camping. Where were they? What did they do? Did they enjoy the experience? ⏱ 10 min

A 🔁 Study the picture for ten seconds and then close your book. With a partner, take turns describing the scene in as much detail as you can. ⏱ 10–15 min

With books closed, tell students they must study the picture very carefully in order to recall as much information as possible. Then tell students to open their books and study the picture. Announce when 10 seconds have passed and have them close their books. Walk around the room listening and making sure pairs take turns describing the picture.

TEACHING OPTION: Support / challenge
One student in each pair should close his or her book and turn so that he or she can't see their partner's book. The partner with the book describes the picture in as much detail as he or she can. The other student draws the picture as it is described. After a few minutes, permit the student who is drawing to see the picture in the book again. How accurate is their drawing? Ask students if there was anything that they couldn't describe because of vocabulary that they didn't know.

B 🔁 Look at the picture again. Answer the questions with a partner. ⏱ 10–15 min

If possible, students should work with a new partner for this exercise. Have pairs ask and answer the questions, then call on students to share their ideas with the class.

C 🔁 What would you do if you were the leader of the group? Make suggestions and explain your answers with a partner. ⏱ 10–15 min

Read the speech bubble with a student to model the dialog. In pairs, students should say what they would do and give reasons for their decisions. As pairs finish, they can join another pair and share ideas. Then ask groups to share any ideas they feel are very good with the class.

EXTRA! Difficult choices
Conduct a discussion with the class about what students would do if confronted with these situations. Use the following suggestions as prompts. ⏱ 20–25 min

If I were stranded on a desert island...

If I were in outer space...

If I had a million dollars...

If I had only one month to live...

If I could meet anyone in the world...

2 SEE IT AND SAY IT

A Study the picture for ten seconds and then close your book. With a partner, take turns describing the scene in as much detail as you can.

B Look at the picture again. Answer the questions with a partner.

1. Who are these people? Where are they?

2. Where are they going or what are they looking for? What time of day is it?

3. What do you think the leader is thinking?

C What would you do if you were the leader of the group? Make suggestions and explain your answers with a partner.

> It's getting late. They should stop. If I were the leader, I'd suggest we sleep in the cave.

> That's one idea. But then again, I think the cave would be too cold. I'd suggest...

3 SARA AND SANDRA

A Read the story about Sara and Sandra. Fill in the missing words.

Sara and Sandra are sisters. They both _____ it rich by _____ the lottery.

Sara decided she could _____ by on very little money. She made a very tight budget for herself. She took 50 percent of the money and _____ it to charities. She also _____ aside the _____ amount in a bank _____.

Sandra, on the other hand, did something different. She _____ her money on jewelry, vacations, and presents for herself. She spent way _____ much money and didn't _____ anything. In one year, she had _____ into debt and _____ afford to pay _____ all the money she had borrowed.

B With a partner, compare your answers in **A**.

C Imagine your friend has won the lottery. Give him or her some financial advice. Use the negative modals in the box.

| don't have to | had better not | shouldn't |

> Well, for one thing, you don't have to tell everyone right away.

4 LISTENING

A Listen to each response. Then choose the question that came before the response. **CD 2 Track 41**

1. a. ☐ What does she look like?
   b. ☐ What's she like?

2. a. ☐ Why did you buy a new car?
   b. ☐ Why do you want a new car?

3. a. ☐ What would you do if you won the contest?
   b. ☐ What will you do when you win the contest?

4. a. ☐ Did you like the painting?
   b. ☐ How long did it take you to paint it?

5. a. ☐ When did they complete the bridge?
   b. ☐ When will they complete the bridge?

6. a. ☐ What do you usually do on Friday night?
   b. ☐ What do you want to do on Friday night?

3 SARA AND SANDRA

WARM UP Ask students to complete this sentence in writing: *If I won the lottery, I would....* Then ask students to share their responses with the class. Would more students save money, spend money, or give it away? ⏱ 5 min

A Read the story about Sara and Sandra. Fill in the missing words. ⏱ 10 min

Students can do this exercise individually. Refer students back to the Vocabulary lessons about money in Unit 10 if necessary. Note that sometimes more than one answer is possible. Do not check the answers yet. That will be done in **B**.

B 🔁 With a partner, compare your answers in **A**. ⏱ 5–10 min

Pair students to compare answers from **A**. Walk around the room and help with any disagreements. If several students have trouble with certain answers, then address these with the class as a whole.

TEACHING TIP: Remembering grammar rules
When working with grammar points, it is often helpful to have students write rules for themselves once they have looked at examples. Explaining in their own words helps them process and understand the structures. Tell students to keep a grammar reference section in their notebook where they can write the rules and make their own examples.

C 🔁 Imagine your friend has won the lottery. Give him or her some financial advice. Use the negative modals in the box. ⏱ 5–10 min

A significant problem for lottery winners is saving their money. Give students a few minutes to review the vocabulary in Lesson B, Unit 10. Tell students to think of their own ideas but that they may refer to Unit 10 if they need to.

EXTRA! Writing prompt
Students can write an email with advice for their friend who has won the lottery. They should put their financial advice into writing using negative modals. ⏱ 15–20 min

4 LISTENING

A 🔊 Listen to each response. Then choose the question that came before the response. **CD 2 Track 41** ⏱ 10–15 min

This exercise calls for students to do the reverse of the usual exercise. Instead of hearing the question and choosing a response, students hear the response and then have to decide between two possible choices for the question. This is a good test of students' abilities to understand the discourse of spoken English. Play the audio twice while students mark their answers. Then play the audio a third time and check answers with the class. Note: In item 1, *What does she look like?* asks about physical appearance. *What's she like?* is a more general question that might relate to personality.

TEACHING TIP: Writing answers on the board
It is helpful for students, especially visual learners, if the answers to exercises are written on the board so they can check that they have them correct in their book. It is more difficult for visual learners if answers are checked only orally.

Instructor's Notes

_____

_____

_____

_____

_____

_____

_____

_____

_____

_____

_____

_____

5 WHILE YOU WERE OUT

WARM UP Ask students if they ever have to take messages. With cell phones and voicemail, they may not have a lot of experience with taking messages. If this is the case, explain the key information that a message should include, such as the caller's name, phone number, reason for calling, etc. ⏱ 5–10 min

A 🔄 Imagine that, while your boss was out, you took several messages. Work with a partner. Using reported speech, give the messages to your boss. Then switch roles and repeat. ⏱ 10 min

Remind students of how verb tenses change in reported speech. Refer to page 166. Note that in Student A, item 2, *won't be* becomes *wouldn't be* and *I'll be* becomes *he'd be*. Remind students that they also need to change relevant pronouns to the third person. In Student B, item 1, *can't* becomes *couldn't*. Also remind students that the use of the word *that* is optional in reported speech.

EXTRA! Answering machine
Teach students how to leave an outgoing message on an answering machine or voicemail system in English. This can be very short: *Hi, this is _____. I can't come to the phone right now. Please leave a message.* Students are also sometimes flustered when they need to leave a voicemail message. Teach them a useful way to leave a message: *Hi, [person's name], this is _____. I wanted to talk to you about _____. Please call me at this number: _____.* Teach students to leave their telephone number very slowly and clearly so that the person listening has time to write it down. ⏱ 10 min

TEACHING TIP: Mixed up sentences
You can reinforce any teaching point by giving students extra examples. To make those examples even more interesting, try giving the sentences with the word order mixed up. In other words, if you are practicing reported speech, an example sentence might be: *She said that she was going to be late to the meeting.* Scramble the word order at random like this: *she late the going was said that to she be to meeting.* You can use this same principle with a number of sentences. For a variation on this method, take a brief story or paragraph and move entire sentences around. The students' task is then to put the sentences in the right order.

6 MAKING PLANS

A 🔄 With a partner, choose a situation and create a conversation of eight to ten sentences. ⏱ 10–15 min

Review with students the Useful Expressions on page 173 for offering another opinion. Ask a strong student to come to the front of the class. Model the conversation with him or her. If you wish to have your students practice speaking, then have them create the conversation verbally only. If you wish to focus more on grammar, have them write down their lines.

B 🔵 Practice your conversation. Then perform it for another pair. ⏱ 10 min

Tell students to stand when performing. Give the listening pair a specific task, such as listening for grammatical accuracy, correct use of vocabulary words, or pronunciation. Tell them to provide feedback to the pair who presented their conversation.

Instructor's Notes

_____

_____

_____

_____

_____

_____

_____

_____

_____

_____

_____

_____

_____

_____

_____

5 WHILE YOU WERE OUT

A  Imagine that, while your boss was out, you took several messages. Work with a partner. Using reported speech, give the messages to your boss. Then switch roles and repeat.

> **Student A:** Give these messages to your boss.
>
> 1. Mary: "The meeting is scheduled for 2:00."
>
> 2. Tom: "I won't be in the office next week. I'll be in China on business."
>
> 3. Copy company: "We're running behind schedule on your job."
>
> **Student B:** Give these messages to your boss.
>
> 1. Celine: "I can't make the deadline."
>
> 2. Dry cleaners: "Your suits are ready."
>
> 3. Mario: "I don't understand your memo. I have questions about it."

> Were there any messages while I was out?

> Yes. There were three. Mary called. She said that...

6 MAKING PLANS

A With a partner, choose a situation and create a conversation of eight to ten sentences.

Situation 1	Situation 2
Student A: There's a Broadway show in town, and your partner wants to see it. You think the show is too expensive.	**Student A:** There's a popular art exhibit at the museum. Your partner wants to see it. You think it will be very crowded and hard to see the paintings.
Student B: There's a Broadway show in town, and you really want to see it. Persuade your partner to go.	**Student B:** There's an exhibition at the museum in town, and you really want to see it. Persuade your partner to go.

B: I really want to see the Broadway show that's in town.

A: Yes, but it's too expensive.

B: That's true, but...

B Practice your conversation. Then perform it for another pair.

UNIT 1 INDOORS AND OUTDOORS

LESSON A

Vocabulary

color
bright ~, dark ~, favorite ~,
  neutral ~, primary ~

combine
get rid of
home improvement
option
overwhelming

rearrange
rebuild
recreate
redo
repaint
repair
replace
restart
work well

Speaking Strategy

Making informal suggestions
With base form
Why don't you <u>fix</u> it yourself?
I think you should <u>fix</u> it yourself.
I know what you should do. <u>Call</u>
  my friend.

With verb + -ing
Have you thought about <u>fixing</u>
  it yourself?
Try <u>calling</u> my friend.

Responding
Strong yes
Good idea!
That's a great idea.
Sounds good to me.

Weak yes
I guess it's worth a try.
Maybe I'll do that.

No
I don't think so.
No, I don't like that idea.

LESSON B

Vocabulary

disturb
litter
no one else's business
preserve

privacy
have (no) privacy

public
the general public
open to the public

public / private
~ conversation, ~ figure,
  ~ life, ~ school, ~ space, in ~

publicly / privately
~ owned business

rights

UNIT 2 MILESTONES

LESSON A

Vocabulary

infant (baby) / infancy
toddler
child (kid) / childhood
adolescent (teenager) /
  adolescence
young adult
adult (grown-up) / adulthood

start a family

Speaking Strategy

Talking about plans
planning + infinitive
  I'm planning to take a driving test.
going to + base form
  I'm going to visit my cousins.
thinking about + gerund
  I'm thinking about taking a trip.

Talking about needs
need + infinitive
  I need (to rent) a car.

LESSON B

Vocabulary

be born
buy a house
enroll (in college)
fall in love
get a job
get divorced
get married
get pregnant
go to school
have children
leave home
raise a family
retire

UNIT 3 GETTING INFORMATION

LESSON A

Vocabulary

argue / argument
        get into an argument
converse / conversation
        strike up / start a
                conversation
        carry on a conversation
chat / chat
        chat with your coworkers
discuss / discussion
        a discussion of (the plan)
gossip / gossip
        the latest gossip
        a piece of gossip
        juicy gossip
share
        share your (feelings / ideas)
talk / talk
        give a talk, listen to a talk

argue / converse / chat / gossip /
  share / talk (*with* someone,
  about something)
discuss (something *with*
  someone)
have a(n) argument / conversation /
  chat / discussion / talk

Speaking Strategy

Interrupting someone politely
Introducing yourself
Excuse me. May I interrupt for
  a moment? My name is…
I'm sorry to interrupt. / I beg your
  pardon.
I just wanted to introduce myself.
  My name is…

Interrupting someone you know
Excuse me. Sorry to bother you,
  (name), but I have a question.
Could I interrupt for a second?
  I just wanted to say / ask
  something.

LESSON B

Vocabulary

media
in the media

news
get (your) news
in the news
tell (someone) the news
(news) source
news **story**
(**local / national / international**)
  news
(**entertainment / sports /
  tabloid**) news
(news) **program / site**
**bad, good, great, sad,
  sensational** (news)
spread the, hear the news

accurate ↔ inaccurate
reliable ↔ unreliable
scandal

word of mouth

UNIT 4 MEN AND WOMEN

LESSON A

Vocabulary

brush your (hair / teeth)
color / **dye** your hair
get a (haircut / manicure / tattoo)
get your ears pierced
have (your nails done / your hair curled / your teeth straightened)
neaten up
shave your (face / head / legs)
straighten your hair
stand out
strike a pose
wear (cologne / perfume / deodorant / makeup / bright colors)

Speaking Strategy

Disagreeing politely
I agree up to a point.
Yes, but… / I know, but…
I'm not sure. / I don't know.
But what about (the cost)?
I'm not sure it's / that's (such) a good idea. Are you sure?
I see what you're saying / you mean, but…
I see where you're coming from, but…

LESSON B

Vocabulary

Separable phrasal verbs
ask (someone) **out**
give (something) up
turn (someone) **down**
turn (something) **on**

Inseparable phrasal verbs
break up (with someone)
cheat on (someone)
get along (with someone)
get over (someone)
go out (with someone)
grow up
make up (with someone)
run into (someone)

UNIT 5 ACROSS CULTURES

LESSON A

Vocabulary

appropriate ↔ **inappropriate**
considerate ↔ **inconsiderate**
crucial
customary
honest ↔ **dishonest**
kind ↔ **unkind**
mature ↔ **immature**
normal
polite ↔ **impolite, rude**
pleasant ↔ **unpleasant**
respectful ↔ **disrespectful**
responsible ↔ **irresponsible**
sincere ↔ **insincere**

Speaking Strategy

Asking about culturally appropriate behavior
Is it OK / appropriate to use my fingers?
Is it OK if I use my fingers?
  Please, go right ahead.
  Absolutely.
  Actually, it's probably better to use a fork.
  Normally, people use a fork.
Is it all right to wear shoes inside?
Is it all right if I wear shoes inside?
  Sure, no problem.
  Yeah, it's fine.
  Actually, it's best to remove your shoes.
  No, you really should take off your shoes.

LESSON B

Vocabulary

body language
discouraged
eating habits
(make) **eye contact**
facial expression
homesick
(have, avoid) **jet lag**
(overcome a) **language barrier**
personal space
(make) **small talk**

UNIT 6 BUSINESS AND MARKETING

LESSON A

Vocabulary

advertise → advertisement →
  advertiser
consume → consumption →
  consumer
develop → development →
  developer
employ → employment →
  employer
invest → investment → investor
manage → management →
  manager
produce → production →
  producer
promote → promotion →
  promoter
purchase
ship → shipment → shipper

Speaking Strategy

Asking about companies
What does your company
  do exactly?
What is the main focus of your
  company?
How do you… ?

Emphasizing important points
I'd like to emphasize that…
Never forget that…
This is a key point.
The bottom line is…

LESSON B

Vocabulary

catchy
clever
a **dramatic increase** / **increase**
  dramatically
get better ↔ get worse
increase ↔ decrease
inspiring
persuasive
profits
recover
a **sharp fall** / **fall sharply**
shocking
a **slight rise** / **rise slightly**
(in a) **slump**
a **steady decline** / **decline**
  steadily
(be) up ↔ (be) down

UNIT 7 WELLBEING

LESSON A

Vocabulary

can't stop + *-ing* verb: I can't stop
 (**coughing** / scratching /
 shivering / sneezing).
feel + adjective: I feel (**dizzy** /
 nauseous / **drowsy** / **exhausted** /
 faint / **weak** / sick).
have + noun: I have (a
 stomachache / an earache /
 a backache / a toothache / a
 cut / a sore throat / a fever / a
 temperature / a cold / the flu).
possessive adjective + noun +
 hurt: My (arm / finger / back /
 stomach) hurts. / My legs hurt.
blink
breathe
chew
make sense
swallow
symptom

Speaking Strategy

Giving serious advice
In my opinion, you should…
I always advise people to…
I think the best idea (for you)
 is to…
If I were you, I'd…

Accepting advice
You're right. Thanks for the advice.
That makes (a lot of) sense. I'll
 give it a try.
I'll try it and get back to you.

Refusing advice
I'm not sure that would work for me.
That doesn't (really) make sense
 to me.
I could never do that.

LESSON B

Vocabulary

care: take ~ of, ~ about

sick: make someone ~,
 call in ~, ~ **day**,
 ~ **of** (something /
 someone), **worried** ~
homesick, carsick, lovesick,
 seasick

well: do ~, ~ **behaved**, ~ **paid**,
might (may) **as** ~

boss around
chaos
cut class
fatigue
gentle
ground (= punish) someone
massage
meditation
paralyze
straightforward
tidy
treat (someone) like (a kid)
yoga

UNIT 8 THE ACTIVE LIFE

LESSON A

Vocabulary

activity:
be into / **be involved in** /
 participate in / **take part in an** ~
spare / leisure time ~
physical, mental, outdoor,
 extracurricular, classroom ~

active:
stay / remain ~
highly / extremely / very ~
fairly, increasingly ~
mentally, **physically** ~

athlete:
amateur, professional, serious ~

Speaking Strategy

**Explaining the set-up and rules
of a game**
It's played with…
You don't need any special
 equipment.
There are 11 players on each
 team. / You compete against
 each other.
One team starts by… / The game
 begins when…
The team with the most points
 wins. / The object is to score the
 most runs.
It's played on a field. / It's played
 all over the world.

LESSON B

Vocabulary

ask for
believe in
dominate
go to your head
head out
learn about
pay for
prepare for
spend on
stay in
warn about

UNIT 9 SOCIAL ISSUES

LESSON A

Vocabulary

as usual
campaign
candidate
citizen
clear (adj)
corporation
enthusiastically
expand
give it your best shot
launch (v)
make progress
never in my wildest dreams
raise taxes
(a) record turnout
reelect
running neck and neck
tax (v)
term
up for reelection
vote (for ↔ against)
voting age
vow (v)

Speaking Strategy

Language for presentations

Stating the purpose
Today, I'd like to talk to you
   about…
I'll begin by (talking about the
   issue). / I'll provide an overview
   of (the issue).
Then I'll list the (two / three /
   four)…

Stating important points
Let's talk first about… / Let's start
   by talking about…
One of the main causes of (traffic)
   is…
Another / A second cause
   of (traffic) is…
And finally…

LESSON B

Vocabulary

a change of scene
depression
destroy → destruction
develop → development
disabled
encourage → encouragement
force → force
improve → improvement
protect → protection
provide
put down roots
rely (on) → reliance
sprawl
spread
suburban
support → support
urban
wait and see
waste → waste

UNIT 10 MONEY

LESSON A

Vocabulary

afford
broke
(make a / have a) budget
borrow ↔ lend (money)
get by
go into debt
owe
pay back
save ↔ spend (money)
short on cash
stick to it

Speaking Strategy

Apologizing
Small accident or mistake
I'm sorry. It was an accident.
Sorry. My mistake.
I can't believe I did that.

Serious accident or mistake
I'm really sorry that I forgot to…
I'm so sorry about damaging…
I want to apologize for what
   happened.

Accepting an apology
Don't worry about it.
Oh, that's OK.
No problem. It happens.
Apology accepted.

LESSON B

Vocabulary

affordable
donate (money)
earn / make (money)
earnings
invest (money)
millionaire
set aside / save ↔ spend
   (money)
squander / waste (money)
strike it rich
valuable
wealthy

C Complete the sentences with the correct form of the words in parentheses.

1. This room needs a lot of work. The walls (crack) _____, and the floor (stain) _____.

2. It rained a lot, and now the house (flood) _____.

3. Don't (jam) _____ the key into the lock. You don't want to (break) _____ it.

4. Someone (break) _____ the window last week, and it _____ still (break) _____.

5. The little boy (throw) _____ something into the sink. Now the drain (clog) _____.

6. What's the best thing to do when your car door (freeze) _____?

7. This key doesn't work because it (bend) _____.

LESSON B

Giving Permission and Expressing Prohibition				
	be	*allowed / permitted / supposed to*	**Base form**	
You	**are**	**allowed to / permitted to**	park	here.
	aren't	**supposed to**		
		Modal	**Base form**	
You	**can**		park	here.
	can't			
	must			
	must not			

Use *(not) be allowed / permitted to* or *can / can't* to give or deny permission to do something.

Use *be supposed to* to say that someone is expected to do something.

(Not) be supposed to means that you are not allowed to do something.

Use *must / must not* for formal rules and warnings. It is more common to use *can / can't* for prohibition in normal spoken English.

No	**Gerund**	*be*	*allowed / permitted*	
	Talking	**is(n't)**	**allowed / permitted**	during the test.
No	**talking**			

You can use a gerund + *(not) be allowed / permitted* to give or deny permission.

No + gerund is often used on signs to say something is not allowed.

A Unscramble the words to make sentences.

1. allowed to / He / an hour of TV a week / watch / is

   _____.

2. isn't / in class / Eating / permitted

   _____.

3. permitted to / stay out / She's / until midnight with her friends

   _____.

4. here / is not / Parking / allowed

   _____.

5. supposed to / to school / aren't / wear shorts / We

   _____.

3. A: Are you going to study at this school next term?

   B: I _____ . I'm thinking about going to another school.

4. A: Is it going to be cold tonight?

   B: I don't know; it _____ . Take a jacket to be safe.

5. A: Are you going to hang out with your friends this weekend?

   B: I _____ , or I _____ stay home and study.

B Cover the answers in **A**. Answer the questions about yourself. Use modals of future possibility.

1. _____

2. _____

3. _____

4. _____

5. _____

UNIT **3** GETTING INFORMATION

LESSON A

Participial and Prepositional Phrases		
Who is Joe Ortega?	He's the guy	**chatting on the phone.** **on the phone.**
Who is Ms. Anh?	She's the woman	**wearing glasses.** **in front of the class.**
Which books are mine?	They're the ones	**lying on the floor.** **in the drawer.**

Use participial and prepositional phrases to identify people and things. These statements answer questions that ask *who*, *what*, and *which one(s)*.

A present participle uses the form verb + *-ing*. It follows the noun it is modifying: *She's the lady <u>talking to the police officer</u>*.

A prepositional phrase starts with *in, on, by*, etc. It also follows the noun it is modifying: *He's the man <u>with the mustache</u>*.

A Look at the picture below. What are the people doing? Give each person a name and write a sentence about him or her. Then label the picture.

Who is _____ ?

He's the man _____ .

_____

_____

_____

_____

_____

_____

B Write questions about the people in the picture. (Use the words in parentheses.)
Start your questions with *Do you know...?*

1. (talk / bus driver) _____ *Do you know the woman talking to the bus driver?* _____

2. (listen / music) _____

3. (skateboard and backpack) _____

4. (school uniforms) _____

5. (talk / phone) _____

6. (suit / briefcase) _____

C 🔊 On a piece of paper, make up your own stories about each person. Use participial and prepositional phrases.

LESSON B

Review of the Present Perfect				
Subject	**have / has** *(not)*	**Past participle**		
❶ I	**have**(n't)	seen	that news program.	
❶ He	**has**(n't)			
❷ I	**have**(n't)	worked	as a news reporter	**for** six months.
❷ She	**has**(n't)			**since** May.

❶ You can use the present perfect to talk about past actions or experiences when the time they happened is unknown or unimportant.

I have seen that news program.

I haven't been to France.

❷ Use can also use the present perfect to talk about an action that started in the past and continues up to now. Use *for* + a length of time. Use *since* + a point in time.

I have worked as a reporter for six months.

I've lived in Paris since May.

Notice the difference:

present perfect: I've worked as a news reporter for six months. I love my job. (action continues)

simple past: I worked as a news reporter for six months after college. (action is finished)

Questions and short answers					
Wh- word	**have / has**	**Subject**	**Past participle**		**Answers**
	Have	you	heard	the news?	**Yes, I have.** I heard it this morning.* **No, I haven't.** What happened?
How long	**have**	you	been	a reporter?	(I**'ve been** a reporter) **for** six months.
	has	she			(She**'s been** a reporter) **since** May.

* When you answer a present perfect question with a specific time expression, use the simple past:

Have you heard the news? Yes, I heard it this morning.

A 🔄 Complete the conversation. Use the present perfect form of the verb in parentheses, a short answer, or *for* or *since*.

A: (1. hear) ____Have____ you _____ the latest news about Leo?

B: No, I (2.) _____. What's up?

A: He's going to be on that reality show *Pop Idol*.

B: Really? How long (3. be) _____ Leo _____ a singer?

A: (4.) _____ high school.

B: I had no idea. (5. see) _____ you ever _____ him perform?

A: Yeah, I (6.) _____. I saw him at a talent show in high school. He was amazing.

UNIT **4** MEN AND WOMEN

LESSON A

Adverbs Used with the Present Perfect			
	With questions	**With affirmative verbs**	**With negative verbs**
ever	Have you **ever** worn makeup?		I haven't **ever** worn makeup.
never		I've **never** worn makeup (before).	
yet	Have you taken a shower **yet**?		I haven't taken a shower **yet**.
still			I **still** haven't taken a shower.
already	Have you **already** taken a shower? Have you taken a shower **already**?	I've **already** taken a shower. I've taken a shower **already**.	
just		I've **just** finished shaving.	

Ever means "at any time." Note: *I haven't ever = I've never*

Never means "not at any time." It is used with an affirmative verb and makes the meaning of the sentence negative. You can add the word *before* for emphasis.

Yet means "up to or until the present time" or "thus far."

Still has a similar meaning to *yet*. It is used for situations that have continued for longer than expected.

Already means something happened and no longer needs to be done. Notice the different placement of *already* in sentences.

Just means "very recently."

A Victor is traveling in Vietnam. Read his email back home. Correct the six errors.

> Greetings from Ho Chi Minh City, Vietnam!
>
> There is a lot to see and do here. We've been already here for two days, but there is so much we yet haven't seen. For example, I've already been to the Ben Thanh Market, but I haven't still visited the famous Jade Emperor Pagoda.
>
> By the way, I've come just back from my first ride on a scooter. It was really fun. I haven't never seen so many scooters on the street before!
>
> When are you going to join us? Have already you packed? I can't wait to see you and explore Vietnam with you!

B Circle the sentence that best follows the first sentence.

1. He's never worn bright colors.
   a. He's adventurous.
   b. He's not a risk-taker.

2. I've just met Paula.
   a. She's nice.
   b. She's an old friend.

3. I've already gotten a tattoo.
   a. Should I do it?
   b. I really like it!

4. I haven't washed my hair yet.
   a. I'd better hurry.
   b. It looks much better.

5. I haven't brushed my teeth yet.
   a. I can't find my toothbrush.
   b. My teeth feel so clean!

6. I haven't seen the doctor yet.
   a. I saw him yesterday.
   b. I hope he comes soon.

LESSON B

Phrasal Verbs	
Please **turn on** the TV. Erin **ran into** Alex yesterday.	English has many two-word (phrasal) verbs. These verbs have a verb (like *turn* or *run*) and a smaller word (like *at, along, back, down, in, on, out, over, up, with*).
Please **turn on** <u>the TV</u>. Please **turn** <u>the TV</u> / <u>it</u> **on**. ~~Please **turn on** it.~~	Some phrasal verbs are separable. This means <u>the object</u> (a noun or pronoun) can separate the phrasal verb. **Note:** With separable phrasal verbs, the pronoun *cannot* follow the phrasal verb.
Erin **ran into** <u>Alex</u> / <u>him</u> yesterday.	Many phrasal verbs are inseparable. This means <u>the object</u> (a noun or pronoun) can *only* follow the phrasal verb.
She **grew up** in Mexico City.	Some phrasal verbs do not take an object.
Do you **get along** with Max? Did Sean **ask** her **out**? When did they **break up**? Have you ever **gone out** with him?	Form questions with phrasal verbs the same way you do with other verbs.

Separable phrasal verbs	Inseparable phrasal verbs	
ask (someone) out give (something) up = "stop doing something" turn (someone) down turn (something) on / off	break up (with someone) cheat on (someone) get along (with someone) get over (someone) go out (with someone)	grow up make up (with someone) = "forgive someone and become friends again" run into (someone)

A Unscramble the questions.

1. up / where / you / did / grow

   _____?

2. you / get / do / along / with your family

   _____?

3. out / you / how often / do / with friends / go

   _____?

4. asked / have you ever / out / someone / on a date

   _____?

5. The music is loud. it / you / can / off / turn

   _____?

6. on the way / you / who / into / did / run / to class

   _____?

B Now answer the questions in **A** in complete sentences. Use the phrasal verbs.

1. _____ .

2. _____ .

3. _____ .

4. _____ .

5. _____ .

6. _____ .

UNIT **5** ACROSS CULTURES

LESSON A

It + be + Adjective + Infinitive; Gerund + be + Adjective						
It	*be*	**Adjective**	*(for)*	**(pronoun)**	**Infinitive**	
It	**was**(n't)	hard	(for)	(me)	to pass	the test.
It's not		normal	(for)	(us)	to eat	with chopsticks.
It isn't		normal	(for)	(us)	to eat	with chopsticks.
Gerund			*be*	**Adjective**	*(for)*	**(pronoun)**
Passing	the test		**was**(n't)	hard	(for)	(me).
Eating	with chopsticks		**is**(n't)	normal	(for)	(us).

It + *be* + adjective + infinitive and gerund + *be* + adjective are two different ways of expressing the same thing.

Some adjectives that are commonly used in these patterns are *easy*, *difficult / hard*, *important*, *impossible*, *necessary*, and *wrong*.

For + pronoun is optional because the pronoun is often understood.

You can also use other linking verbs in the place of *be*: *It <u>seems</u> impossible for us to win the game. / At this point, winning the game <u>seems</u> impossible.*

A Read the information about cultural rules in Norway. For each underlined sentence, rewrite it on page 202.

1. People greet each other by shaking hands. At business meetings, <u>it's customary to shake hands when you arrive and when you leave</u>.

2. Business meetings start right on time. <u>Being late is inappropriate</u>.

3. Close friends and family members may hug each other. <u>Hugging people you've just met isn't typical</u>.

4. When you visit someone's home, <u>it's considerate to bring a small gift</u>.

5. Norwegians don't like to waste food. <u>It's polite to finish everything on your plate</u>.

6. Norwegians don't like to say bad things about each other. <u>Being kind to others is very important for them</u>.

7. If you mention "getting together later" to a Norwegian, <u>not following up with a sincere invitation is rude</u>.

8. Norwegians are proud of their distinctive culture. <u>It's disrespectful to treat Norway and Sweden as the same culture</u>.

1. _Shaking hands when you arrive and when you leave is customary._
2. _____
3. _____
4. _____
5. _____
6. _____
7. _____
8. _____

B 🔁 Now rewrite the sentences in **A** to make similar cultural rules about your country.

Examples:

Bowing when you meet someone is customary.

It's inappropriate to talk to a professor using casual speech.

_____

_____

_____

_____

LESSON B

Present and Future Time Clauses with *before, after, when, as soon as / once*	
Main clause	**Time clause**
❶ In Spain, people often kiss each other	**when** they <u>meet</u>.
❷ Please remove your shoes	**before** you <u>enter</u> the temple.
❸ We're going to go to the park	**after** we <u>eat</u> lunch.
❹ I'll call you	**as soon as / once** we <u>arrive</u>.
Time clause	**Main clause**
Before you enter the temple,	please remove your shoes.*

A time clause shows the order of two or more events:

In sentence ❶: *When* shows that two events happen at almost the same time: At the time you meet someone, you kiss them.

In sentence ❷: You remove your shoes first, and then you enter the temple.

In sentence ❸: We plan to eat lunch first, and then we're going to go to the park.

In sentence ❹: *As soon as / Once* means "right after." We arrive, and then I will call you.

When we use time clauses to talk about facts or other information in **the present** (as in ❶ and ❷), the <u>verbs</u> in the main and time clauses are in the present tense. ❷ uses the imperative form with time clauses.

When we use time clauses to talk about **the future** (as in ❸ and ❹):

the <u>verb</u> in the main clause uses a future form.

the <u>verb</u> in the time clause is in the simple present.

*In <u>writing</u>, when the time clause comes first, put a comma before the main clause.

A Alejandro is starting college in Los Angeles soon. Look at his timeline. Then use the words in parentheses to connect the phrases and make sentences about the future.

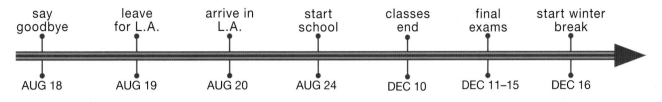

say goodbye	leave for L.A.	arrive in L.A.	start school	classes end	final exams	start winter break
AUG 18	AUG 19	AUG 20	AUG 24	DEC 10	DEC 11–15	DEC 16

1. leave for L.A. / say goodbye to his friends (before)

   _____

2. arrive in L.A. / start school (four days after)

   _____

3. take his final exams / his classes end (once)

   _____

4. start winter break / finish his last exam (as soon as)

   _____

B Complete the sentences below about yourself. Pay attention to the verb forms you use.

1. Before I go home today,

   _____.

2. After I eat breakfast in the morning, I

   _____.

3. I _____ when _____.

4. I'm going to _____ as soon as _____.

5. I will _____ once _____.

<table>
<tr><td>UNIT 6</td><td>BUSINESS AND MARKETING</td></tr>
</table>

LESSON A

The Passive Voice: Simple Present and Simple Past			
Subject	**Verb**	**Object**	**Active voice**
Sound Smart	makes	audiobooks.	In an active sentence, the subject is the *agent* (the one performing the action).

Subject	*be*	**Past participle**	**(*by* + Object)**	**Passive voice**
❶ Audiobooks	**are**	**made**	by Sound Smart.	In a passive sentence, the object becomes the subject, and the subject becomes the object. The subject is not the agent because it doesn't perform an action.
❷ The products	**were**	**shipped**.		
❸ The company	**was**	**founded**	by Beverly Smith.	

(Continued)

The Passive Voice: Simple Present and Simple Past

❶ In a passive sentence, the focus is on the action that happens to the subject, not on who / what performed the action (the agent).

Use *by* + object to indicate the agent: *The Fallingwater house **was built** <u>by Frank Lloyd Wright</u>.*

❷ We don't use *by* + object when the agent is understood, unknown, or unimportant, or when an action is done by people in general.

I'm paid twice a month. (I know who pays my salary. The agent is understood.)

*All of the money **was stolen**.* (We don't know who did it. The agent is unknown.)

*Once a week, her house **is cleaned**.* (We don't care who does it. The agent is unimportant.)

*Portuguese **is spoken** in Brazil.* (Everyone speaks it. It's done by people in general.)

❸ We include *by* + object in sentences where it sounds incomplete without it.

The company was founded. (By whom? When? This sentence sounds incomplete.)

We can also add a time or place phrase. *The company was founded (by Pablo Ruiz) (in Seattle) (in 2004).*

The form of *be* depends on the verb tense. For the simple present, use *am / is / are* (see sentence **❶**). For the simple past, use *was / were* (see sentences **❷** and **❸**).

A Read this profile of Unilever, one of the world's largest companies. Find and circle six examples of the passive.

- Unilever was created in 1930 by a British soap maker and Dutch margarine producer.

- Today 400 brands of home, personal care, and food products are sold by the company.

- Some of the more popular products are Knorr® (soups), Lipton® (tea), and Dove® (soap).

- Lux® soap, which was introduced in 1924, became the first mass-marketed soap in the world.

- Today Knorr® is Unilever's most popular brand. It is sold in over 80 countries.

- The multinational company operates companies and factories on every continent except Antarctica.

- 174,000 people are employed by the company worldwide.

- 160 million times a day, a Unilever product is purchased by someone—somewhere in the world.

B Now rewrite the passive sentences in **A** as active sentences.

1. In 1930, _a British soap maker and Dutch margarine producer created Unilever._

2. Today the company _____.

3. In 1924, a man _____.

4. Today Unilever _____ in over 80 countries.

5. _____ 174,000 people.

6. 160 million times a day, someone in the world _____.

LESSON B

Connecting Ideas with *because, so, although / even though*	
❶ She uses that product **Because** it's the cheapest,	**because** it's the cheapest. she uses that product.
❷ This snack is "100% natural,"	**so** a lot of moms buy it for their kids.
❸ Many people buy that car **Even though / Although** it's expensive,	**even though / although** it's expensive. many people buy that car.

Because, *so*, *although*, and *even though* join two clauses together. A clause has a subject and a verb.

❶ *Because* answers the question *why*. It gives a reason: *Why does she buy that product? (She buys it) because it's the cheapest.*

In conversation, people often give the reason only (*because it's the cheapest*). Don't do this in formal writing. When the clause with *because* comes first, put a comma at the end of the clause.

❷ *So* gives a result: *The snack is "100% natural." The result: A lot of moms buy it.*

In writing, use a comma before *so* unless the two clauses are very short.

❸ *Although* and *Even though* mean the same thing, and they introduce <u>surprising or opposite information</u>: *Many people buy that car <u>even though it's expensive</u>.*

In writing, when the clause with *although / even though* comes first, put a comma at the end of the clause.

A Complete the sentences with *although / even though*, *because*, or *so*.

1. The phone was on sale, _____ so _____ many people bought it _____ they didn't need a new phone.

2. A lot of people buy those shoes _____ a famous basketball player wears them.

3. _____ their product is affordable, it doesn't work as well as ours.

4. The new toy was very popular, _____ it sold very quickly.

5. _____ smoking can kill you, many smoking ads show people smiling.

B Use the connecting words to join the sentences together. Which items can you write in more than one way?

1. That ad is really popular. It has a catchy slogan. (because)

   _____

2. I hate TV commercials. I don't watch much television. (so)

   _____

3. Advertising on TV is very expensive. Companies still do it. (although)

   _____

4. I still bought it. That TV is expensive. (even though)

   _____

5. I decided to try it. My sister liked that shampoo. (so)

   _____

LESSON A

Describing Symptoms						
	have	Noun		Possessive adjective	Noun	*hurt*
I	have	a headache,	and	my	throat	hurts.
	feel / be	Adjective			*can't stop*	*-ing* verb
I	feel / am	tired,	and	I	can't stop	shivering.

Use *have* + noun, possessive adjective + noun + *hurt*, and *feel / be* + adjective to talk about states and conditions.

Use *can't stop* + *-ing* verb to talk about repeated actions that you have no control over.

Other common vocabulary

have + noun: *I have (a stomachache / an earache / a backache / a toothache / a cut / a sore throat / a fever / a temperature / a cold / the flu).*

possessive adjective + noun + *hurt*: *My (arm / finger / back / leg / stomach) hurts.*
                                    My (legs) hurt.

feel / be + adjective: *I feel / am (dizzy / nauseous / drowsy / exhausted / faint / weak / sick).*

can't stop + *-ing* verb: *I can't stop (coughing / scratching / sneezing).*

Questions

How do you feel?

Does your head hurt?

What hurts?

Where does it hurt?

A Read the two conversations and complete the sentences. Use the correct form of *be*, *have*, *feel*, *can't stop*, or *hurt*.

Conversation 1

A: What's wrong?

B: I (1.) _____ exhausted. I didn't sleep well last night.

A: (2.) _____ you sick? Maybe you (3.) _____ a cold.

B: No, I'm fine. It's my husband, Fred—he (4.) _____ the flu.

A: I'm sorry to hear that.

B: Yeah, it's pretty bad. He (5.) _____ coughing. It keeps me awake at night. And now my head (6.) _____.

Conversation 2

A: Mom, my stomach (7.) _____.

B: Do you (8.) _____ a fever?

A: No, I don't think so.

B: Do you (9.) _____ nauseous?

A: No, not at all. But you know, I did have potato chips and peanut butter for dinner.

B Write two sentences about each of the pictures on a separate piece of paper. Use the different grammar patterns for describing symptoms.

LESSON B

Reported Speech: Commands and Requests		
	Quoted speech	**Reported speech**
Command	The doctor said, "Get some rest."	The doctor **told** me **to** get some rest.
	The doctor said, "Don't smoke."	The doctor **told** him **not to** smoke.
	Jane's mom said, "Be home at midnight."	Her mom **told** her **to** be home at midnight.
Request	Jon said, "Please turn off your phone."	Jon **asked** me **to** turn off my phone.
	Maria asked, "Can you help me?"	Maria **asked** us **to** help her.
	Chen said, "Please text me later."	Chen **asked** me **to** text him later.

Quoted speech uses a person's exact words: *"Get some rest," said the doctor.*

Reported speech explains what someone else has said: *The doctor **told** me **to** get some rest.*

A **command** is an order: someone tells you what to do.

To report a command, use *tell* + noun / pronoun + (*not*) infinitive (*to* + verb).

If someone makes a **request**, the person is asking you to do something.

To report a request, use *ask* + noun / pronoun + (*not*) infinitive (*to* + verb). Notice how some underlined words change in reported speech.

A Read each quoted command or request. Then complete the sentences in reported speech.

1. "Clean your room!" my mom says every day.

   My mom is always telling me _____.

2. "No texting in class!"

   Our teacher often tells us _____.

3. "Can you loan me some money?"

   Sometimes my friend asks me _____.

4. "Dad, can you drive me to school?"

   Yesterday, I asked my dad _____.

B Read the sentences with quoted speech. Then rewrite each one in reported speech.

1. Coach Jon said to the team, "Don't give up!"

   _____

2. My friends asked me, "Will you help us?"

   _____

3. Anna said to her older sister, "Don't boss me around!"

   _____

4. The librarian said to Mrs. Green, "Please be quiet."

   _____

5. Professor Lewis asked our class, "Please turn in your papers tomorrow."

   _____

6. The parents said to their children, "Don't talk to strangers."

   _____

LESSON A

The Present Perfect vs. the Present Perfect Continuous					
	***have / has +** (not)*	***been***	**verb + *-ing***		
I	**have**(n't)	**been**	**doing**	much in my spare time.	Use the present perfect continuous for an action that started in the past and continues in the present.
She	**has**(n't)	**been**	**participating**	in the school play.	

Incorrect: ~~I've been taking this test three times already.~~ Correct: **I've taken** this test three times already.	To talk about a repeated action in the past, use the present perfect, not the present perfect continuous.

I've been playing cricket <u>since I was a child</u>. = **I've played** cricket <u>since I was a child</u>.	When you use *for* or *since* to indicate a specific period of time in the past, you can use the present perfect continuous or the present perfect. They have the same meaning.
I've been reading a book on long-distance running. I'm enjoying it. (The action is ongoing.) ≠ **I've read** a book on long-distance running. It was excellent. (The action is completed.)	Some sentences don't indicate a specific time in the past. Use the present perfect continuous for an action that is still happening. Use the present perfect for a completed action. These two sentences have different meanings.
I've been going to the gym a lot <u>lately</u>. <u>Recently</u> **I've been working out** more.	To emphasize that an action has been happening in the recent past up to now, use words like *lately* and *recently* with the present perfect continuous.
Incorrect: ~~I've been owning that car for ten years.~~ Correct: **I've owned** that car for ten years.	As with other continuous tenses, don't use stative verbs (such as *hear*, *like*, and *own*) with the present perfect continuous. Use the present perfect instead.
Incorrect: ~~I've been taking this test three times already.~~ Correct: **I've taken** this test three times already.	To talk about a repeated action in the past, use the present perfect, not the present perfect continuous.

A Tom has started a lot of activities but hasn't finished them. Write five affirmative sentences in the present perfect continuous using the verbs in the box. What is one activity that he hasn't started yet? Write one negative sentence. (Note: The verb *do* is used twice.).

do	eat	study	talk	watch

1. He's been doing his homework. _____
2. _____
3. _____
4. _____
5. _____
6. _____

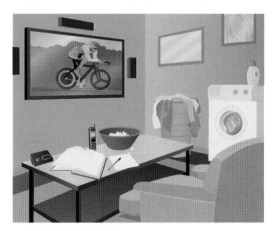

B Circle the correct answer(s) to complete each sentence.

1. I've gotten / I've been getting increasingly active since I joined the judo club.

2. I've belonged / I've been belonging to the club for three months.

3. This is the third time I've taken part / I've been taking part in an extracurricular activity.

4. We've practiced / We've been practicing after school every day since April.

5. My sister has joined / has been joining the photography club.

6. She's taken / She's been taking pictures every day.

LESSON B

Review: The Simple Past vs. the Present Perfect vs. the Present Perfect Continuous		
	Completed past action	**Actions started in the past continuing up to now**
Simple past	❶ I **visited** South Africa <u>in 2010</u>.	
Present perfect	❷ I've **visited** South Africa once.	❸ Fabiola **has skated** for years.
Present perfect continuous		❹ Fabiola **has been skating** for years.

❶ Use the <u>simple past</u> to talk about completed (finished) actions.

❷ You can use the <u>present perfect</u> to talk about past actions if the time they happened is not stated.

In sentence ❶, the speaker says when he was in South Africa: *in 2010*. For this reason, the simple past is used.

In sentence ❷, the speaker has been to South Africa in the past, but he doesn't say when. The present perfect is used.

❸&❹ You can use the <u>present perfect</u> or the <u>present perfect continuous</u> with *for* or *since* to talk about an action that started in the past and continues up to now. Notice that sentences ❸ and ❹ have the same meaning.

Do NOT use the <u>present perfect continuous</u> in the situations below. Use the <u>present perfect</u> instead.

With stative verbs (verbs not used in the continuous like *be, have, like, hate, know, need*):

~~I've been knowing her for five years.~~   I've **known** her for five years.

To talk about actions that happened a specific number of times:

~~She has been winning the gold medal in the event six times.~~   She **has won** the gold medal in the event six times.

A Read about mountain climber Erik Weihenmayer. Complete the sentences with the verbs in parentheses. Use the present perfect or the present perfect continuous.

Erik Weihenmayer (1. be) _____ blind* since he was 13. He (2. climb) _____ since he was 16, and he's still doing it.

Erik (3. climb) _____ Mount Everest. Also, he (4. reach) _____ the top of the Seven Summits—the seven tallest mountains on the seven continents.

Erik (5. develop) _____ his own climbing system. His partners wear bells on their vests. He follows the sounds of the bells.

Erik (6. think) _____ about his next trip for a long time, but he (7. not choose) _____ a place to go yet.

*blind = unable to see

B Circle the correct verb form to complete each sentence. Sometimes, both answers are possible.

I learned / I've learned how to play dominoes from my grandfather many years ago. He taught / He's been teaching me the game during my summer break from school.

My cousin is 20 years old. He played / He's been playing dominoes since he was seven years old. He's been / He's been being in many dominoes competitions. Last year he got / he's gotten second

(continued)

place in a really big contest. He's always done / He's always been doing well under pressure. I think he'll win first prize this year.

My grandfather has played / has been playing the game for 50 years. He says he's played / he's been playing about 20,000 games, and he doesn't plan to stop.

UNIT 9 SOCIAL ISSUES

LESSON A

Too + Adjective / Adverb; *too much / too many* + Noun				
	too	**Adjective / Adverb**	**(Infinitive)**	
You're 17. You're	**too**	young	to vote.	
I can't understand him. He speaks	**too**	quickly.		
	too much / too many	**Noun**	**(Infinitive)**	
	Too much	pollution		is bad for your lungs.
Our city has	**too many**	problems	to solve	in one day.

Too means "to a greater degree than is acceptable." It often has a negative meaning.
It comes <u>before</u> adjectives and adverbs.
Use *too much* <u>before</u> noncount nouns.
Use *too many* <u>before</u> plural count nouns.

Adjective / Adverb + *enough*; *enough* + Noun				
	Adjective / Adverb	***enough***	**(Infinitive)**	
I'm 21. I'm	old	**enough**	to vote.	
These are good seats. I can hear	well	**enough.**		
	enough	**Noun**	**(Infinitive)**	
We have	**enough**	water	to get by	for now.
They have	**enough**	police officers		on the street.

Enough means "as much as you need" or "as much as is necessary."
It comes <u>after</u> adjectives and adverbs.
It comes <u>before</u> nouns (count and noncount).

A Complete the reasons on the right with *too, too much, too many,* or *enough*. Then match the questions with the answers.

1. Why are you so hungry now? _____
2. Why does your stomach hurt? _____
3. Why did you fail the driving test? _____
4. Why didn't you take the driving test? _____
5. Why did you lose the race? _____
6. Why are you running indoors? _____
7. Why did they close the bridge? _____
8. Why didn't you jump off the diving board? _____

a. Because I'm _____ young to drive.
b. Because I ate _____ candy.
c. Because there were _____ people on it.
d. Because it's _____ hot outside.
e. Because I didn't study hard _____.
f. Because I didn't eat _____ breakfast.
g. Because I wasn't brave _____.
h. Because I ran _____ slowly.

B 🔊 Correct the errors with *too* or *enough* below. Check your answers with a partner.

1. I can't button this shirt. It isn't too big.

2. It's not dangerous here. It's enough safe to go out at night by yourself.

3. It's crowded. There are too much people in this little room.

4. These condos are expensive enough to buy. We need more affordable housing.

5. He's only 12 years old. He's old enough to get a driver's license.

LESSON B

Future Real Conditionals	
If clause	**Result clause**
A: What will happen if a woman works? B: If a woman **works**,	(then) a family **will have** more money.
A: What will happen if we don't protect our open spaces? B: If we **don't protect** our open spaces,	(then) future generations **won't have** places to relax.
Result clause	**If clause**
A family **will have** more money	if a woman **works**.

Future real conditionals are used to talk about possibilities or to make predictions. The *if* clause states a possible situation. The result clause says what will or might happen.

The verb in the *if* clause uses the simple present. Don't say: ~~If a woman will work...~~

The verb in the result clause uses a future form. You can also say, for example: *If we don't protect our open spaces, future generations **aren't going to have** places to relax.*

If you aren't certain about the result, you can use *might (not)* or *may (not)* in a result clause:

*If a woman works, a family **may / might have** more money.*

At the start of the result clause, you can use or omit the word *then*. Don't use *then* if the result clause comes first.

The result clause can come first in a sentence with no change in meaning.

In writing, when the *if* clause comes first, put a comma before the result clause.

A Use the simple present or future of the verbs in the box to complete the sentences.

be	~~get~~	make	not pass	not say	not study
educate	have	leave	miss	~~save~~	see

1. You _____*'ll save*_____ money if you _____*get*_____ a roommate.

2. If I _____ all weekend, I _____ the test on Monday.

3. I _____ hello if I _____ him on the street.

4. If you _____ early, you _____ all the fun.

5. It _____ better for the Earth if couples _____ smaller families.

6. If we _____ people, they _____ better decisions.

B Find and correct the mistake in each sentence.

1. If more people will carpool, there will be less traffic on the roads.

2. The school is going to cancel the picnic if it raining tomorrow.

3. If the team won't win tomorrow's game, then they'll be out of the World Cup.

4. You'll make more money in the future if you will go to college.

5. If we destroy the forests, then many animals die.

6. I might visit Italy this summer if I will have enough money.

C For each sentence in **B**, think of one more result and write a conditional sentence. The conditional should be one that follows the sentence in **B**.

1. If there is less traffic on the roads, people will be happier. _____

2. If the school cancels the picnic, _____

3. _____

4. _____

5. _____

6. _____

UNIT **10** MONEY

LESSON A

Wish Statements	
Currently I live in the suburbs. I **wish** I <u>lived</u> in the city.	Use the past tense with *wish* to talk about situations that are not true now.
I **wish** (that) I <u>could</u> lend you some money.	Use *could* + base form of the verb with *wish*. *That* is optional in these sentences.
I **wish** (that) I <u>were</u> richer.	Use *were* for all forms of *be* (not *was*).
I can't stick to a budget. I **wish** I could. I don't live in the city. I **wish** I did.	We often shorten *wish* statements in this way.

A Read this joke about Dumb Dave. Complete the sentences with *wish... could* and the verb in parentheses. Why is the character called Dumb Dave?

One day, a genie appeared to Dumb Dave and his three friends. The genie said, "I will give each of you one wish. Don't waste it!"

The first friend said, "(1. fly) _____." Her wish was granted, and she flew away. The second friend said, "(2. live) _____ in a big mansion." He suddenly disappeared, too. The third friend said, "(3. be) _____ a famous actor starring in my own movie." She, too, disappeared.

Dumb Dave looked around and saw that he was alone. Then he said, "I'm lonely. Where have my three friends gone? (4. have) _____ them back here with me now..."

B Imagine that a genie has given you three wishes. What will you wish for? Write three *wish* statements.

1. _____

2. _____

3. _____

LESSON B

	Negative Modals	Meaning
Impossibility	You **can't** have the winning lottery ticket. I have it!	Use *can't* to say that something is <u>impossible</u>. It shows surprise or disbelief.
Ability	Sorry, but I **can't** lend you any money. I'm broke.	You can also use *can't* to say you <u>don't have the ability</u> to do something.
Necessity	You **don't have to / don't need to** be rich to travel.	*Don't have to* and *don't need to* mean something <u>isn't necessary</u>. You have a choice.
Advice	You **shouldn't** waste money on expensive cars.	Use *shouldn't* to give advice. It means <u>it's not a good idea</u> to do something.
Strong advice	You**'d better not** lose this ring. It's very valuable.	*Had better not* gives strong advice. It means "I'm <u>warning</u> you not to do something. If you do, there will be a problem."

A Choose the best modal for each sentence.

1. A: Is that John over there driving a Porsche?

   B: It shouldn't / can't be. He doesn't have a driver's license.

2. You'd better not / don't have to lend money to Jack. He won't pay you back.

3. We can't / don't have to study for the test. The teacher canceled it.

4. You shouldn't / can't play the lottery. It's a waste of money.

5. If you've finished your exam, you'd better not / don't need to stay. You can leave.

6. Maria and Kim can't / shouldn't go to the concert. It costs $20, and they only have $10.

B Use the negative form of the modal and the word(s) given to answer speaker A.

1. A: I'm going to spend all my money on a new car.

   B: (had better / squander) _____. Save some!

2. A: My friend Mary wants to borrow some money.

   B: (should / lend) _____. She never pays it back.

3. A: Jane really wants the job, but she doesn't speak Japanese.

   B: (need to / speak) _____ Japanese to get the job.

4. A: We're late for our business class.

   B: (can / be) _____. Class doesn't start until 9:30.

UNIT 11 HONESTY

LESSON A

Present Unreal Conditionals	
If clause	**Result clause**
If you **told** the truth,	(then) you **would feel** relieved.
If I **didn't have** a lot of homework,	(then) **I'd go** to the movies.
If I **found** a wallet,	(then) **I'd return** it.
If I **were** a liar,	(then) I **wouldn't have** any friends.
Result clause	**If clause**
You'**d feel relieved**	if you **told** the truth.

Present unreal conditionals are used to talk about imagined or unreal events.

The *if* clause presents an imagined condition. It is not true right now.

The verb in the *if* clause is in the simple past.

With the verb *be*, use *were* for all subjects: *If I were rich, I'd buy a big house.*

In writing, when the *if* clause comes first, put a comma before the result clause.

The result clause presents an imagined result. It can come first or second in the sentence.

The verb in the result clause takes *would* + the base form of the verb.

You can also use *might (not)* (probability) or *could (not)* (ability) in the result clause:

> *If you told them the truth, you might not get into trouble.*

> *If I did something against the law, I could go to jail.*

A Match each situation in **A** to a conditional sentence in **B** and **C**. Use the correct form of the verbs in parentheses.

A	B	C
1. My bicycle is really old.	If I (be) sick,	I (improve / could) them.
2. It's faster to go by subway.	If I ever (lose) it,	I (be / might) late.
3. I feel fine right now.	If I (have) a new one,	I (take / would) some medicine.
4. I love my cell phone.	If I (study) harder,	I (ride / would) it everywhere.
5. My grades aren't very good.	If I (go) by car,	I (buy / would) a new one right away.

1. <u>My bicycle is really old. If I had a new one, I'd ride it everywhere.</u>

2. _____

3. _____

4. _____

5. _____

B Read the sentences. Circle the answers that are true for you.

1. I'm / I'm not rich.

2. I'm / I'm not a teacher.

3. I have / don't have to study English.

4. I speak / don't speak English fluently.

5. I live / don't live with my parents.

6. I take / don't take a bus to school.

7. I have / don't have a lot of free time.

C Now rewrite the sentences in **B** as present unreal conditionals.

1. If I were rich, _____
2. _____
3. _____
4. _____
5. _____
6. _____
7. _____

LESSON B

Reported Statements with *say* and *tell*		
Quoted speech	**Reported speech**	
"I **am** an honest person."		he **was** an honest person.
"I **trust** you."		he **trusted** me.
"I **don't believe** you."		he **didn't believe** me.
"I**'m leaving**."		he **was leaving**.
"You **lied** to me."	He **said** (that)	I **had lied** to him.
"I**'ll call** you tomorrow."	He **told me** (that)	he **would call** me tomorrow.
"We**'ve** never **met**."		we **had** never **met**.
"I **may be** late."		he **might be** late.
"You **must work** harder."		I **had to work** harder.
"You **shouldn't talk** to strangers."		I **shouldn't talk** to strangers.

Quoted speech uses a person's exact words: *"I trust you," said Phil.*

You can report what another person has said using *say* or *tell.*

In reported speech:

The verb tense typically shifts to a past form. Note: *should* usually does not change.

Pronouns change: *"I trust you."* → *Phil said (that) he trusted me.*

The word *that* is optional in the reported sentence.

A Find and correct the error in each sentence.

1. Linda said she will call today, but she didn't keep her word.
2. Denis told to me that he was rich, but that was a lie.
3. Aya says that she had a degree in computer science.
4. Last night, Tim told me he can meet today.
5. Leo said me he spoke French, but he doesn't.

B Gina read Harold's profile on a dating site. She contacted him, and they went on a date. Look at the "real" Harold. Complete what Gina said about him using *say* or *tell.*

(continued)

YOUNG AND HANDSOME GUY LOOKING FOR BEAUTIFUL GIRL	
My interests:	I work out at the gym every day.
My lifestyle:	I don't smoke. I only eat healthy foods. I'm very clean. I drive a sports car.
My talents:	I can speak five languages fluently, and I've traveled all over the world.
	Let's have dinner and get to know each other; I'll pay for the meal!

1. (say) _He said he was young and handsome_, but he's actually middle-aged and unattractive.

2. (tell) _____, but in fact he rides a bicycle.

3. (say) _____, but actually his house was very messy.

4. (tell) _____, but the truth is he eats a lot of junk food.

5. (say) _____, but actually, he doesn't even have a passport.

6. (tell) _____, but in reality he smokes a lot.

7. (say) _____, but in fact he only speaks English.

8. (tell) _____, but I had to pay for dinner!

UNIT **12**   **OUR WORLD**

LESSON A

Embedded Questions	
To *embed* means to put (something) inside something else. Embedded questions are questions that are included within another question or statement.	
What is a tapir?	Do you know **what a tapir is**? I'd like to know **what a tapir is**.
Although we call them embedded <u>questions</u>, they take <u>statement</u> word order.	
How many snow leopards are there? Where do mountain gorillas live? What is the answer?	I wonder **how many snow leopards there are**. Do you remember **where mountain gorillas live**? I'm not sure **what the answer is**.
These phrases are used to start embedded questions:	
Asking for information	**Saying you don't know something**
Can / Could you tell me… Do you know… Do you remember… Do you have any idea…	I don't know / I'd like to know… I'm not sure… I can't remember… I wonder…
An embedded question can sound softer and less direct than a regular question.	
Excuse me, what time is it?	Excuse me, do you know **what time it is**?

A Unscramble the embedded questions.

1. what / wonder / time / I / opens / it

_____

2. are / zoo / animals / in / I / what / don't / the / know

_____

3. I / remember / there / get / how / to / can't / exactly

_____

4. any / animals / zoo / are / what / the / have / in / you / idea / do

_____

5. time / it / sure / I'm / opens / what / not

_____

6. to / do / zoo / you / get / know / to / the / how

_____

B Now use the sentences in **A** to complete the conversation.

A: Excuse me, _____?

B: _____, but I think you take the #2 train.

A: _____.

B: _____, but it's probably open by now.

A: _____?

B: I'm sorry, but _____.

LESSON B

The Passive with Various Tenses		
	Active	**Passive**
Simple present	Engineers <u>build</u> skyscrapers with a steel frame structure.	Most skyscrapers **are built** with a steel frame structure.
Simple past	The Woolworth Company <u>built</u> a skyscraper in 1913.	One of the first skyscrapers **was built** in 1913.
Present perfect	Engineers <u>have built</u> the world's tallest building in Dubai.	The world's tallest building **has been built** in Dubai.
Present continuous	Engineers <u>are building</u> a lot of tall buildings in Shanghai.	A lot of tall buildings **are being built** in Shanghai.
Simple future	Someday they <u>will build</u> a skyscraper without concrete.	Someday a skyscraper without concrete **will be built**.

A Here are some facts about three important structures. Complete the sentences with the verb and tense in parentheses. Use the passive form of the tense provided.

Itaipu Dam

1. The dam (complete / simple past) _____ in 1991.

2. It (visit / present perfect) _____ by more than nine million people.

Akashi Kaikyo Bridge

3. The record for the longest suspension bridge (hold / simple present) _____ by the Akashi Kaikyo Bridge.

4. The bridge (design / simple past) _____ to be 12,825 feet, but it (make / simple past) _____ even longer after a big earthquake.

Chunnel

5. The first passengers on a Chunnel train were surprised when they (transport / simple past) _____ to the other side in only 20 minutes.

6. In the future, experts predict that even more passengers (carry / simple future) _____ through the Chunnel.

7. While repairs (do / present continuous) _____ to the tunnels, they remain open.

B Think of a famous building, structure, or monument in your city. Answer the questions about it using the passive.

1. Where is it located?

_____

2. When was it built?

_____

3. How many people have visited it?

_____

4. Are any repairs (fixes) being done to it now?

_____

5. What repairs will need to be done in the future?

_____

Answers

Communication page 175, A

1. Singapore **2.** Greenland **3.** Angel Falls **4.** Etna **5.** the Andes **6.** Mammoth Cave **7.** Lake Baikal **8.** the Sahara **9.** Canada

Listening Strategies

Build background knowledge: p. 66a

Check predictions: pp. 39a, 66a, 98a

Identify a response: p. 66a

Identify a speaker: p. 80a

Identify (key) details: pp. 163a, 131a

Infer information: pp. 34a, 39a, 98a, 103a, 112a, 131a

Infer meaning: p. 163a

Listen for a speaker's opinion: p. 39a

Listen for context: p. 126a

Listen for details: pp. 6a, 20a, 25a, 34a, 39a, 52a, 80a, 98a, 103a, 112a, 117a, 131a, 144a, 149a, 158a, 163a, 172a, 177a

Listen for feeling: p. 103a

Listen for gist: pp. 20a, 25a, 66a, 71a, 85a, 117a, 126a, 163a, 177a

Listen for gist and details: pp. 112a, 117a

Listen for numbers: p. 172a

Listen for paraphrase: p. 66a

Listen for (the) main idea(s): pp. 80a, 126a, 117a, 158a, 172a

Listen for reasons: p. 131a

Listen for specific information: pp. 52a, 85a

Make and check predictions: p. 6a

Make predictions: pp. 39a, 66a, 98a, 149a

Summarize: p. 144

Take notes / Note taking: pp. 52a, 71a, 85a, 144a

Use background knowledge: pp. 52a, 126a, 144a, 149a, 158a, 172a

Reading Strategies

Check predictions: pp. 12a, 104a

Compare and evaluate: p. 150a

Draw conclusions: pp. 86a, 132a

Give opinions: p. 178a

Guess meaning from context: p. 178a

Identify a point of view: p. 86a

Infer information: p. 132a,

Infer meaning: pp. 12a, 26a, 58a, 104a, 132a, 150a, 164a, 178a

Make connections: pp. 40a, 164a

Make predictions: pp. 12a, 26a, 104a, 132a, 150a, 178a

Read for details: pp. 12a, 58a, 104a, 118a, 132a, 150a

Scan for details: pp. 26a, 86a, 104a, 118a, 132a, 178a

Scan for information: pp. 12a, 26a, 104a, 118a

Sentence insertion: p. 58a

Sequence events: pp. 40a, 164a

Summarize: pp. 40a, 178a

Synthesize information: p. 12a

Take notes on key details: p. 178a

Understand purpose: p. 72a

Understand the main idea: p. 12a

Use background knowledge: pp. 40a, 58a, 72a, 118a, 132a, 178a

Teaching Tips

Unit 1: Working with a partner—p. 5a; Using a dictionary—p. 5a; Intonation patterns—p. 6a; Using role play effectively—p. 8a; Starting and ending pair, group, and class activities—p. 9a; Supporting answers—p. 13a; Encouraging fluency and participation—p. 15a

Unit 2: Using English videos—p. 18a; Using Venn diagrams—p. 19a; Keeping students on task—p. 19a; TOEFL—p. 20a; Inference—p. 21a; Speaking exercises—p. 24a; Organizing group work—p. 26a

Unit 3: Cultural context clues—p. 32a; Dictionary use—p. 33a; Starting and ending group work—p. 37a; Learning new words—p. 38a

Review Units 1-3: Error quiz—p. 44a; Active listening—p. 45a; Active listening—p. 47a; Guest speakers—p. 47a; Pair work—p. 47a

Unit 4: Using English videos—p. 50a; Dictionary use—p. 51a; Reflection—p. 53a

Unit 5: Using English videos—p. 64a; Word stress—p. 65a, Modifying difficulty of listening activities—p. 66a

Unit 6: Using English videos—p. 78a; Learner's dictionary—p. 79a; Learning word forms—p. 79a; Presentation skills—p. 81a; Word choice in writing—p. 89a; Peer editing—p. 89a

Review Units 4-6: Working with dialogs—p. 90a; Standardized tests—p. 92a; Helping groups finish at the same time—p. 93a

Unit 7: Using English videos—p. 96a; Language functions—p. 99a; Error quiz—p. 101a; Word associations—p. 102a; Tone of a reading—p. 105a; Performance targets for speakers in class—p. 107a

Unit 8: Using English videos—p. 110a; Listening for inference—p. 112a; Dictogloss—p. 115a; Jigsaw reading groups—p. 116a; Scanning—p. 119a; Schema building—p. 119a; Students explaining grammar—p. 120a

Unit 9: Using English videos—p. 124a; Ensuring that students listen to presenters—p. 127a; Monitoring pair work—p. 129a; Memorizing vs. speaking—p. 129a; Listening tests—p. 131a; *I learned* statements—p. 133a

Review Units 7-9: Encouraging use of English—p. 136a; Brainstorming—p. 138a

Unit 10: Using English videos—p. 142a; Soda—p. 145a; Unfamiliar vocabulary in reading texts—p. 150a; Extensive reading—p. 151a;

Unit 11: Using English videos—p. 156a; Looking up expressions—p. 157a; Form vs. meaning of grammar—p. 160a; Reconstruct the passage—p. 164a; Paraphrasing instructions—p. 165a; Extensive reading—p. 165a

Unit 12: Using English videos—p. 170a; Writing on the board—171a; Word wheel—p. 173a; End-of-class review—p. 175a; Explaining new vocabulary—p. 176a; Self-evaluation—p. 181a

Review Units 10-12: Fluency vs. accuracy—p. 182a; Graphic organizers—p. 182a; Remembering grammar rules—p. 184a; Writing answers on the board—p. 184a; Mixed up sentences—p. 185a

Unit 1, Lesson A
Page 6, Pronunciation (CD 1, Track 2)

Notice how the final item in the series has a falling intonation.

1. The three primary colors on the color wheel are red, yellow, and blue.

   The three primary colors on the color wheel are red, yellow, and blue.

2. White, black, and gray are neutral colors.

   White, black, and gray are neutral colors.

3. Our living room has a sofa, table, and two chairs.

   Our living room has a sofa, table, and two chairs.

4. You can enlarge a space by using mirrors, light colors, and small furniture.

   You can enlarge a space by using mirrors, light colors, andsmall furniture.

Page 6, Listening (CD 1, Track 3)

When you walk into a room, what's the first thing you notice? Hmm... most people say that it's the colors in the room—you know, the bright blue walls, the red and white rug, the colorful flowers on the table.... Well, in this lecture, I'm going to talk about color. I'll introduce you to the *color wheel* and show you how to use it.

I think you'll see that the color wheel is a helpful tool. It helps us to understand the use of color in art and design and basically, the color wheel shows us how to combine colors in an attractive way.

You probably know this—but, many people use the color wheel. Painters use it in their art. Decorators need a color wheel when they are doing home improvement work. Um, even web page designers use it to create visually appealing websites.

Let's look at the color wheel for a second. Maybe the first thing you notice is... there are three primary colors on this color wheel: red, yellow, and blue. Do you see them?—Here... here... and here. When the primary colors are mixed together, they create the other colors on the color wheel. For example, you can mix this yellow over here... with this red... and create orange.

You can also see that there are warm and cool colors on the color wheel. Warm colors like yellow and red have a lot of energy, so, in a painting, uh, they come forward, toward the viewer. Cool colors, on the other hand, are quiet and calm. They seem to move away from the viewer. Some examples of cool colors are blue and purple.

Page 6, Listening (CD 1, Track 4)

OK, now let's talk about how to combine colors. One way is to use opposite colors together, so... uh... when we say "opposite colors," we mean those colors that are directly across from each other on the color wheel. For example, red and green are opposite each other on the color wheel.... All "opposite colors" work well together, but can sometimes be a little overwhelming if they're used too much in a room, so you should use another color as well.

Page 7, Speaking (CD 1, Track 5)

Emilia:	Thanks for your help, Felipe.
Felipe:	No problem. How do you like your new apartment?
Emilia:	It's great. I love it. There's just one thing...
Felipe:	Yeah?
Emilia:	I found a small crack in the wall.
Felipe:	The wall is cracked? Really?
Emilia:	Yeah. It's not too big, but it's in the living room and everyone can see it.
Felipe:	Why don't you fix it yourself?
Emilia:	Um... I don't think so. I'm not good at repairing things.
Felipe:	I know! Try calling my friend, Sam. He can help you. He's a nice guy and he's very capable.
Emilia:	That sounds like a great idea. Do you have his phone number?
Felipe:	Sure. Hold on a second while I get it...

Unit 1, Lesson B
Page 11, Listening (CD 1, Track 6)

Conversation 1

Boy:	Go on, you talk to her.
Donny:	No, you! I'm too shy to do it. Why don't you?
Boy:	No way. I like her too much. Come on, please!
Donny:	OK. What do I say?
Boy:	I don't know. She *is* really cute.... Ask her if she has a boyfriend.
Donny:	All right.
Donny:	Excuse me. Hi.
Girl:	Hi.
Donny:	I'm Donny, um, from math class.
Girl:	Uh, yeah, I know.
Donny:	My friend and I are wondering... do you have a boyfriend?

Conversation 2

Mother: What are you reading, Paula?

Paula: The latest issue of *Take a Look* magazine.

Mother: Yeah? Shouldn't you be studying?

Paula: I will in ten minutes. You should look at some of the photos!

Mother: OK, let me see.

Paula: Those are pictures of Carla Smith, the actress. You know her, right?

Mother: Of course, I do—she's really famous... I may be your mom, but I'm not *that* old. Wow, how did they get these pictures of Carla Smith in her home?

Paula: Well, you know the paparazzi. They follow her everywhere—and even disturb her at home.

Conversation 3

Man: Welcome to our show.

Woman: Thanks for having me here again.

Man: It's so great to see you. The last time you were here was... I don't know... six months ago.

Woman: That's about right, I think. It was right before my last song was released.

Man: Yes, and that song was a huge hit. It's doing really well! They're playing the music video everywhere.

Woman: I know. It's kind of overwhelming, really. I'm really happy about it.

Man: There have been a lot of changes in your life this year, especially with your family...

Unit 2, Lesson A
Page 20, Pronunciation (CD 1, Track 8)

In English, words that refer to a person, object, action, or characteristic are called *content words*. These words give some kind of information. They are usually nouns, verbs, adjectives, and adverbs. Listen and repeat the following sentences. Notice how the underlined words are stressed.

1. My name is Deena Ravitch, and I'm the CEO of Symtax Corporation.

2. I'm happy to be here.

3. Today is also a time to look to the future.

Page 20, Listening (CD 1, Track 9)

Good afternoon. My name is Deena Ravitch and I'm the CEO of Symtax Corporation. I'm happy to be here. I want to thank Dean Kelley and the faculty for inviting me to speak today.

Today is a very, very special day. We are here to celebrate—to celebrate all of you... and your accomplishments. All of you are making a big step. For four years this campus has been your home. And now you are leaving it. In a sense, you are leaving your adolescence and moving into adulthood. You are joining the work world with all its responsibilities. In short, you are leaving your comfort zone.

Today is a time to look at the past—you studied hard for exams. You spent hours in the library... doing research to write those 20-page essays. You spent hours sitting in class, learning new ideas. You've done a lot of work and it wasn't always easy.

No matter what, though, you were always driven to succeed. And now you are here today. Congratulations.

Today is also a time to look to the future. There will be many challenges coming your way. When times are difficult, you can rely on everything you learned here about working hard, getting along with others... never giving up.

Whatever happens, always do your best—shoot for the moon. Even if you miss it, you will land among the stars.

Page 20, Listening (CD 1, Track 10)

1. For four years this campus has been your home. And now you are leaving it. In a sense, you are leaving your adolescence and moving into adulthood. You are joining the work world with all its responsibilities. In short, you are leaving your comfort zone.

2. Today is a time to look at the past—you studied hard for exams. You spent hours in the library... doing research to write those 20-page essays. You spent hours sitting in class, learning new ideas. You've done a lot of work and it wasn't always easy.... No matter what, though, you were always driven to succeed. And now you are here today.

3. Whatever happens, always do your best—shoot for the moon. Even if you miss it, you will land among the stars.

Page 21, Speaking (CD 1, Track 11)

Yuri: What are you studying for, Max?

Max: Oh, hi, Yuri... just my driving test.

Yuri: Your driving exam? Don't you have a driver's license already?

Max: I had one... but it expired, so I have to take the test again.

Yuri: That's a drag.

Max: Yeah, and I need to get my license soon.

Yuri: How come?

Max: I'm planning to visit my cousins in two weeks. I need to rent a car for the trip.

Yuri: Sounds like fun. Well, good luck with everything!

Unit 2, Lesson B
Page 25, Listening (CD 1, Track 12)

Lindsay:	Hey, Mark. Can you come here for a second?
Mark:	What do you want? Hey, what's that magazine?
Lindsay:	It's *Teen Life*. I want you to take this quiz. It's really fun.
Mark:	OK. Shoot.
Lindsay:	All right, this is how it works. You have to look at this list of life events and choose which one is the best...
Mark:	The best?
Lindsay:	I mean, you have to choose which one you most look forward to. Like, if you're really hoping to get a great job, you would choose "get a job" because you're excited about it happening.
Mark:	OK, so, I choose the one thing in life I'm most excited about. Got it. What kind of things are on the list?

Page 25, Listening (CD 1, Track 13)

Mark:	OK, so, I choose the one thing in life I'm most excited about. Got it. What kind of things are on the list?
Lindsay:	Let's see, there's, like, *get a job,* and *enroll in college* is another one. And there's *get married*...
Mark:	Yuck. I don't want to get married. Ever.
Lindsay:	You say that now! I'll ask you again in five years.
Mark:	Let's see, I think I'd choose *leave home.* Yep, that's my first choice.
Lindsay:	Yeah? Why?
Mark:	Freedom! You can do whatever you want when you leave home. You can stay out late with your friends, oh, and you don't have to clean your room.
Lindsay:	But you have to do your own laundry!
Mark:	Oh. I never thought of that. What's yours?
Lindsay:	Let's see, I can't decide between *get married* or *have a big family.* If I have to choose one, I guess it's *get married.* It seems so romantic. I want a really big wedding and everything.
Dad:	C'mon, kids. It's time for dinner.
Lindsay:	Hold on a minute, Dad. I want you to answer this question. Here, read this...
Dad:	Hmm... I have to choose just one?
Lindsay:	What about *get a promotion*?
Dad:	No, I wouldn't choose that one. But I would choose *retire.* I work too hard. I'm ready to take it easy!

Unit 3, Lesson A
Page 34, Listening (CD 1, Track 15)

Imagine this: You need to buy a new cell phone but don't have a lot of money to spend. Also, you don't have a lot of time—you need to get that phone today! In this situation, what would you do? If you're like most people, you would probably go to your computer and start searching the Web for answers. The Internet is fast, right? But actually, sometimes the Web doesn't have the exact information that you need. You spend a lot of time on your computer and you can't find an answer. And that's frustrating. I'm here to tell you that there's another way. It's an online service called InstaHelp. And it works like this: Your need an answer to a particular question—not a general one, but something specific. You send InstaHelp, an excellent new online service, an email or instant message. InstaHelp immediately sends your question on to your online friends and their acquaintances. What happens next? Within five minutes or so you will have at least one response to your question. Someone in cyberspace knows the answer... and they'll give you some good information. It's that easy! You'll get the best advice from your friends online, with InstaHelp's assistance, of course! So, if you want to directions to the hottest club or a suggestion for a new cell phone, don't worry! Just send your question to InstaHelp and then sit back and wait for the best answer!

Page 34, Pronunciation (CD 1, Track 16)

1. Who do you TALK to when you have a problem?
   Who do you TALK to when you have a problem?
2. What do you TALK about with your friends?
   What do you TALK about with your friends?
3. What is everyone GOSsiping about these days?
   What is everyone GOSsiping about these days?
4. Do you need to disCUSS anything with your teacher?
   Do you need to disCUSS anything with your teacher?
5. Who do you CHAT with the most on the phone?
   Who do you CHAT with the most on the phone?

Page 35, Speaking (CD 1, Track 17)

Ana:	Oh, look... there's Gloria Ruiz. Do you know her?
Jared:	No, I don't. Who is she?
Ana:	She's the VP of Marketing for Global Industries. She's standing right over there.
Jared:	Is she the tall woman in the sweater?
Ana:	No, Gloria is the woman with glasses. She's chatting with the man in the suit.

Jared:	You know, I *am* looking for a job.
Ana:	You should talk to her. Maybe she can help you.
Jared:	That's a good idea. Thanks!
Jared:	Excuse me, Ms. Ruiz? May I interrupt for a moment? My name is Jared Levy...

Unit 3, Lesson B
Page 39, Listening (CD 1, Track 18)

Rex:	And now, for our next story. Here's Liz Demming.
Liz:	Thanks, Rex. I have a question for you. What is the biggest news story you've paid attention to this week? Was it the big news about the job market? The president's meeting in Asia? Or was it the scandal about the soccer player?
Rex:	Hmm... Well I guess we've all been talking about that soccer player who got caught cheating.
Liz:	Right. In fact, polls show that the news about the soccer player has been the most popular.
Rex:	Well, it is an interesting story.
Liz:	True, but when the media spends most of its time covering tabloid stories, like the one about the soccer player, the public isn't getting information that's really important... like the news about the economy.

Page 39, Listening (CD 1, Track 19)

Rex:	And now, for our next story. Here's Liz Demming.
Liz:	Thanks, Rex. I have a question for you. What is the biggest news story you've paid attention to this week? Was it the big news about the job market? The president's meeting in Asia? Or was it the scandal about the soccer player?
Rex:	Hmm... Well I guess we've all been talking about that soccer player who got caught cheating.
Liz:	Right. In fact, polls show that the news about the soccer player has been the most popular.
Rex:	Well, it is an interesting story.
Liz:	True, but when the media spends most of its time covering tabloid stories, like the one about the soccer player, the public isn't getting information that's really important... like the news about the economy.
Rex:	Well, let's face it, a lot of news today focuses more on selling advertising than on educating the public.

Liz:	Good point.
Rex:	And if you want ratings... you know, for a news article or program to be popular, it has to be exciting.
Liz:	And what gets people to read or watch?
Rex:	Things like murder, and uh... sports, and, of course, celebrity gossip and entertainment news.
Liz:	Exactly. People know everything that happened to the soccer player, but very little about what's happening with the economy or the environment. These should be our lead stories, not the celebrity scandals.

Review Units 1–3
Page 46–47, Listening (CD 1, Track 21)

Amy:	John, I've never noticed this old photo of your family before.
John:	My mother just decided to hang it up, I guess.
Amy:	It's really nice. Look at how young you are! How old are you in the photo?
John:	Eight, no wait, I was nine.
Amy:	I guess those two older people standing behind you are your parents?
John:	Yep. They were still married then. They're divorced now.
Amy:	Oh, where are they now?
John:	My mom lives in Toronto. My dad is retired... in Florida.
Amy:	What are their names?
John:	My mother's name is Olivia. She was named after a famous actress. And my father is Joseph.
Amy:	I love the name Olivia. Say, who's that other guy?
John:	Which one?
Amy:	The guy with the mustache. Is he your brother?
John:	No, that's my uncle. Uncle Randy. He and his wife just had their first child.
Amy:	Nice.
John:	My brother is the young guy wearing the tie. His name is Tom. He's doing well. He just bought a house!
Amy:	That's great! Your little sister, Tina, is so cute!
John:	Yeah, she is. She was four or five years old there. Can you believe it? She's graduating from high school next month!

Unit 4, Lesson A

Page 52, (CD 1, Track 22)

Mark: Hi, I'm Mark Green, and we're here today talking with Maria Consuelos. Welcome, Maria.

Maria: Hi, Mark. It's nice to be here.

Mark: I was looking at your Facebook page earlier, Maria, and I noticed something… you have quite a few selfies on your feed. And you look good.

Maria: Thank you.

Mark: Obviously, you are good at taking selfies. That's why we invited you here today to tell us "How to take the perfect selfie."

Page 52, Listening (CD 1, Track 23)

Mark: Hi, I'm Mark Green, and we're here today talking with Maria Consuelos. Welcome, Maria.

Maria: Hi, Mark. It's nice to be here.

Mark: I was looking at your Facebook page earlier, Maria, and I noticed something… you have quite a few selfies on your feed. And you look good.

Maria: Thank you.

Mark: Obviously, you are good at taking selfies. That's why we invited you here today to tell us "How to take the perfect selfie." And let me tell you, I am *not* good at selfies. What am I doing wrong? What's the secret to taking the perfect photo?

Maria: Well, Mark, there are several points to consider. And to make it easy, I divide them into two groups: *before* you take the photo and *while* you're taking the photo.

Mark: OK, sounds good.

Maria: You want to look good in the selfie, right? So you need to practice…practice striking different poses. You can do it in front of the mirror. See which one looks best. It sounds funny, but it really works.

Mark: Do I have to?

Maria: You want to find the best angle for your face and body. And beforehand, comb your hair if you can. Also, check your makeup to make sure everything is OK…. And I like to wear bright colors. That way I stand out in a selfie.

Mark: OK, got it.

Maria: Finally, if you have something new, show it off. Maybe you've just gotten a haircut or had your nails done. That's a good time to take a selfie.

Mark: Those are some great tips to prepare for your selfie. Now what can you do as the photo is being taken?

Maria: Consider your background. You're going to be the main person in the photo, but you still want a pretty scene behind you.

Mark: I think selfies taken in nature look really good.

Maria: Me too. And you can raise the camera a bit to take the photo. We always look better when the camera is pointing *down* at us. And finally, watch out for *photobombers.*

Mark: What's a photobomber?

Maria: That's a person who stands in the background of your photo and makes funny faces in order to ruin the picture.

Mark: Right… well, thank you Maria.

Maria: Oh, and there's one more important thing to remember!

Mark: What's that?

Maria: Grab a friend or two for your selfie. It's always more fun to take a picture with friends!

Mark: I will definitely remember that. Thanks for stopping by, Maria, to tell us all about selfies. It's been great.

Maria: Thanks again for having me.

Page 53, Speaking (CD 1, Track 24)

Chris: Guess what? I'm getting a tattoo… right here on my arm!

Tyler: Really? Are you sure?

Chris: Yeah. My best friend has one. It's really cool. Now I want one.

Tyler: But what do your parents think? Did they say anything?

Chris: They're not too happy. But I know it's going to look great!

Tyler: I see what you're saying, but...

Chris: And I found a really good tattoo artist.

Tyler: But what about the cost? Isn't it expensive?

Chris: No, it's not too bad—and I can pay half now and the rest later.

Tyler: Yeah, but what if you don't like it?

Chris: Don't worry. It's going to look great!

Unit 4, Lesson B
Page 57, Listening (CD 1, Track 25)

Karen: Hey, Alex, come here a second.

Alex: Yeah?

Karen: I need your help. I have a problem.

Alex: Sure, Karen. That's what friends are for. I'll try to help.

Karen: OK, listen, um, I think I—I like Gabe.

Alex: Gabe? Gabe Martin? You're kidding.

Karen: No, I'm serious. Yeah. You know Gabe, right?

Alex: Yeah, of course. Really well. We play on the soccer team together. He's a nice guy—he gets along with everyone. How do you know him?

Karen: We were in the same math class last semester.

Alex: Oh, OK.

Page 57, Listening (CD 1, Track 26)

Karen: Hey, Alex, come here a second.

Alex: Yeah?

Karen: I need your help. I have a problem.

Alex: Sure, Karen. That's what friends are for. I'll try to help.

Karen: OK, listen, um, I think I—I like Gabe.

Alex: Gabe? Gabe Martin? You're kidding.

Karen: No, I'm serious. Yeah. You know Gabe, right?

Alex: Yeah, of course. Really well. We play on the soccer team together. He's a nice guy—he gets along with everyone. How do you know him?

Karen: We were in the same math class last semester.

Alex: Oh, OK.

Karen: And last Friday, he asked me out—to see a movie.

Alex: Great! What are you going to see?

Karen: Um, we're not going...

Alex: You're not?! But you said you liked him.

Karen: I know. I know. I'm so stupid! I turned him down.

Alex: Why did you do that?

Karen: I don't know! I think I was nervous or something. Ugh! Anyway, I really want to go out with him! So I need your help.

Alex: What can I do?

Karen: The next time you have soccer practice, call me on my cell. I'll just show up and "run into" you guys "by accident."

Alex: But it won't be an accident! You're making a plan!

Karen: I know, silly. We're going to *pretend* that we just ran into each other. Then Gabe and I can talk again. Do you understand?

Alex: I guess so... we *do* have a soccer practice tomorrow. I guess I can call you then. Around 3:30?

Karen: That would be great. Thanks, Alex.

Page 60, Pronunciation (CD 1, Track 28)

In each phrasal verb below, the verb ends in a consonant sound. The second word starts with a vowel. In spoken English, these two sounds link together, and the two words sound like one word.

1. ask out
2. break up
3. cheat on
4. give up
5. get along
6. get over
7. run into
8. turn on
9. make up

Page 60, Pronunciation (CD 1, Track 29)

1. Alex cheated on Erin.
2. Turn on a light, please.
3. Don't worry. You'll get over it.
4. He asked her out.

Unit 5, Lesson A
Page 66, Listening (CD 1, Track 30)

Hello, everyone and welcome to the City Zoo. Before we get started, I want to go over some of the rules with you guys, OK? Uh, Johnny, um, sit down, please and Alice, would you please stop talking? Everyone listen up, OK? Please pay attention. So, welcome to the City Zoo. It's a very beautiful and exciting place. It's also a safe place for the many animals that live here. We want to keep it a safe place, so I'm going to tell you all some rules before we start our tour. The first and most important rule is to *not* climb over any fences or walls. Those barriers are there for your protection. OK?

Page 66, Listening (CD 1, Track 31)

The first and most important rule is to *not* climb over any fences or walls. Those barriers are there for your protection. OK?

You will see a path that is painted green. This is the main path in the zoo. There are also special red paths that lead to the exits. Always stay on the red and green paths throughout the zoo. Don't worry, you'll be able to see all the animals easily.

OK, guys, remember, we have to be kind to the animals. Please do not feed them. They have special diets and the staff is responsible for feeding them. Lunchtime for the animals is every day at noon and you can watch. It's a lot of fun!

It's important not to run or scream through the zoo. That is bad behavior and can be inconsiderate to other guests as well as the animals. Does everyone understand? OK? We don't want you to get injured!

You may see different birds walking around the zoo freely. Don't worry—they haven't escaped! They aren't kept in cages but please don't touch or chase them, all right?

Remember, you're not allowed to bring in any food or drink from outside the zoo. However, we do have a nice café on the grounds. You can have lunch here right at the zoo!

And finally, we want to keep the zoo clean, right? After you finish lunch, put everything in the green containers—don't use the regular trash cans. You may not know this, but all of the trash here is recyclable. So, let's do our part to help the Earth, OK?

All right, then, those are some of the rules—the things I *don't* want you to do. Now I'm going to tell you some of the things I *do* want you to do. First, *do* ask a lot of questions. A staff member or volunteer can help you. . .

Page 66, Listening (CD 1, Track 32)

When a word ends in a consonant sound and the next word begins in the same consonant sound, you can say these consonant sounds as one long sound. You don't need to say each sound twice. Listen and repeat.

don't touch

want to

steak came

left twenty

all loved

Tom might

Page 66, Pronunciation (CD 1, Track 33)

Tom, Sue, and I had dinner together. The waiter was polite and considerate. I had the most delicious soup. Tom's steak came out quickly and it was perfectly cooked. We all loved the place. We left twenty dollars for a tip. I would definitely eat there again. In fact, Tom might go there again tonight!

Page 67, Speaking (CD 1, Track 34)

Inez: Wow! Everything smells delicious, Ahmed. How long did it take you to cook all this?

Ahmed: A few hours. But don't worry—I like to cook for my friends. And I like to have dinner parties. Please, sit down.

Inez: Um, can I sit anywhere?

Ahmed: Sure. You're the first guest to arrive. Make yourself comfortable.

Inez: You know, I've never had Turkish food before,

Ahmed: Don't worry. I'll explain everything... Uh, here, try this.

Inez: Um, is it OK if I use my fingers?

Ahmed: Sure, go right ahead. So, what do you think?

Inez: Mmm. It's delicious.

Unit 5, Lesson B
Page 71, Listening (CD 1, Track 35)

Lecture 1

Well, uh, next I am going to show you an example, um, of what I've been talking about. I'm going to play a conversation. Uh, this is a conversation between Jane and Tom. They work together in the same office.

Jane: Oh, hi, Tom. How are you?

Tom: Pretty good.... How about you?

Jane: Good, thanks.... Can you believe this weather? It's so crazy!

Tom: I know. It's so cold for July.... It was really chilly this morning.

As you can see, Jane and Tom are talking informally—about something unimportant, like the weather. It's a popular topic. Other common topics are TV and movies and shared experiences. What is a *shared experience*? Well, it's an experience that both people have in common, for example...

Lecture 2

OK, we've been talking about how to, you know, "read" someone. Can you read or understand a person just by looking at him or her... and how he or she moves? Hmm, well, um, let's see.... Experts say—well, the answer is basically *yes.* For example, if I cross my arms, like this, it may mean *Don't come near me.* I'm using my body to give you a message. You may be surprised—research shows that when we communicate, only 7% of it consists of the words—most of our communication, 93%—can you believe it?—consists of the way our bodies move, not the words we say. This can be seen...

Lecture 3

OK, we've already talked about how to start a conversation and what to say. Now, uh, let's say you're already talking to the person. You want to make a good impression, right? The first thing to remember is to look at the other person—directly. That will show that you are interested in him or her—that, um, you are really listening. But don't overdo it! Don't stare at the person! When you look directly at the person's face for too long, he or she will feel uncomfortable. So, uh, a good idea is to look at the other person for a few seconds and then look to the right or the left for a couple of seconds. When you do this...

Unit 6, Lesson A
Page 80, Listening (CD 1, Track 37)

Lian: Hmm, that's interesting…

Arturo: Hey, Lian. What's interesting?

Lian: Hi Arturo… uh… what?

Arturo: I said, "What's interesting?" What are you reading?

Lian: Oh, it's just this article. It's about our daily online habits.

Arturo: You mean it's about how much time we spend online each day?

Lian: That's only part of it. Let me ask you something. What are your habits? What kind of Internet user are you?

Arturo: What do you mean?

Lian: Well, do you always go online for a specific purpose, like to check your email or to write a paper for school?

Arturo: Hmm… I'm not sure.

Lian: Or do you go online all the time, sometimes for a certain reason, but more often just to find out what's happening online.

Arturo: That sounds more like me.

Lian: Well, a lot of people are like you. In fact, the article says there are basically two kinds of people.

Arturo: What type am I?

Lian: You're the first type. You are online throughout the day, always checking email and social media. More often than not, you're going online for no particular reason. You just want to be connected. And the number of people like you is increasing.

Arturo: That certainly describes me.

Lian: You should try recording how many hours a day you spend online. It could be interesting.

Arturo: I don't think I want to know!... Anyway, what type of Internet user are you?

Lian: I'm in the second group. We only use the internet for certain things: like email for work or school, to purchase things we need, to get specific information, and so on. Once we finish our tasks, we go offline.

Arturo: Well, I don't necessarily like being online all day, but I feel like if I'm not, I'll miss something. Being up-to-date is important. And I like being the first one to hear breaking news as it happens.

Page 80, Pronunciation (CD 1, Track 38)

Sometimes the noun and verb forms of a word have the same spelling, but the stress patterns are different. Take *PRESent* and *preSENT*, for example. The first word, PRESent, is a noun. The second word, preSENT, is a verb. Read the two sentences. Then listen and repeat. Notice how the stress shifts.

1.

How many PRESents did you get for your birthday?

How many PRESents did you get for your birthday?

2.

He preSENTS his ideas to the board at 2:00.

He preSENTS his ideas to the board at 2:00.

Page 80, Pronunciation (CD 1, Track 39)

Practice saying these sentences. Then listen and repeat.

What's your email address?

I need to address this package.

You should check the record.

You should try recording your hours.

There has been an increase in numbers.

The number of users is increasing.

Page 81, Speaking (CD 1, Track 40)

Host: I'd like to welcome Beverly Smith, the CEO for Sound Smart Inc., to our show today.... Welcome, Beverly! So, my first question is, what *does* Sound Smart do exactly?

Beverly: Well, as you know, a lot of people are studying English. And many of them want to be able to study anywhere, so we produce audio books... Maybe you've seen one of our advertisements online?

Host: Yes, I have. What a great idea—how convenient! Can I get one of your audio books?

Beverly: Sure. After you make a purchase, you can download the book online. It's simple.

Host: What is the main focus of your company?

Beverly: Well, we really believe in our employees. The bottom line is that happy employees make a good product. So our company slogan is "People First!"

Host: How exactly do you do that—put people first?

Beverly: Well, for one thing, we have a lot of perks. Our company has its own gym in the building. Also, each of our 100 employees gets the day off on his or her birthday.

Host: Nice! Where can I get an application?

Unit 6, Lesson B
Page 85, Listening (CD 1, Track 41)

1. Are you tired of businesses that rely on a catchy song and slogan? Here at TravelHub, we don't focus on trying to be clever or funny. Our only goal is to make sure you go on the trip of a lifetime. Our people are dedicated to helping plan the most memorable vacations in the world for our customers. The biggest influence on the journey is the person we're working with. You won't find deceptive sales people at TravelHub, only friends that want you to have a trip you'll remember forever.

2. We all know the feeling: you have an amazing experience that you want to share with your friends, but the photos or videos just don't capture it. Well, we can help. Our innovative new software will help you take the events in your life: the happy, exciting, inspiring, and even weird or shocking ones, and make your friends feel like they were right there with you. Click the link to see a sample of our work and get in touch!

3. We all need to stop sometimes, rest up, and get refreshed. For a quick and delicious pick-me-up, after a game of tennis with friends, there's nothing like an icy-cold Diet CR! The sparkling, sweet flavor will leave you wanting more. Every day, more than 20 million consumers choose Diet CR as their drink of choice. Won't you join them and feel refreshed today?

Review Units 4–6
Page 92, Listening (CD 1, Track 42)

1. There's been a slight increase in our profits.
   A) That's terrible!
   B) What a big change!
   C) That's good news!

2. Although I'm doing OK, I think she's really tired.
   A) I don't feel the same way.
   B) She should probably rest.
   C) Why are you tired?

3. Is it OK if I wear my shoes inside?
   A) Sure, take them off.
   B) Basically, it's a rule.
   C) Actually, it's best to remove them.

4. I think I want to get a tattoo.
   A) I'm not sure that's a good idea.
   B) Who is going to get one now?
   C) Did it take a long time to finish?

5. Our company was bought by Google.
   A) Really? Google bought your company?
   B) Wow, your company bought Google?
   C) When does the new employee start?

6. Ouch. I think I chipped a nail.
   A) What color are they?
   B) Does it hurt?
   C) I gave it to her.

Unit 7, Lesson A
Page 98, Listening (CD 2, Track 2)

Man: So, Lea... I heard that you were sick. How are you feeling now?

Lea: Better, thanks.

Man: Whew, that's a relief.

Lea: Yeah, no kidding. I wasn't feeling well for a long time.

Man: If you don't mind me asking... what happened exactly?

Lea: Well, first my lower back started to feel uncomfortable. I also started to feel dizzy and weak.

Man: Oh, no.

Lea:	Yeah… the weird thing is that I noticed these symptoms while I was at work. The pain in my back spread to my neck and shoulders. Everything was hurting…
Man:	That's scary.
Lea:	It was. But I'm doing a lot better now.
Man:	I can tell. You *sound* healthy...
Lea:	Thanks. Anyway, I ended up going to see the doctor. He did a lot of tests and said I was completely fine! Which was weird because I felt so nauseous a lot of the time. My symptoms were so severe.
Man:	You must have been frustrated.
Lea:	I was. Then the doctor asked me a strange question: *How many hours in a day do you spend sitting down?*
Man:	And what was your answer?
Lea:	A lot! When I thought about it, I realized that I sat for an hour on my commute to work on the train. I worked nine hours a day, and I was sitting most of that time. Then I had a one-hour commute home—more sitting. By the time I got home, I felt so exhausted. I would just sit down in front of the TV for 3 or 4 hours… and watch until bedtime.
Man:	That's a lot of sitting!
Lea:	It sure is. And I learned that sitting too much can be bad for your health. It can give you low energy and lots of aches and pains in your muscles.
Man:	I had no idea. What did the doctor suggest that you do?
Lea:	It's simple. He told me to set an alarm for every 60 minutes. When the alarm goes off, I should stand up, stretch, and walk around the office for a couple of minutes.
Man:	So the important thing is to not sit for long periods of time without moving. That makes sense.
Lea:	You got it. Moving your body throughout the day is the most important thing. After I started doing that, most of my aches and pains started going away.
Man:	I'll have to remember that. Most importantly, though, I'm glad you're feeling better!

Page 98, Listening (CD 2, Track 3)

1.

Man:	(male): So, Lea… I heard that you were sick. How are you feeling now?
Lea:	Better, thanks.
Man:	Whew, that's a relief.
Lea:	Yeah, no kidding. I wasn't feeling well for a long time.

2.

Lea:	Thanks. Anyway, I ended up going to see the doctor. He did a lot of tests and said I was completely fine! Which was weird because I felt so nauseous a lot of the time. My symptoms were so severe.
Man:	You must have been frustrated.
Lea:	I was. Then the doctor asked me a strange question: *How many hours in a day do you spend sitting down?*

3.

Man:	What did the doctor suggest that you do?
Lea:	It's simple. He told me to set an alarm for every 60 minutes. When the alarm goes off, I should stand up, stretch, and walk around the office for a couple of minutes.
Man:	So the important thing is to not sit for long periods of time without moving. That makes sense.
Lea:	You got it. Moving your body throughout the day is the most important thing.

Page 99, Speaking (CD 2, Track 4)

Dr. Pena:	OK, Ming, we're finished. As far as I can tell, you're completely healthy!
Ming:	Great!
Dr. Pena:	But I do want to talk to you about one thing.
Ming:	Uh-oh. This doesn't sound good.
Dr. Pena:	No, it's nothing scary. It's just that winter is coming. You need to prepare. I always advise my patients to get a flu shot.
Ming:	Hmm... I could never do that. I'm afraid of needles!
Dr. Pena:	Don't worry, Ming. The shot doesn't hurt at all.
Ming:	Really? Well, maybe...
Dr. Pena:	It will protect you from the flu. You'll be able to swim all year without getting sick. In my opinion, I think you should do it.
Ming:	Well, OK. Maybe I'll give it a try.
Dr. Pena:	Good! I'll tell the nurse to come in and see you. Take care and good luck on the swim team this year!

Page 100, Pronunciation (CD 2, Track 5)

The schwa sound is the most used vowel sound in English, but it doesn't have its own letter. It is an unstressed sound and can be represented in writing by any of the vowel letters. It sounds like "uh." Listen and repeat.

1. I have a cold.
2. I was coughing all the time.
3. I think I have the flu.
4. And my stomach hurts.

Unit 7, Lesson B
Page 103, Listening (CD 2, Track 6)

Mom:	Hello?
Ben:	Uh, hi, Mom.
Mom:	Ben! It's so good to hear your voice! How are you?
Ben:	I'm OK.
Mom:	Yeah? Really? How's school?
Ben:	All right, I guess. It's just my classes. They're kinda hard.
Mom:	Yeah?
Ben:	Especially my math class. I can't stand it. It meets at 8 AM three days a week.
Mom:	That is early and I know you don't like mornings.
Ben:	Yeah, I'm not like you.
Mom:	It's true—I do get up early. Well, anyway, I know you'll do well in that class. Just don't give up. Have you made any new friends?
Ben:	I just got here, Mom... it takes time...
Mom:	I know, I know...
Ben:	But I have met a couple of nice guys, though. And I really like my roommate.
Mom:	Oh, that's good.
Ben:	His name is Sam. He's an international student and I think he's a little homesick.
Mom:	That's too bad. Maybe you can help him out, you know... show him around and everything.
Ben:	Definitely. So, what's going on at home? Anything exciting?
Mom:	No, everything's pretty much the same here. Your younger brother has been surprisingly well behaved. I haven't felt well today—I actually called in sick yesterday.
Ben:	How are you feeling now?
Mom:	Much better, thanks. But I have to go soon. Can I call you back later tonight?
Ben:	Yeah, anytime after eight would be fine.
Mom:	Oh, what are you doing this afternoon?
Ben:	The soccer team is having tryouts. My roommate and I are going to check it out.
Mom:	Well, let me know how it goes.
Ben:	I will. I don't know if I'll like it or not, but I figure, I might as well give it a try.

Unit 8, Lesson A
Page 112, Pronunciation (CD 2, Track 8)

1. BOARD game BOARD game
2. BASKETball BASKETball
3. COMPUTER game COMPUTER game

Page 112, Pronunciation (CD 2, Track 9)

1. Sergei is the national table tennis champion.
2. I want to stay active, so I got a gym membership.
3. How many comic books does he have?
4. I need to practice to get my driver's license in my spare time.
5. I've put the best photos in my photo album.
6. She's good at baseball.

Page 112, Listening (CD 2, Track 10)

Conversation 1

Lucia:	Hello?
Andy:	Hello. Could I speak to Lucia, please?
Lucia:	Speaking.
Andy:	Hi, Lucia. This is Andy Dow and I'm calling from Metro 24-hour Fitness.
Lucia:	Uh-oh.
Andy:	How are you today?
Lucia:	I'm OK, and I know I haven't been going to the gym lately. I've been so busy! I need to get back there...
Andy:	Well, actually, I'm calling because your gym membership is going to expire soon. In fact, it's going to finish... let me see... next Tuesday...
Lucia:	Oh, wow. That's really soon.
Andy:	So, I was wondering... well, if you wanted to renew your membership today, we could do it over the phone.

Lucia:	Well, I guess I should renew it—I mean, I need to stay active, right?
Andy:	Yeah, sure.
Lucia:	But I'm not sure...
Andy:	Well, if it helps—we do have a wide range of new exercise classes this fall. Honestly, there's something for everyone. And we're offering a discount this week for active members who renew.
Lucia:	Oh, really?
Andy:	It's $40 off—a savings of nearly 20 percent.
Lucia:	Sounds good. You know, I think I'll do it! Can I do it in person, though? Say... tomorrow afternoon?
Andy:	Sure. Just look for me—I work the front desk. I'm the only one who wears glasses.
Lucia:	OK, Andy. See you tomorrow... around 2!

Conversation 2

Deo:	Hey, Heidi, can I ask you something?
Heidi:	Sure, Deo, go ahead...
Deo:	Well, you know, my driver's license is coming up for renewal.
Heidi:	I didn't know that, but OK...
Deo:	Yeah, and I'm thinking of not renewing it.
Heidi:	Really? Why?
Deo:	Well, I've decided to sell my car.
Heidi:	You're kidding!
Deo:	No, I'm not. I mean, I hardly ever use it.
Heidi:	What about work? Don't you drive to work?
Deo:	Never. I always take the train, and on weekends, well, I go for casual drives in my spare time. Sunday drives—that kind of thing. But it's not like I *need* a car. I can do all my errands right here in the neighborhood. Everything's within walking distance.
Heidi:	Well, that's good. And if you did sell your car, you could save a lot of money.
Deo:	Exactly. I spend way too much money on parking. It's really killing me! So, if I get rid of the car, I won't need a license either, right?
Heidi:	Hmm, I hear what you're saying...
Deo:	So, you think it's a good idea? To sell my car, I mean...

Heidi:	Yeah, but... I still think you should renew your driver's license.
Deo:	Yeah? Why?
Heidi:	It's just good to have. In case of emergency. You never know when you're going to have to drive.
Deo:	Good idea! I hadn't thought of that. Mmm, I can't wait to get rid of this car once and for all!

Page 113, Speaking (CD 2, Track 11)

Rohan:	Cricket is a great game. I love it!
Ana:	I've never heard of it.
Rohan:	Oh, it's really popular, especially in England, India, and some other countries in Asia.
Ana:	Well, how do you play?
Rohan:	It's played with a bat and a ball. Oh, and you need gloves, too. You start by pitching the ball to the striker.
Ana:	It sounds like baseball to me.
Rohan:	They're similar. But in cricket, there are 11 players on a team. And you play on an oval field.
Ana:	How do you win?
Rohan:	The object of the game is to get more runs than the other team, and... hey, what time is it?
Ana:	Four o'clock. Why?
Rohan:	I have to go. I'm late for cricket practice!

Unit 8, Lesson B
Page 117, Listening (CD 2, Track 12)

Friend:	Hey, Kim. What are you looking at?
Kim:	This article about a guy preparing to go on a parkour trip. He's going to…
Friend:	Parkour?
Kim:	Yeah. It's this sport where people run, jump, and climb to get from one place to another, usually it's done in cities, but people do it all over the place.

Page 117, Listening (CD 2, Track 13)

Friend:	Hey, Kim. What are you looking at?
Kim:	This article about a guy preparing to go on a parkour trip. He's going to…
Friend:	Parkour?
Kim:	Yeah. It's this sport where people run, jump, and climb to get from one place to another, usually it's done in cities, but people do it all over the place.

Friend:	Oh, yeah. I think I've seen videos of that.
Kim:	So, there's this guy and he's preparing for a parkour trip across the country. He'll travel by car, but stop in a bunch of cities and even some parks. There are pictures of him in this one park climbing rocks and jumping over canyons.
Friend:	Sounds dangerous.
Kim:	Yeah, people have warned him about that, but he says he's careful and looks at the areas before he heads out on his runs. He also has his friend nearby. His friend films everything, but also has a first aid kit and a phone in case anything bad happens!
Friend:	So, why is he doing it? I mean… it doesn't seem like something a person just decides to do.
Kim:	This guy started doing parkour when he was a teenager in New York and said that he's always wanted to see the country and that combining his love of parkour with that is a dream come true. He also believes in showing kids ways to stay active, so he's giving tips on how to get started online with the videos.
Friend:	Cool. Hey, can you send me that link? I think I'll follow along.
Kim:	Sure!

Unit 9, Lesson A
Page 126, Listening (CD 2, Track 15)

Doris's speech

Good evening, everyone. Thank you so much for coming. It's great to see you all. You know, when we started ten months ago—well, never in my wildest dreams did I think we would get this far. It's really been unbelievable. You, the citizens of the city, helped me to launch my race for mayor on a cold day last January, and it's been a long and hard campaign. I gave it my best shot, I really did, but today just wasn't our day. I have already called Amelia Smith to congratulate her on winning the election. She's been a fine candidate and will be a fine mayor for our city.

Amelia's speech

Hello, everybody! We did it! I am so honored to be your new mayor. And it's all because of you—the staff and all of our enthusiastic volunteers, that made it possible. As you know Doris and I were running neck and neck in the votes until about two hours ago and then we pulled ahead and won! So, to the voters I say, "Thank you, thank you, thank you!" We saw a record turnout—nearly 95%—and that's a wonderful thing.

Page 126, Listening (CD 2, Track 16)

Amelia's speech

So, to the voters I say, "Thank you, thank you, thank you!" We saw a record turnout—nearly 95%—and that's a wonderful thing. But we can't rest now that we've won. To make progress, we have to keep moving forward.

First of all, we need to rebuild downtown. We can do this by bringing new companies to our city—by vowing not to raise taxes on corporations for the next five years. We need to make our city attractive so these companies will want to do business here.

We need to make our streets safer. I'm asking all citizens to get to know their neighbors—talk to each other and watch out for each other. Teach your children how to call the police in an emergency.

Finally, we have to come together and build more schools. We need to provide our students with good teachers and textbooks—preparing them so they can be successful in the international workforce.

All of our city's problems didn't happen overnight… it's going to take hard work to fix them… but together we can do it! Thank you very much.

Page 127, Speaking (CD 2, Track 17)

Today I'd like to talk to you about rush hour traffic. I'll begin by telling you about the problem. Then I'll list the three things I think are causing this problem.

So, let's start by talking about rush hour traffic in this city. We've all experienced it, and in recent years it's gotten worse. Ten years ago, it used to take about 45 minutes to drive across town. Now it takes two hours. One of the main causes of this problem is too many cars on the road. More cars means more traffic and, of course, more traffic accidents. Another cause of rush hour traffic is…

Page 127, Pronunciation (CD 2, Track 18)

What is one of the biggest problems facing our city today? It's rush hour traffic.

Today we're going to talk about this important problem. I'll begin by telling you about the problem. Then I'll list three things…

Unit 9, Lesson B
Page 131, Listening (CD 2, Track 19)

| Scott: | Hi, this is Scott Johnson. Urban or suburban? That's the question we're talking about today. Which do you prefer? Do you love the fast-paced, glamorous yet challenging urban lifestyle? Or do you prefer the quiet and predictable suburban life? In today's *Just Like You* segment, we're talking to three women about where they live now, where |

they *want* to live in the future, and which they prefer. We'll start with you, Bella. Which is it for you—urban or suburban?

Bella: Well, Scott, I do love my time in the city. I work there. But I prefer the suburbs, where my family and I live now.

Scott: Would you ever consider moving to the city?

Bella: Sometimes I think about it. After all, commuting is a big waste of time. If I lived in the city, I could spend more time with my husband and baby. But the suburbs are cheaper, and the air is *much* cleaner. You know, the pollution in the city is terrible. Also, my husband and I just bought a house outside the city, so I imagine I'll stay here for a long time.

Scott: What about you, Anne? City or suburb?

Anne: I grew up in the suburbs—lived there my entire life. But, last year, at the age of 75, I moved to the city! I made a big change!

Scott: Wow! I'll say. Why did you do it?

Anne: My husband died three years ago. I was lonely in the suburbs, and I have friends in the city. Plus, there are groups you can join for people with certain hobbies or interests. I met a lot of new people that way. It was time to try something new.

Scott: How do you like it?

Anne: I love it! I have no plans to move again, and I encourage other seniors to consider living in the city, too...

Scott: And finally, Mercedes, what about you? Urban or suburban?

Mercedes: I love the energy of the city, but unfortunately, I can't go there as much as I'd like.

Scott: Why not?

Mercedes: I don't have my driver's license yet, so I have to rely on my parents to go into the city. I still live with them, in the suburbs...

Scott: Oh, no!

Mercedes: Yeah. The suburbs are really boring; there's nothing to do. But next year, I'll move to the city when I go to college. I can't wait!

Page 131, Listening (CD 2, Track 20)

Scott: We'll start with you, Bella. Which is it for you—urban or suburban?

Bella: Well, Scott, I do love my time in the city. I work there. But I prefer the suburbs, where my family and I live now.

Scott: Would you ever consider moving to the city?

Bella: Sometimes I think about it. After all, commuting is a big waste of time. If I lived in the city, I could spend more time with my husband and baby. But the suburbs are cheaper, and the air is *much* cleaner. You know, the pollution in the city is terrible. Also, my husband and I just bought a house outside the city, so I imagine I'll stay here for a long time.

Scott: What about you, Anne? City or suburb?

Anne: I grew up in the suburbs—lived there my entire life. But, last year, at the age of 75, I moved to the city! I made a big change!

Scott: Wow! I'll say. Why did you do it?

Anne: My husband died three years ago. I was lonely in the suburbs, and I have friends in the city. Plus, there are groups you can join for people with certain hobbies or interests. I met a lot of new people that way. It was time to try something new.

Scott: How do you like it?

Anne: I love it! I have no plans to move again, and I encourage other seniors to consider living in the city, too...

Scott: And finally, Mercedes, what about you? Urban or suburban?

Mercedes: I love the energy of the city, but unfortunately, I can't go there as much as I'd like.

Scott: Why not?

Mercedes: I don't have my driver's license yet, so I have to rely on my parents to go into the city. I still live with them, in the suburbs...

Scott: Oh, no!

Mercedes: Yeah. The suburbs are really boring; there's nothing to do. But next year, I'll move to the city when I go to college. I can't wait!

Review Units 7–9
Page 139, Listening (CD 2, Track 22)

Your body is made up of mostly water. Did you know that? In fact, 75% of your body's weight is due to water. Now, when the amount of water leaving your body is greater than the amount of water coming in, dehydration occurs. Let me spell that for you—dehydration: d-e-h-y-d-r-a-t-i-o-n.

When you say "I'm dehydrated" it means "I'm thirsty." Your body needs more water because it doesn't have enough.

One way we can become easily dehydrated is by sweating. When you exercise a lot or are active on a hot, sunny day, your body sweats to cool down. You can also lose water just by breathing, too!

There are many symptoms of dehydration. They include experiencing a dry mouth and, for some people, getting dizzy.

It's important to drink plenty of water even when you don't feel thirsty. If we don't do this and we become severely dehydrated, we may have to go to the hospital. Serious complications can occur, such as...

Unit 10, Lesson A
Page 144, Listening (CD 2, Track 23)

Let me ask you a question: Can money buy happiness? That is, if you have *more* money, will you be happier? What do you think?

Page 144, Listening (CD 2, Track 24)

Let me ask you a question: Can money buy happiness? Let's try to answer that question by looking at the following situation. Let me tell you about the Smith family.

Mr. and Mrs. Smith have four children. And money is tight for them. You could say they are barely getting by. Mr. and Mrs. Smith worry a lot about money. They worry about paying their bills and having enough to buy food for their family. They don't want to go into debt.

If you suddenly gave the Smith family some money, would they be a lot happier? I think the answer is *yes*. Why?

Well... to be happy, you need to have your basic needs met. When I say basic needs, I mean the things you need to survive. So, to be happy... you need to have a safe place to live, enough food to eat, and a way to make money. When you can't afford these things, it's difficult to be happy because you are always worrying.

Let's get back to the Smith family. The parents were worried before, but now they feel better because they have more money. They can pay their bills and take care of their children. Their basic needs have been met. The money has made them a lot happier because they have less stress.

Page 145, Speaking (CD 2, Track 25)

Eva: Thanks for picking up lunch, Mike.

Mike: Sure.

Eva: How much do I owe you?

Mike: Your total comes to $10.20. You can just give me ten dollars.

Eva: OK. Oh, wait.... Sorry, I've only got a twenty-dollar bill. I wish I had something smaller...

Mike: Don't worry about it. Why don't we eat first and then you can pay me later?

Eva: Oh, OK. Thanks.

Mike: No problem.... OK, here you go—a hamburger and fries for me... and a turkey sandwich for you.

Eva: Um, where's my soda?

Mike: Oh, no! I forgot your soda. Sorry... my mistake.

Eva: No problem. It happens. I'll just have water instead.

Unit 10, Lesson B
Page 149, Listening (CD 2, Track 26)

Woman: Two researchers studied wealthy people, and they wrote about their findings in a book called *The Millionaire Next Door*. Tell us, what did they learn from the study?

Man: Well, the book talks about many different things, but let's start with their image—that is, how others imagine a millionaire to be.

Woman: OK.

Man: For example, when you think of a millionaire, what do you picture?

Woman: I don't know... uh, a person with expensive clothes, an expensive car, and a big house?

Man: Exactly. That's what most people think. But, *actually*, many millionaires live fairly simple lives. Most don't squander their money on expensive clothes or cars. Instead, many of them wear regular clothes and drive affordable cars, just like you and me.

Woman: Hmm. That's surprising. So, what *do* they do with their money?

Man: A lot of them invest their earnings in things like property. They might buy a home or two, for example. These things increase in value over time.

Woman: What else do they do?

Man: A lot of them also make an annual budget, and they don't spend more money than they make.

Woman: That's important.

Man: It is. That's how they *keep* their money. Most also set aside some of their earnings every year for the future.

Woman: What about donating money? Do many millionaires do it?

Man: A lot of people think they don't, but *in fact*, many of them do. One recent study showed that over ninety percent give some of their money to charity in their lives

Page 152, Pronunciation (CD 2, Track 28)

Listen and repeat. Pay attention to the final /t/ and /d/ sounds.

can't
You can't have the winning ticket.

don't
You don't have to be rich.

shouldn't

You shouldn't waste money.

You'd better not

You'd better not lose this ring.

Unit 11, Lesson A

Page 158, Listening (CD 2, Track 29)

Denise: Hi, Roger.

Roger: Oh, hi, Denise. How's it going?

Denise: Good, good. Hey, I was wondering—where's Cindy today?

Roger: Oh, you didn't hear the news?

Denise: No. I just walked by her cubicle. She's not there. And her desk looks empty.

Roger: Yeah. Well, she's not working here anymore.

Denise: What do you mean? She was fired?

Roger: Yep. It happened on Friday morning.

Denise: You're kidding! I was on vacation last week. I had no idea. What happened?

Roger: Well, to be honest, I don't know the details, but it had something to do with her résumé.

Denise: Her résumé?

Roger: Uh-huh. She lied about her experience. I guess they did some checking and found out that some of her work experience wasn't true.

Denise: Oh, that's not good. I mean, I can understand telling a half truth to avoid hurting someone's feelings. But on a résumé? It's really important to be honest about everything.

Roger: I agree. I don't think her boss was very happy that she had lied to him.

Denise: I can understand that. It's too bad but in all honesty, I'm worried. I don't know what we're going to do. We really needed Cindy. We're already short staffed.

Roger: I wouldn't worry too much. I think they're going to be interviewing this week to find someone new. We just have to be patient.

Page 158, Listening (CD 2, Track 30)

Denise: You're kidding! I was on vacation last week. I had no idea. What happened?

Roger: Well, to be honest, I don't know the details, but it had something to do with her résumé.

Denise: Her résumé?

Roger: Uh-huh. She lied about her experience. I guess they did some checking and found out that some of her work experience wasn't true.

Denise: Oh, that's not good. I mean, I can understand telling a half truth to avoid hurting someone's feelings. But on a résumé? It's really important to be honest about everything.

Roger: I agree. I don't think her boss was very happy that she had lied to him.

Denise: I can understand that. It's too bad but in all honesty, I'm worried. I don't know what we're going to do. We really needed Cindy. We're already short staffed.

Denise: I wouldn't worry too much. I think they're going to be interviewing this week to find someone new. We just have to be patient.

Page 158, Pronunciation (CD 2, Track 31)

Conversation 1

　A: Cindy was fired.

　B: She was fired? Why?

　A: Because she lied on her résumé.

　B: I can't believe it!

Conversation 2

　A: Cindy got into trouble.

　B: She got into trouble? How?

　A: She dented her parents' car.

　B: You're kidding!

Page 159, Speaking (CD 2, Track 32)

Mr. Ward: So, how's the chicken?

Mrs. Ward: Delicious. How about your steak?

Mr. Ward: It's all right...

Mrs. Ward: Are you being honest? You don't sound very happy with it.

Mr. Ward: Well, it's not cooked right. I asked for medium rare. This is well done.

Mrs. Ward: Why don't you send it back?

Mr. Ward: Oh, I don't want to bother anyone. I can eat it, I guess.

Mrs. Ward: But it's expensive. I don't think you should eat it. Let's call the waiter. You won't hurt his feelings!

Mr. Ward: Yeah, but...

Mrs. Ward: If you don't say something, you're not going to enjoy your meal. Excuse me, waiter!

Unit 11, Lesson B
Page 163, Listening (CD 2, Track 33)

Professor: So, as I was saying, everyone lies. In fact, studies show that 60% of people will tell you a lie within ten minutes of meeting you. Often, they do it to make themselves look better in some way. We like to think we're all trustworthy, honest people, but the reality is that most of us tell at least one lie – big or small – every day. The question is *why*. We do it to make ourselves look better, but why else do we lie? Any thoughts? Yes, Diego.

Diego: Well, sometimes people lie so they don't hurt another person's feelings. Like, for example, my sister asked me yesterday, "How do you like my new haircut?" Well, it was terrible but I told her, "Oh, you look good." I mean, it was a lie, but I couldn't really tell the truth.

Professor: OK, that's a great example. It's very common to tell these kinds of little white lies for exactly the reason you give, Diego – so we don't hurt another person's feelings.

Page 163, Listening (CD 2, Track 34)

Diego: Sometimes people lie so they don't hurt another person's feelings. Like, for example, my sister asked me yesterday, "How do you like my new haircut?" Well, it was terrible but I told her, "Oh, you look good." I mean, it was a lie, but I couldn't really tell the truth.

Professor: OK, that's a great example. It's very common to tell these kinds of little white lies for exactly the reason you give, Diego – so we don't hurt another person's feelings. Now, let me ask you a question. When you told your sister that she looked good, did she know you were lying?

Diego: Uhm... I don't know. I hope not!

Professor: Well, research shows that it's often possible to catch someone in a lie. We know someone isn't being truthful because most people act strangely when they lie. For example, Diego, when your sister asked you "What do you think of my new haircut?" what did you do?

Diego: Uhm, I don't remember exactly. I think I hesitated at first. And then I said she looked good.

Professor: Exactly. When we lie, it's very common to pause and speak in an uncertain or nervous way. This is because the brain has to work harder to think.

For this reason, it's actually very difficult for people to lie in a believable way. So when you hesitated, Diego, your sister probably knew you were lying. OK, how else can we tell if a person is lying? Any ideas? Yes, Carla.

Carla: I've heard that people won't make eye contact with you when they're being dishonest.

Professor: That's one common belief, but actually, it's not always true. In fact, many people can look at you right in the eye and lie to you.

Unit 12, Lesson A
Page 172, Listening (CD 2, Track 36)

1. The capybara is a hairy animal that lives near rivers and likes to go underwater. It can hold its breath underwater for up to five minutes! If you don't like rats, you won't like this animal. The capybara is the largest rodent in the world—it can weigh up to 68 kilos. It's long as well—the length of a capybara can exceed 1.2 meters.

2. The tapir also lives near water and spends most of its day underwater. You can often see tapirs with their snouts sticking out of the water so they can breathe. They weigh between 135 and 180 kilos. The tapir is a pig-like animal that is related to a horse. You won't see a tapir during the day, though—they are nocturnal animals.

3. The sloth spends its life in the trees and only comes down to the ground about once a week. In fact, they eat and sleep hanging upside down from tree branches! Sloths have a green color to their fur—this helps to camouflage them so you can't see them easily. Another meaning for the word "sloth" is laziness. Sloths inhabit tropical forests in Central and South America and they eat leaves and fruits.

4. You can see the spider monkey high in the trees of the rain forest. They rarely come down to land. They are called the "acrobats of the forest" because they swing between trees so easily. A spider monkey can leap over 12 meters! Scientists say that spider monkeys are one of the most intelligent monkeys in the forest.

Page 173, Speaking (CD 2, Track 37)

Bart: So, what exactly did you do over the summer?

Gustav: We worked as volunteers at Glacier National Park.

Bart: I've never been there. What's it like?

Carolina: It's beautiful. There are mountains and lakes... and, of course, glaciers!

Bart: How was the job?

Gustav:	We had to do a lot of physical work. It was kind of hard.
Carolina:	That's true, but it was exciting, too! We actually saw bears!
Bart:	Wow! That *does* sound exciting. Maybe I should apply. I'll need a job next summer.
Carolina:	Sorry, Bart, but you can't apply to that program. It's a special program for international students.

Unit 12, Lesson B
Page 177, Listening (CD 2, Track 38)

Interviewer:	Hello, Jamie, and welcome to our program.
Jamie:	Hello. Thank you very much for having me.
Interviewer:	You are a civil engineer, correct?
Jamie:	Yes, that's right.
Interviewer:	You know, when I think of "engineer," I picture someone sitting at their desk, looking at blueprints of buildings... that kind of thing...
Jamie:	Actually, it's funny. I don't work in an office very often.
Interviewer:	Really?
Jamie:	Yeah. I'm out in the field quite a bit.
Interviewer:	Do you mean that you're visiting construction sites... watching buildings as they go up?
Jamie:	Some architects may do that, but that's not the focus of my job. I work with finished buildings. I investigate problems and design solutions to get around those issues.
Interviewer:	Can you give me an example?
Jamie:	Sure. Let's say a building has leaky windows, um, that's not a good thing.
Interviewer:	No, it surely isn't!
Jamie:	So, we want to know what the problem is so that we don't repeat the same mistake. I have to check the windows from the inside *and* the outside, and it's very challenging to see the parts that are outside.
Interviewer:	So, what do you do?
Jamie:	We rappel down the side of the building...
Interviewer:	You rappel? Can you tell our viewers what rappelling is?

Jamie:	Sure. It's a way to get access to places that are hard to reach. You use two ropes and, um, you hook them to the top of a mountain or a building. Then you lower yourself over the edge...
Interviewer:	So, you're just hanging up there in the air from two ropes? It sounds scary!
Jamie:	It is sometimes, especially when it's windy!
Interviewer:	Is it safe?
Jamie:	Yeah, we're very careful about it. It was really scary the first time, but now I'm pretty used to it.

Page 177, Pronunciation (CD 2, Track 39)

We sometimes use negative questions to confirm that something is true.

Listen to these four questions. Notice that the speaker's intonation rises at the end.

Repeat each question. Check your answers.

1.

| Man: | Aren't you an engineer? |
| Woman: | That's correct. I'm a civil engineer. |

2.

| Man: | Don't you work on the second floor? |
| Woman: | No, actually I work on the third floor. |

3.

| Man: | Isn't the Burj Khalifa in the UAE? |
| Woman: | Yes, it is, in Dubai. |

4.

| Man: | Wasn't the Eiffel Tower built in 1900? |
| Woman: | No. It was finished in 1889. |

Review Units 10–12
Page 184, Listening (CD 2, Track 41)

1. She's tall with long, brown hair.
2. My old one broke down. I wish I could afford a new one.
3. I'd jump up and down and scream.
4. It took something like three months to finish.
5. It was finished in 1920.
6. I feel like seeing a movie.

Unit 1

Maybe it's a family out running a lemonade stand.

Hula hooping, jump roping.

Cha cha.

Free haircuts.

There's dodgeball.

A teenager practicing their latest song.

Aerobics.

Yoga.

Advice on nutrition.

Bike.

Dancing.

Or walking.

Kids playing soccer in the middle of the street.

Mike:	Open streets are when you temporarily close a street to people driving and then open it up for people biking, walking, skating, running, pretty much do anything but drive a car. And it's a really amazing way to activate a street and to get a whole wide variety of people together as a community to be, yes, physically active but also social.
Gil:	It's like an exercise in social integration. You get young and old, rich and poor, fat and skinny, you get everybody. You enjoy the [inaudible] of the street all you need is two feet and a heartbeat.
Joe:	All races, all ages, looking each other in the face, smiling, there's sort of like this civic pride of people being together in public space.
Janette:	Well, the notion that streets are for people is a very powerful concept. And I think summer streets underscores that concept. Celebrates the concept that streets are for people. Enrique: It's a wonderful experience for anyone who really live in the city, dominated by cars, just being to enjoy places where never you imagine to be walking. Because cars really take all of our streets.
Gil:	When you take a look at any city from the air, the biggest public space are the streets. So the [inaudible] of a street, it's showing people that the streets can have different uses according to the time of the day, the day of the week, the week of the year.
Mike:	It's a great way to bring in new folks who are maybe interested in biking more and walking more and adding more physical activity to their lifestyle but aren't sure how.

Unit 2

Interviewer:	How old are you?
Woman:	97. I'll be 98 in October. I live in a retirement community. And we used to have a bus here to take people to the grocery store twice a week, and they gave that bus up. I don't know why. So a lot of people were stuck around here. Like my neighbor Joyce who was a very shy person. She said to me, "Well, if they don't get another bus, they'll find another place for me to live." And she says, "I just don't want to go anywhere else." I said, "Joyce, I'll get you to the grocery store every week." But I lost my driver's license because somebody thought I was too old. But I didn't have a mark against me at all. I was heartbroken at that, I really was. It made me feel old, it made me feel useless. I am a good driver, I really am. I'm not fearful when I drive, but I'm very careful.
Interviewer:	Are you a hot-rodder?
Woman:	No.
Interviewer:	Drag race a lot?
Woman:	Well, I drive 65. But I obey the rules, so I went to get it back. You make a promise, it's important for me to keep that promise if it's possible. And I passed it. I'm on the Earth, I'm here. If I can contribute, I should. Shouldn't we all? And not just think of ourselves?
	(to Joyce) It's supposed to get real cold.
	Like I say, I don't have money to give, but I can give myself, and my time. A lot of people in the world who don't have anybody who cares about them. So that's the way I felt. We're asked to love our neighbor, be a friend. That will give you joy. I mean, I don't do this so you think I'm great. I don't even think of that. My daughter says, "Mother, you shouldn't do this, you shouldn't do that." I'll say, "Well, okay." And like I say, I do what I please. I wouldn't do anything dangerous but, you know. How about a cup of tea? Would you like a cup of tea and a muffin?
Interviewer:	Oh, I'm good. No, I'm good, thank you. Sounds like a big wasp coming.
Woman:	Oh, she's trimming. They do the—
Interviewer:	She is trimming.
Woman:	Yeah, they do the yard on Mondays.

Unit 3

Artie: What I like best about living in the quiet zone and it kind of tells the whole story, the quietness. Some people that come here, they'll say, "What do you do?" Well, I just say, "I'm doing it right now, you know." And I say, "Just listen to nature all around you."

Michael: Green Bank, West Virginia is a very unique place. I find it ironic sometimes that, you know, we are working with technology here that's world class, it's world leading. But, yet, no one here has a cell phone.

Karen: So, a radio telescope works just like an optical telescope in that if you build it or have it in an area where there's a lot of radio noise, the signals you're trying to look for would be obliterated by that radio noise in the same way you can't see the Milky Way in downtown New York City.

Michael: The cell phone on Mars would be the brightest radio object to us in the sky. In order to protect the radio atmosphere in this area, Congress created the National Radio Quiet Zone. And that's an area that's 13,000 square miles. There's actually a long list of modern conveniences that we can't utilize here and that generally shouldn't be utilized in the community. Gasoline engines cause a problem. We only use diesels on site. Wi-Fi modems, cordless telephones, no cellular phones, the automatic door opener at the local store, no digital cameras.

Makeia: Piggy, come here. Piggy, come up here. Piggy. Hey! When you go and you tell people stuff like that, they can't believe it. And they're just like, what? Like I called my college roommate and she's like "Well, just give me your number and you'll text you." And if she doesn't have an iPhone and we can't do iMessage. I was like, "Well, we can't text because I don't have service." And they don't understand. They're just like, "How do you live without your phone? Like what do you do?" I mean, it's different like if you don't go from one house to another house with Wi-Fi, you don't have any way to contact other people which is odd.

Joyce: I really enjoy it because it's quiet, it's peaceful, it's beautiful. All these electronic technician things that these kids are sitting and pushing buttons on, don't happen here. Only way you can do that is at home.

Karen: It would be very difficult to create a radio quiet zone these days. Because in order to create it you would have to walk into an area and take things away from people. But living here, people have grown up without it and they've built their homes, and they've built everything around the idea that they will be where they don't have wireless systems. So it's much easier to maintain a setup like this than it would be to create a new setup.

Unit 4

Host: So, ladies and gentlemen, listen carefully. Your gender is counting on you. Take a look at this husband and wife and do your best to listen to everything they're about to say. Because in a minute, we'll have some questions for you.

Todd: Hi, I'm Todd, and this is my wife, Jill. I'm an elementary school teacher, we have two sons, a dog, and a parakeet. And I would say that between the two of us, I'm definitely better at outdoor grilling and tennis.

Jill: Hi, I'm Jill. I teach sign language and raise our two boys, Jared and Keith. I'm definitely better at remembering details. Who's better at tennis? That's debatable.

Host: OK. How well do you think you listened? We'll start you off with some easy questions. What is this man's name? Is it Tom, Todd, or Thad? The answer is Todd. What about his wife's name? Is it Jane, Jen, or Jill? The correct answer is Jill. So how did you do? We're betting pretty well since a majority of the men and women we asked got both of those correct. But remembering names is one thing. Now we're going to test how well you listen to other details. And this time, no multiple choice answers. You'll have to rely on the power of your memory and listening skills just like in your daily life. First question. What does Jill do for a living?

Jill: I teach sign language and raise our two boys.

Host: What kind of pets do Todd and Jill own?

Todd: A dog and a parakeet.

Host: What are their kids' names?

Jill: Jared and Keith.

Host: What sport do Todd and Jill both like to play?

Jill: Tennis.

Todd: Tennis.

Host:	Finally, what did Jill say she was definitely better at?
Jill:	I'm definitely better at remembering details.
Host:	So how many details did you remember correctly? Well, the more you got correct, the more likely it is that you're a woman. That's because the cliché that women are better listeners actually has some science to back it up. Research shows that men listen primarily with the temporal lobe in just the left half of their brain. While women listen with the temporal lobe in both sides of their brain. With both sides firing in the female brain, more neurons are stimulated so more details can be remembered. It doesn't mean men are doing half the work or that women are twice as good at listening. It just means they listen differently. Guys! Next time a woman accuses you of not listening, just tell her, it's your brain's fault.
Man:	I'm OK.

Unit 5

Matthew:	First thing I do when I wake up is grab my phone.
Host:	Thirty-two-year-old Matthew Barrett is never far from his smartphone.
Matthew:	To be honest, it's never without it. I know I'm addicted because I know without it I do have withdrawal.
Host:	And Matthew, a New York City PR executive, isn't the only one living his life almost completely online. As those devices become more integrated in people's lives, psychologists say smartphone users are in danger of becoming addicted.
Man:	If I don't have my phone, I can't really do anything, I can't function right.
Woman:	I can't really go a day without it. If I do go one day without it, I kind of go really psycho. Michael: The more connected we are, the less we're connecting.
Host:	Experts like addiction specialist, Dr. Michael Dall, say that too much smartphone use not only causes people to disconnect from reality, but smartphone withdrawal can cause physical symptoms like anxiety, insomnia, and even depression.
Michael:	And it actually creates a lot of cortisol in the brain and in the body. That stress hormone is actually cardio-toxic. So it's actually very bad not only for your mental health and maybe your relationships, but it can also be bad for your biological health as well.

Host:	But like other vices, for many the power of this addiction outweighs the mental and physical cost. And until something smarter comes along, young people on the move like Matthew show no signs of putting down their smartphones anytime soon.

Unit 6

Host:	In Los Angeles this past Sunday, the line stretched down the block at the first ever Sriracha Festival. There was Sriracha ice cream, Sriracha apples, and even Sriracha cocktails.
Man:	There are certain things that have magic, you know. That sauce has magic. I bet you could get into Fort Knox or the Pentagon easier than you can get into the Sriracha headquarters.
Host:	Ours were the first TV cameras let inside the brand new, $40 million Sriracha plant in Irwindale, California. This month is peak production. Two hundred thousand bottles are filled each day. Sriracha is run by founder David Tran. The rooster on the bottle is his astrological sign.
David:	If you don't like my product, what happened with you? Something wrong. There's something wrong with people? We do the fresh one, the best one, the cheapest one.
Host:	But there are those people who say it's too spicy.
David:	Using less. Using less.
Host:	Just use less?
David:	Yes.
Host:	The main ingredient in Sriracha is spicy head jalapeno pepper. They are grown on this California farm just 70 miles away. Craig Underwood owns the farm and has worked for David Tran for 25 years. They started with 50 acres of peppers. Next year, they'll plant 4,000.
Craig:	From the time they're picked until they're ground, it's about six hours. And that's important to David. He wants it fresh, he wants them red, he wants them spicy, and he wants them tasty.
Host:	When the peppers reach the plant, they are washed, crushed, mixed, and then stored in these blue barrels. How many barrels are in this warehouse?
David:	More than 200,000.
Host:	David Tran drove us around the new 650,000 square foot facility. But now his hot sauce has him in hot water with neighbors near the plant. This week, the City of Irwindale filed a lawsuit asking a

judge to shut down Sriracha until they can figure out how to manage [this] strong chili pepper odor that neighbors say is making them sick.

Woman: We had a bridal shower, we had to have the guests go inside because they were all choking, hacking, it was right in the throat.

Host: There's a lot at stake. Last year, Sriracha sold $60 million worth of sauce and revenue is growing at 20 percent each year. We interviewed Tran before the lawsuit was filed. Did you ever in your wildest dreams imagine you'd be running this?

David: I never thought that we would make big money or do something like that. But keep me busy, always. Every day, make more and more and more product.

Host: He's been perfecting his product for more than 30 years. After the Vietnam War, David Tran fled with his family to the United States. He started mixing hot sauce in barrels on the streets and sold it to LA's growing Asian community. He named his company Huy Fong Foods after the Taiwanese freighter that brought him out of Vietnam. He grew it without the help of any investors.

David: I want to say thanks to the American. They accept me when I refugee. I try to do something, give back to the American.

David: Tran says he wants to be a good neighbor and will work with the city to reduce the pepper smell. But while he may not be popular with his neighbors, to Sriracha fans, this 68-year-old is the hottest thing around.

Unit 7

Narrator: To shake or bump? That, my friends, is the question. Ah, the handshake. For ages, a person's handshake has represented an offering of peace, a sign of congratulations, and a symbol of mutual agreement. But is handshaking the safest or cleanest way of saying hello? Could there be another method? What about the fist bump? Dr. Tom McClellan knows about the importance of clean hands, he's a surgeon. So he conducted a study that's in the Journal of Hospital Infection and asked the question, is it better to shake or bump?

Dr. McClellan: In the hospital environment, we're confronted by handshakes all day. And we know that a handshake is enough to transmit infectious diseases. But what we wanted to learn is

whether a fist bump, which has grown from pop culture obscurity to mainstream popularity, was cleaner than a handshake. Were there actual medical benefits to a fist bump rather than a handshake?

Narrator: So Dr. Tom and his team of researchers set up the following test. They traveled throughout the hospital shaking hands with 20 other health care workers. Along the way, they pushed elevator buttons, used door handles, typical stuff. When they were finished, they planted their hands in a Petri dish to see how many germs they had collected. Then they repeated the entire process but this time instead of handshakes, they fist bumped.

Dr. McClellan: We found that the growth after 72 hours of incubation of bacteria on the hand shakers was four times greater than that on fist bumpers.

Narrator: Think about that. Four times more. You'll have four times less yuck on your hands if you bump instead of shake. Four times less means your chance of spreading, catching, and becoming a walking germ bag is reduced big time.

Dr. McClellan: We think if you're able to reduce the amount of germs on your hands by 400 percent, now that's significant.

Narrator: To learn and see more, visit us at PikewoodCreative.com.

Unit 8

Mark: I started thinking about where I hadn't been before. I found a reference and it said something to the effect of the fascinating and mysterious Musandam Peninsula. And that was about all it said.

Jimmy: Mark Synnott is probably one of the most prolific exploratory rock climbers of his generation.

Mark: What a climb. Succeeded.

Jimmy: He always has a plan to go somewhere that you didn't even know had rock climbing or you didn't even know existed.

Alex: Some of the most interesting stuff I've ever seen in the world. Sort of jagged limestone peaks that just fall straight into the water. Where rock and water and that's it.

Hazel: We should be able to find something good. I mean it's just miles and miles of coastline of rock.

Mark:	We're hoping that the rock is going to be good.
Jimmy:	Soloing is defined by climbing without a rope. And so deep water soloing is soloing rock climbs above deep water.
Mark:	It's a relatively new branch of rock climbing.
Hazel:	Deep water soloing can be dangerous. The water turns into rock when you go high enough. You will really hurt yourself.
Mark:	This is the first time that I've ever deep water soloed.
Mark's friend:	Oh, come on, dude. Oh. Come on, dude. Oh, my god! Oh. You gave up.
Mark:	Climbing with two young guns, as we like to call them, and they're telling me about stories of people who have died, who landed wrong.
Jimmy:	It's kind of an interesting juxtaposition to have Mark, who's this veteran climber, who's climbed all over the world. And so he's kind of at that point in his career where he's brought things down a notch. But then, you have Alex and Hazel who are at the point in their career where they're only bringing it up notches constantly.
Alex:	We tried it in the evening at sort of lowish tide and you could actually hit the bottom.
Mark:	They're pushing me. I've had to expand the boundaries of what I thought was reasonable to climb without a rope on this trip. It's been really cool to experience all these kind of different perspectives on, you know, a landscape that's really different. The climb that we did of this huge buttress above the village of Sibi—we're in for it. I mean, this thing is gigantic—was just an amazing day in the mountains. One of my best experiences because it got us up high. Could see all these limestone fingers extending out into the Persian Gulf. I know that that will be, you know, one of those days that I kind of always look back on as one of the highlights of my climbing career.
	To see the world really is kind of the essence of it for me. The cultural experience and to meet new people. I'm doing this for the adventure.

Unit 9
[music only]

Unit 10

Host:	How many of you have heard of the phrase "If it's too good to be true, it probably is?" Wise words to live by, right? What if we set up an experiment where that wasn't the case? Would people's distrust keep them from taking advantage of a no-strings-attached, guaranteed-win situation? We're about to find out in this next game. This next experiment, we're setting up a booth in a public place. We're going to offer free money to people walking by. They can take as much or as little as they want. We've hidden cameras everywhere. They're in the booth, in the buildings, they're even hidden in the bushes. What do you think people will do? Will they take the cash? So is this the dumbest experiment we've ever done? Of course people are going to take the money. Or will they? Would you like some free money? Excuse me, do you want some money? For free? Hey, you guys want to take this cash? We're giving it away, free money. So what would you do? Would you take some money? Or would your trust detectors go off? Do you want some free money?
Woman 1:	Is it really free?
Host:	It's free money.
Woman 1:	Are you serious?
Host:	I mean, this is all about trust, so you have to trust me.
Woman 1:	Are you serious?
Host:	Yeah. This is about trust. You're smiling.
Woman 1:	Is something going to attack me or like what?
Host:	I promise there's no strings attached.
Woman 1:	Pinky promise?
Host:	I pinky promise there's no strings attached. It's just free money. Just free money.
Woman 1:	Swear.
Host:	It's free. Even when people took the money, they were sure it was a trick. No strings attached.
Woman 2:	I feel like someone's going to pop out— [inaudible]
Host:	No. It's not a practical joke. It's just all about trust.
Woman 2:	Thank you.
Host:	Take care. Hey, you want some money? Would you like some free money? It's free money. Do you trust me?

Man 1:	You're kidding me, right?
Host:	Take as much as you'd like.
Man 1:	What's the catch?
Host:	It's free money. Enjoy. We're giving away free money.
Man 2:	Seriously?
Host:	Yeah, it's free, man.
Man 2:	What's wrong with it?
Host:	Nothing's wrong with it
Woman 3:	[inaudible]
Host:	No. This is about trust. It's not fake, it's about trust.
Man 2:	So can I put in a dollar?
Host:	Can you put in?
Man 2:	Yeah.
Host:	If you'd like, but this is more for you to take. We were giving people a chance to take money, and he's trying to put money in. What's wrong with these people? You would think it would be easier for people to take money. But people just hesitate. What do you think will happen if we change up the experiment and remove me from the booth? Now I'm up in the control room watching the action. Will people be more trusting if I'm not there? Imagine you're on your coffee break. You walk by a booth with a sign saying free money. What would you do? Would you take the cash? And how much would you take?

Unit 11

Dr. Wiseman:	Extend the first finger of your dominant hand and now you've got five seconds to trace a capital Q on your forehead. Some people draw the Q in a way that can be read by somebody facing them with the tail on the left side of their forehead. If you did that, then you tend to be aware of how other people see you. You're happy being the center of attention, and you're a good liar. Other people draw the Q so they themselves can read it with the tail on the right hand side of their forehead. If you did that, then you tend to be more of an introvert and not very good at lying. So if you want to gain a quick and fun insight into somebody, just ask them to draw a Q on their forehead.

Unit 12

Walter:	I will get up about 7:30, try to put my artwork out for the general public to see. Put some bird seed out. I'll walk down to the beach, and I'll also do a bird survey. My name's Walter Fuller, and I'm the steward for Ormond Beach. I've had another title, protector of birds of Ormond. But the steward, I like the title better. I was a janitor for 28 years when I was still working at Point Mugu. I would be coming here on my days off and then my time off. That's when I first started out here.
Carmen:	Ormond Beach, in particular, is pretty much the last wetlands on the Southern California coast.
David:	Ormond Beach are these important pieces of habitat left because these species now have been so confined and there's limited numbers of places where they can breed. And without a presence there to reinforce what the regulations are and sort of keep an eye on these places these birds are just not going to survive.
Walter:	You know what, I would recommend you go down the trail and go around that way…
Carmen:	I knew he was a volunteer, completely volunteer person out here trying to protect the wetlands when we didn't have and we still don't have enough protection for it. And he would come out here and talk to the people and try to engage them about bird watching.
Walter:	Cindy Hartley is a bird monitor; she's out there right now doing a quick survey.
Carmen:	About not doing negative things on the beach that would hurt the environment, hurt the endangered species.
Woman:	When you see one, who do you call?
Walter:	I call Marine Mammal Rescue.
Carmen:	The word was starting to get out, and more and more he's become a legend. And we count on him and hopefully can get him a little more help.
Walter:	The last year of my high school, my science teacher asked me to do a project for earth science, and I picked the eagle family. I got my pair of binoculars, got my field guide, and off to the mountains I went. That gave me the inspiration to watch and study birds in the wild. Here's a picture, one of the pictures of my bald eagle that we had out here, number 67.

Carmen: I don't think of him as quote unquote "caretaker." I like what's on his uniform, it says steward. It's a person who takes the protection of whatever they're responsible for very seriously.

Walter: [Inaudible] put a nest down right here. First they're walking with the sun beating down on them, they just calmly walk by and step on it, and they wouldn't even think about it.

Man: The coastline is to Oxnard what I think Yosemite National Park is to Californians. It's arguably some of the most beautiful parts of not just the State of California, but anywhere in the United States, if not the world. This should become a national seashore. And I see that Walter Fuller is the one, he is the guardian of that.

Walter: You got to be in the documentary.

Man 2: Well, you don't mind?

Walter: Come on!

What motivates me? Nature motivates me. I love being out in nature, I love taking care of nature. That what motivates me. I'm the steward for Ormond Beach, but technically we're all stewards for this earth.

A Quick Guide to Using the *World Link* Videos

The *World Link* Videos

The *World Link* video program provides stimulating and exciting video material, offering both audio and visual input as well as opportunities for follow-up conversation practice. Each *World Link* video unit features four video segments: the new in-unit **Warm-Up videos**, as well as **Good Morning World**, **City Living**, and **Global Viewpoints**.

- The **Warm-Up videos** are new to this edition of *World Link*. These videos were curated for English language learners from a variety of sources, including National Geographic and YouTube.

- **Good Morning World** is a morning show program featuring interviews, discussions, and demonstrations in the style of talk shows. The hosts, Jay Jones and Kim Kimal, welcome many guests and discuss various topics associated with the themes and language presented in the *World Link* student books.

- **City Living** is a series of original dramatic episodes, filmed in an engaging sitcom-like style. They focus on the lives of six young people from a variety of international backgrounds living in New York City. Each episode reinforces and expands upon the language presented in the corresponding unit of the student books.

- **Global Viewpoints** are real-life interviews in which a wide range of students and professional people from around the world present their personal views on issues related to unit topics.

The *World Link* Video Worksheets

The **Warm-Up video** program is included as an introduction to each unit's theme. Careful scaffolding is provided in the lesson planner, so that teachers have the support they need to successfully teach each video. Additionally, the video page is fully extractable from the student book unit, making it ideal for classroom use or, in a flipped-classroom model, independent student work at home. The 36 printable video worksheets that correspond to the three remaining video units are available on My World Link Online and the teacher companion site as a downloadable resource. The worksheets are designed to facilitate effective use of the *World Link* videos in the classroom or outside of class, for homework or extra practice. There are three worksheets per unit, one for each video segment. The first worksheet focuses on **Good Morning World**, the second on **City Living**, and the last on **Global Viewpoints**. The worksheet activities integrate pre-viewing, viewing, and post-viewing activities into complete video-based lessons.

Using the Good Morning World Segments

The **Good Morning World** worksheet includes two viewing activities and one communicative activity.

- Viewing activities (1A/1B) focus on video comprehension by asking students to watch and listen for specific information. Activity formats vary from unit to unit but typically take the form of true / false, multiple choice, circling, checking, or sentence-completion exercises.

- Communicative activities (1C) encourage students to apply in the classroom what they learned in the video. These activities are intended to motivate students to think about the practical applications of the topics and the language presented in the video.

Using the City Living Segments

The **City Living** worksheet contains three activity types: pre-viewing, viewing, and post-viewing.

- Pre-viewing activities (2A) usually take the form of a schema-generating discussion question ("Are you nervous at job interviews? Why or why not? Tell a partner.") or a brainstorming activity ("Why do people use smartphones so often? List all the reasons you can think of."). Pre-viewing activities are most effective when presented in class as discussion-generating exercises and sufficient time is allowed for all students to present and discuss their views.

- Viewing activities (2B) focus on video comprehension. As with **Good Morning World**, students are asked to watch and listen for specific information. Discussion is invited by having students compare answers with a partner. More involved classroom discussion may be stimulated by asking students to give reasons for their answers.

- Post-viewing activities (2C) encourage students to express their personal opinions and reactions to the characters and events in the **City Living** episode. As with the viewing activities, more elaborate discussion can be encouraged by asking students to provide reasons for their answers. In some cases, postviewing activities can be used as the basis for optional writing assignments. For example, students can be asked to write a paragraph explaining one or all of their answers.

Using the Global Viewpoints Segments

The **Global Viewpoints** worksheet contains two activity types: two viewing activities followed by a communicative activity.

- Viewing activities (3A/3B) are similar to those found in the **Good Morning World** and **City Living** worksheets. In the **Global Viewpoints** worksheet, these activities typically take the form of true / false, multiple choice, circling, checking, or sentence completion activities.

- Communicative activities (3C) are always fun or game-like exercises designed to stimulate conversation in pairs, groups, or the whole class. Activities often take the form of opinion surveys and discussions that encourage students to share personal experiences, ideas, and feelings related to the themes explored in the unit.

General Suggestions for Using the *World Link* Videos

- Familiarize yourself with the videos. Before showing a segment to the class, view it yourself and try doing the activities. In this way, you will be able to anticipate questions students may have about the segment.

- Allow students to view the videos more than once. The video icon indicates activities during which the video should be shown. In order to carry out these viewing activities, students may need to view an individual segment several times. Play the segment as often as the students feel is necessary to complete the activity.

- Clarify directions for viewing activities. Focus students' attention more effectively on the task at hand by making sure they understand the directions before you play the video segment.

- Know your video equipment. Practice with the computer or DVD player you will be using in class, so that you can easily locate and play the appropriate segment.

Using Video in the Classroom

Video is one of the most useful aids available for language teaching. It is motivating. It shows how people speak to each other. It is excellent for teaching both behavior and body language. It shows the culture of the people using the language. It is one of the best ways of communicating meaning and stimulating student discussion. But how can you exploit these advantages most effectively in the classroom? There are several useful techniques you can use to add variety to your classroom lessons and to make more effective use of video in the classroom.

The following are descriptions of five basic techniques for using video in the classroom: silent viewing, pause / freeze frame, sound only, split viewing, and normal viewing. These tactics have been incorporated into the lesson planner scaffolding for the new **Warm-Up videos**. With these descriptions are suggestions for specific teaching activities based on each technique.

1. *Silent Viewing*

This technique, which involves playing the video with the sound off and showing only the images, can be used to stimulate student interest and language use about what is being shown on the screen (rather than what can be heard) or to get students to focus on what is being said through the use of a variety of guessing and prediction tasks. Playing a short video sequence with the sound turned off not only helps students concentrate on the situation, but it also stimulates their imagination. Some classroom activities based on the Silent Viewing technique are:

- **What are they saying?**
  Show a dramatic scene with short exchanges of dialog, where the action, emotions, setting, and situation give clues to what is being said by the characters. Students watch the scene with the sound off and guess or predict what the characters are saying. Then they watch the scene with the sound on and compare their guesses and predictions with what the characters actually say.

- **What's happening?**
  Write the following three questions on the board, or dictate them to students:
  Where are the people?
  Who are they?
  What's happening?
  Students watch a dramatic scene and use the questions as a guide to help them guess the gist of the situation rather than the exact words used by the characters.

- **What's the conversation?**
  Students watch a dramatic scene, preferably one involving a conversation between two people. Then they work in pairs and try to write an appropriate dialog to accompany the pictures. Students practice their dialog in pairs and then take turns performing the dialog in front of the class. Finally, students watch the scene again, this time with the sound on, and compare their dialog with the dialog that is actually used in the video.

- **What did you see?**
  Students watch a video sequence and then write a descriptive commentary on what they see.

2. *Pause / Freeze Frame*

This technique, which involves using the pause button to stop the video while keeping a still picture frozen on the screen, can be used with either the sound on or off. The Pause / Freeze Frame technique is useful for concentrating on a single image or sentence in a video sequence. It is ideal for studying language in detail. For additional language reinforcement, it can be used in conjunction with displaying the subtitles that accompany each *World Link* video sequence. Some classroom activities based on the Pause / Freeze Frame technique are:

- **Listen and say**
  Students watch a video sequence twice with the sound on. During the first viewing they simply follow the story. During the second viewing, use the pause function to stop the video from time to time so that students can repeat the line just spoken. Encourage students to use the same intonation and stress patterns as the speakers. Offer opportunities for individual students to repeat the lines, as well as for the whole class to repeat the lines in chorus.

- **Tell me what you see**
  Play a video sequence with the sound off and pause at a convenient point to show a still image. Students work in pairs and take turns describing what they see. As a variation, instead of using a single image, you can pause at several different points where specific items come into prominence.

- **Guess the next line**
  Students watch a dramatic sequence, preferably one involving a dialog between two characters, with the sound on. During the viewing, pause the video at several different points, always just after one character has asked a question or said a sentence to which the second character is expected to respond. Students guess what the second character will say in response to what the first character has said. After eliciting suggested responses from the students, play the video and allow students to hear the actual response used in the video. After going through a sequence in this manner, play the entire sequence again straight through without pausing, so that students have a chance to follow the dialog spoken at its natural pace.

3. *Sound Only*

This technique involves playing the video with the sound on and no picture. (Cover the screen with a cloth, a coat, or a large piece of paper.) With Sound Only, students listen and concentrate on what they hear, rather than on what they see. As with Silent Viewing, the creation of an information gap stimulates the imagination and student language use. Some classroom activities based on the Sound Only technique are:

- **Describe the person**
  Choose a video sequence in which one character speaks continuously for at least 10 or 15 seconds. On the board, write a list of words that students are likely to need to describe the character; for example: *old, young, tall, short, nice, mean.* Play the video sequence with sound only. Students listen and write down the words they feel describe the character. Students then work in pairs or small groups, comparing and giving reasons for their answers. Elicit some answers (and reasons for them) from the class. Then replay the sequence with sound and picture so that students can modify or confirm their original answers.

- **Describe the scene**
  Select a video sequence with a soundtrack in which some clues are given as to the location, number of characters, and general situation of the scene. Write the following questions on the board, or dictate them to the students:
  Where does the scene take place?
  How many characters are in it?
  How are they dressed?

What are their ages?

What is their relationship?

What are they doing?

Play the sequence with sound only. Students listen and then work in pairs or small groups asking and answering the questions and giving reasons for their answers. Finally, play the scene again, this time with sound and picture. Students discuss the questions again, taking into consideration the new information they now have from the pictures.

4. *Split Viewing*

The technique of Split Viewing involves having some students see a video sequence and hear the soundtrack, while other students only hear the soundtrack. Some activities based on the Split Viewing technique are:

- **Tell me what happened**

  This activity is a lot like a game. Divide the class into pairs. One student in each pair is a listener who faces away from the screen. The other student is a watcher who faces the screen. Play the video. Listeners listen only. When the sequence ends, the watchers have three minutes to tell the listeners what they saw. At the end, encourage one or two listeners to sum up the story. Then replay the episode for all students to watch. At the end, the listeners and the watchers compare their earlier versions with what actually happens in the video.

- **Find out what happened**

  This activity follows a procedure similar to that described above, but instead of watchers telling listeners what happened, the listeners have to ask the watchers questions to find out what happened. After listeners have interviewed watchers, call on listeners to report the information they find out. This is all useful practice in asking questions and reporting information.

5. *Normal Viewing*

As you would expect, the technique of Normal Viewing involves watching the video with sound and picture, the way most people normally watch TV or a video. There are numerous activities based on this technique, and only a few of them are listed here. The most common and popular techniques that involve Normal Viewing are:

- **Role-play**

  Select a video sequence with a dialog involving two or three characters. Divide the class into groups composed of the same number of students as there are characters in the video sequence. Play the sequence twice. The students' task is to study the situation in the video and then role play the same situation using whatever words or other means they wish. After students have viewed the sequence twice, allow the groups five minutes or so to practice role-playing the situation in the video. Finally, groups take turns performing their role plays for the class, using their own words, actions, and gestures. Role playing is an excellent way of having students use the language they have learned. With role plays, students concentrate not just on the language people use but also on how they behave.

- **Change!**

  This is a variation of role-playing (above). In large classes, each group prepares the role of one character. It then nominates one of its members to play that character. During the role play, members can be substituted by the teacher calling "Change!" or by another group member tapping the role player on the shoulder and replacing him or her.

- **Behavior study**

   In this activity, students watch a dramatic sequence, imagine a similar situation in their own country, and examine the differences in behavior. Select a video sequence that illustrates two or three incidents of behavior that are culturally different from the students' own culture. Ask the students to observe the video carefully. Play the video sequence and pause after each incident. Elicit information about what the people in the video said and did and how this differs from the students' culture. For, watch how the people greet each other. Play the relevant part of the sequence and elicit from the class:
   a. where the people are.
   b. what they say.
   c. what they do.
   d. what their relationship is.
   e. how they would act differently in the students' own culture, using the students' native language.

- **Comparing situations**

   Two or three incidents or sequences can be contrasted to allow the students to compare behavior in two different situations (e.g., people greeting each other at a party and people greeting each other at a business meeting).

- **Prediction**

   Before having students watch a scene, tell the class where the scene takes place and ask them to predict eight to ten things they might see in the video. For example, for a scene that takes place in a kitchen, students might predict the following: *an apple, a cake, a cook, a stove, a table, a spoon, a sink, a chair, a refrigerator.* Play the video. Students watch and call out the names of the predicted items as they see them on the video.

- **Thinking and feeling**

   As much as the words we use, our body language—such as posture, gestures, and facial expressions—conveys what we really think and feel. An interesting and valuable activity involves describing what characters in a video are thinking and feeling, using clues from the dialog and the body language they use. To carry out this activity, start by pre-teaching a number of words students can use to describe feelings exhibited by a character or characters in the video, for example, *angry, irritated, furious, curious, surprised, disappointed, unhappy, worried.* The students' task is to watch the video and name the feelings being expressed. Play the video, stopping at crucial points to focus on a character. Ask students which word describes the character's emotions or feelings at that point, and have them give reasons for their answers.

- **Telling the story**

   Students can watch a video and then produce an oral or written summary of the story. Alternatively, they can watch a video and make up a story about the events leading up to what they saw on the video or about what may happen next. Using video to get students to make up a story is an excellent way of getting students to recycle language they have learned and use it in original ways for their own purposes.

Unit 1, Lesson A:

1. Vocabulary
A. 1. e 2. d 3. h 4. a 5. f 6. c 7. b 8. g 9. i
B. 1. rearrange 2. work well 3. home improvement
   4. combine 5. get rid of 6. neutral 7. repair
   8. option 9. overwhelming 10. repaint 11. redo

2. Conversation
A. Conversation 1: 3, 5, 1, 6, 2, 4 Conversation 2: 3, 7, 5, 2, 8,
   6, 1, 4 / 3, 5, 7, 2, 8, 4, 1, 6
B. Answers will vary.

3. Grammar
A. 1. cracked 2. flooded 3. stained 4. jammed
   5. bent 6. burned 7. clogged 8. fixed
B. 1. froze / frozen 2. surprised / surprised 3. forbade /
   forbidden 4. written / wrote 5. excite / excited
   6. spoken / spoke 7. confused / confused 8. broke /
   broken

Unit 1, Lesson B:

1. Vocabulary and Grammar
A. 1. c 2. e 3. a 4. d 5. g 6. f 7. b 8. h
B. 1. private citizen 2. general public 3. right 4. private
   conversation 5. public 6. privacy
C. Answers will vary.

2. Reading and Writing
A. 1. calm 2. planters 3. illegal 4. pedestrians
   5. crosswalks 6. bike lanes 7. speed bumps 8. contact
B. 1. good idea 2. good idea 3. bad idea 4. good idea
   5. good idea 6. bad idea
C. 1. biggest 2. like 3. much 4. safer 5. Another
   6. some 7. nothing 8. build
D. Answers will vary.

Unit 2, Lesson A:

1. Vocabulary
A. 1. f. 2. a 3. d 4. h 5. e 6. g 7. c 8. b
B. People: toddler, grown-up, teen, kid, infant; Stages of Life:
   childhood, adulthood, adolescence
C. Answers will vary.

2. Conversation
A. 1. What are you doing? 2. I'm buying a plane ticket on the
   Internet. / I'm on the Internet buying a plane ticket.
   3. Where are planning to go? 4. I'm going to visit my
   friends in Cuba. 5. What will you do there? 6. We're
   thinking about driving down the coast together.
B. Answers will vary.

3. Grammar
A. 1. b 2. c 3. b 4. a 5. a 6. d 7. c 8. a 9. b 10. a
B. 1. arrives 2. will take 3. will arrive 4. are taking 5. am
   bringing 6. is going to be 7. will see
C. Answers will vary.

Unit 2, Lesson B:

1. Vocabulary and Grammar
A. 1. h 2. f 3. b 4. a 5. e 6. c 7. d 8. g
B. Answers may vary. Adolescence: go to high school,
   leave home, get your first job, start college; Adulthood:
   get married, fall in love, buy a house, get divorced, have
   children, retire
C. Answers will vary.

2. Reading and Writing
B. *quinceañera:* Mexico; a girl's 15th birthday; 15-year-old-girls;
   go to church; have a big party with music and dancing; a
   fancy dress and a cake. Retirement party: United States; last
   day of work; people who are retiring; dinner, entertainment;
   presents. Coming-of-Age Day: Japan; second Sunday
   in January; 20-year-olds; dress up, go to City Hall, hear
   a speech; presents. *Schulanfang:* Germany; first day of
   school; six-year-old children; take pictures, party for parents;
   Zuckertuetes
C. 1. is getting 2. will be / is 3. are going to have / are
   having 4. are going to look 5. are going 6. are
   planning 7. will be / is going to be 8. will be / is going
   to be
D. Answers will vary.

Unit 3, Lesson A:

1. Vocabulary
Across: 1. talk 3. share 7. gossip 8. converse
          9. discussion 10. chat
Down: 2. argue 4. argument 5. conversation 6. discuss

2. Conversation
A. 1. Sorry to bother you. 2. May I interrupt for a moment?
   3. I'm sorry to interrupt. 4. I beg your pardon. 5. I just
   wanted to say something.
B. Conversation 1: 1, 4, 2, 3 Conversation 2:. 2, 4, 3, 1
   Conversation 3: 3, 1, 4, 2
C. Answers will vary.

3. Grammar
A. 1. Do you know who the actor is? He's the guy with the long
   hair. 2. Can you tell me who the photographer is? She's the
   woman carrying the camera bag. 3. Do you know the news
   anchor? He's the one in the blue suit.
B. Answers will vary.

Unit 3, Lesson B:

1. Vocabulary and Grammar
A. 1. tabloid 2. sports 3. local 4. International
   5. entertainment 6. sensational 7. mouth
   8. national 9. spread 10. programs
B. 1. started, have read 2. have eaten, went 3. has lived,
   lived 4. was, has been 5. has not been, went 6. have
   known, were 7. came, have met 8. have not received,
   bought

2. Reading and Writing

A. 1. They Couldn't Communicate   2. A Dangerous Dinner
   3. Silent Beauties   4. A Very Busy Thief
B. 1. g   2. b   3. a   4. f   5. c   6. h   7. d   8. e
C. 1. has taught   2. worked   3. has had   4. graduated
   5. started   6. became   7. was   8. went   9. studied
   10. has been   11. has written   12. have bought
D. Answers will vary.

Unit 4, Lesson A:

1. Vocabulary

A. 1. e   2. h   3. c   4. f   5. a   6. d   7. g   8. b   9. i
B. 1. colors   2. teeth   3. manicure   4. curled   5. perfume
   6. dye   7. straighten   8. hair
C. Answers will vary.

2. Conversation

A. 1. I'm not sure that's such a good idea.   2. I don't know.
   3. I see what you're saying.   4. I agree up to a point.
   5. I see where you're coming from.   6. But what about
   the cost?
B. 8, 6, 2, 4, 5, 1, 7, 3
C. Answers will vary.

3. Grammar

A. Answers may vary. 1. She hasn't had the dentist
   appointment yet.   2. She has already bought a present
   for Mom.   3. She still has to write the report.   4. She
   hasn't called Francisco yet.   5. She has already gone to the
   bank.   6. She has just had lunch with Carla.   7. She has
   already called her mom.   8. She still has to answer emails.
B. 1. already   2. still   3. just   4. yet   5. ever   6. never
C. Answers will vary.

Unit 4, Lesson B:

1. Vocabulary and Grammar

A. 1. break   2. cheat   3. get   4. ask   5. go   6. get
   7. run   8. turn   9. turn   10. grow
B. 1. Marco ran into Rita last Friday.   2. Marco asked her
   out.   3. Did she call him back?   4. Did she cheat on
   him?   5. Did she go out with him?   6. Marco broke up with
   Rita.   7. Rita got over it.   8. They turned on the lights when
   they got home.

2. Reading and Writing

B. 1. b   2. d   3. a   4. d
C. 1. relaxed = relaxed   2. dateing = dating
   3. coleague = colleague   4. personallity = personality
   5. intrests = interests   6. oppinion = opinion
   7. ofice = office   8. togehter = together
D. Answers will vary.

Unit 5, Lesson A:

1. Vocabulary

A. 1. inconsiderate   2. polite   3. disrespectful
   4. inappropriate   5. insincere   6. dishonest   7. unkind
   8. irresponsible   9. unpleasant   10. immature
B. Answers will vary.

2. Conversation

A. 1. You should call and ask the family.   2. Well, normally
   people sit on the floor.   3. Actually, it's best to try a little bit
   of everything.   4. Sure. No problem. We use forks, too.
B. Possible answers: 1. A wedding in Saudi Arabia

Mary: Is it OK if I wear pants to the wedding?
Fatima: No, you should really wear a dress.
Mary: Is it appropriate for me to dance at the party?
Fatima: Sure. Go right ahead.
Mary: Is it all right for me to shake hands with the bride?
Fatima: Absolutely.
Mary: Is it all right for me to bring my boyfriend to the
   wedding?
Fatima: Only people who receive an invitation come to a
   wedding.
   2. Answers will vary.

3. Grammar

A. Answers will vary.
B. Answers will vary.
C. 1. It's dangerous to drive very fast in bad weather. / Driving
   very fast in bad weather is dangerous.   2. Learning
   new words every day is important. / It is important to
   learn new words every day.   3. It's expensive to eat at a
   restaurant every night. / Eating at a restaurant every night is
   expensive.   4. Studying in a foreign country is not easy. /
   It's not easy to study in a foreign country.   5. It's respectful
   to take off your hat inside. / Taking off your hat inside is
   respectful.   6. Traveling for work every week is tiring. / It is
   tiring to travel for work every week.

Unit 5, Lesson B:

1. Vocabulary and Grammar

A. 1. e   2. g   3. a   4. h   5. c   6. d   7. b   8. f
B. Answers may vary.
   1. 1, 2; She'll give the product presentation before she'll
      attend the company dinner. / She'll attend the company
      dinner after she gives the product presentation;
   2. 1, 2, As soon as she arrives in Toronto, she'll take a taxi to
      the meeting. / She'll take a taxi to the meeting as soon as
      she arrives in Toronto;
   3. 1, 2, She'll have lunch with Mr. Carter before she writes
      her report. / She'll write her report after she has lunch with
      Mr. Carter;
   4. S, S, As soon as she has free time, she'll go shopping. /
      She'll go shopping as soon as she has free time. / She'll
      go shopping when she has free time.

2. Reading and Writing

A. 2, 1, 5, 3, 4

B. 1. culture shock stage   2. honeymoon stage   3. mental isolation stage   4. integration stage   5. initial adjustment stage
C. 1. Before   2. As soon as   3. After / Once   4. While   5. As soon as   6. While
D. Answers will vary.

Unit 6, Lesson A:

1. Vocabulary Workout
Across: 1. ship   5. develop   7. advertise   8. promote
        9. employ   11. purchase   12. investor
        13. promotion
Down: 2. invest   3. consumer   4. consume   6. manage
        8. produce   10. shipment

2. Conversation
A. 1. The key point is that   2. I'd like to emphasize that
    3. The bottom line is that   4. Never forget that
B. 7, 4, 1, 3, 5, 6, 8, 2
C. Answers will vary.

3. Grammar
A. 1. started   2. built   3. taught   4. made   5. found
    6. written   7. visited   8. done   9. sent   10. cooked
    11. read   12. eaten
B. 1. Two hundred people are employed by the Smith Corporation.   2. The World Cup was won by Germany.
    3. The products were shipped yesterday by the factory.
    4. Chinese is spoken by over 1 billion people.   5. That book was written by two women.   6. Excellent coffee is grown by farmers in Mexico.
C. 1. is spoken   2. visit   3. is checked   4. celebrate
    5. is learned   6. is used   7. provides   8. is celebrated
    9. reads   10. are found

Unit 6, Lesson B:

1. Vocabulary and Grammar
A. Positive: increase, recover, rise
    Negative: decline, down, fall, get worse, slump
B. 1. increase   2. steady   3. slump   4. dramatically
    5. slightly   6. recover
C. Answers may vary. 1. Because the car crashed into it, the tree was destroyed.   2. The woman was angry, so she shouted at Pete.   3. The woman was angry because the tree was destroyed.   5. Although the car was damaged, Pete could still drive it.

2. Reading and Writing
B. 1. spread   2. significance   3. supporters   4. pressured
    5. consumerism
C. Answers may vary.   1. Buy Nothing Day   2. Not buy anything   3. Canada, Japan, Australia, the U.S., the U.K.   4. Canada   5. It's the first day of the Christmas shopping season.   6. They feel pressured to buy a lot.
    7. They want people to shop less and live more.
D. 1. so   2. because   3. Although   4. because
E. Answers will vary.

Unit 7, Lesson A:

1. Vocabulary
A. 1. exhausted   2. cough   3.drowsy   4. shiver   5. chew, shallow   6. breathe   7. blink   8. dizzy   9. weak
    10. make sense
B. Verb: blink, breathe, chew, shiver, swallow, cough
    Adjective: dizzy, drowsy, exhausted, weak
C. Answers will vary.

2. Conversation
A. 1. I always advise people to rest.   2. I'll give it a try.
    3. That doesn't make sense to me.   4. I could never do that.   5. If I were you, I'd rest.   6. In my opinion, you should go home.   7. I'm not sure that would work for me.   8. I'll try it and get back to you.
B. Conversation 1: 2, 4, 1, 5, 3   Conversation 2: 4, 2, 1, 5, 3

3. Grammar
A. 1. I have a cough and my throat is sore. / My throat is sore and I have a cough.   2. Greg feels really cold and he can't stop shivering. / Greg can't stop shivering and he feels really cold.   3. Barb feels terrible because she has the flu.
    4. I have a headache and I feel faint. / I feel faint and I have a headache.   5. I can't stop coughing, so I should stay home.
B. 1. a sore throat   2. a cut   3. cold   4. a fever
    5. nauseous   6. exhausted   7. drowsy   8. scratching
    9. sneezing   10. shivering   11. ear   12. eyes

Unit 7, Lesson B:

1. Vocabulary and Grammar
A. 1. e   2. h   3. j   4. c   5. g   6. d   7. b   8. f   9. l
    10. m   11. i   12. k   13. a
B. 1. My instructor asked me to learn five new words every day.   2. The doctor told Carlos to eat more fruits and vegetables.   3. Our boss told Jenny to finish the report by Friday.   4. My mother asked me to call more often.
    5. The police officer told Dave not to drive so fast.
C. Answers will vary.

2. Reading and Writing
B. 1. –   2. X   3. +   4. –   5. –   6. +   7. –   8. +   9. X   10. +
C. 1. d   2. e   3. f   4. a   5. c   6. b
D. 1. sleep   2. stop   3. get   4. Reduce   5. have   6. go
    7. do   8. wake   9. feel
E. Answers will vary.

Unit 8, Lesson A

1. Vocabulary
A. 1. active   2. activities   3. active   4. action   5. activity
   6. activities   7. action   8. active
B. 1. Most teens enjoy physical activity.   2. Many students are involved in sports teams.   3. Alexis Sanchez is a professional athlete.   4. The school has a wide range of sports teams.   5. Older people should stay active.
   6. I have several leisure time activities.   7. You need to do an outdoor activity.   8. Luis is a serious athlete.

2. Conversation
A. 3, 5, 1, 2, 4, 6
B. Answers will vary.

3. Grammar
A. 1. How long has Bill been studying in Japan? He's been studying there since April.   2. How long has your brother been talking on the phone? He's been talking for more than two hours.   3. How long has Sandra been working at the hospital? She's been working there since 2011.   4. How long has that dog been barking? He's been barking for a few hours.
B. Answers will vary.
C. 1. work = working,   2. has = have,   3. since = for,
   4. taken = taking   5. when = since   6. I = I've

Unit 8, Lesson B:

1. Vocabulary and Grammar
A. 1. head   2. ask, pay   3. spend   4. warn   5. prepare
   6. believe   7. stay   8. learn
B. 1. have seen   2. has enjoyed   3. have been studying
   4. has been raining   5. have read   6. has been writing
   7. has taken   8. have been working
C. 1. learned = been learning   2. visited = has visited
   3. C   4. C   5. have been listening = listened
   6. cooked = been cooking   7. C   8. going

2. Reading and Writing
B. 1. NG   2. T   3. F   4. T   5. NG   6. F   7. T   8. NG
C. 1. taking   2. traveled   3. visited   4. like   5. gotten
   6. haven't stopped
D. Answers will vary.

Unit 9, Lesson A:

1. Vocabulary
Across: 3. corporation   7. usual   8. expand   9. citizen
     12. vote   13. launch
Down: 1. vow   2. enthusiastically   3. candidate
     4. reelect   5. term   6. raise   10. tax   11. clear

2. Conversation
A. 1. c   2. e   3. b   4. a   5. d
B. 5, 4, 1, 3, 6, 2
C. Answers will vary.

3. Grammar
A. 1. enough   2. too much   3. too many   4. enough
   5. too   6. enough
B. 1. I don't like taking the bus. There are not enough buses in our city.   2. I don't like my math class. There is too much homework every day.   3. I don't like this department store. There are not enough clothes in my size.   4. I don't like the beach on weekends. There are too many people there.   5. I don't like my apartment. There are not enough windows.   6. Answers will vary.
C. 1. too much   2. too many   3. enough   4. enough
   5. Too many   6. enough   7. enough

Unit 9, Lesson B:

1. Vocabulary and Grammar
A. 1. e   2. g   3. a   4. l   5. h   6. k   7. b   8. d   9. i
   10. j   11. c   12. f
B. +   +   −
   +   −   −
C. Answers will vary.

2. Reading and Writing
A. 1. Where are they located?   2. How bad are conditions in these sweatshops?   3. Can we stop sweatshops with new laws?   4. What should we do?   5. Are the prices much higher?   6. Where can we get information about companies?
B. 1. must   2. rich and poor   3. lose their jobs   4. many
   5. a little more   6. buy from good companies
C. Answers will vary.

Unit 10, Lesson A:

1. Vocabulary
A. 1. afford   2. short   3. save   4. borrow   5. get by
   6. back   7. broke   8. owe   9. debt   10. budget, stick
   11. lend   12. spend
B. Answers will vary.

2. Conversation
A. 1. b   2. e   3. f   4. c   5. a   6. d
B. 3, 1, 4, 5, 2
C. Answers will vary.

3. Grammar
A. 1. I wish I had a lot of money.   2. I wish I could swim.
   3. I wish I didn't have a headache.   4. I wish I were good at math.   5. Tom wishes he had a girlfriend.   6. I wish I didn't have homework every night.   7. Elena wishes she could find a good job.   8. Mrs. Kim wishes she were organized.   9. I wish I were on vacation now.   10. I wish my children would clean their rooms.
B. Answers will vary. Possible answers: 1. She wishes she were on the beach.   2. She wishes she could lose weight.
   3. She wishes she were president of the company.
   4. She wishes she had a new car.
C. Answers will vary.

Unit 10, Lesson B:

1. Vocabulary and Grammar

A. 1. e 2. c 3. b 4. f 5. a 6. d

B. 1. strike it rich 2. earnings 3. invest 4. squander
5. donate 6. set aside

C. Answers will vary.

2. Reading and Writing

B. Mary would agree with statements 2, 4, and 6.

C. 1. volunteering 2. marina 3. fraction 4. mortgage
5. maintaining 6. considering

D. When I was a university student, I bought my first car. It wasn't very expensive because it was really old. It was a little white car.
I worked in a restaurant during summer vacation and in the fall I finally had enough money. I bought the car from my friend's father. I took all my friends driving around every weekend and we had so much fun. A year later, I had an accident. I wasn't hurt, but the car was destroyed. I still miss my first car.

E. Answers will vary.

Unit 11, Lesson A:

1. Vocabulary

A. 1. against the law 2. hurt 3. honest 4. punish
5. the truth 6. obvious 7. rewarded 8. an exception
9. circumstances 10. liar

B. Answers will vary.

2. Conversation

A. 1. d 2. e 3. b 4. a 5. c

B. Conversation 1: 3, 1, 2, 5, 4 Conversation 2: 1, 4, 3, 5, 2

C. Answers will vary.

3. Grammar

A. 1. weren't 2. spoke 3. would tell 4. had 5. would
feel 6. could

B. Answers will vary.

C. 1. ~~was~~ = were 2. ~~give~~ = gave 3. ~~will~~ = would
4. ~~bought~~ = buy 5. ~~will~~ = would

Unit 11, Lesson B:

1. Vocabulary and Grammar

A. 1. I have confidence in my country's banks. 2. I always keep my word. 3. The boss is counting on us to do good work. 4. I don't trust my brother with my car.

B. 1. Rosa said she worked in a big office. 2. Mohammed said he didn't like watching sports very much.
3. Cathy said she was studying computer science at the university. 4. The president said he / she had many ideas for our country.

C. 1. She said she couldn't talk about the story. 2. She said she would go to Mexico after the movie was finished.
3. She said she didn't know what she would do there.
4. She said she was learning to speak Spanish.

2. Reading and Writing

B. 1. Akiko 2. Kevin 3. Carrie 4. Melissa 5. Ron

C. 1. were 2. would tell 3. is 4. don't say 5. could
6. were 7. would you feel

D. Answers will vary.

Unit 12, Lesson A:

1. Vocabulary

Across: 2. habitat 3. endangered 5. protected
8. environment 9. rarely 10. illegal 11. remain

Down: 1. wild 4. decline 5. dense 7. increase

2. Conversation

A. 1. That's true, but the mountains are also relaxing. 2. Yes, but on the other hand, it's crowded. 3. Even so, it's a lot of fun. 4. But then again, it's really expensive.

B. Answers will vary.

3. Grammar

A. 1. Do you remember where my backpack is? 2. Can you tell me where Oaxaca is? 3. I'm not sure when the dodo bird became extinct. 4. I wonder what time it is. 5. I'd like to know when Jamaica became a country. 6. Do you have any idea where aardvarks live?

B. Answers will vary. 1. I don't remember your roommate's name. 2. Can you tell me what he's like? 3. Do you know where his family is from? 4. Do you have any idea where he is now? 5. I wonder who lived here before you. 6. Do you remember how much the rent was?

Unit 12, Lesson B:

1. Vocabulary and Grammar

A. 1. V 2. V 3. N 4. A 5. V 6. N 7. N 8. V 9. A
10. V 11. V

B. 1. proposed 2. withstand 3. efficient 4. construction
5. accommodate 6. consider 7. goods 8. get around
9. sustainable 10. transport 11. obstacle

C. 1. That health book was written by two doctors. 2. The class party has been planned by the students. 3. The reporter's questions weren't answered by the president.
4. Several dangerous criminals have been arrested by the city police. 5. Music will be played by the school orchestra. 6. I wasn't surprised by the bad news.

2. Reading and Writing

Place	Louvre Museum	Kyoto Station	Millennium Dome
City	Paris , France	Kyoto, Japan	London, the United Kingdom
Date	1989	1997	2000
Architect (s)	I. M. Pei	Hiroshi Hara	Richard Rogers and Mike Davies
Purpose	more space for visitors	bigger railroad station	to celebrate the new millennium
Special element of design	a glass pyramid	a high, wide, modern building	a gigantic dome
Positive comments	Some said it was a piece of art.	It brings new life into the city center.	It is an important symbol of modern life.
Negative comments	Some found it ugly.	It destroys the traditional look of the city.	It was too expensive.

C. 1. has   2. are made   3. were designed   4. used   5. were finished   6. were   7. has   8. is   9. like   10. show
D. Answers will vary.

Instructor's Notes

Instructor's Notes

Instructor's Notes

Instructor's Notes

Instructor's Notes

Instructor's Notes

Instructor's Notes

Instructor's Notes